have done for Woodland church,

CW00918919

Vera xx
Michael

Nick Thornley.

THE FURNESS RAILWAY

A HISTORY

by

Michael Andrews

PREFACE

In the academic year 1954-5 London University ran its first course in railway history studies, a Thursday evening tutorial followed by a Saturday site visit. The tutor was Dr Edwin Course, now doyen of the academic study of railway history, and course members were encouraged to prepare a dissertation on a subject of their choice. The author chose the Furness Railway. But in the short time available it was only possible to complete the history of the railways of Barrow-in-Furness. This dissertation was lodged in the Barrow Library reference department and, in 2003, was published by the Cumbrian Railways Association as *"The Furness Railway In and Around Barrow"*.

Over a period of 50 years, research at the Public Record Office has led to the completion of the Furness Railway story. In view of the copious literature on Furness Railway locomotives and rolling stock, particularly that contained in the CRA publication *"Furness Railway 150"*, the author has chosen only to touch on this subject. However, the story of the Whitehaven Junction Railway has been included as, from 1852 to 1866, it was worked jointly with the Whitehaven & Furness Junction Railway. Also included is the story of the Cleator & Workington Junction Railway which was, in the main, worked by the Furness Railway.

"The Furness Railway: A History" is now presented in the form it had reached at the time of Dr Andrews' untimely death in September 2010. It represents a lifetime of patient research and is now published by Michael Andrews' family and friends as a contribution to transport study and in memory of a Barrovian with a passion for his local railway.

One of Michael's favourite photos from his own collection is this one of Shipyard Station at Barrow. This view would have been taken in 1963 when two workmen's trains were run and are here seen ready for the evening departures. On the left is the southbound train for stations to Grange and on the right the train going north to Silecroft. (Author: MAA33)

FRONT COVER

'Furness Railway No.80 at Roanhead' – a painting completed in 2002 by the late Edward Paget-Tomlinson. (By kind permission of Mrs P.L. Paget-Tomlinson)

TITLE PAGE

The Furness Railway badge as carried on locomotives from around 1898 until the Grouping in 1923. The crest within the garter is a facsimile of the seal last used to surrender Furness Abbey to King Henry VIII in 1537. The motto 'Cavendo Tutus' means 'Secure by Caution'. (George Taylor collection)

Published in 2012 on behalf of the Executors by Barrai Books, Barrow in Furness

ISBN 978-0-9569709-0-9

Text © the Executors of Michael Andrews
Maps and line illustrations © Alan Johnstone
Photographs © as credited

All rights reserved. No part of this publication may be reproduced, stored in a retrieval system or transmitted in any form or by any means, electronic, mechanical, photocopying, recording or otherwise without the prior permission in writing from the publishers.

Printed by Ashford Colour Press, Gosport, Hampshire
Design and production by Trevor Preece: trevor@epic-gb.com

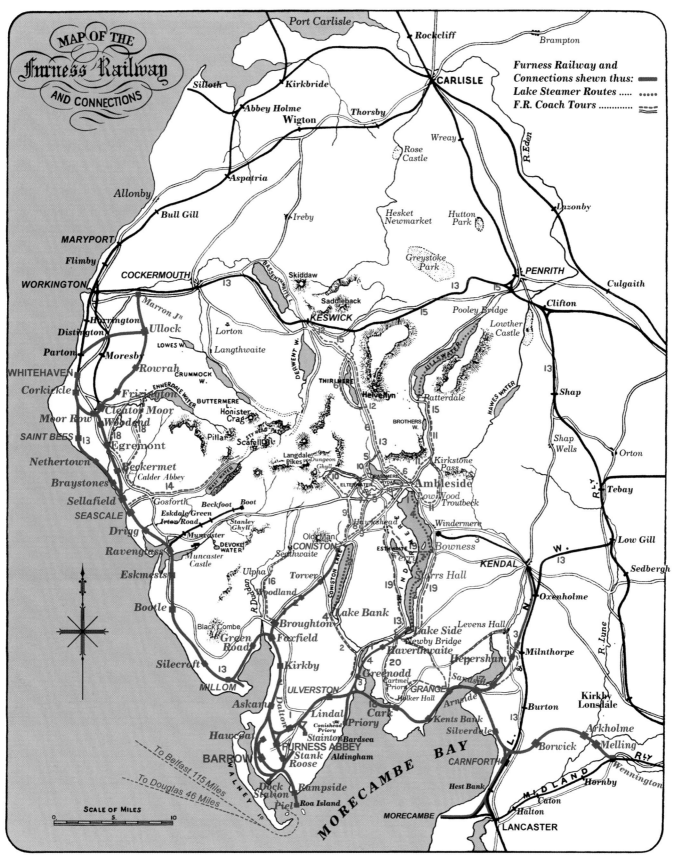

The Furness Railway system in its heyday with the tours to extend the boundaries beyond the railheads.
(Holiday Resorts of the Furness Railway, John Hext collection)

CONTENTS

Note: *In the earlier years of the 19th century the spelling 'Ulverstone' was popularly used. However when the local newspaper Soulby's Ulverston Advertiser, was launched in 1848, it used the historically correct spelling in its masthead. The author has only used 'Ulverstone' where it appears as such in legal documents, for example 'Ulverstone & Lancaster Railway'. Similarly, early references to Lindal often have an added 'e'.*

MICHAEL JOHN ANDREWS
OStJ, MRCP, MRCS, FFOM: 1932-2010

AN APPRECIATION

Michael and I first met in the Spring of 1941, in the very darkest days of the War, at school in Barrow. We became firm friends and in the succeeding wartime years and their immediate austere aftermath, spent many happy times together.

Towards the end of the War, we had a joint experience that may have affected the course of both our lives subsequently when we were invited, after Sunday School, to visit Walney Ferry signalbox. The box controlled one of the routes into Barrow shipyard and in those wartime days worked seven days a week. Even though it dealt with nothing more than local shunting, I think the ability to command the movements of trains appealed to both of us. From then on our interest in railways, already showing itself in train observation and the collecting of engine numbers, included what would now be known as the infrastructure (then of course a totally unknown word).

We rapidly learnt that taking up positions close to signalboxes gave us a much better idea of traffic movements than simply waiting at the lineside. Salthouse Junction and Park South were among the earlier sites. Others followed and soon we had several acquaintances among friendly local signalmen.

Life was not then burdened with excessive regulation. H&S, CRB, high visibility clothing, etc were unheard of. Signalmen, used to working alone and unsupervised were able, most of them, to take a balanced view of the extent to which the Rules regarding signalbox entry were to be interpreted. Consequently we boys, showing an intelligent interest, were often invited into the box and learnt about the intricacies of block signalling first hand, often taking over the box under the kindly eye of the signalman. We became expert amateur signalmen, or thought we were.

School years pass all too soon and events began to influence both our lives. In 1947 our ways parted but Michael and I kept closely in touch. He already had medical interests and once when he was visiting, my Father arranged for him to have a talk with the works Doctor, an event which, he told me later, first kindled his interest in industrial medicine.

With the completion of schooling in 1950 Michael left Barrow for London to do his medical training at St Mary's Hospital. Later, while he was finishing training and occupying Registrar and Senior Registrar posts, we met many times and attended an evening course on railway history together, another seminal moment as it has turned out, leading after more than fifty years, to this his *magnum opus*.

Over the succeeding years and decades our friendship continued at long-distance; he in London, I away in the North. Nevertheless whenever we met, even sometimes after intervals of years, we were able to talk about our mutual interests as if no time had intervened.

After several years occupying posts at various London hospitals and shipping organisations Michael became a Railway Medical Officer, first on what was then the Southern Region of British Railways, covering the south-east of England, and then later moving to the London Midland Region with his office in a corner of the station buildings at Euston station. Finally he achieved the top job in railway medicine, that of Chief Medical Officer, with an office at Railways Board HQ on Marylebone Road. I know from talking to other railway MOs that he was well liked by his colleagues.

Throughout all this period Michael continued his special interest in railway signalling, begun all those years ago at Walney Ferry; writing a paper on signalmen's working conditions and the design of signalling panels, and, on the side, accumulating a notable collection of signalling equipment which is now at Kidderminster Railway Museum. He also published several works on the railway history of Barrow and district, the first an article in the *Railway Magazine* as long ago as 1959. Michael was a long-time member of the Cumbrian Railways Association and enjoyed their meetings and contributing to the on-line chat group.

Finally I am sure Michael would have wished me to pay a tribute to the memory of those signalmen who through their kindly interest set him on the long road that has resulted in this book, and me on a very different but equally rewarding railway career. They included Charlie Helm (Relief Signalman: Barrow Central South and several others), Bob Cumming (St. Luke's Junction/Barrow Central North), Joe Sim (Plumpton Junction), David Evans (Salthouse Junction), Billy Penrith (Park South/Buccleuch Dock/Loco Junction), *Chinny* and *Cuffty* (real names lost: Ulverston Station).

Brian Whitehouse

Another of Michael's favourite photos from his own collection and where he spent many happy hours in his youth. Plumpton Junction is seen on 4th May 1963. This was the junction for the Lakeside and Priory branches. Ex-MR 0-6-0 2F No. 58116 (22902) of Barrow shed runs on to the Lakeside branch with a trip train to Greenodd, Haverthwaite and Lakeside. Black Five 4-6-0 No.45326 of Carnforth (24L) shed eases its Carnforth – Ulverston freight trip train back on to the Priory branch prior to leaving for Carnforth. (Author: MAA84)

From an early age Michael was fascinated by signalling and illustrated here in Plumpton Junction box are a pair of Tyers 1 wire 3 position instruments as used by the Furness Railway from 1906 onwards. These instruments survived in everyday use until being superseded by more modern standard BR instruments during the 1970s, which are still in use. (Author: MAA848)

Where it all began. The box on the 'Low Road' from Hindpool to Barrow Island, seen here in April 1973, changed little on the outside between its opening in April 1905 and its down-grading to ground frame status in November 1972. When Michael first saw the inside there would be levers controlling the layout and a large wheel to swing the gate closed to stop road traffic when a train required to cross the old caisson between the original entrance basin and the main Devonshire Dock. (G. Holme: GH100-1-1)

INTRODUCTION

When the Furness Railway became part of the London, Midland & Scottish system in 1923 it was a well known company serving the steelmaking and shipbuilding town and port of Barrow-in-Furness, the industrial and mining belt of West Cumberland and the southern part of the Lake District. Its main line ran from Carnforth, on the main West Coast route of the London & North Western Railway, to Whitehaven, a distance of 74 miles. It owned the Wennington-Carnforth line jointly with the Midland Railway and the Whitehaven to Moor Row, Rowrah and Marron Junction lines jointly with the LNWR. It operated a large dock system at Barrow and steamers on Windermere and Coniston Water. In 1922 its capital exceeded £8 million.

Its origin, some 80 years before, was as a single line of 14 route miles promoted by the principal Furness landowners, their associates and agents, to bring down to the coast the slate from Kirkby Moor and the hematite iron ore from mines above Dalton, for shipment to the Mersey, the Dee and the Severn. The original capital, in 1844, was £100,000. The line was extended to Broughton in 1848 and to Ulverston in 1854. Its financial soundness allowed it to purchase the Ulverstone & Lancaster Railway in 1862 and the Whitehaven & Furness Junction Railway in 1866. Its Barrow Docks were completed in 1879 at a capital cost of some £2 million. In 1878, after tough negotiations with the

LNWR, it obtained, jointly with that company, ownership of the Whitehaven, Cleator & Egremont Railway and, in 1879, it commenced working the main line traffic of the newly opened Cleator & Workington Junction Railway.

The shipping place of Barrai or Barrayhead on the southwest tip of Furness had, in 1844, the year in which the FR was incorporated, a population of less than 100. By 1881 it had become an industrial town of some 47,000. The story of the Furness Railway was not one of continuing prosperity, as towards the end of the 19th century, advances in steelmaking technology eliminated the supremacy of hematite iron, which had been essential for the pioneering Bessemer steel-making process. Further, the Furness iron mines were becoming worked out and the accumulation of water in old workings rendered the remaining mines increasingly expensive to operate. The iron and steel industry of Furness and West Cumberland lurched from financial crisis to financial crisis. Barrow became more and more dependent on the shipbuilding industry founded, in 1870, by railway and steelworks proprietors. The FR itself became increasingly expensive to operate as the Board of Trade introduced safer working practices. A second generation of railway managers developed the tourist traffic but profits continued to decline, the 10% dividends of the early 1870s falling to around 3% from the turn of the century.

ABBREVIATIONS

BL	British Library
BNFL	British Nuclear Fuels Ltd, Sellafield
BRO	Barrow Archive & Local Studies Centre (formerly Record Office)
BTHR	British Transport Historical Records
C&WJR	Cleator & Workington Junction Railway
C&WJR&FR	Cleator & Workington Junction Railway & Furness Railway Joint Committee
C&WR	Cockermouth & Workington Railway
CK&PR	Cockermouth, Keswick & Penrith Railway
CM	Committee Meeting
CR	Caledonian Railway
CRA	Cumbrian Railways Association
CWAAS	Cumberland & Westmorland Antiquarian & Archaeological Society
DM	Directors Meeting
DRS	Direct Rail Services
F&M	Furness & Midland Railway
FR	Furness Railway
FRCM	Furness Railway Committee Meeting Minutes
FRDM	Furness Railway Directors Meeting Minutes
FRSM	Furness Railway Shareholders Meeting Minutes
FRT	Furness Railway Trust
F&WR	Furness & Windermere Railway
F&YUR	Furness & Yorkshire Union Railway
HLRO	House of Lords Record Office
HSLC	Historic Society of Lancashire & Cheshire
JCM	LNW & Furness Joint Committee
K&WR	Kendal & Windermere Railway
L&CR	Lancaster & Carlisle Railway
LBSCR	London, Brighton & South Coast Railway
LLWR	Low Level Waste Repository, Drigg
LMSR	London Midland & Scottish Railway
LNWR	London & North Western Railway
L&SWR	London & South Western Railway
L&YR	Lancashire & Yorkshire Railway
M&CR	Maryport & Carlisle Railway
MR	Midland Railway
NBR	North British Railway
N&CR	Newcastle & Carlisle Railway
NDA	Nuclear Decommissioning Authority
NGRS	Narrow Gauge Railway Society
NWR	('Little') North Western Railway
PRO	Public Record Office National Archives, Kew
P&WR	Preston & Wyre Railway
R&CHS	Railway & Canal Historical Society
R&ER	Ravenglass & Eskdale Railway
R&KFR	Rowrah & Kelton Fell (Mineral) Railway
SD&LUR	South Durham & Lancashire Union Railway
S&DR	Stockton & Darlington Railway
SJR	Solway Junction Railway
SM	Shareholders Meeting
SRO	Scottish Record Office
UFLCR	Ulverstone, Furness & Lancaster & Carlisle Union Railway
U&LR	Ulverstone & Lancaster Railway
VCH	Victoria County History
W&FJR	Whitehaven & Furness Junction Railway
W&FJLER	Whitehaven & Furness Junction Lancashire Extension Railway
WJR	Whitehaven Junction Railway
WC&ER	Whitehaven Cleator & Egremont Railway

TIMES OF DEPARTURE OF THE OVER SANDS
COACHES,
FOR THE MONTH OF SEPTEMBER, 1848,
Between ULVERSTON & LANCASTER.

Lancaster to Ulverston. SEPTEMBER.			H. M		Ulverston to Lancaster. SEPTEMBER.			H. M
Friday	1st		7 30 a m		Friday	1st		6 30 a m
Saturday	2nd		8 0 a m		Saturday	2nd		7 0 a m
Monday	4th		9 0 a m		Monday	4th		8 0 a m
Tuesday	5th		9 30 a m		Tuesday	5th		9 0 a m
Wednesday	6th		10 30 a m		Wednesday	6th		9 0 a m
Thursday	7th		10 30 a m		Thursday	7th		11 0 a m
Friday	8th		11 0 a m		Friday	8th		11 30 a m
Saturday	9th		1 30 p m		Saturday	9th		1 0 p m
Monday	11th		2 0 p m		Monday	11th		2 30 p m
Tuesday	12th		3 0 p m		Tuesday	12th		5 0 a m
Wednesday	13th		3 30 p m		Wednesday	13th		5 30 a m
Thursday	14th		4 0 p m		Thursday	14th		6 0 a m
Friday	15th		6 30 a m		Friday	15th		6 0 a m
Saturday	16th		7 0 a m		Saturday	16th		6 30 a m
Monday	18th		8 0 a m		Monday	18th		6 30 a m
Tuesday	19th		9 0 a m		Tuesday	19th		7 30 a m
Wednesday	20th		10 30 a m		Wednesday	20th		9 0 a m
Thursday	21st		10 30 a m		Thursday	21st		10 0 a m
Friday	22nd		1 30 p m		Friday	22nd		11 30 a m
Saturday	23rd		1 30 p m		Saturday	23rd		1 0 p m
Monday	25th		2 30 p m		Monday	25th		2 30 p m
Tuesday	26th		3 0 p m		Tuesday	26th		5 0 a m
Wednesday	27th		6 0 a m		Wednesday	27th		5 30 a m
Thursday	28th		6 30 a m		Thursday	28th		6 0 a m
Friday	29th		7 0 a m		Friday	29th		6 30 a m
Saturday	30th		7 30 a m		Saturday	30th		6 30 a m

The Coaches will arrive at the Hest Bank Station in 2 hours after leaving Ulverston.
PLACES OF DEPARTURE:
LANCASTER..KING'S ARMS INN, AND BEAR AND STAFF INN.—ULVERSTON..SUN INN, AND BRADDYLL'S ARMS.
PROPRIETORS.......... MESSRS. BLAYLOCK, BUTCHER. & Co.

J. JACKSON, PRINTER, MARKET-PLACE, ULVERSTON.

A contemporary timetable for September 1848 shows there to have been one coach daily in each direction with times dictated by the state of the tide. Each crossing was accompanied by the official Guide and, even in these enlightened times, crossing the sands must never be attempted unless in the company of the Queen's official Guide.

2

BEFORE THE FURNESS RAILWAY

urness, together with Cartmel, once a part of the County Palatine of Lancashire, is a largely isolated region, separated from the mainland of the county by the sands of Morecambe Bay. This physical separation can, even today, be determined by the indirect route of the main road between Lancaster and Barrow, a heritage of the turnpike age.

Although the Kirkby Kendal – Kirkby Ireleth turnpike trustees had improved the old road between Kendal and Ireleth, under an Act of 1763[1] and subsequently, in 1820, the Ulverstone – Carnforth Turnpike was opened[2], residents of Furness were not deterred by the hazards of the traditional 'oversands' route from Lancaster.

Full-time guides were employed and the wealthy did not hesitate to use their coaches on the oversands route, saving some 12 miles[3]. Coaches also provided the public transport, the first recorded being a chaise which commenced running between Lancaster and Ulverston in 1781[4]. Fortunately the coastal position of Furness more than compensated for the difficult land access, therefore, although remote, the district was able to enjoy a moderate prosperity from the export of its produce by sea.

The town of Ulverston (the spelling, 'Ulverstone' dropped out of use in the mid 19th century), situated a mile or so from the sea in the shelter of hills, was sufficiently prosperous for its inhabitants to engage John Rennie (1761-1821), engineer of the Lancaster Canal, to design a ship canal to enable coastal vessels to come up to the town for discharge and loading. The Ulverston Canal was opened on 18th November 1796, but because of navigation difficulties in Morecambe Bay, made worse by frequent changes in the course of the channel of the River Leven, the canal company was not financially successful, no dividend being paid until 1836[5].

The most important of the Furness shipping places was Piel, off the south-west coast of Furness, taking its name from Pile of Fouldrey, a castle built by the monks of the Abbey of St Mary of Furness to protect their shipping trade in iron and wool. Piel, in the lee of the south end of Walney Island, was an ancient harbour of refuge and was used by mariners to escape the ravages of the westerly gales that are a feature of the Irish Sea. The harbour was particularly appreciated by the masters of vessels bound for the Ulverston canal. However, some three miles north of Piel, between the mainland and Old Barrow Island, another shipping place had grown up at a village with a population of 65 in 1806[6], which became known as Barrow.

The industry of Furness was, at this time, largely agricultural but there was also slate quarrying at Kirkby Moor, copper mining at Coniston and iron ore mining north-east of Dalton, which yielded a particularly rich hematite iron ore, much sought after in the traditional iron industry districts of Staffordshire, Shropshire and the Bristol Channel area. The records of Furness

Until the opening of the Ulverstone & Lancaster Railway in 1857, the shortest route from mainland Lancashire to the isolated Furness peninsula was by coach and horses or on foot across the treacherous sands of Morecambe Bay. An engraving based on J.M.W. Turner's painting 'Lancaster Sands'.

Abbey show that mining of iron ore dated back at least to the 12th century, but the modern iron industry dates from 1711, when water-powered blast furnaces were erected at Cunsey, on the west bank of Windermere, and at Backbarrow, on the River Leven. Ironmasters from the traditional ironmaking districts were attracted by the plentiful supply of charcoal, burned in the coppice woods of High Furness, resulting in ore, charcoal, and pig iron, together with some finished iron products, being exported, by water, principally from the port of Greenodd. Stemming from this, a regular trade was developed by the Quaker ironmasters, between Furness and the Bristol Channel. Abraham Darby, of Coalbrookdale, visited the Backbarrow furnace in 1712, but his pioneering use of coke for iron smelting – a method he

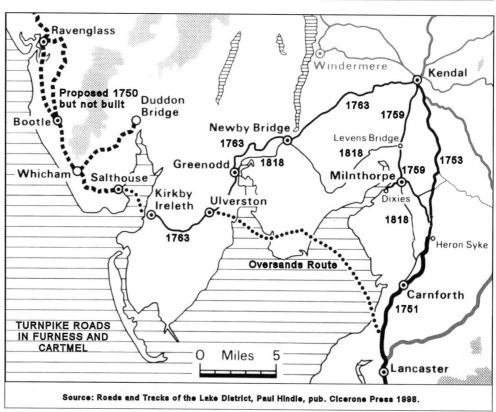

Source: Roads and Tracks of the Lake District, Paul Hindle, pub. Cicerone Press 1998.

Furness Turnpikes, from "Roads and Tracks of the Lake District" by Paul Hindle (Cicerone Press). (reproduced by kind permission of the Author)

had commenced in 1709 and which was to lead to the decline of the charcoal iron industry – was destined not to be adopted in Furness for another 150 years.

During the eighteenth century a coastal shipping trade developed between Furness and the established iron industry locations via the rivers Mersey, Dee, Stour and Severn. The demand for hematite ore reached a peak between 1780 and 1790, by which time the Furness ironmasters had concentrated their ship-

ping activities at Barrow[7], a decision which was to place an increasing burden on the narrow parish road between Dalton and Barrow.

Barrow, Burlington and Buccleuch

The Backbarrow Company built an iron ore floor at Barrow in 1776 and, in 1782, the principal iron firm in Furness – the Newland Company of Newland Furnace, east of Ulverston, (later

The coaches plied between Hest Bank, near Morecambe, and Kents Bank, near Grange over Sands. This 1890s photograph shows the landfall on the Furness side of the bay. (North Lonsdale Magazine: Dec. 1898)

known as Harrison, Ainslie and Company) – built the first jetty at Barrow for loading iron ore into ships. The jetty was opened on 22nd February 1782, in celebration of which '24 shillings worth of ale was consumed'. This jetty reduced the cost of loading ore from 6s 4d to 1s 4d per 20 tons[8]. After trade peaked, at the end of the eighteenth century, a period of depression set in and the Furness iron industry did not revive until 1825[9]. Thereafter there was a steady increase in Furness ore production, shown by the output from the Duke of Buccleuch's mines:

1825	7,658 tons
1826	15,808 tons
1840	35,093 tons
1841	39,962 tons[10]

Although traffic on the Ulverston canal increased, Barrow consolidated its position as a Furness port with a second jetty being built in 1833, a third in 1839 and a fourth in 1842[11]. Iron ore was not the only export of the Furness district. The rapid increase in house building in the nineteenth century led to an increase in the demand for slate from the quarries at Kirkby and Coniston and it was at the Kirkby slate quarries that the first railway in Furness was constructed. R.W. Dickson in his *"General View of the Agriculture of Lancashire"* (1815) states *'In the quarry wrought by Mr Fisher the metal [slate] is conveyed in small four-wheeled wagons on an iron rail-way.'*[12] Nevertheless it was the transport problems at Kirkby slate quarries which drew the attention of their owner, Lord Burlington, to the transport needs of the Furness industry in general. William Cavendish, second Earl of Burlington (1808-1891) who was to become Chairman of the Furness Railway Company and the major investor in Barrow industry, was the grandson of the first Earl, Lord George Cavendish of Holker Hall, Cartmel. (1754-1834). William's father was killed in an accident at Holker in 1812, before he was able to succeed to the title - the first in a series of tragedies that were to mar William's life. His wife, the former Blanche Howard, died on 27th April 1840[13] at the age of 28.

William Cavendish was a mathematician and a senior wrangler at Cambridge University, which he represented in Parliament, but, following the death of his wife, he turned his energies to the improvement of his estates and the education of his four young children. His cousin, the sixth Duke of Devonshire, died without issue in 1858 and Burlington inherited the Chatsworth estates to become the seventh Duke. In 1882 his second son, Lord Frederick Cavendish, who had been groomed to take over the Cavendish interests in Furness, was assassinated in Phoenix Park, Dublin, and his third son, Lord Edward Cavendish, died, of natural causes, at Holker in 1891. William Cavendish was a brilliant, essentially philanthropic, but introspective man who was destined to do more for the district of Furness and its industry than any other individual. His diary, kept from 22nd January 1838 until a short time before his death, provides a unique record of this fascinating period.

Walter Francis Montagu Douglas Scott, fifth Duke of Buccleuch and seventh Duke of Queensberry (1806-1884), was Lord of the Manor of Furness, his ancestors having inherited this right which was granted by Charles II to the Duke of Albemarle. His lands included Hawkshead, Blawith, Ulverston and Dalton. Throughout his life, Buccleuch, who, from 1842-1846, was Lord Privy Seal in the second Peel administration, remained largely aloof from his Furness estates leaving their control, including his mining interests, to able agents. Among these were Edward Wadham of Millwood, a mining engineer and John Iltid Nicholl

and his son Frederick, his legal advisors, all of whom were also Furness Railway directors.

West Cumberland

Industry had been well developed in West Cumberland before the first blast furnaces were built in Furness. The West Cumberland coalfield had its origins in antiquity, with mining being recorded by the Priory of St Bees in the thirteenth century. At an early date coal was easily won from the upper seams of the coalfield, which outcropped on the west side of the St Bees valley, whilst the later-worked, deeper seams extended from Mealsgate in the north to Whitehaven in the south, where they ran out to sea.

It was after the acquisition of the manor of St Bees, by Christopher Lowther (created 1st baronet in 1642), that the first serious mining operations were carried out. A pier for loading coal for export to Ireland was built at the seaside hamlet of Whitehaven in 1634. Sir John Lowther (1642-1705) extended the coal workings, sinking the pits forming the Howgill colliery and employing engines for pumping water. North east of Whitehaven, which was now expanding into a town, the Whingill colliery was also developed.

From these two collieries coal was at first carried to the harbour in sacks on horseback. But the Lowthers, recognising the need for improved transport, built in 1683, through their agent John Gale, a 'coalway' between Woodagreen Pit and the harbour consisting of a 'causey' or causeway, bounded on either side by wooden baulks, on which cart wheels could run.

A significant development was the construction by John Spedding, principal steward of the Lowther estates, of a wooden 'waggonway' between a shaft at Ravenhill, on the high ground south of Whitehaven, down to the south side of the harbour, which was first used to carry coal from the Saltom Pit on 15th November 1735. A second waggonway was opened on 4th August 1738 from the Parker Pit, in the Howgill colliery, to the harbour[14]. It seems that Carlisle Spedding, younger brother of John, had learned the principles of waggonway construction during the time he spent in the collieries on the Tyne, where he had posed as a miner to learn the local technologies. From this period the use of the waggonways spread throughout the West Cumberland coalfield[15].

By 1750 the Lowthers were operating coal pits at Clifton, near Workington, and at Distington, as well as at their Whitehaven mines. Other landowning families: the Curwens of Workington and the Fletchers of Moresby, also joined in this mining activity. The shipping of coal was extended to ports developed at Harrington and Workington, whilst at Ellenfoot, the Senhouse family constructed a port which was named Maryport. However, Whitehaven retained its premier position as the principal West Cumberland port, exporting an average of 81,940 chaldrons (1 chaldron = approx. 2 tons) of coal between 1781 and 1792, compared with 70,870 chaldrons at all the other West Cumberland ports[16]. The population of Whitehaven had increased from 250 in 1634 to 9,000 by 1762 and in 1750 the port of Whitehaven was second only in tonnage to the port of London: London 146,187 tons and Whitehaven 100,068 tons[17].

In the eighteenth century coal was the main industry of West Cumberland, however, the district also contained deposits of hematite iron ore similar to those of Furness. The first mining of hematite was at Egremont, south of Whitehaven, and the iron-field was found to extend from Lamplugh in the north to Hodbarrow in the south. Hematite production increased from 20,000 tons in 1791 (an almost identical output to that of

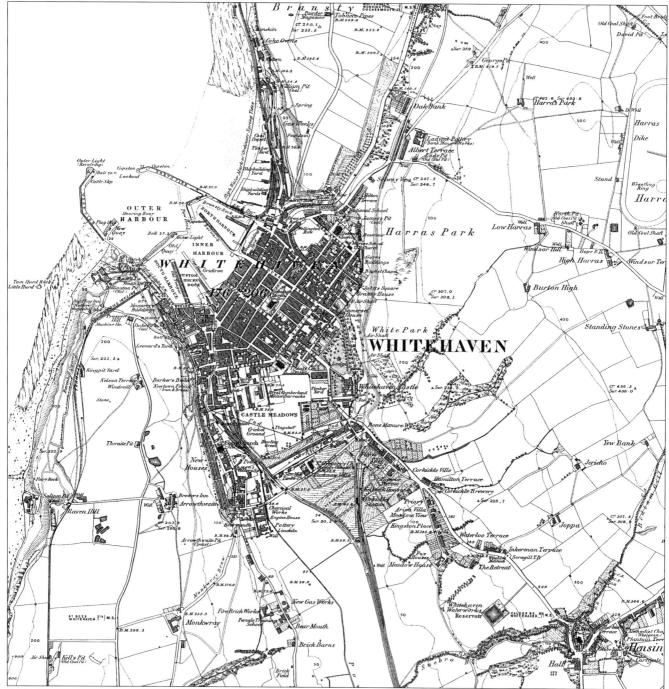

Whitehaven OS map 1863.

Furness at that time) to 100,000 tons in 1849. The West Cumberland iron ore was taken to Whitehaven harbour in carts and stored there until it was shipped.

The coincidence of coal and iron would normally have led to the early development of an iron smelting industry, but West Cumberland coal produced a soft and sulphurous coke that was relatively unsuitable for iron making as a result of which coke made from Durham coal was to become indispensable for the iron trade of the region. Nevertheless, the first West Cumberland blast furnace, built at Little Clifton in 1723, used coke made on site from West Cumberland coal. A second blast furnace was constructed by a partnership including Furness iron-masters, at Maryport in 1752 and utilised coke made on the site. However the blast furnaces built at Barepot, near Seaton, in 1763 used charcoal imported from Scotland.

The first modern ironworks in West Cumberland was that of the Whitehaven Hematite Iron Company at Cleator Moor, built by Thomas Ainsworth (1804-1881) in 1841. His partners included Samuel and Joseph Lindow[18]. Ainsworth's Cleator Moor Iron Mines were the most productive in West Cumberland, raising 30,000 tons per annum by 1846[19], but the West Cumberland iron and steel industry was not properly established until the coming of the railway opened up the district.

Cumberland Coast Route proposals 1836-1842

During the first half of the nineteenth century Whitehaven had become a major port for coal and iron ore exportation as well as having a flourishing import trade from the Colonies. It was not surprising therefore that the town became a focus for railway speculation. The energies of the Whitehaven railway promoters were directed towards the opening up of the district by means of a main line route and, in 1837, during the construction of the Newcastle and Carlisle Railway (N&CR), George Stephenson (1781-1848), the most famous engineer of his day, was

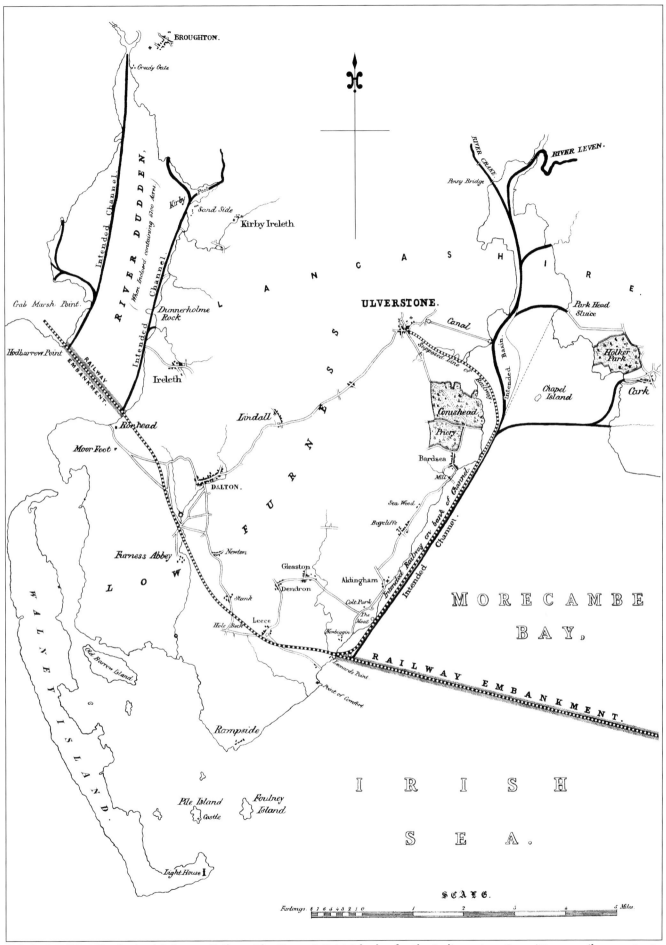

Caledonian, West Cumberland & Furness Railway. The Hague & Raistrick plan for the Parliamentary Committee on railway routes to Scotland, 19th May 1840. Ulverston was to be served by a branch off the main line and a new channel was to be cut for the Ulverston Canal. (Geoff Holme collection)

Early railway schemes across Morecambe Bay and Furness 1837-1840.

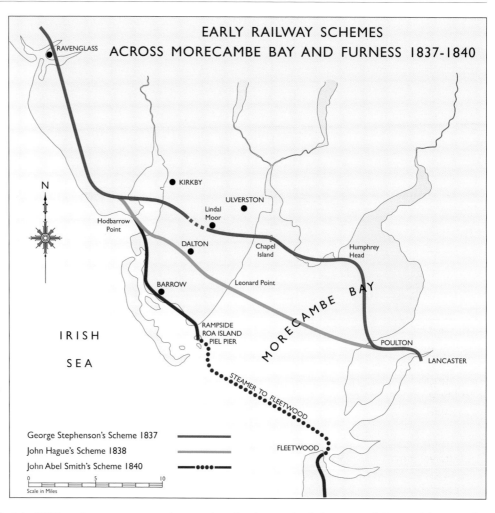

EARLY RAILWAY SCHEMES
ACROSS MORECAMBE BAY AND FURNESS 1837-1840

George Stephenson's Scheme 1837
John Hague's Scheme 1838
John Abel Smith's Scheme 1840

0   5   10
Scale in Miles

approached to survey an extension of the N&CR from Carlisle into West Cumberland. He reported to the Committee of the Maryport & Carlisle Railway (M&CR), on 12th October 1836, recommending that the line be continued as far as Whitehaven, but it was decided to take the line only to Maryport, the now established port of the Senhouse family, which would provide a western outlet for north-east coast produce. On 1st September 1836, while Stephenson was surveying the M&CR, he was asked by a committee formed in Whitehaven to survey a much more ambitious route for a projected line of railway from Lancaster to Scotland by way of Furness, Whitehaven and Carlisle, to be known as the Grand Caledonian Junction Railway[20]. He was unable to accept this commission at that time but was approached again in the following year, 1837, by which time the M&CR had been sanctioned (12th July 1837) and a separate survey carried out for a Whitehaven & Maryport Railway by Hall, presumably a surveyor acting for Stephenson.

George Stephenson's report of 13th March 1837 to the committee of the Whitehaven, Workington and Maryport Railway proposed the course of a line from the M&CR to Whitehaven and, on 6th June 1837, Stephenson agreed to make a preliminary survey of both inland and coastal routes from Lancaster to Carlisle. He started out from Lancaster on 1st August 1837, crossed oversands into Furness and over the Duddon Sands into Cumberland, returning from Carlisle to Lancaster by way of Penrith, Shap Fell and Kirkby Lonsdale. He reported to the Committee of the Grand Caledonian Junction Railway on 16th August 1837[21]. and in a covering letter to the committee he set out his practice:

'The principle I have always kept in view in laying down a line of railway has been the same as in this, namely keeping the lower level although it may be a greater distance, unless some prosperous country or large town is to be gained by a higher line.'

Stephenson's report recommended a line commencing at the terminus of the Lancaster & Preston Junction Railway at Lancaster, via Green Ayre to Torrisholme, reaching the coast of Morecambe Bay north of the village of Poulton (forerunner of the later resort of Morecambe). Two sea embankments were proposed, the first crossing the sands to Humphrey Head in Cartmel and the second traversing the Leven Estuary via Chapel Island to the Furness coast at Sandhall, west of the basin of the Ulverston canal. (Stephenson is strangely silent on the topic of

the canal navigation, and of the port of Greenodd, given the Admiralty's obsessional interest in the preservation of coastal navigation).

From Sandhall the line was to pass west of the town of Ulverston and east of Pennington village, where the rough ground would need cutting and tunnelling under Kirkby Moor. After crossing the Duddon Sands to Holborn Hill (later known as Millom) Whitehaven was reached by a route following the line as later built. In accordance with his stated principles, Stephenson was opting for the level, but longer, route instead of the steep route over Shap, despite the unknown problems of extensive sea embankments. The Whitehaven committee accepted Stephenson's plans[22] and a meeting in Ulverston gave further support. Another meeting in Ulverston, on 20th December 1837, led to a petition, drawn up in Whitehaven, being signed by a number of Furness merchants and ironmasters[23].

However, Stephenson had provided no more than an outline plan and, in the early weeks of 1838, the decision was taken to ask John Hague to carry out a detailed survey of Morecambe Bay and Duddon Sands. Hague, who had experience of reclamation work in Lincolnshire, accepted the commission, reporting to Sir Humphrey le Fleming Senhouse and the Provisional Committee of the Caledonian, West Cumberland and Furness Railway, on 3rd November 1838, from his office at 36 Cable Street, Wellclose Square, London[24] recommending a direct crossing of Morecambe Bay from Poulton to Furness. The overland parts of the route were surveyed by John Urpeth Rastrick (1780-1856), engineer of the London & Brighton Railway[25].

This scheme had already received significant support in Furness. A circular from the Committee Room, Ulverston, dated 14th April 1838, which was signed by R. Francis Yarker, Honorary

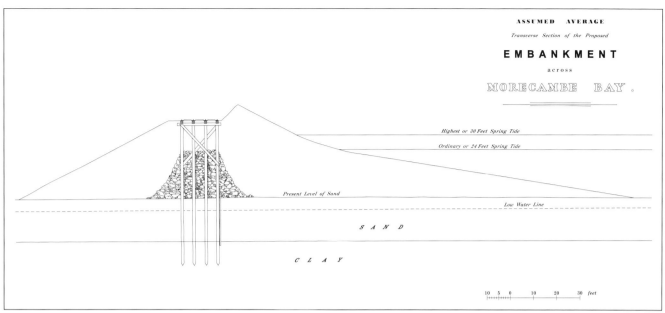

Cross-section of the proposed embankment across Morecambe Bay. (redrawn by Alan Johnstone)

Secretary, invited subscriptions to the Caledonian, West Cumberland and Furness Railway Committee and requested those interested to attend a meeting at the Sun Inn in Ulverston on 1st May, as *'small sums are equally acceptable with large'*. The Subscription List which reads...

'We the undersigned subscribe the sums against our respective names for the purpose of raising a sufficient sum for the purpose of obtaining a survey of the line of railway between Lancaster and Maryport[26].'

...included the well-known West Cumberland names of Henry Curwen, F.L. Ballantyne Dykes, Humphrey Senhouse, Henry Christian and Thomas Ainsworth together with Furness notables, James Stockdale of Cark, John Barratt, proprietor of Coniston Copper Mines, and Anthony Gaskarth of Coniston Hall.

Lord Burlington, whose Holker Estate in Cartmel, North Lancashire, embraced some five miles of Morecambe Bay coast line, could not avoid serious concern over a plan to embank the Bay and he noted in his diary on 18th May 1838:

'Capt Hague called this morning. He is about to go to Lancashire to survey the proposed line of railway over Morecambe Bay. He treats all the objections very lightly and considers that the object will be effected without difficulty. I reserve my opinion until further information on the subject.'

On 5th July 1838 Burlington commented:

'Jopling (his mineral agent) has ... his thoughts much engaged on the oversands railway. ... My own opinion is the railway is a very wild scheme.'

Joseph Jopling wrote to Ulverston solicitor

R.F. Yarker, on 18th August 1838, pointing out the great advantages to Ulverston which would be achieved by building the branch railway to the town[27].

Lord Burlington returned from his year-long 'Grand Tour' of Europe in June 1839 and, on 29th June, in a less critical mood noted:

'Mr Rastrick and Mr Hague called upon me ... They of course see no objections. I am sorry the measure has been brought forward but I doubt it will be so great an Injury to Holker as I feared at first. I still doubt its practicability.'

Detail of piling for proposed embankment. (redrawn by Alan Johnstone)

A prospectus was issued in October 1839, by which time the title of the line had become the West Cumberland Railway, being later revised again to the West Cumberland, Furness and Morecambe Bay Railway.

As it was the intention to introduce a Bill in the 1840 session of Parliament, detailed plans, sections and a book of reference of owners and occupiers on the course of the line, were compiled. A feature of the proposed line, as shown in the plans, was a branch from the Furness coast near Rampside to Ulverston, which would enclose a waterway to connect with the Ulverston Canal. In Furness, the line was to tunnel under Yarlside, pass Furness Abbey to the east, and then follow the Goldmire valley to Ireleth where a further embankment would cross the Duddon Sands to Holborn Hill. Rastrick's line then followed the line as subsequently built, except that the town of Whitehaven was to be crossed by a viaduct before passing Parton, Harrington and Workington, to end at the M&CR at Maryport. The plans were duly deposited, but no Bill appears to have followed.

These Cumberland coast proposals elicited swift response in the towns of Kendal and Penrith, the opposition being summarised in a pamphlet by Cornelius Nicholson, Secretary of the Kendal Railway Committee. Entitled *"The London and Glasgow route through Westmorland and Cumberland – the Interests of Kendal considered[28]"* it extolled the virtues of the inland route, which produced several competing schemes set out in detail by Brian Reed in his book "Crewe to Carlisle".

However, all the various schemes for a main line from Lancaster to Scotland were overtaken by the appointment of a Commission to inquire into the various projects to connect London with Scotland and Ireland. Hitherto it had been accepted that the Government's attitude on railway matters should be one of laissez faire and in opposition to the motion for a Commission, Poulett-Thompson, President of the Board of Trade, stated:

'Such an attempt would be productive of no practical good. (It was) decidedly better to leave railways ... in the hands of those who were willing to embark their capital on such speculations subject always to the scrutiny and control of Parliament[29].'

Nevertheless, the Commission was duly appointed under the chairmanship of Lt Col. Sir Fredrick Smith (appointed in the next year as Inspector General of Railways to the Board of Trade) and Professor Peter Barlow.

The Commission's Report, dated May 1840, complimented Hague and Rastrick on the way they had drawn up their plans for the coast line, but the Commissioners rejected their scheme on the grounds of the engineering problems associated with the construction of the sea embankment and the cost[30].

The title 'West Cumberland Railway' again appeared in a plan, dated 1842, by Rastrick in association with the Piel Pier proposal of that year. This proposal for a pier in the Piel Channel at Roa Island was made nominally by Sir Percy Hesketh Fleetwood of the Preston & Wyre Railway Company (P&WR), but it appeared that a shareholder, London banker John Abel Smith, was really behind the scheme. The Rastrick scheme proposed two alternatives for lines between Hodbarrow, on the north shore of the Duddon, to Rampside. The first, subsequently adopted by the Furness Railway, ran on a route through Furness Abbey, the second followed a more seaward course through the village of Barrow[31].

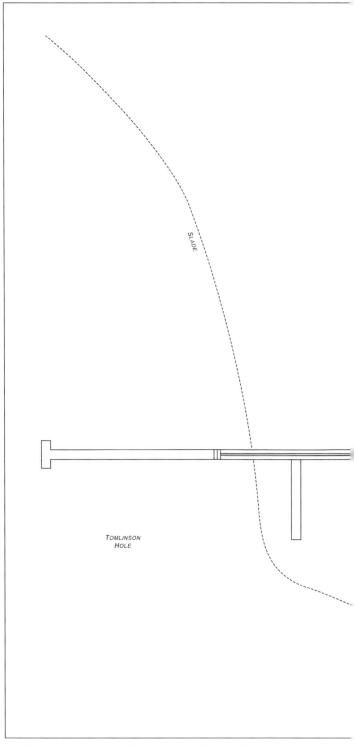

This revival came to the notice of the *Cumberland Pacquet* which, on 8th February 1842, having previously noted and supported the opposition in Ulverston to the Piel Pier plan, commented:

'We learn that during the last few days some stir has been making in this town and neighbourhood to revive public feeling on the subject of the Western Line of railway from Lancaster to Scotland. ... We opine that this subject, like the sluggard, will only be roused, to go to sleep again.'

The formal Notice of Application to Parliament for a railway from Rampside to Maryport (untitled) appeared in the *Cumberland Pacquet* of 15th February 1842. Subsequently, the withdrawal of the Piel Pier Bill, due to opposition, was noted on

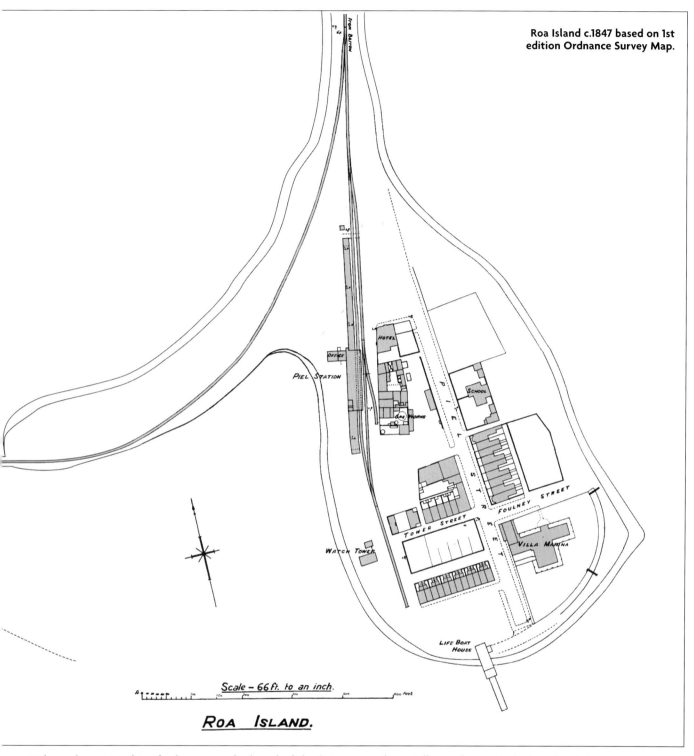

Roa Island c.1847 based on 1st edition Ordnance Survey Map.

Scale – 66 ft. to an inch.

ROA ISLAND.

26th April 1842. Nothing further was to be heard of the 'West Cumberland Railway'.

The winter of 1841-42 was one of the worst periods, industrially and economically, through which the country had ever passed. Lord Melbourne's Whig administration had fallen, in 1841, to be replaced by the Conservatives under Sir Robert Peel. The state of the nation was appalling, nearly one fifth of the population was in receipt of poor relief and the supply of money was virtually non-existent[32]. Peel re-introduced income tax, reduced indirect taxation, and the return to prosperity commenced. By 1844 the condition of the economy had been turned round to one of increasing prosperity, setting the stage for the era of the Railway Mania.

By the time Abel Smith presented his revised Bill, in 1843, for 'Pile Pier' ('Pile' being the archaic spelling of Piel), the Furness

Railway Bill was being drafted and opinion in Whitehaven favoured an allied scheme, which was to become the Whitehaven & Furness Junction Railway.

The Fleetwood Route and Piel Pier

During the period when the abortive plans for a West Cumberland main line to Scotland were being proposed, a separate venture was successfully undertaken and, for a number of years, provided the principal route into Furness. In 1835 the Preston and Wyre Railway, Harbour and Dock Company obtained an Act for the construction of a railway from Preston to the west side of the River Wyre and for building a harbour there. The line between Preston and the new port of Fleetwood was opened on 15th July 1840[33].

In its early years, the company got into financial difficulties and was lent £80,000 by John Abel Smith, who was later repaid in P&WR shares, thereby becoming a principal shareholder. Fleetwood, named after the principal landowner and P&WR promoter Sir Peter Hesketh Fleetwood, became a focal point for shipping services to Dublin, Belfast, Londonderry and Ardrossan for Glasgow.

The company built the North Euston Hotel at Fleetwood to cater for this traffic and the shipping services were operated by the North Lancashire Steam Navigation Company. However, as early as 1835, the steamer *Windermere* had been introduced to ply between the River Wyre and Bardsea, near Ulverston[34]. In 1838 the Fleetwood shipping agent, Frederick Kemp, and Abel Smith, produced their own plan for a route to Scotland proposing a train ferry from the port at Fleetwood, then being constructed, to a pier at Piel Harbour some three miles southeast of the village of Barrow, from whence the Rastrick route to West Cumberland would be followed. Abel Smith purchased Roa Island in Piel Harbour in 1840[35] and, in 1841, petitioned for a Bill, in the 1842 session of Parliament, for the construction of 'Pile Pier', together with a causeway from Roa Island to the mainland at Rampside.

Abel Smith's Bill provoked determined opposition in Ulverston. A public meeting was held in the Sun Inn Ulverston on the 8th January 1842 with Richard Roper, a partner in the Newland Company of ironmasters, in the chair. The introduction of harbour dues at Piel, proposed in Abel Smith's Bill, was the principal cause of complaint and it was agreed that the Bill should be petitioned against. A subscription list was opened to meet the cost[36], and some three months later the *Cumberland Pacquet* gave more details of the Piel Pier scheme:

'The mode of crossing the Bay by those who are at present urging forward this great undertaking, and which we cannot but regard as fatal to it as a national line or as a communication with the North is this: steam vessels are to be used in crossing the Bay from Pile to Fleetwood and to be so constructed that the whole train, engine, tender, trucks, carriages and luggage vans may be run on board and steamed across the Bay which under ordinary circumstances may be accomplished in an hour and a half.'

The *Pacquet* pointed out, on 19th April 1842, the problems associated with the tides and bad weather in Morecambe Bay and the same newspaper, on 26th April 1842, was able to report that the Pile Pier Bill had been withdrawn due to opposition. The new Pile Pier Bill, presented in the next session, was examined by a Commons Committee, on 5th May 1843, which was satisfied that the proposal would not interfere with the harbour as a refuge but would provide much needed accommodation for the traffic in the district. The Pile Pier Act received Royal Assent on 27th June 1843.

The completed Piel Pier was inspected by Major General C.W. Pasley of the Board of Trade Railway Department, on 3rd August 1846, during his inspection of the Furness Railway. His report states:

'I was accompanied in this inspection by Mr McClean, Engineer of the Furness Railway ... and Mr Samuel P. Bidder, Engineer of the Preston & Wyre Railway who attended to explain the details of the Viaduct and Embankment which works in connection with the Furness Railway, were constructed for Mr John Abel Smith under his superintendence[37].'

It should be noted that Samuel Bidder was also 'Joint Engineer' to the Fleetwood Preston & West Riding Junction Railway (Preston to Clitheroe) with George Parker Bidder, his elder brother, as 'Engineer in Chief'[38]. George (1806-1878), famous for his prodigious feats of mental arithmetic and known as 'The Calculating Boy' from an early age, was an engineer of wide experience who went on to be Engineer of the Victoria Dock, London, and it is likely that Samuel Parker Bidder drew up the plans for Piel Pier[39].

Abel Smith's railway was a continuation of the Furness Railway Rampside branch and ran on to the pier which extended south-west from Roa Island into the Piel Channel, allowing passengers to join steamers at all states of the tide[40]. The pier was opened on 24th August 1846, the date on which the Furness Railway was opened for passenger traffic and the Fleetwood-Piel route provided the only connection with the main railway system of Lancashire and the south until the opening of the Ulverstone & Lancaster Railway in 1857.

CHAPTER 1 REFERENCES

1   Hobbs J L, 1956. "The Turnpike Roads of North Lonsdale" *CWAAS Transactions* NS Vol. LVI p.287.
2   Ibid. p.266.
3   Lord Burlington, 1851. Evidence on the Ulverstone & Lancaster Railway Bill, 13th May.
4   *Cumberland Pacquet*, 11th Sep. 1781.
5   *Ulverston Advertiser*, 12th Sep. 1871.
6   Marshall J.D., 1958. *Furness and the Industrial Revolution* p.88.
7   Lord Edward Cavendish. Reported in *Barrow Times* 27th July 1878.
8   Fell A, 1908. *The Early Iron Industry of Furness.*
9   Lord Edward Cavendish. Reported in *Barrow Times* 27th July 1878.
10 Marshall J.D. *Op. cit.* p.93.
11 Ibid. p.94
12 Dickson R.W., 1815. *General View of the Agriculture of Lancashire* British Library 7075 bb4.
13 Diaries of William, 7th Duke of Devonshire, for date as stated (hereafter *Devonshire Diaries*).
14 Scott-Hindson B., 1989, edited by Austin A. "Early Wooden Waggonways at Whitehaven", *CRA Journal* Vol. 8 No. 1 Feb. 2004 pp.4-10.
15 Ibid.
16 Coal Commission Report, 1871. Vol. 3, p.13.
17 Hay D., 1966. *Whitehaven: a Short History* p.29.
18 Lancaster J.Y. & Wattleworth D.R., 1977. *The Iron and Steel Industry of West Cumberland* p.37.

19 Caine C., 1916. *Cleator & Cleator Moor: Past & Present* p. 210.
20 Kendall W.B. Collection of Papers at BRO. Ref. ZK. (hereafter *Kendall MSS*).
21 *Kendall MSS.*
22 *Cumberland Pacquet*, 26th Aug. 1837.
23 *Lancaster Gazette*, 23rd Dec. 1837.
24 Melville J. & Hobbs J.L., 1951. *Early Railway History in Furness* p.6.
25 Marshall J., 1978. *A Biographical Dictionary of Railway Engineers* p.177.
26 Author's collection.
27 G. Holme collection.
28 *Westmorland Gazette*, 9th Dec. 1837.
29 Parris H., 1965. *Government and the Railways in 19th Century Britain* p.26.
30 Reed B., 1969. *Crewe to Carlisle* p.113.
31 Ibid.
32 *Railway Magazine*, Vol. 25 p.505.
33 Ibid.
34 Porter J., 1876. *History of the Fylde of Lancashire.*
35 Melville J. & Hobbs J.L. *Op. cit.* p.13.
36 *Cumberland Pacquet*, 11th Jan. 1842.
37 PRO: MT6/3/53.
38 *Bradshaw's Railway Manual 1848.*
39 J. Holmes-Higgin, personal communication.
40 PRO: MT6/3/53.

THE ORIGINS OF THE FURNESS RAILWAY

The port of Barrow had, from 1772 onwards, been developed by the Furness ironmasters. The increase in Furness hematite ore production from 1825 onwards, put great pressure on local transport. Ore, in 15cwt loads, was carried from the mines to Barrow in horse-drawn carts, with convoys of carts reported to reach two miles in length, on the narrow parish road between Dalton and Barrow, during the summer months[1].

In his manuscript notes on the history of the Furness Railway, W.B. Kendall (who worked for the Furness Railway between 1867 and 1883, after which he joined the staff of the company's consulting engineer, Frank Stileman) recorded that *'In January 1825 considerable interest was taken in certain experiments and trials made on colliery tramways near Newcastle.'*[2]

Nothing seems to have come of this, but on 6th April 1838, Lord Burlington noted in his diary:

'Currey came today and suggested the propriety of letting the new slate quarry (at Kirkby). He had mentioned the subject to Mr Kemp, agent of the Fleetwood Company, who says there would be no difficulty in doing so but thinks that a railway to Pile Harbour must be made.'

Burlington seems to have decided to make a start by building a railway at Sandside, noting, on 5th July 1838: *'My own railway is advancing along the sands'*. He then departed for the best part of a year on a 'Grand Tour' of Europe. On returning he says:

'...the railway now extends about ¼ mile over the sands and it will soon stop till we know what is done respecting the oversands railway. We must require them to make a branch railway.'[3]

In 1839, an energetic newcomer was added to the ranks of the Furness ironmasters. William Henry Schneider (1817-1887) was descended from a Swiss family, one of whose members migrated to London and founded a merchanting business in 1769, which became principally associated with mineral exploration both in the United Kingdom and abroad, primarily in Mexico and South America[4].

Schneider met Joseph Jopling and his son Charles Michael, who were advisers to Lord Burlington. The outcome of that meeting was that Schneider leased mining rights on Burlington's Park Farm estate, some three miles north of Barrow village. The Park Farm royalty and that at Plumpton, near Ulverston, proved unrewarding, which led to Schneider purchasing established mines at Whitriggs and Orgrave, northeast of Dalton.

In 1842 Schneider and his partner James Davis built the fourth jetty at Barrow for the export of iron ore and, according to Schneider's much later account of 1884: *'In the years 1840-41, an effort was made to get a tramway from the mines to the port of Barrow.'*[5]

Schneider approached the Duke of Buccleuch, the principal royalty owner in Furness, for a loan of £40,000 for this purpose, to which Buccleuch acceded, provided that an agreed rate of interest was paid on the loan. In Schneider's own words, *'So little was spirit of the times that the guarantee was not forthcoming'*, and the matter lapsed. It might be claimed that Buccleuch was short-sighted in this matter, having much to gain from the expansion of the Furness ironfield, but he was no doubt guided by his professional advisers and their agents who would not wish to expose their master to what they thought might have been a risky investment.

Road transport to Barrow became increasingly difficult as ore production increased so much during the early 1840s, that in 1842, the Furness ironmasters commissioned Job Bintley, the Kendal surveyor, who had been involved in the surveying of the Kendal railway route between Lancaster and Carlisle, to examine a possible route for a tramway between the mines and Barrow. Bintley suggested two alternatives for a tramway commencing at Lindal and passing via Dalton, to Barrow. The first was to run from Furness Abbey via Newbarns and the second via Millwood

Looking south at Kirkby station in the 1930s. In the foreground is the railway built by Lord Burlington, in the period 1838-42, to carry slate from the Burlington Slate Quarries to Kirkby Pool for shipment. (CRA: Pattinson collection)

and Sowerby Woods. These schemes invoked local opposition because of the frequent level crossing of roads – the parish road between Dalton and Barrow being crossed, on the level, five times within four miles.

However, the ironmasters' proposals for a tramway were in the process of being overtaken, as Burlington began to examine the reclamation of land on Salthouse Sands and in the Duddon Estuary, as part of the development of his estates. In 1841 he commissioned the civil engineer, James Walker, (1781-1862) to examine reclamation prospects and the improvement of his slate quarries at Kirkby Moor. Walker had been associated with a number of civil engineering projects and was shortly to become President of the Institution of Civil Engineers, where the length of his tenure of the appointment was to invite peer criticism[6].

In October 1841, Walker and Burlington's Furness agent, Joseph Jopling, examined the district. A survey was carried out by Walker's assistant, J.R. Wright, and a report was submitted in which a number of suggestions were made. The report pointed out that both transport and reclamation projects would inescapably involve the other two manorial lords – the Earl of Lonsdale, in the Duddon Estuary, and the Duke of Buccleuch, in Furness.

Lord Burlington's wife Blanche, daughter of the 6th Earl of Carlisle, died unexpectedly on 27th April 1840 after a short illness. This left him devastated and, with the responsibility of four young children, business affairs were conspicuously absent from his diary for a long time.

One of the first subsequent entries recorded his visit to the Kirkby slate quarries, on 12th August 1841, to meet his solicitor, Benjamin Currey, who was carrying out an examination of the state of the quarries.

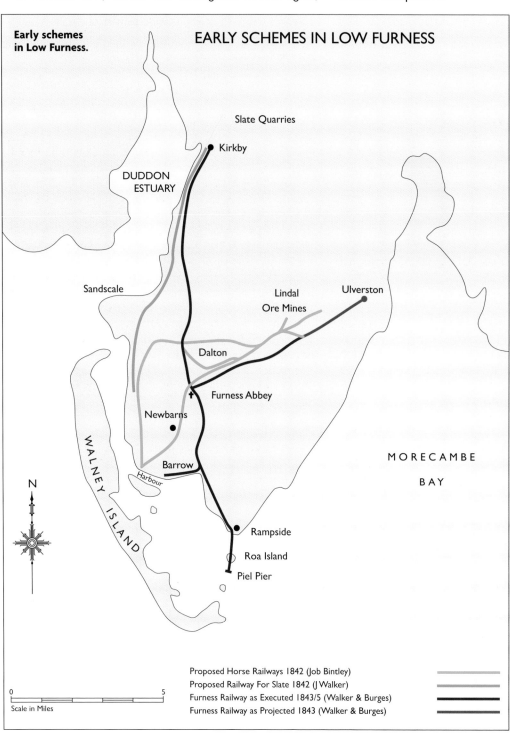

Early schemes in Low Furness.

EARLY SCHEMES IN LOW FURNESS

Slate Quarries

Kirkby

DUDDON ESTUARY

Sandscale

Lindal Ore Mines

Ulverston

Dalton

Furness Abbey

Newbarns

WALNEY ISLAND

Barrow

Harbour

MORECAMBE BAY

N

Rampside

Roa Island

Piel Pier

Proposed Horse Railways 1842 (Job Bintley)
Proposed Railway For Slate 1842 (J Walker)
Furness Railway as Executed 1843/5 (Walker & Burges)
Furness Railway as Projected 1843 (Walker & Burges)

0   5
Scale in Miles

The Furness Railway Bill

On 20th August 1842 Burlington noted:

'I have received Mr Walker's report and plan on the Duddon embankment and it appears sensible and recommends less than had been expected.'

On 11th September 1842 he went to Furness and Barrow:

'...to examine some of the portions of sand Mr Walker proposes to embank and also space for wharves etc if a railway is carried here from the iron and slate works.'

As a result Walker received a second commission, from Burlington and Buccleuch jointly, to examine the possibilities for a railway, from the Kirkby slate quarries and the Furness iron mines, to Barrow. The report was made by James Walker and his partner Alfred Burges, on 1st June 1843, from their office at 23 Great George Street Westminster, and is entitled *'The Furness Railway'*. (The enclosure of Salthouse Sands was the subject of an Act of 1846 which received Royal Assent on 18th August

1846.) The Furness Railway proposal was for a railway from Kirkby to Rampside, with a branch from Roose to Barrow village, together with an 'iron ore railway' connection, commencing near Millwood and running north of Dalton to the Whitriggs and Lindal Moor mines. A branch to Stainton mines was also included.

However, by the time the Bill, plans and sections had been prepared, in September 1843, the 'iron ore railway' had been replaced by a main line railway to Ulverston[7]. A prospectus was issued and a Bill deposited, the statutory notices appearing in the London Gazette on 8th, 18th and 25th November 1843. Burlington noted on 19th December 1843:

'Mr Coward (manager of the quarries) is very much against this railway and so is everyone in the neighbourhood, but Currey is confident they are mistaken.'

Coward later contributed £100.

The Subscription Contract was signed on 25th January 1844 listing:

Duke of Buccleuch, Montagu House, London	£15,000
Earl of Burlington, 10 Belgrave Square, London	£15,000
Henry Hoyle Oddie, 65 Portland Place, London	£1,500
Charles Rivers Freeling, 43 Weymouth Street, London	£1,000
John Iltid Nicholl, Doctors Commons, London	£1,000
Robert Wheatley Lumley, 9 Charles Street, London	£3,000
Frederick John Howard, 1 Belgrave Square, London	£1,000
Benjamin Currey, Old Palace Yard, London	£15,000
William Pott, 6 Bridge Street, Southwark	£3,000[8]

After the deposit of the Furness Railway Bill, the following additional contributions were made:

Robert Wheatley Lumley	£1,000
John Iltid Nicholl	£1,000
William Pott	£2,000
Lord Brooke, Warwick Castle	£1,100
Joseph Hallam, 29 Devonshire Hill, Hampstead	£500
Benson Harrison, Montague Ainslie, Richard Roper } of The Newland Company	£1,000
William Jennings, Eversholt, Dorset	£1,000
John Robinson McClean, 17 Great George Street, London	£1,050
Joseph Paxton, Chatsworth	£1,000
Edward Coward, Kirkby	£100
John Cranke, Ulverston	£250
James Walker, 23 Great George Street, Westminster	£5,000
Marchioness of Ailesbury, 41 Grosvenor Gardens, London	£3,500

This was very much an "in-house" list with some of Burlington's friends and relatives - Howard was his brother-in-law. Among the less familiar names were William Pott, a vinegar manufacturer, and his solicitors, Oddie and Lumley. Nicholl was a proctor (gatherer of tithes and estate dues) employed by the Duke of Buccleuch. J.R. McClean (1813-1873) was a junior partner of James Walker and was to become the FR Engineer, architect of the Barrow Docks and, in 1864-5, President of the Institution of Civil Engineers.

The Furness Railway Bill came before a House of Lords

Standing Orders Committee on 2nd March 1844 and, with amendments relating to the level crossing of a turnpike road, was allowed to proceed. It was examined by the Lords Committee on Railway Bills on 6th May 1844. As no petitions against the Bill were presented and, subject to a speed limit of 6 mph on the crossing of the Dalton – Newton road, it was passed and received Royal Assent of 23rd May 1844.

The Act authorised the four branches from Little Mill (later known as Millwood Junction) to Piel, Barrow, Lindal and Kirkby Ireleth, the latter being described as *'terminating by a Junction with an existing Railway or Tramroad at or near Sandside in the Parish of Kirkby Ireleth'*. This was Lord Burlington's own railway, commenced in 1838 but held up pending a decision on the railway across Morecambe Bay which was abandoned in 1840.

On 18th August 1845 Burlington met FR engineer J.R. McClean and Captain Stephen Eddy (the Duke of Devonshire's lead mine captain from Grassington, who was advising Burlington on the development of the Kirkby Quarries) at Kirkby regarding the course of the branch down from the quarries. On 10th October Burlington noted *'The Incline to connect the quarries with the railway is decided and will commence soon'*. McClean prepared the plans and the FR contractor Tredwell carried out the work of construction. By July 1847 the incline was in operation, and on 29th September Burlington reported *'went up my incline in a slate wagon'*.

The Railway Mania

The first meeting of the shareholders of the new Furness Railway Company was held at Benjamin Currey's offices, 6 Old Palace Yard, Westminster on 10th July 1844, when Currey, representing Burlington interests, was elected Chairman and the following Directors were appointed:

Robert Wheatley Lumley, of the firm of Oddie and Lumley, Solicitors of 18 Carey Street, London, representing share-holder William Pott,
John Iltid Nicholl Barrister and proctor of Doctors Commons, London, representing the interests of the Duke of Buccleuch
Frederick John Howard, of 1 Belgrave Square, London, Burlington's brother-in-law.
Arthur Currey (Benjamin's son) was appointed Secretary.

Currey told the meeting of James Walker's resignation as engineer to the Company and, on Walker's recommendation, the appointment of John Robinson McClean as his successor.

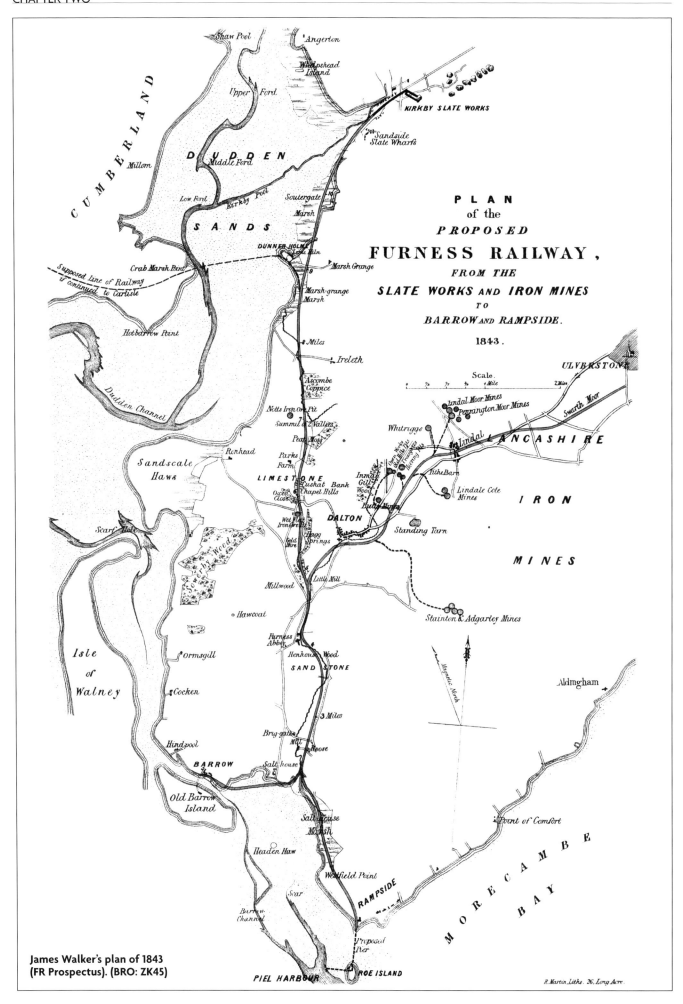

James Walker's plan of 1843
(FR Prospectus). (BRO: ZK45)

McClean had already recommended a number of improvements to the line of the Furness Railway and these had been incorporated into the Act. Benjamin Currey proposed that the seal of the dissolved monastery of St Mary of Furness be adopted by the Company together with the motto *Cavendo Tutus* (Secure by caution) – that of the Cavendish family.

The first meeting of the Directors was held on 17th July 1844 at Currey's offices with Currey, Lumley and Nicholl present. The detailed business of constructing a railway had begun.

The two years which it took to construct the Furness Railway embraced a period of unprecedented railway promotion which has become known as the 'Railway Mania', the evolution of which inevitably impinged on the Furness Railway's directors' objectives and decisions in both general and local contexts. The general effects were caused by the sheer scale of railway promotion in the 1845 and 1846 Parliamentary sessions. The 1844 session, in which the Furness Railway and the Lancaster and Carlisle Railway were authorised, had been busy enough, taxing the Parliamentary processes for Private Bills sufficiently to lead to measures being taken for the improvement of these procedures.

William Gladstone, President of the Board of Trade and a protagonist of railway regulation, required that a committee of the Board's railway department, chaired by the Board's Vice-Chairman, Lord Dalhousie, should examine and report to Parliament, on all railway Bills with a view to agreeing their compatibility with the national interest. This committee was soon overwhelmed as 248 Bills were deposited in November 1844 for the 1845 session of Parliament. Further, the committee came under pressure to receive the lobbyists for these Bills and to listen to their respective cases. An additional problem was that the decisions of Dalhousie's board had a profound effect on the value of 'scrip' – the shares in promoted railways. This led to criticism of the Board of Trade's powers and to allegations of corruption, although such allegations were without foundation as the records of the Board of Trade's railway department show. Nevertheless, both Dalhousie and the law secretary, Samuel Laing, suffered health breakdowns due to the pressures upon them. Board of Trade scrutiny of railway Bills lapsed in 1845 and the policy was subsequently abandoned[9].

Another problem was the severe pressure put on the available resources for engineering, surveying and plan making, owing to the hundreds of new lines of railway, with the result that many plans and sections for new lines were incompetently prepared, leading to successful petitions, by rivals, that the plans failed to comply with the Standing Orders of Parliament. Also, the number of Bills deposited outstripped the availability of capital required to execute them. Shares were acquired by a deposit of 10 per cent, often on a speculative basis, overstretching the ability of many scrip holders to meet subsequent calls on the shares. Many shares were forfeited and deposits lost for non-payment of calls, as a result, numerous individuals were financially ruined.

For example, the Whitehaven and Furness Junction Railway, authorised in the 1845 session, had obtained approval for its line by Dalhousie's board and was duly sanctioned. However, by 1847, no fewer than 11,652 of the 17,360 shares were in arrears on the third call[10]. Fortunately for the Furness Railway Company, the modest objectives of its 1846 Bill, to extend the line to Broughton and to Ulverston, were well within the resources of its affluent proprietors.

Matters grew worse in the 1846 parliamentary session, when some 561 Bills were presented, but only 271 received Royal Assent. These included 24 for amalgamation, 7 for the enlargement of the facilities of existing companies, 131 for branches to existing companies and only 109 for new companies[11].

It was, however, the local implications of Railway Mania which were of greater significance to the Furness Railway. Various schemes were proposed both east and west of the Lancaster & Carlisle Railway (L&CR). The first of several major railway amalgamations had taken place in 1844 when, after a period of almost suicidal rate cutting, the Midland Counties Railway (Rugby to Derby), the Birmingham and Derby Junction Railway (Birmingham to Derby) and the North Midland Railway (Derby to Leeds) joined forces, under the chairmanship of George Hudson, to form the Midland Railway[12]. This system sought an outlet to Scotland and, as the terrain north of Newcastle was not conducive to railway construction, the obvious choice was to extend north-west from Leeds, by way of the Aire and Lune valleys, to join the Lancaster and Carlisle Railway.

The Leeds and Bradford Railway had been authorised in July 1844[13] and, in 1845, drafted a Bill for an extension to Skipton and Colne to connect with a branch of the East Lancashire Railway. The connection between Skipton and the Lancaster & Carlisle was the objective of a separate company, the North Western Railway, which had a Bill in the 1845 session. This company, in addition to connecting with the L&CR at the head of the Lune Valley at Orton (Low Gill), proposed to serve the town of Lancaster by connecting with the nominally independent Morecambe Bay Harbour & Railway (Lancaster to Poulton, with a harbour for Irish steamer traffic) and to provide a means of communication with Furness and West Cumberland.

The course of this latter connection was influenced by the schemes west of the Lancaster & Carlisle line, however, by the time the North Western Railway Bill came before the Parliamentary Committee, on 29th April 1846, no scheme west of the L&CR had been approved and the NWR proposal for a branch to Milnthorpe was struck out. The North Western Railway Act of 26th July 1846 gave powers to build the line from Skipton to Low Gill, on the L&CR, with a branch to Lancaster, and with offers of financial support from the NWR, the Morecambe Harbour and Railway Act was passed, its title having been amended by the exclusion of the word "Bay". Eventually its powers were taken over by the NWR[14].

Also, east of the Lancaster and Carlisle line, were several proposals for lines from the north east into Lancashire and from Yorkshire to Scotland. After various deals and scheme amalgamations only the Northern Counties Union Railway was authorised for a line from Thirsk, on the York & Newcastle Railway, to Clifton on the Lancaster & Carlisle Railway, with branches from Bishop Auckland to Kirkby Stephen and from Kirkby Stephen to Tebay. This line was never built but, at a later date, was completed in part by the South Durham & Lancashire Union and Eden Valley Railways.

The Furness Railway directors had to consider three proposals for lines between the Lancaster & Carlisle Railway and Furness. In its original prospectus of 1844, the Whitehaven & Furness Junction Railway indicated its intention to seek powers for an extension from Dalton, on the Furness Railway, to the Lancaster & Carlisle line. On 9th May 1845 it issued a Notice for its Lancashire Extension[15] and a prospectus was published in Herapath on 31st May 1845. The provisional committee was chaired by Lord Lonsdale and included Benjamin Currey, Chairman of the Furness Railway. George Stephenson was the Engineer. The Whitehaven & Furness Junction Railway Lancashire

Extension (WFJRLE) petitioned to bring in its Bill, with proposed capital of £350,000, in time for the 1846 Parliamentary session. There were a number of petitions in favour of the WFJRLE, including the inhabitants of Ulverston, Whitehaven, Workington, Maryport and Harrington, together with the Maryport & Carlisle Railway. These petitions also objected to the rival Ulverstone, Furness & Lancaster & Carlisle Railway Bill[16]. However, two petitions against the WFJRLE Bill were received, one of which was from the Lancaster & Carlisle Railway, on the grounds that the Standing Orders of Parliament had not been complied with. The Chairman of the Select Committee on Petitions for Private Bills reported to the Commons, on 3rd April 1846, with a long list of the WFJRLE's non-compliance with Standing Orders. The principal failure was that the Parliamentary plans[17] showed two lines, one directly across Morecambe Bay to Hest Bank and an alternative running inland from Flookburgh, via Grange-over-Sands and Silverdale village, to a junction with the Lancaster & Carlisle at Dertred Yeat (Carnforth), although the Bill described only the latter line. A large number of detailed errors occurred in the plans, for example, the Bill referred to bridges at crossings of public roads, whereas the plans showed level crossings, in contravention of the Railway Clauses Consolidation Act 1845, and there were a large number of omissions of properties from the Book of Reference. The L&CR petition was referred to the Select Committee on Standing Orders which, on 4th May 1846, reported that Standing Orders should not be dispensed with. Consequently the WFJRLE Bill failed.

The main competing Bill was that of the Ulverstone, Furness & Lancaster & Carlisle Railway (UFLCR). Its Notice, published in Herapath on 3rd May 1845, proposed a line from Ulverston to Milnthorpe, on the L&CR, which would form *a communication between Furness & West Cumberland and the manufacturing districts of Lancashire and Yorkshire'*. The engineers were Joseph Locke FRS and John Errington MInstCE. The provisional committee included Lord Burlington, the Duke of Buccleuch, Benjamin Currey and Robert Wheatley Lumley, all Furness Railway proprietors. A prospectus was published in Herapath on 17th May 1845. The inclusion of Benjamin Currey, Chairman of the Furness Railway Company, in the list of the provisional committee of two competing lines, the FR and UFLCR, is a matter for speculation. The UFLCR line was to run from Milnthorpe, on the L&CR, by way of the Derby Arms at Witherslack and a tunnel, 2,255 yards long, to Newby Bridge, thence by the Leven Valley to Greenodd and north of the basin of the Ulverston Canal to a junction with the Furness Railway[18]. Joseph Locke's report on the proposed line was published in Herapath on 5th July 1845.

Locke commented on the previous Hague scheme and on the rival WFJRLE project:

'The construction of an embankment in that situation would certainly be hazardous and its maintenance would be both expensive and subject to much risk by the injurious action of the sea.'

He also alluded to the strong possibility of Admiralty objections. Subsequent events proved Locke to be right on both counts.

The capital proposed was £350,000 and the value of the connection with the Windermere steamers at Newby Bridge, for the tourist traffic, was highlighted. Finally, Locke referred to the avoidance, by his scheme, of any interference with the navigations of the rivers Kent and Leven[19]. One petition against this Bill

survived, that of Benson Harrison and others. The petitioners were Benson Harrison of Green Bank, Westmorland, Ironmaster; Montague Ainsley of Ford Lodge, Lancashire, Ironmaster; and Richard Roper of Gawith Field, Lancashire, Ironmaster; (all of the Newland Company): John Fell of Spark Bridge, Lancashire, Gentleman, Contractor and Timber Merchant; Joseph Walker of Ulverston, Lancashire, Merchant; and Stephen Stephenson of Lowick Bridge, Lancashire, Merchant. Their case was that the proposed line would run close to the Backbarrow Ironworks where it was necessary to store large amounts of charcoal, which would be a fire hazard and that nearby premises at Greenodd would be damaged.

The UFLCR scheme had been the subject of an editorial in the *Whitehaven Herald* of 28th February 1846. It referred to a 'well-timed' letter by Thomas Ainsworth, the West Cumberland ironmaster of The Flosh, Cleator and continued:

'It will be remembered that the W&FJR were the first projectors of the undertaking (to connect West Cumberland with the L&CR) and the directors of the L&CR impressed with notions of its practicability, convened a meeting and put out a prospectus in which they proposed a competition line which was to extend to Ulverstone and join their line near Milnthorpe. Both Companies have their schemes before Committees of the House. The U.F.& L.& C.R. having passed the Standing Orders Committee and the W.&.F.J.R. Lancashire Extension being now before them, coming on for hearing next week. A Petition to the House of Commons is in the course of signature. The line of the W.& F.J.R.L.E. is shorter by upward of 8 miles.'

Thomas Ainsworth's letter which prompted those remarks was dated 21st February 1846. It read:

'You are aware that we already enjoy a railway communication from Carlisle to Workington which will soon be extended to Whitehaven and that Cockermouth will soon be connected with this line, and that a railway is under formation connecting all these lines with the Furness District. To carry this communication forward into the commercial districts of Lancashire must be the wish of every resident of West Cumberland and Lonsdale North of the Sands. This the W.&.F.J.R. wish to do by their Lancashire Extension or "Coast Line". But a party have planted themselves down between Ulverston and Milnthorpe 8 miles longer than the Coast Line, with worse gradients and at a cost of construction greater. I consider I am only doing my duty in warning you of the penalty which is impending and which maybe enacted, unless you petition against it.[20]'

In 1846, Parliament ruled that railway Bills must be approved by a special meeting of provisional shareholders before being enacted, to ensure that an adequate provision of capital was available to complete the scheme[21]. Such a meeting was convened by the provisional committee of the UFLCR and its report was noted by Herapath's *Journal* on 9th May 1846. The failure of the North Western Railway's Milnthorpe branch, together with that of the WFJRLE Bill were also noted.

The meeting was in favour of continuing with the Bill, but at a subsequent meeting in London, on 19th May 1846, where 9,429 shares were represented, more than the third required by the new Sessional Orders, there was a five to three vote in favour of discontinuing the railway. It was unanimously resolved to wind

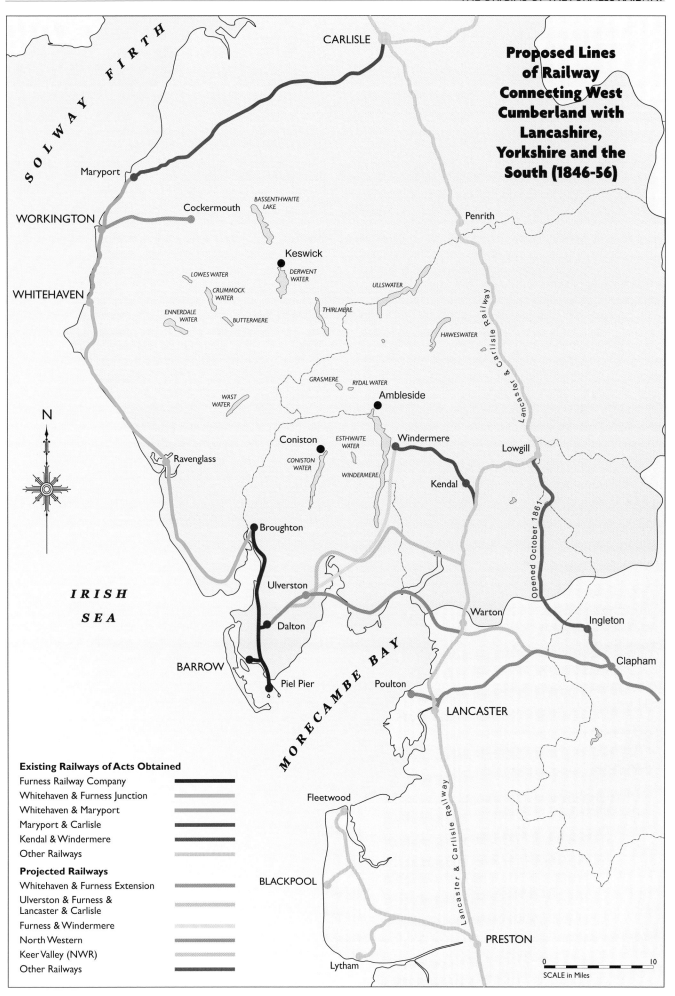

Proposed Lines of Railway Connecting West Cumberland with Lancashire, Yorkshire and the South (1846-56)

SOLWAY FIRTH

CARLISLE

Maryport

Cockermouth

BASSENTHWAITE LAKE

Penrith

WORKINGTON

Keswick

LOWES WATER

DERWENT WATER

ULLSWATER

WHITEHAVEN

CRUMMOCK WATER

THIRLMERE

HAWESWATER

ENNERDALE WATER

BUTTERMERE

Lancaster & Carlisle Railway

GRASMERE

RYDAL WATER

N

WAST WATER

Ambleside

Coniston

ESTHWAITE WATER

Windermere

Lowgill

Ravenglass

CONISTON WATER

WINDERMERE

Kendal

IRISH SEA

Opened October 1861

Broughton

Warton

Ingleton

Ulverston

Dalton

Clapham

BARROW

Piel Pier

Poulton

MORECAMBE BAY

LANCASTER

Existing Railways of Acts Obtained

Furness Railway Company

Whitehaven & Furness Junction

Whitehaven & Maryport

Fleetwood

Maryport & Carlisle

Kendal & Windermere

Other Railways

Projected Railways

Whitehaven & Furness Extension

BLACKPOOL

Ulverston & Furness & Lancaster & Carlisle

Furness & Windermere

North Western

Keer Valley (NWR)

PRESTON

Other Railways

Lancaster & Carlisle Railway

0 ____ 10

SCALE in Miles

Lytham

up the project[22] and a supper was held, on 21st May 1846, to celebrate the winding up of the Company[23].

The third contender west of the L&CR was the Furness and Windermere Railway (F&WR). This was not actually a direct competitor as it was promoted by Kendal interests to provide a railway link with Furness and West Cumberland to enhance Kendal's trade with Ireland, and it was, in fact, considered to be complementary to the WFJRLE line. Its deposited plan[24] was for a line from Birthwaite (later Windermere Town) to Ulverston via Newby Bridge. Herapath, of November 1845, noted that the F&WR now proposed to join the WFJRLE at Newland, east of Ulverston. The FR board had recorded, on 28th February 1846, that 'The proposed F&WR is before Parliament and in the event of its promoters obtaining an Act will bring a great deal of traffic to your line.' On 9th May 1846 Herapath reported that the F&WR had abandoned its line between Birthwaite and Newby Bridge, an action noted by the L&CR at its meeting on 28th August 1846. In conclusion it should be noted that Herapath's list of Bills referred to an Ulverston & Milnthorpe Union Railway. A Prospectus has survived in Preston Records Office, showing that the provisional directors were nearly all from Northern Ireland, but it does not appear to have reached Bill stage[25].

All that remained in the 1846 Parliamentary session was the Furness Railway Extension Bill[26] proposing extensions from Kirkby to Broughton-in-Furness and from the FR terminus at Crooklands to the Urswick Road at Ulverston, with branches from Crooklands to the Butts mines and from Lindal Cote to the Whitriggs mines. The line to Lindal, authorised by the 1844 Act, was abandoned.

Further capital of £100,000 was proposed and was taken up according to the subscription contract as follows:

Duke of Buccleuch	£14,000
Earl of Burlington	£12,200
Benjamin Currey	£10,560
James Walker	£4,000
J.R. McClean	£260
John Brogden	£560
Alfred Burges	£900
Marchioness of Ailesbury	£3,300
Benson Harrison	
Montague Ainslie of The Newland Company	£600
Richard Roper	
John Cranke	£260
Edward Coward	£100

Only the Kirkby Kendal – Kirkby Ireleth Turnpike Trustees petitioned against the Bill which received Royal Assent on 27th July 1846. The subscribers were those of the original FR Bill of 1844 with the exception of John Brogden of Sale, Manchester, a contractor who was destined to play a major role in the development of the railways of Furness.

Building the Furness Railway

The first meeting of the FR Directors took place on 17th July 1844. On 7th August, the newly-appointed engineer to the Company, John Robinson McClean, advised a deviation of the line at Millwood to allow the building of a curve between the Kirkby and Dalton branches of the FR, which would provide for through traffic from Whitehaven should the proposed Whitehaven & Furness Junction Railway be built. On 7th September McClean further advised that the sharp curve at Furness Abbey might be improved by the construction of a

tunnel, 100 yards long, at a cost of £300, a momentous recommendation as its acceptance by the board saved the destruction of part of the ruins of Furness Abbey. Additional improvements in the line, suggested by McClean on 13th November, were a more inland course between Salthouse and Barrow and the termination of the line at Rabbit Hill, short of Barrow village. He also advocated that the other end of the line should terminate at Crooklands, a half mile east of Dalton, from where cheap tramways to the various mines could be made.

At the shareholders' meeting on 26th February 1845, the Directors reported that:

'The portion of the line which the Company had originally intended to carry from Lindal to Ulverstone was abandoned prior to the application to Parliament, the undertaking not having met with sufficient encouragement from that Town to justify its adoption.'

On 12th February the FR Board meeting, attended by Currey, Lumley and Nicholl, considered the tenders for the construction of the line for completion by 30th September 1845. These were:

Messrs Tredwell	£47,788 19s. 6d.
John Brogden	£59,722 2s. 6d.
Messrs Betts & Son	£65,000 0s. 0d.

On McClean's advice, a reduced tender from Tredwell, of £46,287 19s. 6d. for completion by 31st December 1845, was accepted and, on 19th March 1845, McClean's recommendation that the trackbed of the Furness Line should be made to accommodate a double line of railway was also accepted.

It is abundantly clear that this 31 year old Ulsterman's engineering prowess greatly impressed the FR Board. He was to go on to become the architect of Barrow Docks, the lessee with John Brogden of the South Staffordshire Railway, and President of the Institution of Civil Engineers in 1865. McClean was the first of a number of brilliant professional people who were destined to support William Cavendish, second Earl of Burlington and seventh Duke of Devonshire, in his commercial activities within the region. Other significant figures were James Ramsden, FR Manager; Josiah Smith, Barrow Hematite Steel Works Manager; and William Currey, his solicitor and guardian of his finances. The Duke likewise found himself important aides in his other fields of activity, for example, on the Cavendish estates at Buxton and at Eastbourne.

Construction of the Furness Railway began at Salthouse under the direction of Francis Croughton Stileman (1824-1889), one of McClean's pupils, who in 1849, was to become his partner. The firm of McClean & Stileman remained as consulting engineers to the FR until the death of McClean in 1873, after which, Frank Stileman, son of F.C. Stileman, joined the practice and resided in Barrow.

The line's construction had a great effect on the local economy, excavators were paid 3s. 3d. per day[27] and Burlington noted in his diary, on 6th March 1845, that he was obliged to increase the rates of pay to his quarrymen at Kirkby, 'Mainly owing to the Furness Railway which is in progress and on which large wages can be earned.' Day labourers on a farm near Dalton had been paid 1s. per day in 1844, but by 1845 were receiving 1s. 1d or 1s. 2d. and, by 1846, 1s. 6d.[28] The FR Board noted that progress on the line had been slowed by a strike of workmen in May, but they were back at work in June when Wordsworth visited Furness Abbey. He wrote on 21st June 1845:

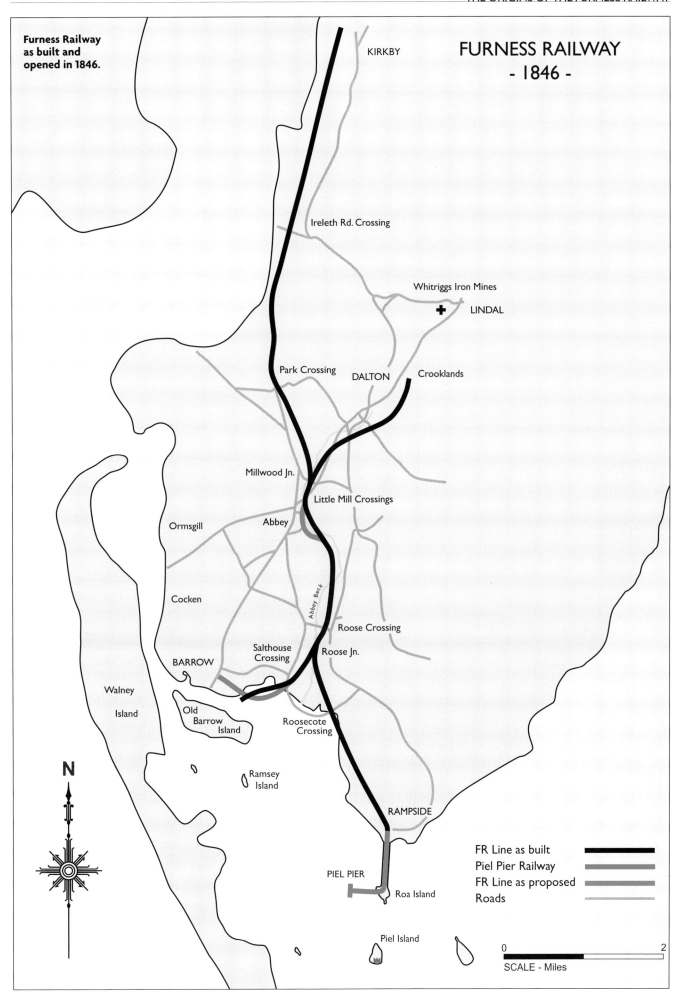

Furness Railway as built and opened in 1846.

FURNESS RAILWAY
- 1846 -

KIRKBY

Ireleth Rd. Crossing

Whitriggs Iron Mines

LINDAL

Park Crossing

DALTON

Crooklands

Millwood Jn.

Little Mill Crossings

Ormsgill

Abbey

Cocken

Abbey Beck

Roose Crossing

Roose Jn.

Salthouse Crossing

BARROW

Old Barrow Island

Roosecote Crossing

Walney

Island

Ramsey Island

RAMPSIDE

N

PIEL PIER

Roa Island

FR Line as built
Piel Pier Railway
FR Line as proposed
Roads

Piel Island

0   2
SCALE - Miles

Furness Abbey tunnel, c.1935. This view from the south portal shows its short 67 yard length, the construction of which saved part of the ruins of the nearby Abbey from destruction. Rebuilding with the present brick portals took place between 1956 and 1959 when tracks were interlaced to allow trains to continue running whilst reconstruction took place. (CRA: Pattinson collection)

'Well have your Railway Labourers to this ground
Withdrawn for noontide rest. They sit, they walk
Among the ruins, but no idle talk
Is heard; to grave demeanour all are bound.
And from one voice a Hymn with tuneful sound
Hallows once more the long deserted quire
And thrills the old sepulchral earth around.
Others look up and with fixed eyes admire
That wide spanned arch, wondering how it was raised
To keep so high in air, the strength and grace.
All seem to feel the spirit of the place,
And by general reverence God is praised.
Profane Despoilers, stand yet not reproved
While there, these simple-hearted men are moved?' [29]

The Furness Railway, having accepted McClean's recommendation to avoid the ruins by a short tunnel, soon recognised the attractions of Furness Abbey and a station was built there, followed by a hotel, a conversion of an existing Manor House.

Burlington noted, on 12th August 1845, that the line had made much progress, being in some parts nearly finished. He was not the only interested visitor. He found *'Currey and his sons and Paxton looking at the line.'* [30] By December the Board was anticipating an opening of the line between Dalton and Barrow in March 1846, but the Furness winter, with its gales and rain, delayed progress, so that by 25th February McClean had revised his estimate of completion to 1st May 1846.

Early in 1846 there had been two important arrivals in Furness. On 23rd July 1845, the Board had ordered two standard Bury bar-framed 0-4-0 locomotives from Bury, Curtis & Kennedy of Liverpool at £1,495 each. This class of locomotive had been employed on the London & Birmingham Railway (L&BR) with some success and the first locomotive was brought over from Fleetwood, in March 1846, on the deck of a tugboat. This ran up alongside Henry Schneider's pier at Barrow where the unloading was supervised by Thomas Fisher on the instructions of Benjamin Currey, the FR Chairman, who was about to leave for London. Fisher recalls:

'Next morning when the tide was at a height that left the tugboat on a level with the pier, we got to work, put a line of rails from the pier on to the boat, got the engine placed on the rails, made fast our ropes and chains on to it and with a long pull and a strong pull and a pull altogether of about 100 hands, landed it safely on the hill to a position about the top part of St George's Square!' [31]

At the FR Board Meeting of 16th January 1846, consideration was given to the appointment of a Locomotive Superintendent and the applications of a certain James Ramsden and one other were considered. McClean was asked to interview Ramsden and, on 29th January reported that the second applicant had been seen, but as *'the person appointed should be intimately acquainted with locomotive engines'* that applicant was unsuitable. The directors duly appointed James Ramsden who immediately advised the purchase of two further locomotives *'of a more powerful nature',* together with additional passenger coaches and ore wagons. [32]

James Ramsden (1822-1896) was born at Bolton on 23rd February 1822, the son of a millwright. He had served his apprenticeship with Bury, Curtis & Kennedy and when the FR had ordered its first locomotives from that firm, was working at the London & Birmingham Railway's works at Wolverton. (Ramsden's L&BR driver's ticket has survived in the CRA Walker Collection held at Kendal Records Office.) Ramsden was destined to serve the FR for 50 years, becoming Secretary and Manager in 1850 and Managing Director in 1866. He became involved in the municipal affairs of Barrow, being appointed its first Mayor in 1867. He was knighted in 1872.

The FR General Offices, designed by Lancaster architect, Edward Paley, were built in stages, between 1855 and 1857, on a site adjacent to the original Barrow station. In the right foreground is the 1863 engine shed, built on the site of the 1846 station. Later the engine shed became engineering workshops. This building still stands but the General Office building has long gone. (Author: MAC33)

Opening of the Line

By the beginning of June 1846 the permanent way was nearing completion and it was decided to open the line for goods and mineral traffic. The *Kendal Mercury* of Saturday, 6th June 1846 recorded:

'FURNESS RAILWAY. This railway was opened on Wednesday last (3 June 1846) for traffic betwixt Dalton and Barrow, large quantities of iron ore, malt etc. were sent down the line for shipment at Barrow where a splendid pier has been erected by the Furness Railway Co. That part of the line betwixt Barrow and Rampside is not yet finished. No part of the line, for passengers, will be opened until that is completed which may be about the latter part of June or beginning of July.'

Notice of an opening of the FR to passenger traffic on 1st May 1846 had been given to the Board of Trade on 27th March, but due to delays this had to be revised to 31st July 1846. The Inspector General of Railways, Major General C.W. Pasley, inspected the line on 3rd August 1846 in the company of Samuel P. Bidder, engineer of the Preston & Wyre Railway and of Abel Smith's Pier, and Arthur Currey, son of the FR Chairman.

Pasley kept a diary[33] in which he recorded his visit to Fleetwood and Furness, one of his last inspections before leaving the Railway Department. He had arrived at Preston, after business in Manchester, where he was met by an engine sent by Samuel Bidder. He reached Fleetwood at 4.30pm and noted that it was extremely hot and humid. He stayed at the North Euston Hotel which was *'quite full'* and bathed in the hotel's swimming pool, at that time something

On the branch to Piel a panorama of Rampside station looking north c. 1900. On the left is Rampside siding and the stationmaster's house. A train is leaving for Piel. (Wyn Anderson, original postcard. Geoff Holme collection: WH 4-2-2)

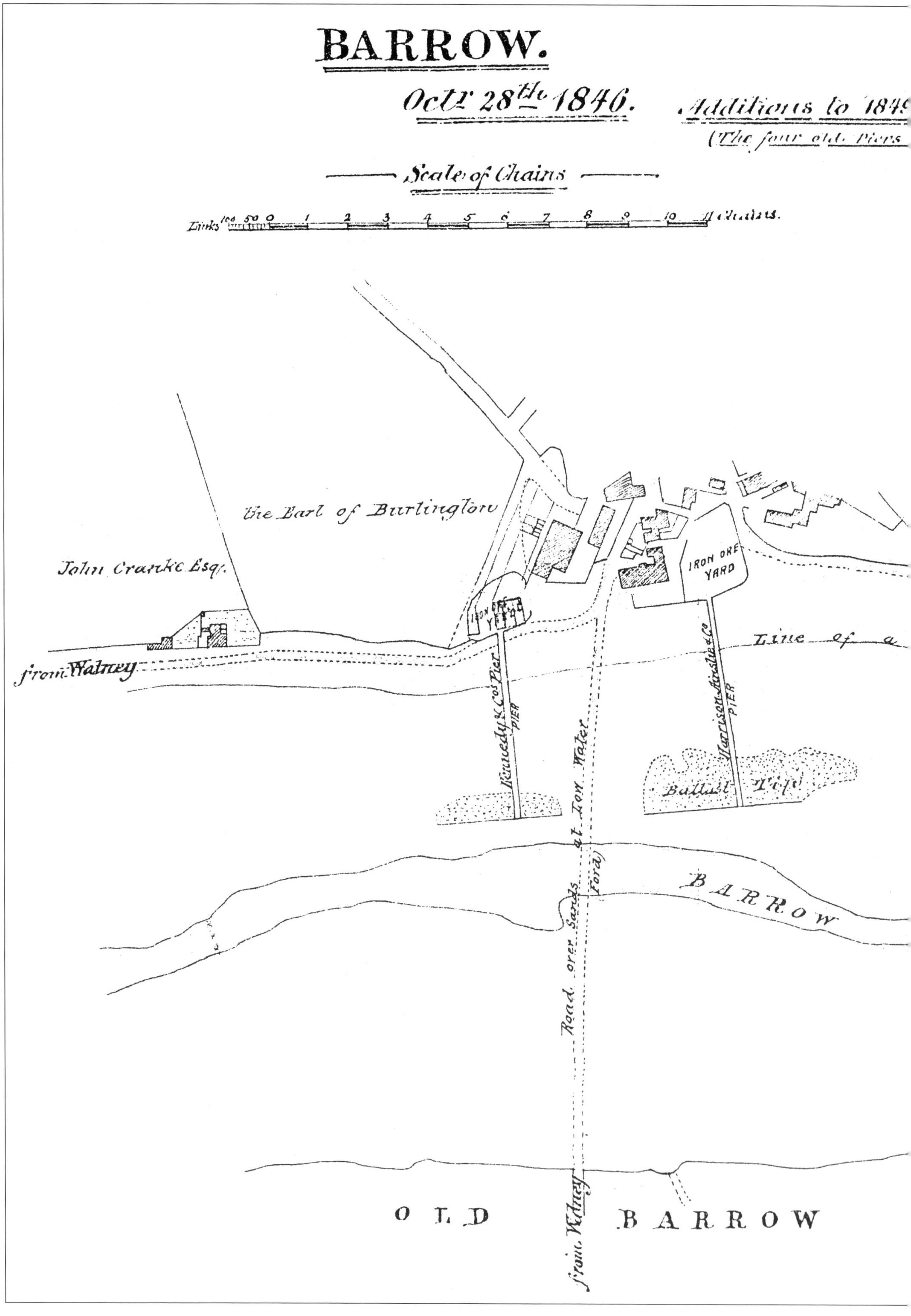

BARROW.

Octr 28th 1846.

Additions to 1849
(The four old Piers

— Scale of Chains —

Links 100 50 0   1   2   3   4   5   6   7   8   9   10   11 Chains.

the Earl of Burlington

John Cranke Esqr

from Watney

IRON ORE YARD

IRON ORE YARD

Kennedy & Co's Pier PIER

Harrison Ainslie & Co PIER

Line of a

Ballast Tip^d

Road over Sands at Low Water (Ford)

B A R R O W

O L D   B A R R O W

from Watney

William Barrow Kendall (1851-1919) was the son of a Salthouse farmer and became the most distinguished Furness antiquarian of his generation. When James Ramsden arrived in Barrow, he lodged with the Kendall family, which may explain how their eldest son went to work in the offices of the Furness Railway engineer in 1867. This drawing by W.B. Kendall shows in detail the small community that was Barrow in 1846 and the four ore loading jetties. To it Kendall has added (in red on his original) the location of the new railway terminus and pier inspected by Major General Pasley in August that year and shows the early facilities provided: a booking office, carriage shed, engine shed and the two rows of railway cottages.

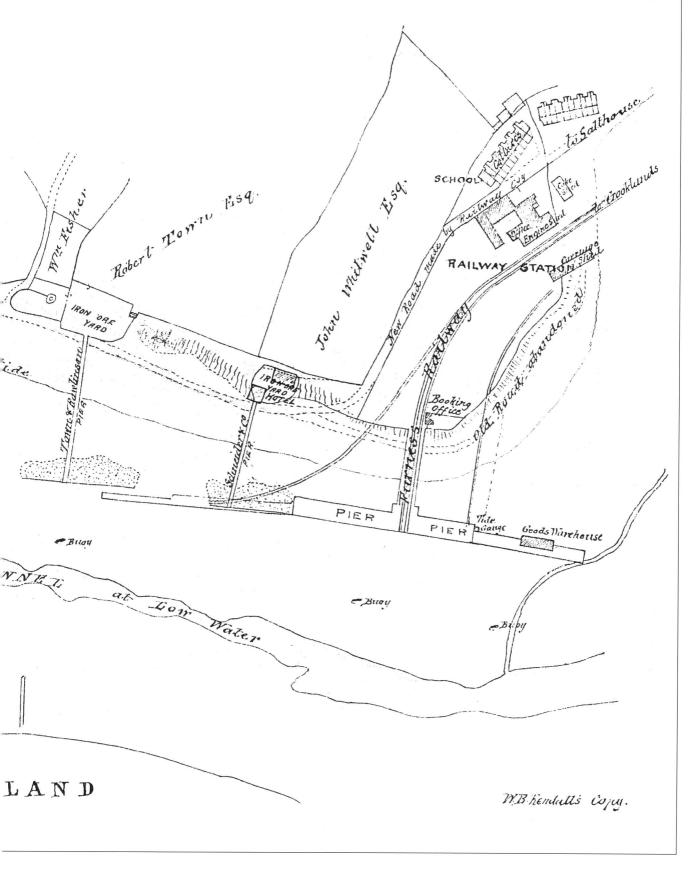

of a novelty. He described it as being 20 feet by 36 feet and sloping downwards from the middle from a depth of 3 feet to 16 feet. The next day he set out on the steamer *Nile* for 'Roe (sic) Island' where:

> 'Mr. Bidder has made a fine pier 1,500' long and an embankment to the mainland. Thence see the Furness Railway and its branches made by Mr. Maclean (sic) and got to Dalton where there are iron ore mines and to Lord Burlington's slate works and afterwards to Barrow, the port for both. The railway is good. See Furness Abbey, a very fine ruin ... a collation and champagne accompanied by Mr. Currey, son of the Chairman. Returned to Fleetwood in the evening for a swim.'

A day later, Pasley inspected the 3½ miles of the double line of the Preston & Wyre Railway and then returned to London by train arriving home at 9.30pm.

Pasley's report on the Furness Railway was dated 3rd August 1846 and was compiled at Fleetwood on Wyre[34]. It is a classic example of the reports of this period and merits quoting in full:

> 'I this day inspected the finished portions of the Furness Railway, the main line of which extends in a Northerly direction from Rampside on Morecambe Bay until it approaches the little town of Dalton to the North Eastward of which it terminates for the present, communicating with the rich iron mines in that neighbourhood at a point from whence it will be continued to Lindal and Ulverstone.

> About 2¼ miles from Rampside Station a short Branch diverges to the westward to Barrow, a small tide harbour long frequented by coasting vessels, and at a distance of about 4¾ miles from Rampside, another Branch in a northerly direction forks off from the main line in the form of a letter 'Y' and, passing to the westward of Dalton, terminates for the present at the slate quarries at Sandside on the estuary of the River Duddon in the Parish of Kirkby Ireleth from whence it will be continued to Broughton.

> The iron ore from Dalton and the slates from Sandside may, by this railway, either be embarked in coasting vessels at Barrow, where the Company are making a convenient pier, extending from the shore with two lines of rails to the distance of 200 feet where it branches out perpendicularly both to the right and left in the form of a letter 'T making a frontage of 400 feet, in which space three lines of rails are to be established and 12 turntables for goods wagons laid down, or at Roe Island which has been connected with the Rampside Station of the Furness Railway by a wooden viaduct upon piles over a little creek called Concle Hole near that station and an embankment over the sands south of that creek which were always dry at low water.

> Concle Viaduct Bridge consists of 16 bays of 12 feet span to admit the free passage of the tides, which in other parts are intercepted by the above mentioned embankment the length of which is nearly 3,000 feet. Upon arriving at Roe Island a fine wooden pier 1,500 feet long has been constructed on piles which is called Piel Pier from a ruined castle of that name on an island opposite. It had originally been proposed to extend this pier from Roe Island to Piel

> Island nearly in a straight line, which was prevented by the Admiralty, who considered that a free passage between these two small islands was necessary for the navigation. Hence the present pier has been laid out in a westerly direction nearly at right angles to the embankment from which it proceeds by a sharp curve and is in three levels, the highest of which commencing from Roe Island admits of iron ore, slates and other goods being put on board steamboats and coasting vessels at high water, the two lower levels which lead into deep water are for passengers to embark when the tide is low. A line of rails in continuation with the Furness Railway has been extended to the southward over the embankment and viaduct and also along the upper portion of Piel Pier which works have been erected at the expense of Mr John Abel Smith who proposes to build an Hotel on Roe Island which will be very convenient for passengers about to cross over from Fleetwood to travel by the Furness Railway especially after the latter shall have connected with Whitehaven and other places to the northward on the same coast by the Whitehaven Junction Railway.

> I was accompanied, in this inspection by Mr. McClean, Engineer of the Furness Railway and by Mr Timperley and Mr. Stileman his assistants as well as by Mr Tredwell the Contractor and Mr. Samuel P. Bidder engineer of the Preston & Wyre Railway who attended to explain the details of the Viaduct and Embankment which works, in connection with the Furness Railway, were constructed for Mr. John Abel Smith under his superintendance.

> The main line of the Furness Railway from Rampside to Dalton is 6 miles 4 chains while the branch to Barrow is 1 mile 20 chains and that to Sandside 6 miles 64 chains to which is added about 53 chains for the extension of the main line from Rampside to Piel Pier, and the whole will amount to nearly 15 miles in length over which a single line of rails only has been laid for the present, except at Barrow Pier as before mentioned and at Piel Pier on the upper level of which two lines of rails with proper switches are to be laid, but the bridges and tunnels that will afterwards be described have been made wide enough and sufficient land has been taken to admit of a second line of rails, which I have no doubt will eventually be required.

> Several of the gradients are steep, being at the rate of 1 in 100 but most of them descend from Dalton, near which the iron mines are situated, towards Rampside as well as towards Barrow, the two points of embarkation which will be in favour of the waggons laden with iron ore for the conveyance of which this railway was chiefly constructed. Two gradients of the same steep rate of inclination on the Kirkby Branch ascend from the slate quarries there towards the junction with the main line after which point the gradients are generally descending as before observed.

> The curves are rather sharp, one of 8 chains radius in particular, near the pier at Barrow, which however, is only 5 chains long. The next sharpest has a radius of 15 chains and is 15 chains in length, besides which there are 15 of 25 chains radius, 1 of 27 chains, 6 of 30 chains, 2 of 35 chains, and 2 of 40 chains radius respectively, intermixed with a smaller number of straight portions for several of the

curves are serpentine as will be seen by the table. The sharpest of these curves being at the end of the Branch terminating on the sea and all being on a line where great speed is not required, will render them unobjectionable. They have been rendered necessary by following the course of the narrow valleys in this district from which the railway could not have deviated without enormous expense.

The cuttings and embankments are generally moderate with few exceptions, the deepest of the former being 21, 27, 43 and 55 feet respectively, the two last being each at the mouth of a Tunnel. None of the other cuttings and none of the embankments exceed 18 feet in extreme depth or height. All the cuttings have been excavated, either in sandstone rock of an excellent quality for building, or in limestone rock, or compact gravel or sand mixed with clay favourable to stability, so that no slips are to be apprehended. One of the embankments on the main line, commencing about 1½ miles from Rampside Station and rather more than 1 mile in length, has been formed over part of the Salthouse Sands covered at high water by materials obtained from the adjacent beach, having a slope of 3 to 1 towards the west, which has been protected by a pitching or pavement of flat stones on edge, after part of the same embankment before that precaution was adopted had been carried away by high tides. Above this pitching, a sloping bank or parapet, also of material procured on the beach and faced with sods on both sides has been raised about 4½ feet higher than the level of the rails to shelter the passengers when the wind blows inshore.

One bridge only, for the turnpike road from Dalton to Barrow, has been erected over the railway, having stone abutments with eight iron girders cambered or raised in the centre in a segmental form, the intermediate spaces being covered with iron plates strengthened by flanges to support the gravel for the roadway. These girders have a span of about 30 feet owing to the obliquity of the road which crosses the railway at an angle of 54 degrees, though the perpendicular width between the abutments is only 24 feet. Under the railway there is only one small semi-circular archway of 12 feet span and another opening of 10½ feet span covered with wooden beams.

There are two tunnels on the main line, the first of which called the Abbey Tunnel commencing at the distance of 3 miles 76 chains from Rampside is 73 yards in length. The arch is semicircular having a span of 24 feet and a clear height of 22 feet above the rails with perpendicular side walls, the former lined with brickwork 18 inches thick, the latter cut out of the sandstone rock. The second called the Dalton tunnel commencing at the distance of 5 miles 30 chains from Rampside, has an arch of semi-elliptical form with segmental side walls and measures 22 feet in clear width at the level of the rails increasing to 24 feet at the

FR 2-4-2 tank engine No.75 has arrived at Piel station on Roa Island with a train from Barrow c.1910. In the left background is the curved embankment which led to Piel Pier used, from 1846, by the FR steamer service to Fleetwood and, from 1867, by the Barrow Steam Navigation Company's Belfast and Isle of Man services. The latter were transferred to Ramsden Dock station in 1882 and the Piel Pier was demolished c.1892. (Lawrence Allen collection)

The original station at Furness Abbey, which dated from the opening of the Furness Railway in 1846, was rebuilt in 1866 with staggered platforms, a down loop and an up bay to enable the exchange of traffic between the lines to Carnforth and to Whitehaven. In 1873 this exchange was moved to a rebuilt Dalton station. (George Taylor collection: KNO 007)

springing of the arch with a clear height of 22 feet. The arch is of brickwork laid in cement, the side walls partly of brickwork and partly of stone rubble both about 2 feet 3 inches thick.

A mansion house adjoining to the grounds of Furness Abbey close to which the main line passes to the eastward, has been purchased and converted into a station, which will have every convenience, including a large refreshment room, it being expected that numerous visitors will be attracted to that magnificent ruin during the summer months and therefore that this will be the principal passenger Station of the railway. The other stations at Rampside, Barrow and Dalton, besides one for Kirkby Ireleth and another a little beyond it at the slate works, the latter of which forms the present terminus of that Branch, though not quite finished, are all in a state for reception of passengers. Turntables have been provided in sufficient number to prevent the necessity of any of the trains travelling tender foremost and self acting switches of an approved pattern have been laid at all the crossings.

The whole of the works of the Furness Railway, including the Bridges and Tunnels that have been described, as well as those of the extension of that line to the Southward, viz. Concle Viaduct bridge, the embankment thence to Roe Island, both sides of which have been pitched or paved, as before described, and Piel Pier, are safe and strong and creditable to the two engineers by whom they were designed and under whose superintendance they have been erected as well as the respective contractors and workmen. The rails, chairs, sleepers etc. are everywhere in a safe and efficient state and have been travelled over by wagons conveying iron ore, slates or contractors materials

for some months which has consolidated every part of this railway and its branches. The Company also gave due notice of their intended opening for passenger traffic to this Department as required by Act of Parliament, the first of one month dated the 27th of March to open on the 1st of May last, which design they afterwards abandoned having resolved to carry goods only for some time, but not without giving me timely notice of the change to prevent a premature inspection; the second was a ten-days notice of their readiness for inspection dated the 20th of July so that as I have now been enabled to form a favourable opinion of the Furness Railway and of its branches and extension, I see no reason why they should not be authorised to open it for public traffic a week from this date as they propose.

I have the honor to be, My Lord, Your Lordship's most obedient humble servant,
*   C.W. Pasley, Major General,*
*   Inspector Genl. of Railways.'*
*   (Authorised opening 12th August)*

The proposal was to open the Furness Railway for passenger traffic on 12th August 1846, which was duly recorded by the *Cumberland Pacquet* of 11th August and the *Kendal Mercury* of 22nd August, both of which suggested that the line had opened on this date. At the FR Directors Meeting on 19th August, it was recorded:

'The Directors approved an undertaking which the Chairman had entered into on behalf of the Company to bear one half of the expense of hiring and working for a period of two months a steamboat to ply between Fleetwood and Piel Pier in consequence of Mr Smith's boat not being ready.'

The Chairman stated that the other half of the expense had been arranged to be divided between Mr. Fell of Spark Bridge and some friends and the Preston & Wyre company. John Barraclough Fell (1815-1902) was a contractor and timber merchant of Spark Bridge on the River Crake near Greenodd where he had a sawmill. He carried out contracts for the Furness Railway, on its extensions to Broughton and Ulverston, in partnership with Charles Michael Jopling (1820-1863), the son of Burlington's former Furness agent, Joseph Jopling. Fell and Jopling operated horse drawn omnibuses between the FR terminus at Dalton and Newby Bridge to connect with the lake steamers operated on Windermere by the Windermere United Steam Yacht Company.

In 1852 Fell went to Italy where, in collaboration with Jopling and the contractor Thomas Brassey, he constructed several railways. Fell developed an interest in centre-rail systems for mountain railways and his system was adopted for the Mont Cenis Railway, opened in 1868. He also developed a monorail system, an example being constructed locally from the Yarlside mine to a point near Roose on the FR[35].

The FR passenger service commenced on 24th August 1846 as confirmed by the Company's subsequent return to the Board of Trade and by the diary of William Fisher, a Barrow farmer. The *Cumberland Pacquet* of 25th August 1846 recorded:

'A powerful steamer now runs twice daily between Fleetwood and Piel and succeeds in performing the trip across the Bay in about 45 minutes.'

The *Westmorland Gazette* of 22nd August 1846 noted that:

'The Ayrshire Lassie *plies daily, weather permitting, Fleetwood depart 11am and 2pm and Piel depart 12.30pm and 3.30pm in connexion with the 6.45pm Fleetwood Mail Train to Preston. Conveyances connect with the steam yachts* Lord of the Isles *and* Lady of the Lake *to Bowness and Ambleside.'*

However, prior to the official opening, an interesting diversion was recorded in the *Cumberland Pacquet* of 28th July 1846:

'Such was the violence of the wind on the Furness Coast last week that a carriage consisting of a few boards about five feet square supported by four wheels was frequently driven upon the finished railway from Roa Island to the mainland near Rampside at the rate of a mile in two minutes by the force of the breeze alone. Several parties who were sojourning in the district enjoyed this somewhat novel atmospheric mode of railway travelling.'

Lord Burlington's diary entry for 9th September 1846 gives his account of a visit to the new Furness Railway that day:

'I rode over to Kirby (sic) very early this morning and have been all over the railway. First down from Kirby with a cargo of slate to Barrow. There is no convenience yet for shipping slate but it will be ready before long. The iron ore seems well managed. Then we went to Piel. The steamer arrived with a number of passengers from Fleetwood. This part is not at present going on quite right as the steamer has several times been aground but it is only a temporary one and another will be employed next year drawing less water. From Piel we went to

The Manor House at Furness Abbey was converted to an hotel from the opening of the Furness Railway in 1846. It was extended, in stages, to the designs of Edward Paley. This view dates from pre-1866. (Original print. Geoff Holme collection)

PILE PIER, RAMPSIDE, WITH BARROW IN THE DISTANCE.
From the Sea.

Piel Pier. An artist's impression, c.1850. While the height of the hills in the background has been exaggerated, the three levels of the original pier, opened in 1846, are shown. No photographs of this or of its 1868 successor have been found. (BRO: BD Sol/4/14/57)

the Abbey. Numbers of people about. No doubt its quietness and seclusion is gone but I hardly know whether it is to be regretted so many holiday people from the great towns have an opportunity of seeing it. In the afternoon after the train returns to Piel all the mob vanishes. The railway seems doing well for the time it has been opened but many things are in an unsettled state.'

It now only remained to have the mandatory opening ceremony. For some reason, possibly the Parliamentary recess which would allow Benjamin Currey to take his vacation, this was delayed until 20th October 1846. The *Cumberland Pacquet* of 27th October reported the event:

'On this day the Furness Railway, which was opened for traffic in July and for passengers in August, was formally opened and the event was celebrated by the Directors with an excursion along the line and a grand banquet at the Furness Abbey Station. ... The Chair was occupied by Benjamin Currey Esq. who was supported by the Earl of Burlington, the Directors and a number of the most respectable gentlemen in the neighbourhood. The usual loyal and constitutional toasts having been disposed of, the after dinner proceedings became extremely animated and we are glad to observe that the necessity for extending this railway in a southerly direction was both universally admitted and generally advocated by the different speakers who addressed the meeting.'

CHAPTER 2 REFERENCES

1   Fisher J, 1891. *Popular History of Barrow-in-Furness* p.36.
2   Melville J & Hobbs J.L. *Op. cit.* p.1.
3   *Devonshire Diaries*, 3rd Aug. 1839.
4   Banks A.G., 1984. *H W Schneider of Barrow and Bowness.*
5   Cumberland & Westmorland Association for the Advancement of Science, 1884/5. *Transactions 10* p.105.
6   *Herapath's Railway Journal*, 25th Jan. 1845.
7   Melville J & Hobbs J.L. *Op. cit.* p.27.
8   *Kendall MSS.* Ref. ZK40/1.
9   Parris H. *Op. cit.*
10 WF&JR SM, 26th June 1847.
11 Tuck H, 1848.. *The Railway Shareholders Manual*, 8th edition.
12 Williams F.S, 1886. *The Midland Railway.*
13 Tuck H. *Op cit.*
14 Baughan P. 1966. *North of Leeds.*
15 *Herapath*, 10th May 1845.
16 *Commons Journal*, Mar. 1846.
17 HLRO, 1846-W51.
18 HLRO, Parliamentary Plan, 1846/Ul.
19 *Herapath*, 5th July 1846.
20 *Whitehaven Herald*, 28th Feb. 1846.
21 Parris H. *Op. cit.*
22 *Herapath*, 23rd May 1846.
23 *Westmorland Gazette*, 23rd May 1846.
24 HLRO: Parliamentary Plan, 1846/F2.
25 L.R. Gilpin, personal communication.
26 HLRO: Parliamentary Plan, 1846/F4.
27 Melville J. & Hobbs J.L. *Op. cit.* p.24.
28 Marshall J.D. *Op. cit.* p.180.
29 Hopkins K, 1966. *The Poetry of Railways* p.266.
30 *Devonshire Diaries*, 3rd Sep. 1845.
31 Fisher J. *Op. cit.* p.86 seq.
32 FRDM, 25th Feb.1846.
33 British Library, Additional Manuscript 41992.
34 PRO: MT6/3/53.
35 Rigg A.N., 1996. *John Barraclough Fell, CE* pp 66-8.

THE FURNESS RAILWAY
EARLY YEARS: 1846-1857

As noted in Chapter Two, the Furness Railway opened for goods and mineral traffic between Kirkby Slate Wharf and Barrow Pier with a branch from Millwood Junction to a mineral terminus at Crooklands, half a mile north of Dalton, on 3rd June 1846. After some delay, passenger traffic commenced on 24th August 1846 between John Abel Smith's railway at Piel Pier and Dalton, and on the Barrow and Kirkby lines in connection with a steamer sailing between Piel Pier and Fleetwood.

The Furness Railway Company made its first return to the Commissioners of Railways[1], as the Railway Department of the Board of Trade had become in 1846, recording that the total number of passengers carried between 24th August and 31st December 1846 was 15,948, made up of 2,838 first class, 4,620 second class and 8,490 third class. Some 306 passenger trains were run, but in addition, third class passengers were also carried on 635 mixed trains. A total of 46,799 tons of freight was carried of which 43,955 tons was iron ore[2]. This traffic allowed the FR Directors to pay a first dividend of 4% per annum for the half year on the £75,000 worth of ordinary stock. This was regarded *as (being as) favourable as could be expected under the difficulties they had to contend with* [3].

Difficulties arose from the operation of some twelve trains a day on a single line with four branches, no signalling, and, initially, only two locomotives, but by the end of 1846 engines No.3 and No.4 had also arrived[4]. At their meeting on 27th February 1847 the FR board authorised the doubling of the line between Dalton and Roose Junction first envisaged on 4th November 1846. This work was completed by May 1847, inspected by Captain Simmons, the Railway Inspector, on 22nd May 1847 and authorised for passenger traffic[5]. The board also authorised the purchase, by FR nominees, of the steamer *Helvellyn* of Glasgow at a cost of £3,500[6] for the Piel – Fleetwood service, due to recommence in the spring of 1847. The traffic returns for the first half of 1847 showed a reduction in passenger traffic, but a freight tonnage increase to 46,797 and the dividend was maintained at 4% per annum for the half year.

In January 1846 the FR board authorised the building of various cottages, four at Barrow, two at Roose Junction, two at Millwood Junction, together with *'ten small cottages at Barrow to be built as cheaply as could be, the price of which, if possible, not to exceed £100 each'.* [7] The ten small cottages were built, in two terraces, on the north side of Salthouse Road, separated by the future Rawlinson Street and the westernmost of these cottages became the office of the Furness Railway, with Thomas Fisher, the first cashier, occupying the back room[8] and James Ramsden the front room. The original passenger station was constructed in wood, with a single platform and various offices on a site in St George's Square. A later sandstone building on this site still stands at the present time.

The year 1847 was relatively quiet after the excitement of 1846, the opening year of the Furness Railway. Lord Burlington's travel arrangements between his favourite seat Holker Hall (he called it home), and London, were greatly improved by the opening of the Lancaster & Carlisle Railway which had a station at Milnthorpe.

On 15th July he rode to Millwood to see Arthur Currey and commented that the railway *'seems doing pretty well'.* Soon after, on 4th August, he was again in Furness to see Currey. *'I went with him all over the railway; everything seems to be doing well'.*

He rode over to Furness yet again to meet Currey and McClean, on 16th August and noted in his diary:

'I saw the packet come in and as the tides are favourable being midday high water and the weather fine, it brought over a great many passengers. McClean and Currey are thinking of deepening the passage to Barrow so as always to have water sufficient to come up.'

The financial crisis of 1848

As early as 21st October 1847, Burlington noted in his diary: *'In London, money matters are getting worse every day.'*

At the beginning of 1848 the FR Directors began to view the Company's financial situation with some anxiety. The sudden death of the company Chairman, Benjamin Currey, in March 1848, deprived the FR of the man who had shouldered so much of the responsibility for the authorisation, building and early running of the line. Burlington noted on 14th March 1848:

'I have been greatly grieved today by the news of poor Currey's death. He was seized with an apoplectic fit yesterday in the House of Lords and died in a few hours. He was a high minded honourable man and I shall deeply feel his loss.'

At the board meeting on 19th April 1848, Burlington was elected the new Chairman, a position he was to hold until 1887 when, because of advancing age, he handed over to his eldest son the Marquis of Hartington. He found the company *'in a deplorable state'* [9] and enlisted the help of Joseph Paxton, who together with some Midland Railway officials, belonging to the then George Hudson empire, attempted to identify the FR's problems. They found *'great fault'* with the original expenditure and the mode of management[10]. Work on the Ulverston extension, which had been let to the local contractors Fell and Jopling, was stopped and the contractors compensated. The FR's problems mirrored that of most railway companies at this time, in the wake of the collapse of the Railway Mania, the neighbouring Kendal and Windermere Railway had to report to its shareholders:

'The disastrous state of commercial affairs has unquestionably discouraged traffic and the Directors had determined to adopt a stringent system of economy.' [11]

On 10th October 1848 the FR board took the first steps to remedy these alleged ills, characteristically passing the increased costs to the consumer, the local iron masters, by raising the tolls for iron ore from 1/6d per ton to 2/- per ton. A Committee of Inspection was formed consisting of Burlington, R.W. Lumley, Joseph Paxton and James Walker. Paxton and Walker were appointed FR Directors and, after the meeting, McClean noted: *'Had a most successful meeting. Ramsden will be cut down to £120.'* [12] The FR board studied the recommendations of the Committee of Inspection on 21st November 1848 and ordered sweeping reductions in staff and rates of pay.

Ramsden escaped personal criticism and, although his salary was reduced, he was given an incentive bonus by which his salary would be increased in proportion to the dividend paid. At the same time the board decided that a meeting of directors would be held every six weeks, at the Furness Abbey Hotel, until further notice. They further resolved that:

'Goods and mineral traffic shall be primarily considered and provided for and passenger traffic to be only regarded as an auxiliary source of profit. When Barrow Pier is completed no trains will run to Piel as the passenger traffic is insufficient to defray expenses.'

On 19th February 1849 Burlington noted:

'Mr Ramsden came over this morning to lay before me a scheme that Mr McClean and another person have for leasing our line. The terms offered are I think very much too low but I hope they may be improved and then I should greatly like a scheme of this kind.'

Burlington clearly favoured the possibility of getting the Furness Railway, with all its recent problems, off his back but he was sensible enough to expect the right price.

The FR Board met on 27th February and rejected the McClean offer, the terms of which were considered *'miserably low'*. There can be no doubt that *'another person'* was John Brogden, as McClean and Brogden together took a lease of the South Staffordshire Railway the following year.

By 23rd May 1849 Burlington was able to note: *'The line is at present doing well.'* The financial crisis was over and the stage set for the extension to Lindal and Ulverston. However no dividend had been paid for the year 1848.

The Furness Railway and Piel Pier

In the 1840s it may have seemed doubtful whether the Furness economy could support three transport operators. The position of the Ulverston Canal Navigation Company at the time was less affected as the extension of the Furness Railway from Dalton to Ulverston was delayed until the next decade. However, the Pile Pier Company had been established in 1843, a year before the Furness Railway, and the FR proprietors found it necessary to build a branch to Abel Smith's causeway at Rampside. On 27th February 1846, the FR board reported the result of a meeting with Abel Smith at which it was proposed to establish a twice daily steamer service between Fleetwood and Piel Pier.

The FR agreed to provide station buildings at Rampside and to run trains over Abel Smith's causeway to the pier to connect with the steamers[13], with Smith paying a toll to the FR for the use of the carriages and locomotives. Smith stated his intention to build an inn on Roa Island.

The iron ore traffic was not mentioned, although it was clearly the intention of the FR to handle the ore traffic at Barrow, but by July 1846 it had become clear that Abel Smith's

co-operation was not forthcoming. The steamer promised for the opening of the FR did not materialise and, after some delay, the steamer *Ayrshire Lassie* was chartered, jointly by the Preston & Wyre Railway, the Furness Railway and John Barraclough Fell, for a service commencing on 24th August 1846.

During the initial two month season of 1846, 2,838 first class and 4,620 second class passengers were carried on the FR, many of whom must also have been steamer travellers. In May 1847 the FR offered Abel Smith five possible arrangements for the use of Piel Pier, which included a Furness Railway lease. Abel Smith demanded either a toll of 6d per passenger, or a share in the FR ore traffic receipts at 1½d per ton, whether shipped at Piel or Barrow. Understandably anxious to maintain its steamer traffic, the FR agreed, under protest, to pay an additional toll of 3d per passenger out of mineral receipts but took Counsel's opinion concerning its rights at Piel[14]. Counsel's opinion was favourable to the FR. However, at the shareholders' meeting on 28th August 1847, it was reported that steamboat traffic had recommenced from Barrow on 24th May 1847 on a tidal basis, using the steamer *Helvellyn* and that the irregularity of the service had hampered traffic. At the shareholders' meeting on 29th February 1848, it was reported that:

'Passenger & mineral traffic has suffered from the depression and from Piel Pier not having been opened but an arrangement with the owner of Piel has been made and the pier will open immediately.'

At the beginning of the crisis year of 1848, the FR made an agreement with the contractors Fell and Jopling to run a steamer between Furness and Liverpool[15] as a result of which the Liverpool, Fleetwood and Furness Steam Packet Company bought the steamer *Zephyr* and commenced running from Piel Pier on 1st March 1848[16]. The steamer *Helvellyn* was chartered for six months by Fell and Jopling to run daily between Fleetwood and Piel Pier, from 1st April 1848[17]. The latter service had hardly commenced from Piel Pier than it came under the scrutiny of the Committee of Inspection and was pronounced not remunerative, so it was decided that the accommodation at Barrow would be improved and the steamer services would be run from there.

Consequently, in 1849, the Fleetwood steamer was again diverted to the tidal Barrow pier, but by this time the financial position of the FR was improving and the FR board looked again to Piel Pier with its natural advantages. An agreement with Abel Smith was reached and the Fleetwood steamer was transferred from Barrow to Piel Pier on 30th July 1849[18]. The FR board commented:

'The working of the trains to Piel would, during the Summer season, be more than covered by the additional passenger receipt ... Mr Fell stated he expected a considerable reduction in the tolls from those charged last year.' [19]

For the winter of 1849-50 the Fleetwood steamer reverted to Barrow, but from 1850 Piel Pier seems to have been regularly used and an uneasy peace prevailed.

By 1851 Abel Smith was again making unreasonable demands and he wrote to the FR seeking an agreement for the use of Piel Pier for iron ore traffic[20].

The FR stated its willingness to issue a two-year agreement, if this would make extra tonnage available, with the provision of a screw steamer for this traffic but Abel Smith decided on an

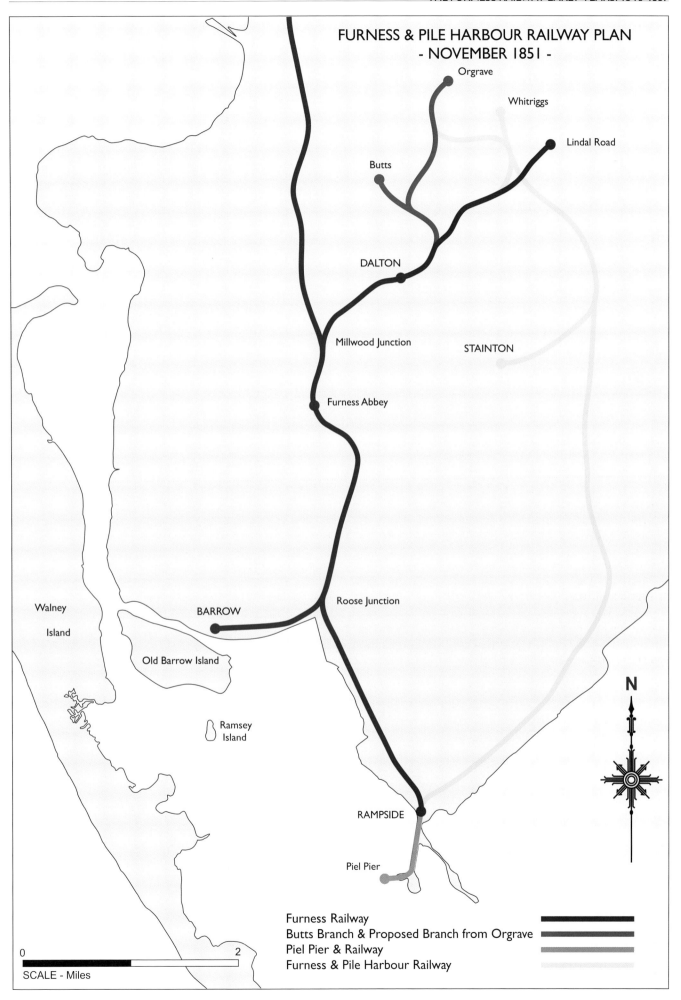

FURNESS & PILE HARBOUR RAILWAY PLAN
- NOVEMBER 1851 -

Orgrave

Whitriggs

Lindal Road

Butts

DALTON

Millwood Junction

STAINTON

Furness Abbey

Walney
Island

BARROW

Roose Junction

Old Barrow Island

Ramsey
Island

RAMPSIDE

Piel Pier

N

Furness Railway
Butts Branch & Proposed Branch from Orgrave
Piel Pier & Railway
Furness & Pile Harbour Railway

0   2

SCALE - Miles

Lindal Railway Station.

The permanent station at Lindal, shown here c.1910, stands on the site of the temporary Lindal Road station. On the left is the up goods loop between Lindal Cote and Lindal West signalboxes used to work empty ore wagons into Lindal Ore Sidings. (Original postcard by Hoskins of Dalton. Geoff Holme collection: N 952)

alternative aggressive policy, based on an alliance with the discontented Furness iron masters and, in November 1851, Abel Smith brought into Parliament a Bill entitled the 'Furness & Pile Harbour Railway and Branch to the Orgrave Tramway'. The parliamentary plan[21] showed a main line running from the Abel Smith causeway at Rampside to Lindal Moor, crossing under the authorised FR Ulverston Extension near the future Lindal Station. A branch to Stainton Mine was proposed, together with a connection with the FR Butts Branch at Dalton. Effectively this line would have tapped the whole of the Furness ironfield and Abel Smith had allies in the persons of J.B. Fell (who had been

bought off his contract for the Ulverston Extension,) and Charles Kennedy, the Ulverston ironmaster, who had supported Abel Smith's original application to Parliament in 1843. The FR petition against the Furness & Pile Harbour Bill failed to comply with Standing Orders but Abel Smith withdrew his Bill and discussions with the FR began in June 1852[22].

The saga of the competitive line to Piel Pier was watched by Lord Burlington at close quarters from his Holker Hall residence and recorded in his diary:

'Had a visit from Mr Fell yesterday. He is irritated at not having got the last contract (Crookland to Lindal) and is devising a new line to Piel Pier to put us out and be a rival in the Iron Trade. He says he is acting with Mr Smith's concurrence and no doubt they will both try to extort something out of us.' [23]

'Mr Smith is still threatening a rival line to Piel but we think he can make nothing of it.' [24]

'Mr Ramsden came over this morning to speak about Mr Smith's proposed railway to Piel. Fell has been telling him Mr Smith is resolved to persevere and expects to

Fowler 4F 0-6-0 44083 slogs up the 1 in 107 incline of Lindal bank at Lindal East c.1962, assisted by an unidentified banking engine. Near this point was the temporary Ulverston Road station used pending the completion in 1854 of the line into Ulverston. (Author: MAA75)

The fine Ulverston terminal of 1854 is seen here in June 1971. Designed by Lancaster architect, Edward Paley, whose firm was by this date providing plans for all FR buildings. Until around 1860 this station was used by both FR and U&L trains. Once the through station was opened the fine FR building became the goods station and is now a car showroom. (Author: MAA861)

get an Act. He is trying to get Lords Derby and Muncaster and the iron merchants to support him but I have no great fears.' [25]

'Mr Smith is persevering with his Bill but I trust we may defeat it.' [26]

'Mr Smith's Bill is going on and I fear it will give us much trouble.' [27]

'We walked over part of Smith's line. McClean thinks we have a strong case against it.' [28]

'I find that many of the iron merchants have partly engaged themselves in his favour ... It seems they are quite duped by his promises.' [29]

'Mr Smith appears to be losing ground with [the ironmasters] on account of his Bill not corresponding with his promises.' [30]

'I had ... an interview this morning with Mr J.A. Smith ... He is evidently very desirous we should take a perpetual lease of his Pier and I think McClean is rather in favour of it but I doubt our coming to terms.' [31]

'Smith is declining to take a payment once for all and is requiring a rent. I called on him this morning but settled nothing.' [32]

'(At Ulverston) met Mr Swift, the referee on the Piel Pier purchase. Mr Smith was there with Bidder and Martin, two engineers, Nelson his solicitor and Fell ... McClean and

Ramsden were examined as to the passenger traffic at Piel. Fell attempted to give evidence for Mr Smith but it was a failure.' [33]

Matters were brought to a conclusion by a severe storm on 27th December 1852 which badly damaged Piel Pier. Abel Smith accepted the FR offer of £15,000 for his works and this sale was ratified by the Furness Railway Act of 4th August 1853.

The Furness Railway extensions

In the Railway Mania year of 1846, the Furness Railway was successful in obtaining powers to extend its line from Kirkby to Broughton and from Dalton to Ulverston. On 4th November 1846 the FR board decided to double the line between the ore terminal at Crooklands, north of Dalton, and the junction between the Barrow and Piel branches at Roose, which was necessary to allow the safe 'and convenient working of the iron ore and passenger trains'. This work was authorised on 27th February 1847. Tenders were invited for the building of the Broughton extension with completion by 1st May 1847, also for the tunnel at Lindal and for the Ulverston extension as far as Lindal, the remainder of this line being left over for the time being, as it was anticipated that the Lindal tunnel would take some 15 months to build.

The Broughton line tenders were all considerably more than McClean's estimate of £6,950, so the work was divided into small contracts and re-let[34]. Local contractors, Fell and Jopling, completed the line for £7,200.

The doubling of the main line was inspected by Captain Simmons of the Commissioners of Railways, successors to the Board of Trade Railway Department, on 22nd May 1847. He was more demanding than his former chief, Pasley, and commented:

A first generation 'heritage' DMU is seen leaving the east end of Lindal tunnel in 1975 with a train from Barrow bound for Lancaster. The tunnel, as built, was 439 yards long but due to unstable ground conditions which gave many problems during its construction it was shortened at the west end by about 25 yards during the spring of 2011. (Author: MAA965)

'The line was incomplete in signals, there being none fixed at the periods of my inspection at the Piel Branch Junction nor at the junction with the branch to Burlington Slate Works. At the latter signals were being fixed and were stated to be made for the Piel Junction ... A Certificate shall be forwarded as soon as they are completed. In other respects the line is in every way ready for opening for public traffic.' [35]

Signals were soon erected and the line sanctioned for opening for both freight and passengers two days later on 24th May 1847. Simmons returned, on 23rd February 1848, to inspect the Broughton branch, a three-mile single line extension from Kirkby, where he noted a bridge over Kirkby Pool as being built of timber on piles with nine openings of 13 feet. He sanctioned the opening for public traffic and it appears that the Broughton branch was opened for passenger traffic immediately[36].

The Lindal extension was also let to Fell and Jopling in June 1847[37] but, as already noted, Burlington stopped this work when he took over as Chairman after the death of Benjamin Currey. The contractors were compensated at 10% on their plant, worth £1,500[38], but relations between the FR and Fell were soured by this event and Fell subsequently formed an alliance with the Furness ironmasters and Abel Smith which led to the rival Furness and Pile Harbour Railway project.

An improvement in the financial position of the FR after the crisis of 1848 led to the Lindal extension being revived in 1849, supported by loans of £5,000 each from Harrison, Ainslie & Company and the Ulverston Mining Company, who sought rail access from their mines at Lindal Moor and Lindal Cote respectively, to Barrow harbour. A contract was let to Wheatcroft at £7,920 including the Lindal tunnel and the line as far as Lindal Road[39], but the contractor was soon in difficulties and required an advance payment[40]. In July 1850 the FR bought Wheatcroft's plant and continued the work themselves, when it was discovered that the Lindal tunnel required more lining than had been estimated and that Wheatcroft's figure was £2,000 too low. The contract was re-let to Chappel & Company[41].

The Lindal Road terminus was designed with accommodation for passengers *'... to be on the smallest possible scale.'* [42] The first mineral train passed through the Lindal tunnel on 6th May 1851 with ore from the Lindal Cote mine[43]. Captain Wynne inspected the mile-long extension on 22nd May 1851, authorised the opening for passenger traffic from 1st June with one engine only and the provision of the electric telegraph through the tunnel[44]. Passenger trains began running to Lindal Road on or about that date.

Lord Burlington reported on 17th July 1851:

'I went over early to Furness this morning. Got onto the Railway at Lindale (sic) and went to Barrow – the first time I have been over the Lindale Extension. The traffic on our line seems somewhat increasing but the iron ore is at present nearly stationary. Ramsden expects it to increase. A little traffic with the North of Ireland is carried on through Whitehaven ... The line to Ulverston is commencing but is rather delayed from difficulty in getting possession of land.'

It now remained to complete the line to Ulverston as by this time the Ulverstone and Lancaster Railway Bill had passed the Parliamentary Committee, receiving Royal Assent on 24th July 1851. Tenders were invited for completion of the line from Lindal to Ulverston and McClean, now acting for both the FR and the U&LR, was asked, by Burlington, to report on the junction between the two lines at Ulverston. He reported on 20th June 1851 that it was in the interests of both concerns to make a junction at the site of the proposed FR terminus, although this would be on a falling gradient. The FR agreed, in its Lindal to Ulverston contract, to build the first part of the U&LR line as far as the bridge over the Ulverston canal, as the spoil from the Pennington cutting could be used for the embankment east of Ulverston station. Boulton won the contract from under the noses of Fell and Jopling, thereby increasing the antipathy of the latter firm to the FR. However, he had significantly underestimated the costs. Boulton proceeded with the Ulverston

LINDAL TUNNEL.
ON THE FURNESS RAILWAY.

PLATE 4 VOL. XIX.

M? CLEAN AND STILEMAN, ENG?S

KELL,BRO? LITH?S CASTLE S? HOLBORN

Minutes of Proceedings, Institution of Civil Engineers, Vol. XIX. Session 1859-60.

Lindal tunnel during doubling of the track. This line illustration shows the method employed in this difficult project. The new double-track tunnel was excavated while traffic still passed along the original tunnel. When a section of the new tunnel was completed the old roof was demolished. During the operation holes would be broken through the old lining to allow the removal of spoil. (Institution of Civil Engineers Proceedings: Vol. XIX, 1959-60 p238)

Extension and when the Ulverston road, east of Lindal, was reached, a second temporary terminus replaced that at Lindal Road. Captain Galton inspected the line to Ulverston Road on 19th May 1852[45].

He described a single line with earthworks for a double line and approved opening for public traffic, provided that the one engine principle applied to the Lindal Road extension was continued. The line to Ulverston Road was opened for passenger traffic on 27th May 1852[46].

The line beyond Ulverston Road proved difficult. Delay occurred in the Pennington cutting and there was settlement of the embankment beyond Ulverston, as a result of which Boulton was allowed an extension of time until 31st March 1854[47]. McClean examined the works in February 1854 and reported that, while the line to Ulverston Road was in good working order, Boulton's work had *'occasioned great delay'*. He considered that coal and timber traffic might safely be run over the

line by 31st March 1854, but a full opening would be delayed until 1st May 1854[48].

The line to the new FR terminus at Ulverston was opened for freight traffic on 4th April 1854 with the arrival of two wagons of coal from Whitehaven[49]. Passenger traffic commenced on 7th June 1854[50] with passenger trains running into the platform of the FR high level station, then being completed. Lower level platforms for through trains to the Ulverstone & Lancaster line were built later, after which the higher level station was used solely for goods traffic. Captain Wynne had inspected the new line on 2nd June 1854[51], and approved the opening, provided that the electric telegraph was utilised. Burlington noted on 15th July 1854:

'I went to Barrow this morning, the first time I have been over the newly opened portion of our line. Barrow looks amazingly busy.'

Park North signalbox and crossing house c.1890, showing the inclined plane serving North Pit of the Park iron mine. Replacing in 1883 an earlier box, this box was built to a design of Paley & Austin. Slightly larger, similar structures survive at Park South and St Bees. The ring on the signal denotes that the up loop was a goods line. These were dispensed with in 1896. (Barrow Library)

Thus, by June 1854, the main line of the Furness Railway was complete. All that remained to be built were two 'expedition curves' needed to avoid the reversals at Furness Abbey and Broughton, following the opening of the Whitehaven & Furness Junction Railway to Broughton in 1850, and the Ulverstone & Lancaster Railway from Ulverston to Carnforth in 1857. The Millwood curve was opened on 1st July 1858 and that at Foxfield (Broughton) on 1st August 1858[52].

The single-line Lindal tunnel soon became a constraint on the traffic in iron ore between Lindal and Barrow. On 20th February 1855 the FR board approved the doubling of the line between Crooklands and Ulverston and a contract was let to William Tredwell for this work, which including the doubling of the Lindal tunnel.

The latter work was carried out to a plan devised by F.C. Stileman, McClean's partner, the original tunnel lining being retained, to allow traffic to continue, as a new lining was constructed around it. Work commenced in June 1855, but was interrupted by a serious fall of masonry, blamed on the use of substandard materials by the contractor. Because of this, passenger trains were discontinued between January and October 1856 and an omnibus service between Lindal and Dalton was operated at the expense of the contractor. Nevertheless this work aroused interest among the civil engineers of the day and was the subject of a paper read to the Institution of Civil Engineers, by Stileman, on 24th January 1860[53].

The Furness Railway and the Ironmasters

The position of the Furness ironmasters was difficult. Their royalty owners were also the proprietors of the means of transport between the mines and Barrow harbour but they had not subscribed to the Furness Railway to the extent that their shareholding carried any weight in the formation of the rates policy. One royalty owner, the Duke of Buccleuch, was prepared to include, in his mineral lettings, a clause requiring the exclusive use of the Furness Railway for the carriage of ore[54]. The FR prospectus had quoted a rate of 1s 6d per ton for the carriage of ore between Dalton and Barrow and this was confirmed in a communication to the ironmasters early in 1846, which indicated that this rate included the terminal charges for loading at Barrow. Some of the ironmasters expressed dissatisfaction at an early date, Harrison, Ainslie & Co. (who were FR shareholders)

asking for a guarantee that the rates would not be increased when the branches to the mines from Dalton were constructed. The FR was not prepared to give such an undertaking unless Harrison, Ainslie & Co. in return, guaranteed to send an agreed tonnage by the FR[55].

The ironmasters continued to carry some of their ore to Barrow by road and offered to stop this practice on 12th December 1848, provided that the FR reduced the toll from the 1848 crisis rate of 2s per ton to 1s 9d. The FR declined. The accounts of Harrison, Ainslie & Co. for a later period show that of the 11s per ton obtained for ore, 1s 4d was merchant profit, 1s 4d royalty, 2s wages and 2s railway toll[56]. The merchants' profit, a healthy 12%, was better than that of the Furness Railway. In fact the steady increase in the output of the Furness ironfield between 1849 and 1856, from 182,000 tons to 464,853 tons[57], would not have been possible without the railway. In 1849 an agreement was reached between the FR and the ironmasters for a rate of 1s 9d per ton on the completion of the Lindal tunnel[58]. As noted previously, Harrison, Ainslie & Co. and the Ulverston Mining Co. agreed to take £5,000 each in preference shares.

The Lindal extension progressed slowly and, by the time the Lindal tunnel opened in May 1851, Abel Smith was promoting his Furness & Pile Harbour Bill, supported by the ironmasters and by John Barraclough Fell, who had lost out twice on contracts for the extension of the FR to Ulverston. However, as noted, Smith's proposals failed and, in 1852, after the storm damaged his pier, he agreed to sell out to the FR.

By the time the Ulverstone & Lancaster Railway was nearing completion the ironmasters renewed their attack on the FR, setting out their grievances in writing and suggesting remedies:

'Newland Furnace, Ulverston
July 31st 1857

My Lord Burlington and the
Directors of the Furness Railway Company

Gentlemen,
We beg respectfully to address you on the subject of a reduction of rates of carriage of iron ore by your line of railway and we think this a fitting time for such reduction as the opening of the Lancaster- Ulverston line must soon take place. We wish to remind you that before the railway was opened the carriage of iron ore from the mines to Barrow was done at as low a rate as you have hitherto charged on your railway and that when the railway was first projected and the first Prospectus issued 1s 6d per ton was the maximum rate proposed for the iron ore from the several mines to Barrow and we think no higher rate would have been needful had the line been confined to Mineral Purposes and thinking thus the additional rate has not been submitted to us with any great cheerfulness.

Again when John Abel Smith Esq. came among us and gave an assurance that he would carry our ore down to Piel at 1s 6d per ton if we would promise him our influence and give him a chance of our trade, two reasons operated on us to continue our full adherence to your line. One was that fact that some of the Lords of our Manors had embarked considerable sums in the old line and the other was the promise given to us on that occasion that if we discountenanced Mr Smith's line a modification of your Mineral Tariff would follow. Again we have been assured that when the line paid 5% the modification would take place. So far our expectations based on these various grounds have not been fulfilled but we now hope that a more liberal spirit will prevail on this subject in your counsels and the reduction we now respectfully but earnestly ask for will be made. We ask you to fix your rates as follows:

From all stations down to Barrow 1s 6d per ton From all stations to Ulverston Junction 1s 3d per ton and we think we can show you that you can meet our wishes and still keep your dividend at its present very exceptional proportion. We assume that you carried 425,000 tons to Barrow last year at 2/- = £42,000. We now calculate our yearly trade will not be less than 600,000 tons. 400,000 tons of this to Barrow at 1s 6d = £30,000 and 200,000

FURNESS RAILWAY.
FURTHER OPENING OF THE LINE TO LINDAL,
WITHIN THREE MILES OF THE TOWN OF ULVERSTON.

This line affords the SHORTEST and CHEAPEST route from Maryport, Cockermouth, Workington Whitehaven, Ulverston, and the Lakes.—to Lancaster, Skipton, Leeds, Preston, Liverpool, Manchester, London, &c.

Time Table.—On and after the 1st Nov., 1851,
AND UNTIL FURTHER NOTICE.

[Timetable content — Furness Railway, Up and Down trains, Week Days and Sundays, Barrow Branch, and General Notices. Detailed tabular figures reproduced from the advertisement.]

General Notices.
On Thursdays, Return Tickets will be issued at all stations for ONE FARE, to persons attending the Ulverston and Whitehaven Markets.

Omnibus Fare:—Lindal to Ulverston, 9d.—DAY TICKETS, 1s.

Return Tickets are issued to 1st and 2nd Class Passengers for ONE FARE AND A HALF on Weekdays.

The SUNDAY TRAINS will stop at ROOSE and IRELETH Gates to take up and set down passengers when required.

Passengers from Underhill, Sylecroft, Eskmeals, Ravenglass, Drigg, Braystones and Netherton, will have to re-book at Broughton Station.

Trains leave Whitehaven for Maryport and Carlisle. For particulars see Whitehaven Time Bills.

COACHES to Coniston and Windermere Lakes
Run as follow, in connexion with the Trains (on week days) viz;—from BROUGHTON STATION at 1 p.m., passing through Coniston, Hawkshead, and Ambleside; arriving at the Windermere Railway Station at 5 0 p.m.; and FROM the Windermere Railway Station at 8 a.m., arriving at Broughton at 12 noon.

FARES PER COACH from
Broughton to Coniston....OUTSIDE 2s.—INSIDE 3s. | Broughton to Ambleside..OUTSIDE 4s.—INSIDE 5s.
" Hawkshead.. " 3s. " 4s. | " Birthwaite " 5s. " 6s.

Barrow, General Manager's Office,
Nov., 1851.

BY ORDER,
JAMES RAMSDEN.

Furness Railway timetable from Soulby's "Ulverston Advertiser", 27th November 1851. (Geoff Holme collection)

tons to Ulverston Junction at 1s 3d = £12,000. The Ulverston rate we consider equivalent to the Barrow rate as the former is free of terminal charges and this very little additional charge will accrue from carrying this additional quantity and by adopting these rates no competition can arise to you from carting by road is now the case from the mines to Canal Foot. If you think it desirable we will not object to enter an agreement to continue to pay the above named rate for five years from the opening of the Ulverstone & Lancaster Railway unless any mining company not now in existence and not party to this agreement should effect better terms with you in the meantime... You see that we propose to give equivalent to 3½d per mile for the carriage of a mineral which passes over other lines at ½d, ¾d and ⅞d per ton. The ironmasters of Whitehaven have recently effected a saving equal to 1s per ton being the difference of cost of carriage between coast and rail and they have an advantage over us in the market. May we solicit your early and special attention to these proposals?

My Lords & Gentlemen: Your faithful and obedient servants,

Harrison, Ainslie & Co. Schneider, Hannay Co. Joseph Rawlinson
Adgarley & Stainton Co. Kennedy Brothers George Ashburner'

The FR board minute was short and to the point:

'It was resolved after discussion that further consideration of the question should be postponed.' [59]

The Furness ironmasters continued to make occasional protests on rates, but the Furness iron industry was about to enter a period of unprecedented boom and so great were the profits of the Bessemer era for all concerned, that differences were forgotten. It was a similar letter, written by the ironmasters from Ulverston in 1878 (21 years later), which spelt out the end of Furness supremacy in the iron trade due to the importation of cheap Spanish hematite ore. In this very same year Sidney Gilchrist Thomas was carrying out his experiments in basic steel making which, a year later, rendered hematite ore no longer essential. The privileged position of Furness and West Cumberland royalty owners, ironmasters and carriers was then at an end.

Furness Railway results 1846-1856

During the years 1846 to 1856 the Furness Railway Company consolidated its position and developed its resources to a level never contemplated at the time of its formation. Its prime function remained the same, namely the transportation of iron ore from mine to ship and by 1856 the FR had become a very successful undertaking. The capital had been increased from £75,000 to £460,000 and the return on this capital, after a slow start due to the depression in trade which followed the Railway Mania, can only be regarded as highly satisfactory. The comparative position of the FR can be seen from the following table:

	FR	M&CR	LNWR	MR
1846 (half year)	2%	0%	10%	7%
1847	3%	3%	8½%	7%
1848	0%	0%	7%	5½%
1849	2%	0%	6½%	2¾%
1850	2¼%	1½%	5¼%	2%
1851	3%	3½%	5¾%	2⅞%
1852	3½%	3½%	5¼%	3⅛%
1853	4½%	3½%	5%	3¼%
1854	6%	3¼%	5%	3⅛%
1855	6%	3½%	5%	3⅝%
1856	8%	4½%	5½%	4⅛%

The basis of this success was the expansion of the Furness iron industry which, by 1856, had reached an output of 464,853 tons of Furness ore.

CHAPTER 3 REFERENCES

1 Parris H. *Op. cit.*
2 PRO: BTHR SPC 14/35.
3 FRDM, 27th Feb. 1847.
4 Pettigrew W.F., 1901. *Transactions of the Institute of Mechanical Engineers.*
5 PRO: MT6/4/31.
6 FRSM, 27th Feb. 1847.
7 FRDM, 16th Jan. 1846.
8 Fisher J. *Op. cit.* p.100.
9 *Devonshire Diaries,* 20th May 1848.
10 *Devonshire Diaries,* 11th Sep. 1848.
11 *Herapath*, 1848, p.842.
12 *Kendall MSS.* Ref. ZK133.
13 FRDM, 27th Feb. 1846.
14 FRDM, 12th May 1847.
15 FRDM, 19th Jan. 1848.
16 *Ulverston Advertiser,* 2nd Mar. 1848.
17 FRDM, 16th Feb. 1848.
18 *Ulverston Advertiser,* 26th Feb. 1849.
19 FRDM, 13th July 1849.
20 FRDM, 14th Oct. 1851.
21 HLRO: Parliamentary Plan, 1852/F2.
22 FRSM, 15th Aug. 1852.
23 *Devonshire Diaries,* 22nd July 1851.
24 *Devonshire Diaries,* 6th Aug. 1851.
25 *Devonshire Diaries,* 30th Aug. 1851.
26 *Devonshire Diaries,* 19th Feb. 1852.
27 *Devonshire Diaries,* 26th Feb. 1852.
28 *Devonshire Diaries,* 6th Mar. 1852.
29 *Devonshire Diaries,* 11th Mar. 1852.
30 *Devonshire Diaries,* 24th Mar. 1852.
31 *Devonshire Diaries,* 7th May 1852.
32 *Devonshire Diaries,* 2nd July 1852.
33 *Devonshire Diaries,* 27th Oct. 1852.
34 FRDM, 23rd Jan.1847.
35 PRO: MT29/6/152.
36 PRO: MT29/7/66.
37 FRDM, 2nd June 1847.
38 FRDM, 19th May 1848.
39 FRDM, 3rd Oct. 1849.
40 FRDM, 25th June 1850.
41 FRDM, 12th Feb. 1851.
42 FRDM, 1st Jan. 1851.
43 *Ulverston Advertiser,* 8th May 1851.
44 PRO: MT29/12/47.
45 Ibid.
46 *Whitehaven Herald,* 29th May 1852.
47 FRDM, 26th Aug. 1853.
48 FRDM, 23rd Feb. 1854.
49 Marshall J.D. *Op. cit.* p.215.
50 Melville J & Hobbs J L. *Op. cit.* p.43.
51 Marshall J.D. *Op. cit.* p.215.
52 FRSM, 4th Sep. 1858, *Engineer's Report.*
53 Stileman F.C., 1860. *Proceedings of the Institution of Civil Engineers* Vol. XIX, p.238.
54 Marshall J.D. *Op. cit.* p.205.
55 FRDM, 22nd Apr. 1846.
56 Marshall J.D. *Op. cit.* p.207.
57 Ibid.
58 FRDM, 27th Feb. 1849.
59 FRDM, 27th Aug. 1857.

CHAPTER FOUR

THE WHITEHAVEN JUNCTION RAILWAY

Black 5 4-6-0 45460 runs into Bransty station at Whitehaven with a south-bound stopping train on 2nd July 1955. On the right are the buildings and chimney of William Pit. (Author: MAC241)

West Cumberland – with its coal and iron industries and a considerable general trade passing through its ports of Whitehaven, Workington and Maryport – was destined to spawn a number of small, independent railways and in this respect it resembled South Wales. Only two of these lines were destined to become part of the Furness system, the Whitehaven and Furness Junction (W&FJR) and the Whitehaven, Cleator and Egremont (WC&ER), the latter jointly with the LNWR. However, the Whitehaven Junction Railway, (WJR)[1] running from Maryport to Whitehaven, was always closely associated with the W&FJR having the same Chairman, the second Earl of Lonsdale, and several directors in common and was, from 1854 to 1866, operated jointly with the W&FJR.

When, in 1865, the amalgamation of the West Cumberland railways was being negotiated, it was Lord Lonsdale's intention that the WJR and the W&FJR would become part of the Furness Railway system, but petty squabbling led to the little Cockermouth & Workington Railway (C&WR) falling into the hands of the LNWR and the prosperous WJR went with it. Nevertheless, the story of the Furness Railway would be incom-

plete without some account of the Whitehaven Junction Railway.

The local enthusiasm for a trunk rail route from West Cumberland to the south, which had resulted in George Stephenson's survey of 1837 and the plans of Hague and Rastrick the following year, was not eclipsed by the failure of the latter scheme to satisfy the Parliamentary Commissioners, who favoured an inland route as subsequently built by the Lancaster & Carlisle Railway. The Maryport and Carlisle Railway (M&CR) was opened between Maryport and Arkleby on 15th July 1840 and on to Aspatria on 12th April 1841, with opening throughout taking place on 10th February 1845[2]. Local interests, led by William Lowther, second Earl of Lonsdale (1787-1872), proprietor of the Whitehaven Collieries and owner of coal and iron mining rights throughout West Cumberland, promoted an extension of the M&CR to Whitehaven.

Known at first as the Whitehaven & Maryport Railway, it was authorised as the Whitehaven Junction Railway in 1844[3], with George Stephenson as its engineer, but the line was laid out by his long time assistant, John Dixon (1796-1865), whose estimated

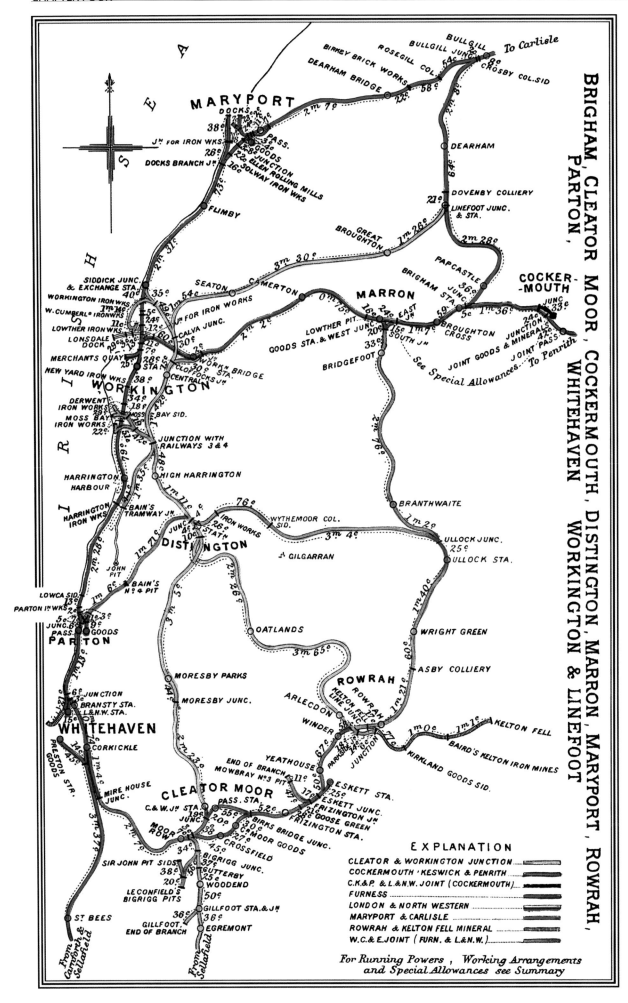

The Railway Clearing House plan of c.1901 shows the ownership of the railways of West Cumberland. Together with a book of distances, this provided the basis on which traffic revenues were apportioned.

cost was £100,000. Commencing at a junction with the M&CR at the south end of Maryport station, the line followed a coastal course. The Act noted that Henry Curwen of Workington Hall, proprietor of a number of coal mines in West Cumberland, had recently commenced a colliery at Whins, near Harrington and proposed to build a tramway from the mine to Harrington harbour, which required the WJR to build a bridge over their proposed line at Harrington to carry this tramway.

The WJR also crossed Lord Lonsdale's waggonway from his William Pit, north of Whitehaven, to Whitehaven harbour. Henry Curwen was the principal petitioner against the WJR Bill, no doubt to protect his rights at Harrington harbour, but he was placated by the clause requiring the tramway bridge at Harrington and the subsequent agreement allowing the Cockermouth & Workington Railway, in which he had a large interest, joint use of the WJR's Workington station[4].

Building and Opening the line

The contracts for the construction of the Whitehaven Junction line were let as follows:

Maryport – Workington: Jacob William Ritson of Hexham.
£10,568

Workington – Harrington: Jacob William Ritson of Hexham.
£7,604

Harrington – Whitehaven: Welch Brothers of Newcastle.
£25,006

For completion by 10th November 1845.

The shareholders' meeting of 30th August 1845 was acrimonious, the Chairman, Robert Jefferson, referring to the removal of four of the company's directors over *'differences'*. One of these directors, a Reverend Mr Key, stated that *'he was glad to go out'*, and that the whole of the directors, with the exception of Lord Lonsdale's agents, were in agreement.

It was said that *'The differences were over a mere culvert'*. William Miller, the deputy Chairman and a Lonsdale functionary, commented that the four directors were going out because they had failed to carry out their duties. Mr Key retorted that:

'They were going out, not because they had failed to carry out their duties but because they would not bend to Lord Lonsdale's purpose.'

Whether this dispute was due to the authoritarian personality of the second Earl, or the longer standing friction between the 'Town' and 'Castle' political groups in Whitehaven, is a matter of conjecture.

There can, however, be no doubt about the second Earl's domineering character. The completion of the first section of the Whitehaven Junction Railway, between Maryport and Workington, was to lead to discord at the highest level between the Board of Trade Railway Department and Lord Lonsdale. Commenting on the situation, Henry Parris notes:

'Parties of sufficient influence and standing could appeal to the President to repudiate his Inspector's report and revoke its order. This is what happened in the case of the Whitehaven Junction Railway.' [5]

The newly completed line between Maryport and Workington was inspected by Captain Joshua Coddington RE (Assistant Inspector 1844-6, Inspector 1846-7 and Secretary of the Caledonian Railway from 1847) on 12th November 1845. His report states:

'The line for the most part consists of a low embankment from 5 to 10 feet in height which has been formed of gravel carted from the sea beach along the side of it. The rails are attached to chairs fixed in stone blocks bedded in the gravel and where the embankment exceeds 5 feet in height, cross sleepers have been used ... The gauge is 4' 9" ... The chairs are set in stone blocks which are more liable to shift their position so as to disturb the gauge than sleepers would be and render these parts insecure. In fact on the day on which I inspected it ... the leading wheels of the engine got off the line and when I returned to gauge its rails I found a difference of ½" in some places.' [6]

Coddington also criticised the use of inside keys on the grounds that loose material could accumulate on top of the chairs leading to derailment of wheels and also commented on the long period of consolidation which would be required by a gravel formation. He concluded that the line was not safe for opening to the public:

'... until further precautions should be taken either by the substitution of transverse sleepering or longitudinal baulks ... in place of stone blocks.'

Major General Pasley, the Inspector General of Railways, passed Coddington's Report to Lord Dalhousie, now the President of the Board of Trade, with a recommendation that the line should not be opened in its present state. This decision was passed to the Chairman of the WJR who sought the opinion of the line's consulting engineer, George Stephenson. Stephenson reported back to Lord Lonsdale and his reply was passed to Captain Coddington who commented, on 18th December 1845:

'Mr Stephenson admits to the accuracy of every point I have advanced and he only differs from me in considering that the remedies may be applied during the traffic to the risk of the public instead of the line being put in proper order before being opened.'

Meanwhile Dixon, the line's engineer, had considered the Coddington report and had, in response to it, produced, on 18th December 1845, a seven-page reply plus appendices. Dixon referred to the radii of 15 chains on parts of the line and stated that the 4' 9" gauge had been adopted by a number of railways, including the Chester & Crewe and the London & Brighton. Dixon went on to defend inside keys which, he stated, had advantages in the resistance of rail loading and in the ease of inspection by platelayers. He did however accept the instability of stone blocks and reported that:

'... sleepers have been introduced to a considerable extent and the remainder will shortly he completed.'

Dixon concluded his report:

'I cannot see wherein the Railway I have constructed at Whitehaven should be considered less safe than others nor why the Company should suffer the expense and myself the disgrace of having it to alter.'

Pasley recorded in his diary on 24th December 1845, that Lord Dalhousie had written to him:

'Lord Lonsdale and Mr George Stephenson were insolent to him and said:
"What could Railway Inspectors possibly know about railways?"'

With a degree of diplomacy born of long years of experience, Major General Pasley decided to carry out the re-inspection for himself and this took place on 26th December 1845. He went to great pains to assess the criticisms of his junior colleague Coddington, even conducting an experiment in which stones were crushed by the locomotive flanges with *'so little effort that I could not feel anything like a shock nor hear any noise ... whilst I was riding on the engine.'* This, together with the introduction of ties between the stone blocks and adjustment of the gauge, allowed Pasley to recommend that opening of the line would not be a danger to the public.

Opening for passenger traffic took place between Maryport and Workington on 19th January 1846.

William Miller chaired the shareholders' meeting, held on 27th February 1846, and reported the opening of the line to Workington which was to be worked, under agreement, by the M&CR. At the shareholders' meeting, held on 28th August 1846, chaired by Lord Lonsdale, it was reported that the line from Workington to Harrington had been opened on 18th May 1846.

The Harrington – Whitehaven contract, let to Welsh & Brotherton, was delayed as a result of the embankment between Harrington and Lowca being destroyed by high tides, and because of this the contract price had been increased from £25,006 to £57,737. It was also suggested by Dixon that there should be a deviation of the line on this section, a suggestion which incurred the displeasure of George Stephenson. He wrote to the Earl of Lonsdale on 7th February 1846:

'George Stephenson
Tapton House
7th February 1846

My Lord,
I have just returned from Whitehaven. I particularly examined the line of railway from Harrington to Whitehaven and I must say that no satisfactory reason could be given me for causing the deviation. When I enquired into the character of the wall I found that it was only a temporary one and unfinished and loose at one end when the sea got in behind it and brought it down piece by piece. Mr Dixon has not had experience in sea walling. He has therefore been frightened into this deviation. In the deviation line a tunnel has been proposed to be made through a shattered and unsound rock and it will be quite uncertain when such a tunnel could be finished. Beside it would be very expensive and the ground would be very bad to deal with on the east side of the tunnel. I therefore consider it quite out of the question to have any tunnel at that place ... I am bound to recommend to your Lordship that the line be carried out in the way I have proposed.'

By the opening date, (18th May 1846) two locomotives had been delivered to the line by Tulk and Ley of the Lowca Foundry and the working agreement with the M&CR was terminated.

The Harrington to Whitehaven section was inspected by Captain Simmons on 11th February 1847. His report noted that the line was single throughout but that space had been made for a double line. He recommended that *'a watch should be kept on the cuttings because of the danger of falling rock'.* The Harrington to Whitehaven section of the line was opened for freight traffic on 15th February 1847 and opening for passengers took place on 19th March 1847, after an official ceremony the previous day.

At the time of the opening of the WJR to Whitehaven, William Miller was deputy Chairman and also a member of the board of the W&FJR. Other common directors were John Peile of Whitehaven and George Pew RN. The official opening was recorded in the *Whitehaven Herald* of 20th March 1847:

'The opening of the Whitehaven-Maryport Railway. On Thursday last 18th March 1847 the Whitehaven Junction Railway was opened throughout, an event which was celebrated with joy commensurate with the dimensions of the work, having great present and prospective advantages to the Harbour and Town of Whitehaven. At 12 o'clock three locomotives were attached to the trains. The first train which was drawn by the 'Lowther' engine contained the following:

'Earl of Lonsdale; William Miller Esq.; Rev. Henry Lowther, Distington Rectory; F.L.B. Dykes Esq., Ingwell; Rowland Pennington Esq., Scotch Street; John Peile Esq., Somerset House; Thomas Mitchell Esq., Roper Street; William Jackson Esq., Roper Street; William Lumb Esq., Meadow House; George Stephenson Esq., Chief Engineer; John Blenkinsop Esq., Resident Engineer; John Musgrave Esq., of Armistead & Musgrave, Solicitors; J.S. Yeats Jnr. Esq., Secretary; Robert Gibson Esq.; and William Grisedale Esq., auditors.

The second train which started a minute after was drawn by the 'Whitehaven' engine and the third train was drawn by an engine marked '33' without a name.'

The identity of the latter engine has been the matter of speculation, but the *Whitehaven Herald* of 30th January 1847 noted that one of a number of Crampton engines, built by Tulk & Ley of Lowca works, was to be tried on the WJR line.

Early difficulties

On 24th April 1847 the *Whitehaven Herald*, the newspaper supporting the 'Town' party in Whitehaven (the *Cumberland Pacquet* supported Lord Lonsdale's Conservative 'Castle' Party) expressed dissatisfaction with the new line in its editorial:

'We learn from a letter which appears in this paper ... that the most unpleasant feelings have been engendered among the principal merchants and traders of the town and neighbourhood arising from the determination of the Board of Directors of the above line (the Whitehaven Junction Railway) to monopolise the cartage of goods to and from the station. We are ready to express our extreme sorrow, after all the bunglings which have taken place in the construction and completion of the line, that the Directors should be so short sighted and really blind to their own interests as to inconvenience and grossly offend their customers.'

Eleven months later the *Whitehaven Herald* of 25th March

A view looking north at Parton c.1962 with a 4F waiting to take a coal train south. The signal for the Gilgarran branch of the former LNW & Furness Joint line was removed when the line was reduced to a siding to Harrington No.10 Pit at Lowca. (Author: MAA186)

1848 contained an editorial blasting the *Cumberland Pacquet*:

'Much has been said in the 'Pacquet' in praise of the Earl of Lonsdale in connection with the prosecution of that important undertaking the Whitehaven Junction Railway. We are willing to give the noble Earl every credit for his powerful aid in extending to this town the advantages of railway communication and we will further admit that without such aid it is more than probable that the desideratum would never have been accomplished but we cannot subscribe to the assertion that His Lordship thereby incurred great sacrifice of property. We do not think for instance that the sale of the site for the station at 5s 6d per yard or the sum of £1,655 was a very great sacrifice nor do we think that the sale of 12,617 yards of old sea walling for £2,217 was a great sacrifice of property especially when most of the land on which it was erected became double protected by a new wall … We also take leave to remark that the whole of the line between Harrington and St Bees is the very worst that could have been selected both with regard to the curves and to the quality of the foundations … And when we turn our attention to the unsightly and awkward viaduct which passes through Harrington we cannot but conclude that the whole is most disgraceful … that the directorate have placed the unsightly and inconvenient thing there.'

Notwithstanding this criticism, the WJR obtained powers to extend its line to Whitehaven Harbour and to deviate it at Parton. The WJR Alteration and Extension Act, which also provided for the raising of funds to double the main line of the

A fine panoramic view, looking south, c.1920, showing Harrington station, the lower town and harbour, with Harrington ironworks in the distance. (Sankey archive: 6822)

A double-headed United Steel Co. train from Lowca, bound for Moss Bay sidings via Harrington Junction, crosses the Whitehaven Junction line at Moss Bay Ironworks. (Author: MAO0905)

Company, received Royal Assent on 22nd July 1848.

The *Whitehaven Herald* of 16th September 1848 contained the following letter:

'The vast extent to which the shareholders have suffered through the bad management of the Directors is unhappily too well known but there are some Companies in which the remuneration received by the directors is so dispropor-tionate to the trifling dividend which they earn for their shareholders that the public attention ought to be drawn to the injustices of the case.'

The *Herald* noted on 23rd February 1850:

'I am not at all surprised to learn from the Report of the Directors that a dividend of 21/- per £20 share has been declared. The tradesmen of this town have frequently had goods put upon trucks at Whitehaven on a Saturday expecting them to arrive for the market and they have not reached the Cockermouth station until the market was over.'

The *Whitehaven Herald* of 31st January 1852 recorded the destruction by gales, on 24th January, of the line between William Pit and Redness Point – the wall between Lord Lonsdale's private waggonway and the railway being 'thrown down' to a considerable extent. The previous winter the sea walls at Harrington and Lowca had been damaged and William Rendell was employed as a consultant civil engineer to report. He stated:

'There is but too much reason to believe that unless the whole of the line of wall between here and Parton be substituted by something very different from the frail structure existing at present, calamities will by no means be a rare occurrence.'

At the shareholders' meeting on 21st February 1852, the Chairman warned the shareholders that the expense of repairing the sea damage to the line would prevent any hope of an increase in the dividend for some time to come. In fact, 4/- per £20 share (2%) was paid in March and 3/- per share (1½%) in September 1852.

Bradshaw's *Railway Manual* for 1853 records that the 30 yards of line washed away between Whitehaven and Parton had been rebuilt under the direction of Mr Rendell at a cost of £1,380 and, as faulty construction was blamed, £796 had been charged to the capital account.

The year 1852 was memorable for the completion of the Whitehaven tunnel between the W&FJR at Corkickle and the WJR at Bransty. This tunnel had been authorised by the W&FJR Act 1846 but had been overtaken by a much more ambitious plan in 1848. The W&FJR Amendment Act 1848 authorised a main line connection between its line near Preston Street to the WJR near Bransty to be built on arches.

Partly due to the financial stringency of the times and also to the objection of the Town and Harbour Trustees, this line did not proceed. The *Whitehaven Herald* of 18th September 1852 recorded that wagons were now passing through the tunnel. Captain Wynne, of the Commissioners of Railways (Railway Department), inspected the Whitehaven tunnel on 24th September 1852 and it was formally opened for traffic. The final development which affected the WJR was the authorisation of the W&FJR, in its Act of 1853, for a tramway from Preston Street station to Whitehaven Harbour. The first wagons passed along the new tramway on 27th January 1854[7].

The Joint Committee

The shareholders' meeting of the WJR, held on 15th August 1854, was notable. The Chairman, Lord Lonsdale, stated that:

'they had experienced many great disappointments and gone through various vicissitudes, first from the bad construction of the line when respectable contractors were difficult to meet with, next they had experienced a series of accidents, followed by bad times and stagnation of trade and a variety of other things which had all served to keep them back, particularly the injuries done to the line in consequence of it being constructed as many of them orig-inally thought too near to the sea.

The Company had now weathered these misfortunes and they now had a brighter prospect of approaching improvement to a considerable extent. He hoped that this was the last time he would have to mention the sea wall for he was convinced that it was a subject with which the shareholders must be completely nauseated ... Their repairs had cost about £11,000 and of this £4,000 had been taken out of revenue instead of being divided as profits.'

The Chairman announced that an agreement had been entered into with the Whitehaven & Furness Junction Railway for the joint working of the traffic on the two lines and he had much pleasure in stating that this arrangement was working satisfactorily, enabling the Company to carry more and much larger traffic than they would otherwise have been able to handle[8].

The year 1854 also was a turning point for the company in other respects. On 16th June 1854 the Whitehaven, Cleator & Egremont Railway Act received Royal Assent for a line from Mirehouse, one mile west of Corkickle on the W&FJR, to Egremont, with a branch from Moor Row to Frizington, tapping the West Cumberland ironfield. The traffic from this line, which opened for goods on 11th January 1856[9] between Frizington and Whitehaven and, on 1st July 1857, for passenger traffic, was to revolutionise the financial position of both WJR and W&FJR.

This was, however, two years ahead and the tribulations of the WJR continued. The *Cumberland Pacquet* of 26th August 1856 recorded the meeting of the Whitehaven Junction Railway shareholders on that day. The report stated:

'The large increase in the locomotive expenses in the present half year's accounts of £985 above those of the corresponding half of the previous year have, the Directors regret to state, been occasioned by the inefficiency of previous repairs. The defective state of the engines have induced the Directors to submit them to the examination of an eminent locomotive engineer.

Guided by his counsel, the Directors took immediate steps to remedy the then existing evil and during the Half Year the expense has been incurred of hiring engine power at a charge of £308/6/5d while at the same time they were largely repairing the engines belonging to the Company. The whole of the traffic is now worked by the Company's own engines and the Directors have contracted to purchase two new engines and in part payment to sell to the contractor two least useful of the old ones. The Directors have well founded hopes that this department will hereafter be conducted in a more efficient and economical manner.'

The accountants, Messrs Quilter, Ball & Co. reported:

'We find considerable irregularity in the accounts relative to the Company's goods traffic and so far as our investigation has gone it does not appear that there are balances due to the Company at the several stations to represent these items.'

Lord Lonsdale then said that the report and statement of accounts had been made as clear as possible. It was a very great grief to him that the affairs of the Company should have been allowed to get into such a state and that the directors were not in a position to present the report to the shareholders before the meeting. He said, on behalf of the directors, that it might be thought they had not paid the attention to the interests of the Company they might have done otherwise the irregularities of which they now had to complain would have been detected sooner. He further said that the Company now had a new set of officers who understood the nature of the duties they had to perform and he believed that they would be active and intelligent in looking after the shareholders' interests. New Shareholders' and Directors' Minute Books were opened on 26th August 1856 which recorded the appointment of Henry Cook, as Secretary and General Manager, and William Meikle, as Locomotive Engineer.

These officers were appointed to the same posts on the W&FJR under the joint working agreement.

The year in which the management of the Whitehaven Junction Railway was put on a proper professional basis was also the year in which the Whitehaven, Cleator & Egremont Railway was opened for traffic. Mineral traffic commenced on 11th January 1856 and up to 30th June 54,303 tons of iron ore were carried. Bradshaw's *Shareholders' Guide* reported that as a result receipts on the W&FJR and the WJR had increased by 30%.

The Cockermouth & Workington Railway (C&WR) had been opened on 28th April 1847[10] and an agreement made with the WJR on 25th May 1846 for the joint use of Workington station[11]. The principal shareholder of the C&WR was Lord Lonsdale, thereby creating a close link with the WJR and the W&FJR.

However, the most active shareholders were John Wilson Fletcher of Greysouthen, ironmaster, and John Steel, solicitor, of Cockermouth. In 1857 the C&WR board approached the WJR with a proposal for a lease of their line at 3½% for two years, 4% for five years and 4½% in perpetuity. The WJR board noted on 31st July 1857 that *'Lord Lonsdale considered the terms too high'*. With the benefit of hindsight, it is clear that this was a major blunder by Lonsdale, as the C&WR line was to become pivotal in the plans for mergers, which developed in West Cumberland, in 1864-65.

On 23rd July 1858 the WJR obtained powers to build branches to Maryport harbour; to Seaton Moor colliery; and the north and south sides of Workington harbour, for which work an additional capital of £65,000 was authorised. The branch to Maryport harbour was opened in August 1859, but the building of the other branches seems to have been abandoned, although the line to Seaton Moor Colliery was built as a private tramway.

The branches to Workington harbour were overtaken by Lord Lonsdale's 1863 Act to build the Lonsdale Dock and rail branches[12].

The Subscription Contract for the 1858 Bill has survived and shows the following contributors:

William Lowther, Earl of Lonsdale	Peer	15 Carlton Terrace	£24,500
William Miller	Banker	Whitehaven	£2,500
John Moore	Gentleman	Retreat, Whitehaven	£2,500
George Buckham	Ship Owner	Whitehaven	£2,500
Samuel Lindow	Iron Merchant	Whitehaven	£2,500
William Clarke	Surgeon	Whitehaven	£2,500
William Lumb	Gentleman	Whitehaven	£2,500
John Spencer	Esquire	Whitehaven	£2,500
John Hodgson	Clerk in Orders	Stamford Hill, Whitehaven	£2,500
Henry Lowther	Clerk A.M.	Distington Rectory	£2,500
George Pew	Royal Navy	Whitehaven	£2,500

A view of the early Whitehaven Junction Railway station at Workington in LNWR days. The increase in traffic in the 1870s led to the station being rebuilt in its present form. (CRA: Pattinson collection)

Increasing traffic led the WJR Board to consider the doubling of the line and, late in 1859, a contract was let for a double line between Harrington and Workington[13]. By 1860 the double line was open between Flimby and Harrington[14], and the double line throughout was completed in 1861[15].

The doubling process was not without incident. In December 1860 the Railway Department (Commissioners of Railways) received a memorial, dated 5th December 1860, from the residents of Harrington regarding the state of the railway viaduct there. Captain Tyier carried out an inspection, noting in his report that the viaduct:

'having been standing for some sixteen years ... is worn out and the Company are renewing it. The planking is thoroughly rotten and it yields 1⅝ inches under a heavy engine. ... one of the upright timbers gave way during the passage of a goods train on 4th December 1860. I observe that a large proportion (of the viaduct) is being renewed in timber ... I would therefore recommend that the Directors are not acting wisely in renewing the viaduct with timber and they would do better even now if they were to employ materials of a less perishable nature. ... The continued employment of this material in the present instance, by the Directors of a Company, in such good circumstances as that to which I refer and whose receipts, I see by the latest returns, are at the rate of £53 per mile per week, is quite inexcusable.' [16]

From 1864 the WJR became involved in the major political upheavals which embraced north Lancashire and Cumberland, nevertheless, they continued their dispute with the W&FJR over the terms of the joint working agreement and James Allport, General Manager of the Midland Railway, was appointed Arbitrator.

The progress of the WJR can be seen from its dividend record.

THE WHITEHAVEN JUNCTION RAILWAY

Dividends on Ordinary Stock as percentage per annum for each half year

1847 1st	2¼%	1857 1st	3¼%
1847 2nd	3%	1857 2nd	4%
1848 1st	1%	1858 1st	3½%
1848 2nd	1⅞%	1858 2nd	5%
1849 1st	1%	1859 1st	6%
1849 2nd	1%	1859 2nd	8%
1850 1st	2%	1860 1st	8%
1850 2nd	2%	1860 2nd	8%
1851 1st	0%	1861 1st	6%
1851 2nd	2%	1861 2nd	5%
1852 1st	1½%	1862 1st	5%
1852 2nd	1½%	1862 2nd	7%
1853 1st	1½%	1863 1st	7%
1853 2nd	3%	1863 2nd	10%
1854 1st	4%	1864 1st	10%
1854 2nd	5%	1864 2nd	10%
1855 1st	3%	1865 1st	10%
1855 2nd	3%	1865 2nd	10%
1856 1st	1½%	1866 1st	10%
1856 2nd	3½%		

CHAPTER 4 REFERENCES

1   Shareholders' and Directors' Minute Books of the WJR and the Directors' Minute Book of the W&FJR for the period 1844-56 were not passed to the successor Companies in 1866 and consequently are not in the British Transport Historical Records of the PRO. Recourse has had to be made to local newspapers and railway periodicals for data for those years. *(Author's Note)*

2   Joy D, 1983. *A Regional History of the Railways of Great Britain* Vol. 14 pp.145-7.

3   7&8 Vic Cap 64, 4.7.1844.

4   WJR SM, 30th Aug. 1845.

5   Parris H. *Op. cit.* p. 91.

6   PRO: Rail1053/6, MT6/2/71&72.

7   *Cumberland Pacquet*, 31st Jan. 1854.

8   *Cumberland Pacquet*, 22nd Aug. 1854.

9   *Bradshaw's Shareholders' Guide 1856* p.40.

10   *Bradshaw's Railway Manual 1856* p.40.

11   C&WR SM.

12   WJR SM, 27th Feb. 1863.

13   WJR SM, 28th Feb. 1860.

14   WJR SM, 30th Aug. 1860.

15   WJR SM, 28th Aug. 1861.

16   PRO: MT29/21 p.453.

CHAPTER FIVE

THE WHITEHAVEN & FURNESS JUNCTION RAILWAY

During the years of the railway mania, the ambitions of the Whitehaven landowners and merchants for a trunk route to the south, were added to those of the railway speculators, including the railway contractor John Brogden of Sale, Manchester, who had a number of successful railway contracts to his credit, including part of the Manchester & Leeds Railway and the Peterborough branch of the London & Birmingham Railway.

The Stephenson and Rastrick/Hague schemes for a trunk route from Lancaster to Carlisle, by way of Furness and West Cumberland, had failed to gain Parliamentary approval, but, in 1844, the Shap Fell route of the L&CR was authorised. Also in 1844, the extension to the coastal route from Maryport to Whitehaven received Parliamentary sanction in the form of the Whitehaven Junction Railway[1].

The prospectus of the W&FJR envisaged a line running down the Cumberland coast to Holborn Hill (later known as Millom), thence across the Duddon Sands, through Kirkby Moor by a tunnel, passing north of Ulverston, and finally crossing Morecambe Bay from Humphrey Head, in Cartmel, to a junction with the Lancaster & Carlisle Railway at Bolton-le-Sands. The Bill, deposited in 1844 was, however, limited to a line forming a junction with the already authorised Furness Railway at Ireleth, the extension to the L&CR being left to the next Parliamentary session.

The proposed capital was £350,000 plus loans of £166,600 and a Parliamentary Committee examined the Bill on 30th May 1845. The promoters estimated the traffic as £23,154 per annum from existing sources, to which could be added a further sum deriving from the opening up of railway communication, making in all £33,884. However, such a figure was not achieved until 1861, and then was largely due to local traffic from the Whitehaven, Cleator and Egremont Railway. George Stephenson, consulting engineer to the line, appeared before the Committee to expound on the engineering features of the line and the Committee was also shown the prospectus for the Whitehaven & Furness Junction Lancashire Extension line, the cost of which was estimated at £350,000. The W&FJR Bill was approved by the Committee and received Royal Assent on 21st July 1845.

The first meeting of shareholders was held at 3 Guildhall Chambers, Basinghall Street, London, on 29th September 1845. Among those present were Benjamin Currey, John Brogden (from his London address, 10 Sussex Gardens, Hyde Park) and John Barraclough Fell of Spark Bridge, Furness. The Subscription Contract showed that the principal subscriber was John Brogden (£40,000) compared with Lord Lonsdale's £10,000.

Brogden was not elected a director and his motives may be discerned from his subsequent activities on the South Eastern Railway, of which he became a director on 17th July 1846 and, on the 20th October 1846, the contract for the eastern section of the North Kent Line was let to his eldest son, John Brogden Jnr, although his tender was not the lowest. These events were repeated when the contract for the western section of the North Kent line was let. Subsequently a dispute developed between the Brogden firm and the South Eastern Railway[2].

In 1846 the W&FJR had a local Bill in Parliament to provide a connection with the Whitehaven Junction Railway at Whitehaven and whilst the Lancashire Extension Bill failed to comply with Standing Orders, the local Bill for the Whitehaven tunnel was successful[3].

The Whitehaven & Furness Junction Railway soon ran into financial troubles typical of the railway mania period, accounts for the second half of 1846 indicating that of the 17,500 shares, acquired for a deposit of £1, at least 6,460 had not yielded the first call of £3[4]. The failure of the Lancashire Extension Bill triggered a dispute between the London/Whitehaven and the Manchester shareholder groups. The Manchester shareholders sent two representatives to the meeting on 6th May 1846 and demanded to be told why such little progress had been made since the passing of the Act.

A Mr Neil Bannatyne warned that:

'...the Chairman and Directors were perhaps not aware that great dissatisfaction existed in Lancashire on the subject of this railway and he was sorry to think that the answers given were not likely to remove it. One eighth of the Capital had already been called up and another call was now being made without the slightest commencement having taken place in the works. The shares were stationary.'

Mr Levy, replying on behalf of the London proprietors, said that this was not the first occasion, in his experience, where the 'Northern Lights' had taken a different view and he saw no cause for gloom. John Brogden admitted that he had advised postponement of land purchase until the outcome of the Lancashire Extension Bill was known, and Richard Till of Whitehaven said that exorbitant prices had been asked for land. The difficulties over land were discussed at the next shareholders' meeting, on 27th August 1846, when it was admitted that land for only 13 miles of the line had been obtained. The Manchester faction now made an all out attempt to place three of their number on the Board, but were defeated by 538 votes to 240. John Brogden was not amongst the votes listed, suggesting that he had sold his shares before prices fell.

In February 1847 the collapse of the railway mania had led to an easing in land prices, most of the land had been acquired and work was proceeding on five of the construction contracts. John Brogden was not among the appointed contractors. Robert Stephenson had succeeded his father as engineer and was engaged in a more detailed examination of the Duddon Sands crossing.

The financial position of the Company remained shaky. By February 1847, 945 shares had been forfeited for non-payment of calls and, by August 1847, this number had risen to 11,652, from a total of 17,360. Seven of the thirteen contracts for construction of the line remained unlet and at the meeting of 26th February 1848, a mood of depression prevailed. The Directors' Report opened:

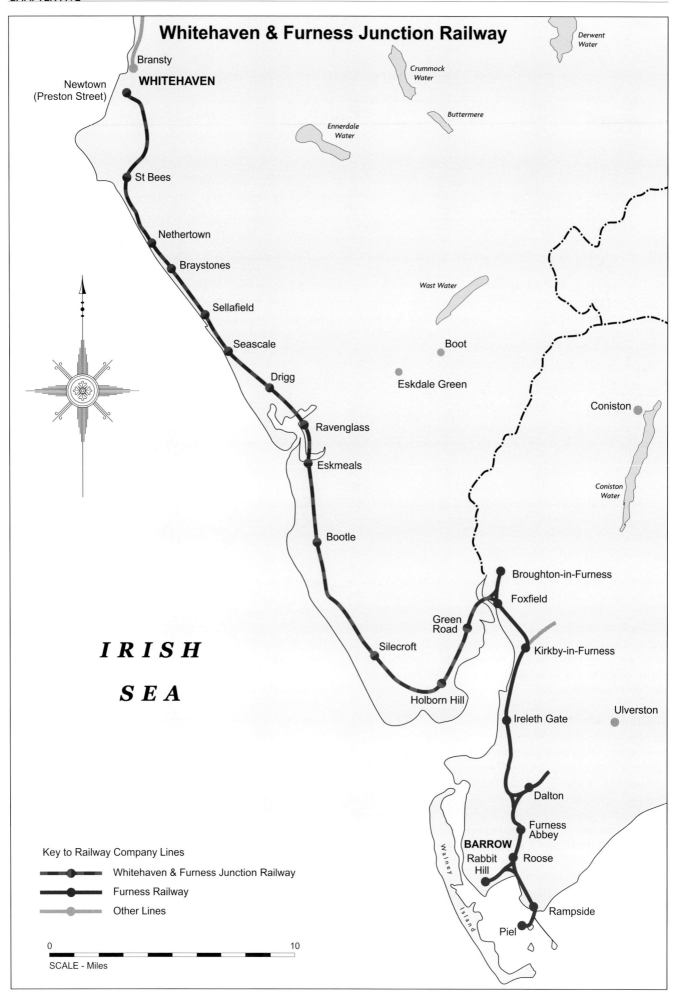

Whitehaven & Furness Junction Railway

Bransty
WHITEHAVEN
Newtown
(Preston Street)

St Bees

Nethertown

Braystones

Sellafield

Seascale

Drigg

Ravenglass

Eskmeals

Bootle

Derwent Water

Crummock Water

Buttermere

Ennerdale Water

Wast Water

Boot

Eskdale Green

Coniston

Coniston Water

Broughton-in-Furness

Foxfield

Green
Road

Silecroft

Kirkby-in-Furness

Holborn Hill

Ulverston

Ireleth Gate

I R I S H

S E A

Dalton

Furness
Abbey

BARROW

Rabbit
Hill

Roose

Walney Island

Rampside

Piel

Key to Railway Company Lines

━━●━━ Whitehaven & Furness Junction Railway

━━●━━ Furness Railway

━━●━━ Other Lines

0   10

SCALE - Miles

Joint Locomotive Committee 2-4-0 No.6 "Phoenix" about to leave St Bees for Whitehaven c.1860. (Geoff Holme collection: GH 255-5-4)

'The shareholders will be prepared to find that the events which have happened ... have influenced the affairs of the Company as they have those of every other railway in the country.'

Familiar remedies resulted, the first being abandonment of the Duddon viaduct in favour of the circuitous route via Foxfield, on the Furness Railway Broughton extension, which was estimated to save £35,000. On the fourth call on shares, 14,144 out of the 17,360 total were in arrears. The Amendment Act authorising the abandonment of the Duddon crossing and the deviation of the line via Foxfield was passed without opposition on 14th August 1848[5].

Opening and early years

By February 1849 the board was able to report that the line had been opened for goods traffic between the Mirehouse station, one mile from Whitehaven, and the River Calder. Work had also commenced on the section between Bootle and the Furness Railway. The line between Whitehaven and Ravenglass was opened for passenger traffic on 19th July 1849, from Ravenglass to Bootle on 8th July 1850, and the remainder of the line, to a junction with the Furness Railway facing towards Broughton, on 1st November 1850.

Captain Simmons inspection of the Whitehaven to Ravenglass section, on 5th June 1849, found that temporary wooden viaducts had been built at two of the river crossings and these were approached by sharp curves requiring a speed restriction of 5mph. In addition one brick arch had settled badly. He went on to say:

'scarcely any ... sidings were completed and there was no

signal on the line and not one station completed or even in an advanced state; in several instances they were not even begun.'

The line was single throughout. Captain Simmons refused to sanction opening and a further inspection took place on 4th July, by which time the essential work had been done. Inspection of the Ravenglass – Bootle section, on 8th June 1850, revealed weak cast iron girders, which had to be replaced. The final section to Foxfield Junction was inspected on 24th October 1850, when Lieutenant Galton spotted that the junction had been made towards Broughton instead of towards Dalton, as authorised in the Act, but he advised no action on this matter. He commented favourably on the *'signal at the junction ... which is admirably adapted to be seen in every direction'.* Passenger trains to Broughton commenced on 1st November 1850.

The Whitehaven & Furness Junction Railway, when completed, was a very different undertaking from that contemplated in 1837. A local group led by William Miller of Whitehaven, banker, merchant and a Trustee of the Town and Harbour of Whitehaven, had now taken over the active direction of both the WJR and the W&FJR under the virtual dictatorship of the Earl of Lonsdale.

An important link between the Whitehaven railways was James Dees (1815-1875) who went to work in West Cumberland when he was 30 and, as his 'Memoir' in the Proceedings of the Institution of Civil Engineers patronisingly remarked:

'by the exigencies of the time he was raised to the surface during the railway mania when the demand for civil engineers exceeded the supply of those regularly trained in the profession.'

Where the road from the Duddon Sands to The Green crossed the W&FJR a station named Green Road was provided in 1850. Seen c.1962, this station remains open as an unstaffed halt. (Author: MAO 0109)

Whitehaven Preston Street station in the 1930s. This was the northern terminus of the W&FJR from 1849, until the formation of the Joint Locomotive Committee in 1854, when passenger traffic was concentrated on Bransty and goods at Preston Street. (CRA: Pattinson collection)

Dees became resident engineer on the construction of the W&FJR in 1848 and, on completion of the line in 1850, was appointed engineer to both Whitehaven companies and manager of the W&FJR[6]. Dees' report to the W&FJR shareholders' meeting on 26th February 1851, showed his insight into the problems of the company – 'The want of a junction with the Whitehaven & Maryport line has been sorely felt.'

A tunnel had been authorised by the 1846 Act, but a more ambitious scheme was authorised by the W&FJR Amendment Act of 1848, involving a line from near Preston Street terminus, through a short tunnel of 210 yards, then by arches across Quay Street, to form a junction with the dock extension of the WJR, a branch to the New Tongue of the harbour was also sanctioned. As the Town and Harbour Trustees did not favour this scheme, the tunnel plan was implemented.

Dees advised that:

'the tunnel would do away with the necessity of carrying the loaded trucks upon wagons drawn through the streets by horses. A very large quantity of iron ore is annually carted from Cleator and the neighbourhood to be shipped there or put in wagons and sent by railway.'

Dees then made a most important recommendation:

'The whole of the iron ore could be carried along seven miles of your railway from Nethertown into the iron district ... The branch could be made for £50,000 ... I strongly advise some steps be taken to accomplish that desirable object.'

In favour of this suggestion was the fact that it would give rail access to the rapidly expanding Cleator ironfield, but against it was the very roundabout route, which might have run into difficulties when the Bill was examined in Parliament. However, the connection with the WJR was considered to be more important and it was left to an independent company, the Whitehaven, Cleator and Egremont Railway (WC&ER), to obtain powers, three years later, for a more direct line into the ironfield. James Dees became its engineer until 1856, when the line was completed, becoming interested in mining at the same time. He was appointed a director of the WC&ER in 1857 and continued in the post until his death in 1875.

By August 1851 construction of the Whitehaven tunnel was proceeding[7]. At the meeting of 25th February 1852, it was noted that the tunnel works had been impeded by old coal workings which had to be brick-arched. However, at the next meeting, on 30th August, completion of the tunnel was recorded and the permanent way was being laid.

The *Whitehaven Herald* of 4th September recorded that the Whitehaven tunnel had been completed and that 'wagons were passing through almost daily'. The tunnel was inspected by Captain Wynne of the Railway Department who reported, on 24th September 1852:

'The extension commences 1,100 yards south of the present terminus of the WFJR at which point it branches off eastward, the entire length of the extension being 1,955 yards. At 470 yards from the commencement the line passes under the Town of Whitehaven by means of a tunnel 1,317 yds in length and 168 yds north of the tunnel the junction is made with the WJR. The formation through the tunnel is constructed in the coal measure and is for single line only.

Side walls are of stone and the arch is partly brick and partly stone. As far as can be judged from appearances, the work is well constructed.

The WJR and the WFJR are both single lines and have until now of necessity been worked independently of each other. The traffic on each is worked by two engines ... and the trains ... are timed to pass each other at a central point. ... On the opening of this extension some of the present trains will be made through trains but the engineer and manager of the WFJR, Mr Dees, informed me that the same principle would be continued in working the through traffic ... The Electric Telegraph (is) provided through the tunnel.' [8]

Captain Wynne recommended the opening of the line for passenger traffic, and this took place on Thursday 30th September 1852.

The W&FJR now turned its attention to a direct communication between its station at Preston Street and Whitehaven Harbour. There had been local opposition to such a plan, but so great was the need that the W&FJR introduced a Bill into Parliament, for the 1853 Session, proposing a tramway from Preston Street to the 'Old Tongue' of the harbour with a branch to the 'New Tongue'. The Bill came before a Parliamentary Committee on 30th May 1853.

William Miller gave evidence before the Committee stating that some 500 to 600 carts a day arrived at the harbour causing great obstruction in the streets. He referred to the proposal for a railway from the Cleator district and the fact that such a line would cause worse congestion in the town unless the tramway was built. William Thompson, MP for Westmorland, stated that he was the owner of the Pen-y-Darren Ironworks in South Wales and that he received only 500 tons of ore from Whitehaven, but could use 50,000 tons. James Dees said that the line, some 600 yards in length, would cost £2,200. The opposition's case rested on the inability of the existing arrangements at Whitehaven harbour to accommodate the increased traffic and the interference this would cause with traffic in the town. The Bill was approved with amendments and passed, the tramway being opened for traffic on 27th January 1854[9].

That the financial position of the W&FJR remained poor was attributed 'to its isolated position',[10] and the opening of the Harbour Tramway held a prospect of good traffic from the proposed WC&ER, but the main obstacle to progress was seen as the lack of communication between the Furness Railway and the main railway system. The Ulverstone & Lancaster Railway had been authorised in 1851, but little progress was being made on the line by the Brogdens. The secretary and manager of the two Whitehaven companies wrote to John Brogden, Chairman of the U&LR:

'John Brogden Esq.

Whitehaven 26th August 1854

Sir,

I am desired by the directors of this Company to say that having reference to the slow progress of the works on the Ulverstone & Lancaster Railway to which your attention has already been called ... if you fail to complete your line within the time specified in your Act of Parliament, thereby rendering a fresh application necessary, they will avail themselves of that opportunity of opposing your

Holborn Hill station was opened by the W&FJR in 1850. The growth of the industrial settlement to support the iron mining and smelting, led to its change of name to Millom. Extensive down sidings were provided. (W. Pinch collection)

application and of applying to Parliament to concede the line to themselves or to some other bona fide projectors. ...
J.S. Yeats Jnr
Secretary'

However, not until the next year was the W&FJR Board satisfied that the U&LR works were being satisfactorily progressed.

The Joint Committee, improving fortunes

Late in 1853 – with the WJR in various difficulties and paying very low dividends and the W&FJR with a low level of traffic paying no dividends at all – consideration was given to the joint operation of the two lines, which would allow a rationalisation of both rolling stock and management. An agreement was signed for operation of the two lines, from 31st December 1853, under the jurisdiction of a Joint Committee formed of directors from each company. J.S. Yeats and James Dees were appointed Secretary/Manager and Resident Engineer respectively to the Joint Committee which continued in operation until the WJR passed to the LNWR and the W&FJR to the Furness Railway in 1866.

However, further trouble was to strike the joint companies. The financial irregularities identified by the accountants regarding the WJR, also involved the W&FJR and the joint Secretary and Manager, J.S. Yeats Jnr., was discharged by both companies, to be replaced, in August 1856, by Henry Cook. Cook was destined to have a distinguished career as Traffic Manager of the Furness Railway, when that company amalgamated with the W&FJR, in 1866. William Meikie was appointed Joint Committee Locomotive Superintendent.

The opening of the Whitehaven, Cleator and Egremont Railway for goods and mineral traffic from Mirehouse Junction, on the W&FJR, to Frizington, on 12th January and to Egremont on 30th April 1856, transformed the fortunes of the W&FJR. Although the distance over which the WC&ER traffic was carried was small – some two miles between Mirehouse Junction and Whitehaven harbour or Bransty Station – the volume of this traffic, together with a toll of 8½d per ton, led to a significant increase in receipts. For the second half years these receipts were

1853	£2,240
1854	£3,519
1855	£3,663
1856	£6,019

During the period to the end of 1856 the W&FJR had been unable to pay any dividend on its Ordinary Stock and the first dividend was 1½ per cent per annum, for the second half of 1857.

Captain Tyler inspected the additional line between Mirehouse and Corkickle and reported on 27th June 1857:

'This portion of the railway is a single line a mile and a half long running alongside the WFJR and forming the termination of the WCER towards Whitehaven. I had occasion to refer to it in reports in August and September 1856 as having been constructed by the WCER upon the land of the WFJR and as requiring extra siding accommodation, improved arrangements for working and some repairs. The engineer has undertaken to complete the two precautionary measures referred to in the enclosed certificate within two weeks ... The Company pledge that only one engine will be allowed on the line at one time.' [11]

After the FR took over the W&FJR in 1866, the original primitive stations were replaced during the 1870s by substantial buildings designed by the FR architects, Paley & Austin. Drigg, seen in July 1968, is a typical example. (Author: MAA 759)

Captain Tyler recommended the opening of the new line. Passenger traffic commenced on the WC&ER on 1st July 1857[12].

The 'expedition curve' between the WFJR and FR lines at Foxfield was opened on 1st August 1858. A station, sidings, engine shed and turntable were built at Foxfield jointly by the two companies for the mutual exchange of traffic[13]. The joint use of the stations at Foxfield and Broughton was the subject of an agreement, operative from 1st January 1860, but which was not formally signed by James Ramsden, for the FR and Henry Cook for the WFJR, until 1st January 1861[14]. A 'small platform' was erected at Drigg in 1859. Owing to lack of traffic it was decided to close the stations at Underhill and Green Road from 1st January 1860, but a memorial, signed by 206 persons, led to the reprieve of Green Road station[15]. Also in 1860, a permanent station was built at St Bees by J. Townley of Whitehaven at a cost of £436[16].

In 1862 the WC&ER proposed to double its line and the WFJR resolved to lay a second line of rails, for the Cleator company's traffic, between Mirehouse and Corkickle[17]. On 1st February 1864 a double line of rail was opened between Corkickle and Moor Row, the WC&ER extension from Frizington to Rowrah was opened on the same day.

During the period from 1856 to 1864 the WFJR board considered a number of other issues. On 18th January 1858 it received a letter from Lord Lonsdale recommending a reduction in passenger trains – a further example of his authoritarian character – and resolved:

'That the timetable submitted be adopted for the month of February in deference to the wishes of the Chairman but

the Directors present are unanimously of the opinion that it would have been better not to have diminished the number of trains so soon after the opening of the new route southwards and for such small a saving as is likely to be effected.'

A rider to this is recorded by the board on 15th February 1858:

'Authorised that the schoolboys be allowed to return from St Bees in the van of the goods train until the passenger trains were again suitable.'

A joint meeting, held in Ulverston on 20th December 1858, agreed that the iron ore rates to South Staffordshire from March 1859 should be:

From Ulverston and Barrow	10/6 per ton
From Whitehaven	13/- per ton

The West Cumberland ironmasters considered these rates detrimental to traffic, which continued largely by sea from Whitehaven, at a rate 1/- per ton less[18].

On 30th June 1863 the W&FJR board resolved:

'That ... the alterations at Preston Street (station) which they had agreed to make for the joint use of both Companies having been completed for some time past, the Board now call upon the WJ Board to carry out their part of the agreement by covering the Bransty Station with a roof which is so much needed to protect the carriages and passengers from the inclemency of the weather.'

A panorama of Millom Ironworks, looking north, in October 1962, and showing the experimental "spray steel" furnace. (Author: MAO 0202)

Final years

The board meeting of 22nd September 1863 presaged the beginning of the final era of the W&FJR. They received a report from the engineer, Thomas Drane, on the cost of making a line of railway across the Duddon estuary from Holborn Hill to the FR. But it was decided that the 1863 traffic levels did not merit an application to Parliament in the next session.

This final era of the W&FJR saw the continuation of parochial squabbling with its Cumberland neighbours, the WJR board noting, on 8th July 1864:

'The WFJ Board were determined to have the present arrangements for the use of the two stations (at Whitehaven) cancelled and a new agreement on a totally different basis entered into.

Resolved: The deputation having failed to come to a settlement of the question of rent contained in the Report of the Investigation Committee, the WFJ Board be requested to give the requisite notice that the present arrangement for interchange of traffic and the use of the two stations as well as the Locomotive Agreement be terminated. The WJR will be glad to receive the W&FJR's proposals for a new agreement.'

All that happened was that James Allport, General Manager of the Midland Railway, was appointed arbitrator, an interesting choice in view of the rumours, which were soon to circulate, regarding the Midland Company's ambitions in West Cumberland.

The second local dispute was with the WC&ER. The communication between the WC&ER and the rest of the railway system was, at this time, totally in the hands of the W&FJR, between Mirehouse and Corkickle, with the bulk of the W&FJR revenue coming from this traffic, as has already been seen. In 1864, the WC&ER proposed a line from their southern terminus at Egremont, to the W&FJR at Sellafield, which would allow a direct route for West Cumberland ore to the furnaces at Barrow. The initial response by the W&FJR was to wheel out James Dees' earlier plan for a line from Nethertown to Egremont. However, on 10th October 1864, the W&FJR board gave serious consideration to the requirements of the WC&ER, proposing that mineral tolls be reduced from 8½d to 6½d per ton, and, for minerals going south, the reduction should be from 8d to 3d per ton. This offer was subject to the WC&ER abandoning its plan for an Egremont – Sellafield line and an agreement that the WC&ER would not oppose the W&FJR Duddon Crossing plan. An agreement between the W&FJR and the WC&ER was sealed by the W&FJR Board on 14th November 1864.

The progress of the W&FJR was not as spectacular as that of the WJR, mainly because of the relatively light traffic on the main portion of the line between Mirehouse and Foxfield.

When it became clear that the Furness Railway was to take over the Whitehaven & Furness Junction Railway, the Whitehaven, Cleator & Egremont Railway reopened negotiations on the proposed Egremont to Sellafield line. On 9th October 1865, the W&FJR board noted that it had met James Ramsden of the Furness Railway and that Ramsden had suggested a line from Egremont to half a mile north of Sellafield, which would be jointly owned.

The W&FJR agreed to abandon its plans for a line to Nethertown and a Bill was rapidly prepared, proposing a joint

A Fowler 4F 0-6-0 passes Corkickle No.2 signalbox with a northbound freight, c.1957. (Author: MAC 216)

committee of three W&FJR and three WC&ER directors. The Cleator & Furness Act 1866 received Royal Assent on 28th June 1866. Colonel C.S. Hutchinson inspected the Cleator & Furness line and found a line 4 miles 61 chains in length which was single throughout. He noted that a turntable was to be provided at Sellafield, but was unable to recommend an opening and re-inspected on 28th May 1869[19], at which time he was able to recommend opening for passenger traffic, provided that the station at Sellafield was completed.

The Cleator & Furness line was opened on 1st August 1869 with an intermediate station at Beckermet[20]. The Furness Railway progressively doubled its main line north of Barrow, which was completed, as far as the junction with the Cleator & Furness line, in August 1874[21].

WHITEHAVEN AND FURNESS JUNCTION RAILWAY

Dividends on Ordinary Stock as Percentage per Annum for each Half Year

Year	Half	%	Year	Half	%
1850 to 1856		0%	1861	2nd	2¾%
1857	1st	0%	1862	1st	2½%
1857	2nd	1%	1862	2nd	3%
1858	1st	0%	1863	1st	5%
1858	2nd	1½%	1863	2nd	5½%
1859	1st	1¾%	1864	1st	7½%
1859	2nd	2½%	1864	2nd	8%
1860	1st	3%	1865	1st	8%
1860	2nd	4%	1865	2nd	8%
1861	1st	3½%	1866	1st	8%

CHAPTER 5 REFERENCES

1   Shareholders' and Directors' Minute Books of the WJR and the Directors' Minute Book of the W&FJR for the period 1844-56 were not passed to the successor Companies in 1866 and consequently are not in the British Transport Historical Records of the PRO. Recourse has had to be made to local newspapers and railway periodicals for data for those years. *(Author's Note)*
2   Dr E. Course, personal communication.
3   9&10 Vic Cap 320.
4   W&FJR SM, 18th Feb.1846.
5   11&12 Vic Cap 128.
6   W&FJR Public Timetable. 1st Nov. 1850.
7   W&FJR SM, 30th Aug. 1851.
8   PRO: MT29/12 p.142.
9   *Cumberland Pacquet*, 31st Jan. 1854.
10 W&FJR SM, 26th Aug. 1853.
11 PRO: MT29/18.
12 *Bradshaw's Shareholders' Guide 1858.*
13 W&FJR SM, 25th Feb. 1859.
14 BRO: Andrews Collection, Plan E.250.
15 W&FJR SM, 5th Dec.1859.
16 W&FJR DM, 7th May 1860.
17 W&FJR SM, 27th Feb.1863.
18 W&FJR DM, 20th June 1859.
19 PRO: MT29/30.
20 *Barrow Herald*, 21st Aug. 1869.
21 *Barrow Herald*, 22nd Aug. 1874.

On the left, Fowler 4F 0-6-0 No.44065 stands in the Joint Line bay at Sellafield in August 1964 with a workmen's train to Moor Row. 4F No.44377 leaves with ore empties for Egremont. (Derek Cross: FM 186)

The signals at Braystones, seen in the 1930s. were used to protect a level crossing giving access to the foreshore. (CRA: Pattinson collection)

THE WHITEHAVEN, CLEATOR & EGREMONT RAILWAY: 1854-1866

Compared with the West Cumberland coalfield, which extended from Aspatria, in the north, to Whitehaven, in the south, the West Cumberland ironfield was relatively circumscribed, running from Rowrah, in the north, to Beckermet, in the south; with the large Hodbarrow deposit being considered, geologically, as part of the Furness ironfield. The West Cumberland hematite ore was, like the Furness ore, of high iron content and free from phosphorus, making it eminently suitable for the Bessemer steel-making process. Iron mining in the Egremont area was first recorded in the twelfth century, but substantial quantities of ore were not raised until the mid-eighteenth century. Apart from some local use at furnaces, such as that at Little Clifton, the bulk of the ore was shipped at Whitehaven harbour to merchants in South Wales, Chester and Scotland.

A significant development was the opening of the Whitehaven Hematite Iron Company's works at Cleator Moor, in 1841, by Thomas Ainsworth, an owner of iron and coal mines in the Cleator district. In 1850 the total ore output of West Cumberland was 100,000 tons. By 1856, the year in which the Whitehaven, Cleator and Egremont Railway opened, it had risen to 200,000 tons[1].

West Cumberland had been put on the railway map by the opening of the WJR and the W&FJR, which were eventually connected by the Whitehaven tunnel. Yet the Cleator ironfield remained isolated from this railway system, although James Dees had advised the shareholders' meeting, on 26th February 1851:

'A large quantity of iron ore is annually carted from Cleator and the neighbourhood to be shipped at Whitehaven or put on waggons and sent by Railway.'

He suggested a branch line to Cleator from the W&FJR at Nethertown, but nothing was done until 1853 when Lord Lonsdale and Anthony Benn Steward, a Whitehaven solicitor, who was reputed to have recognised the need for such a line by observing the congestion caused in Whitehaven by iron ore carts passing through the town on their way to the harbour, instigated remedial action.

They proposed a line of railway from the Whitehaven & Furness Junction line at Mirehouse, to Egremont and Frizington in the ironfield. A Bill for the Whitehaven, Cleator and Egremont Railway was prepared, passed by a Committee of the House of Lords[2], and Royal Assent was granted on 16th June 1854. The authorised capital was £50,000. The subscribers included Colonel Henry Wyndham, owner of mining royalties at Egremont; Samuel Lindow, iron mine proprietor, and William Miller, director of both WJR and W&FJR. The first meeting of the new company was held at the Town Hall, Whitehaven, on 14th September 1854[3].

On 29th December 1854, a group consisting of the Cleator Iron Ore Company; the Eskett Iron Ore Company; John Stirling Esq.; Richard Barker Esq.; the Parkside Mining Company; John Tyson Esq.; and William Cormack Esq.; sent a memorial to the Trustees of the Town and Harbour of Whitehaven urging the improvement of Whitehaven Harbour[4].

On 24th July 1855 the *Cumberland Pacquet* reported:

'There cannot be two opinions upon the importance of the influence of the railway now in course of construction from Whitehaven through the iron ore districts is calculated to exercise on the welfare of the commerce and industrial property of Cumberland. The progress on the line has been watched with considerable interest consequent upon its acknowledged importance.

The new railway will form a junction with the Whitehaven & Furness Railway about a mile and a half from the town, a short distance from Mirehouse ... On leaving the Furness line, the new line will climb at 1 in 52 in the direction of Scale Gill on the Whitehaven to Egremont Turnpike. A single line only is being laid down but the embankment is being made sufficiently wide to admit of a double line should the traffic of the district increase to such an extent to require additional transport accommodation. The contract is being undertaken by Atkinson & Blane. Crossing the Turnpike we come to that portion of the line being undertaken by Messrs. Brotherton & Rigg. From this point the permanent way is laid to the terminus of the Frizington Branch. At the place where the Egremont Branch turns off by a gentle curve, the permanent way has been laid for a distance of ¾ mile.'

On 28th August 1855 the *Cumberland Pacquet* reported on the meeting of the WC&ER and on the comments of the company chairman:

'There is reason to regret that the accommodation for the iron ore (at Whitehaven Harbour) has not been provided as we were led to expect ... Two jetties could have been erected in the South Harbour at a cheap rate and along with other contemplated improvements would not only have been sufficient for the traffic of the railway but would have been of general advantage to the trade of the town ... Preparations have already been made for conveyance of ore by the railway to the east coast and to Scotland and arrangements may also be made into the southern and midland districts.'

This is further evidence of the conservative attitudes in Whitehaven, compared with the progressive activities being demonstrated at Barrow, at the time.

Opening the line

On 11th December 1855 the *Cumberland Pacquet* recorded:

'On 6th December a locomotive engine with a train of

The centre of the WC&ER was Moor Row, where the line to Sellafield via Egremont and the line to Marron Junction via Rowrah divided. A workshop and engine shed were built which became part of the Furness Railway when the LNW & FR Joint Line was formed in 1878. A freight train from the Rowrah line is bound for Whitehaven in the mid 1930s. (Ken Norman collection)

trucks passed over the entire length (of the WC&ER). Mr. Dees, the engineer, and Mr. Linton, the Secretary, accompanied by Mr J.S. Yeats, Mr. Gibson, assistant to Mr. Dees, along with several other gentlemen were accommodated with places on the engine and the result of the trip was most satisfactory to all parties. ... 100 mineral trucks have arrived for use on the line.'

The *Cumberland Pacquet* of 15th January 1856 reported:

'On Friday last (11th January) the WC&ER was formally opened for mineral traffic to the Frizington Branch. A train of wagons, laden with iron ore from the Parkside Mine, was brought to Whitehaven and passed forward, over the Whitehaven Junction Railway and other railways, without change of carriage, direct to consumers in Scotland. On the first trip the amount of ore brought down was 70 tons. On Saturday a second trip was made when the engine took up 40 heavy Newcastle cauldron waggons and brought back a train with 124 tons of ore ... The incline was descended at a rate of 6mph without the application of any break except to the engine.'

The branch to Egremont was completed and opened for mineral traffic on 30th April 1856[5]. Anthony Steward reported to the Half Year meeting on 28th August, that big improvements had been effected at Whitehaven harbour and that a branch railway to the Bulwark had been opened on 28th July. He also stated that the railway had been inspected for the Board of Trade, but because of the lack of siding accommodation at Corkickle and the lack of a working agreement with the W&FJR, together with the failure of the WC&ER to provide its own passenger carriages, opening for passenger traffic had not been sanctioned. Over 54,000 tons of iron ore

and 10,000 tons of other traffic had been carried since the opening of the line.

The Board of Trade inspection referred to had been carried out by Captain H.W. Tyler on 18th August 1856. He reported:

'This new line runs over the land and alongside the single line of the Whitehaven & Furness Junction Company from Corkickle, a small station near Whitehaven, for a mile and a quarter. It then diverges from the line of the latter Company and ascends on a gradient of 1 in 52 for two miles to the Moor Row Junction whence the main line runs on for 2¼ miles to Egremont and a branch for two miles to Frizington. The Whitehaven & Furness Company should give notice of the opening of the section running over their land. The siding accommodation is as yet insufficient for working the passenger traffic and the heavy and increasing mineral traffic of the two Companies into and through the small station which is awkwardly situated at the mouth of a long tunnel traversed by a single line of rails, and satisfactory financial and working arrangements between the two Companies have still to be decided upon. It will evidently not be desirable to open the WC&ER until a permanent Agreement should have been completed upon these points between the two Companies and sanctioned by their Directors because whatever measure may be adopted by the Egremont Company for securing the safety of their passengers they are liable otherwise to be thwarted at any time by the views of the Company on whose property they encroach and in whose power to a certain extent they at present are.

For some months a considerable goods and mineral traffic has passed over the line and will much increase from the

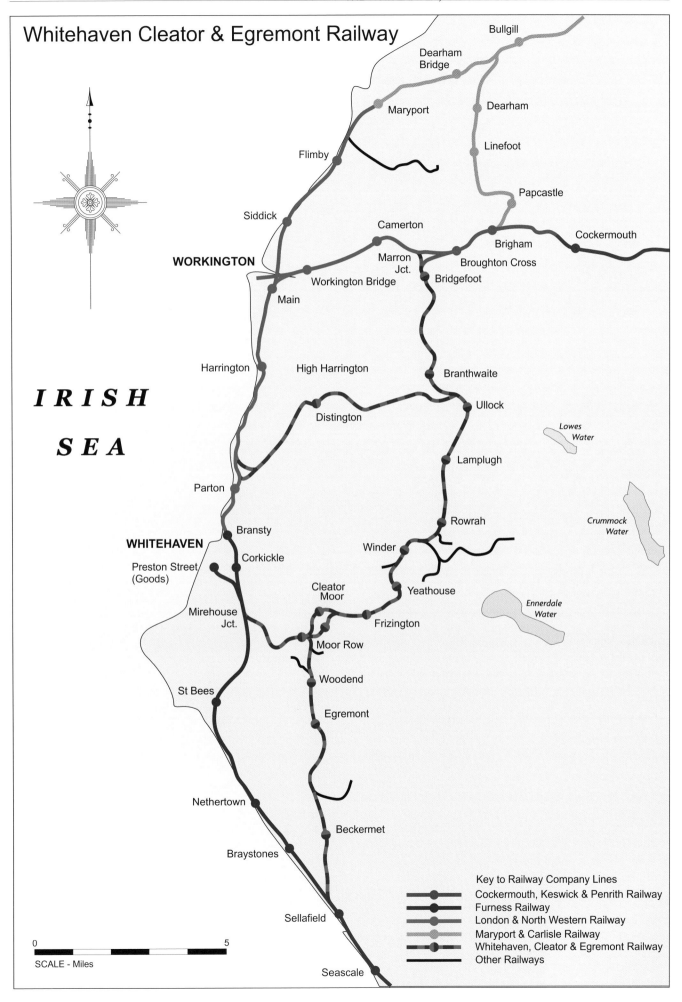

Whitehaven Cleator & Egremont Railway

Bullgill

Dearham
Bridge

Maryport

Dearham

Linefoot

Flimby

Papcastle

Siddick

Camerton

Cockermouth

Brigham

WORKINGTON

Marron
Jct.

Broughton Cross

Workington Bridge

Bridgefoot

Main

Harrington

High Harrington

Branthwaite

Ullock

Lowes
Water

Distington

Lamplugh

Parton

Crummock
Water

Rowrah

WHITEHAVEN

Bransty

Winder

Corkickle

Cleator
Moor

Yeathouse

Ennerdale
Water

Preston Street
(Goods)

Frizington

Mirehouse
Jct.

Moor Row

Woodend

St Bees

Egremont

Nethertown

Beckermet

Braystones

Key to Railway Company Lines
Cockermouth, Keswick & Penrith Railway
Furness Railway
London & North Western Railway
Maryport & Carlisle Railway
Whitehaven, Cleator & Egremont Railway
Other Railways

Sellafield

0   5

SCALE - Miles

Seascale

IRISH

SEA

The WC&ER was double-tracked between Egremont and Gutterby, north of Woodend, as seen here c.1962. (Author: MAA156)

pits of red hematite ore which abound in the neighbour-hood but they possess only two engines one of which is disabled, and no passenger carriages. It appears that they intend to procure another engine and to borrow carriages from the Whitehaven & Furness Company until they can purchase a sufficient number of their own. On application to the latter Company I find that their means of lending are rather precarious and I should therefore recommend the former Company to procure a proper stock of their own before attempting to carry passengers.

The engine they employ is not well suited in some respects to the circumstances of the line; they should obtain engines of a different construction for working passenger traffic. The present engine is a tank engine of great power, six coupled, and weighing 36 tons creating a great strain on the permanent way and has been six times derailed. The few signals present on the line are of an inferior descrip-tion. More siding accommodation is wanted at Moor Row as well as a platform and shed for the use of passengers. Some special arrangement will have to be adopted at the bottom of the incline leading up to the junction to prevent accident in case of carriages or waggons or even whole trains breaking away. The opening of this line must be attended with danger to the public.'

Captain Tyler carried out a further inspection on 29th June 1857[6]. He reported:

'In consequence of my reports of 18th August 1856 and 13th September 1856 the WC&ER were induced to withdraw their Notice of Opening. Since that time they have produced an extra engine and three passenger carriages and a break van fitted with 'Newall's Break'. They have made a better arrangement with the W&FJR for the working of the traffic into and out of the Corkickle Terminus. I may add, however, that it appears exceedingly desirable that the supply of rolling stock should be increased, that a double line of rails should be constructed between Moor Row and Corkickle and that a telegraph wire should be laid between those places.

Opening advised.'

The line was opened for passenger traffic on 1st July 1857[7].

In 1857 the WC&ER applied to Parliament for an Act to increase its capital by £25,000, plus loans, to complete its railway. The Act received Royal Assent on 21st March 1857, but did not authorise any new lines. The Directors' Report to the shareholders' meeting in August 1857 recorded:

'The quantity of coke, iron, coal and other merchandise amounted to 32,226 tons showing an increase compared with the corresponding period of last year of 97% on iron ore and 195% on the remaining articles of traffic.'

For the half year to 31st December 1857 the WC&ER paid a dividend of 7% p.a. on its ordinary stock, which, by 30th June 1860, had risen to 10% p.a.

The Whitehaven, Cleator & Egremont Railway must have contributed to the increasing output of the West Cumberland ironfield. New ironworks began to spring up as the innovative Bessemer steel process increased the demand for the phospho-rus-free Furness and West Cumberland hematite pig iron.

Ironworks at Oldside (Workington) and Harrington opened in 1857 and, in 1872, the giant West Cumberland Iron & Steel Works at Workington went into production. During the six years from 1855 to 1860 the output of the West Cumberland ironfield was:

1855	200,788 tons
1856	259,167 tons
1857	323,812 tons
1858	331,544 tons
1859	400,306 tons
1860	466,851 tons

The extension to Marron

This highly profitable railway now gave consideration to extending its Frizington branch northwards, to tap the newer iron mines at Eskett; the quarries at Yeathouse and Winder; and the northern part of the Cumberland coal field in the Lamplugh area. Powers were also sought to double the existing line. The WC&ER Act[8] authorised these works together with an increase in capital of £45,000, and the Lamplugh extension was opened for mineral traffic in November 1862. However, by 1862, the advantages of extending the line to a triangular junction with the Cockermouth and Workington Railway (C&WR) at Marron, became apparent.

The extension of the C&WR line from Cockermouth to Penrith, to connect with the South Durham and Lancashire Union and Eden Valley Railways, had been authorised, in 1861, as the Cockermouth, Keswick & Penrith Railway. The Marron extension was authorised by an Act of 8th June 1863, which also permitted new capital of £75,000, and granted a necessary devi-

ation between Moor Row and Frizington because of mining subsidence on the original line, although the old main line remained open as the Crossfield loop, serving the Whitehaven Hematite Iron Company's works.

The extension from Frizington to Lamplugh was inspected by Captain F.H. Rich of the Board of Trade Railway Department, on 28th December 1863, the extension line being three miles, 53 chains in length and single throughout, although the bridges had been built for a double line. Rich noted that stations were provided at Frizington, Eskett, Winder, Rowrah and Lamplugh, and the opening was authorised, with passenger traffic commencing on 12th February 1864.

Captain Tyler inspected the deviation between Cleator Moor and Birks Bridge Junction and the doubling of the line onwards to Frizington, on 26th September 1864[9]. He required a signal box to be provided at Birks Bridge Junction, but his re-inspection, on 27th February 1866[10], was unsatisfactory, which further delayed the opening of the deviation line for passenger traffic. It was finally opened, together with a new Cleator Moor station, on 19th April 1866[11].

On 27th February 1866 Captain Tyler also inspected the 8¼-mile extension from Lamplugh to Marron Junction on the Cockermouth & Workington line, at which junction there were east and west curves, the east curve providing a direct line to the Maryport & Carlisle Railway's Derwent branch, authorised in 1865 and opened on 1st June 1867[12]. Intermediate stations, between Lamplugh and Marron, were provided at Ullock, Branthwaite and Bridgefoot, with the WC&ER proposing to use the platform at Marron, built by the C&WR, at the west junction. The platform was on the eastbound side of the single Cockermouth & Workington Railway, which meant that WC&ER trains had to

Cleator Moor Junction, seen in the mid-1930s, was where the Cleator & Workington Junction line to Workington and Siddick Junction branched off the WC&ER. A LNWR 2-4-2 tank engine is signalled to Rowrah with a Bransty to Workington train. FR 0-6-0 No.119 is shunting in the sidings. (CRA: Pattinson collection)

One of the few photographs known to have survived of this curious and little-used station at Marron Foot at the northern end of the WC&ER line from Rowrah where it joined the Cockermouth & Workington line at a triangular junction. (CRA: Pattinson collection)

cross a mineral branch to reach it. Captain Tyler disapproved of this arrangement and declined to sanction opening. The WC&ER promptly provided a separate platform for their trains. The Marron extension was opened for passenger traffic on 2nd April 1866, opening for goods and minerals having already taken place on 15th January 1866[13]. Tyler noted that the Marron east curve was not yet in use. Lamplugh station was renamed Wright Green in 1866, but reverted to Lamplugh in 1901.

The dividends, per half-year, for the first ten years of the Whitehaven, Cleator and Egremont Railway speak for themselves:

WHITEHAVEN, CLEATOR & EGREMONT RAILWAY

Dividends on Ordinary Stock as Percentage per Annum for each Half Year

1856	1st	4%	1861	2nd	10%
1856	2nd	4%	1862	1st	5½%
1857	1st	4½%	1862	2nd	10%
1857	2nd	7%	1863	1st	15%
1858	1st	7%	1863	2nd	12%
1858	2nd	7%	1864	1st	13%
1859	1st	8%	1864	2nd	12%
1859	2nd	8%	1865	1st	10%
1860	1st	10%	1865	2nd	10%
1860	2nd	10%	1866	1st	10%
1861	1st	10%	1866	2nd	8%

These results were among the best of all the railway companies in the United Kingdom and they no doubt influenced the Directors to stand aloof from the amalgamation plans of 1865.

CHAPTER 6 REFERENCES

1 Lancaster J Y & Wattleworth D R. Op. cit.
2 Cumberland Pacquet, 30th May 1854.
3 Cumberland Pacquet, 19th Sep. 1854.
4 Cumberland Pacquet, 9th Jan. 1855.
5 Cumberland Pacquet, 6th May 1856.
6 PRO: MT29/18.
7 Bradshaw General Railway Guide, 1st July 1857.
8 Royal Assent, 7th June 1861.
9 PRO: MT29/25 p.625.
10 PRO: MT29/27.
11 Joy D, 1983. Op. cit. pp.166.
12 Simmons J, 1947. The Maryport & Carlisle Railway p.20.
13 PRO: MT6/68/10.

THE LONDON & NORTH WESTERN RAILWAY INVADES WEST CUMBERLAND

October 1864 marked the peak of the Earl of Lonsdale's supremacy in West Cumberland railway affairs. On 19th October, his Whitehaven & Furness Junction Railway board approved the terms of an agreement for the handling of their principal source of traffic – the iron ore from the Whitehaven, Cleator & Egremont Railway. The Cleator Company had been able to reduce its tolls for iron ore, thus attracting to rail the hematite still carried by road to Whitehaven harbour.

A day earlier, the offer of the board of Lonsdale's Whitehaven Junction Railway to lease to the now strategically important Cockermouth & Workington Railway was accepted at 10%. The C&WR would become a trunk route to the north-east on the imminent completion of the Cockermouth, Keswick & Penrith Railway line. Within just two days, Lonsdale appeared to have added, to his north-south line, a new east-west link, with its promise of an east-bound traffic in hematite ore and pig iron and a west-bound traffic in Durham coke – at that time an essential commodity for the blast furnaces of West Cumberland. At the same time he had contained the Whitehaven, Cleator & Egremont Railway by controlling its northern outlet at Marron Junction and its southern outlet at Mirehouse Junction.

However, Lonsdale had not anticipated the aggressive policies of the Maryport & Carlisle Railway's secretary and general manager, John Addison, who had been appointed in 1858[1] and, by the end of May 1865, the 77 year old Lonsdale had lost his entire railway empire.

In the early 1860s West Cumberland was industrially much more developed than it had been in the pioneer days of its first railways. In 1849 the ore output was some 100,000 tons, which had risen to 467,000 tons by 1860, and was destined to continue to rise to its peak of 1,700,000 tons by 1882[2].

The through-route formed by the Maryport & Carlisle, the Whitehaven Junction and the Whitehaven & Furness Junction Railways had been augmented, in 1847, by a single line from the WJR station at Workington, to Cockermouth. The Cockermouth & Workington Railway remained, for many years, of purely local significance, transporting coal from pits in the valley of the River Derwent to Workington harbour for shipment, although, from its earliest days, the possibility of this line forming part of a route to the east had been recognised.

In 1845 a group of shareholders formed an independent Cockermouth & Workington Extension Railway and, in 1846, obtained powers to build a line to Keswick[3]. The following year

Looking south at Derwent Junction in the mid-1930s. In the centre foreground, the line to Workington Docks curves to the right, whilst centre left is the signalbox and the line giving access to the dock from the Cockermouth direction. In the distance is the junction between the the Whitehaven Junction line and the Cockermouth & Workington line. (CRA: Pattinson collection)

they tried to interest the Kendal & Windermere Railway (K&WR) and the C&WR in joining them to make a line between Cockermouth and the K&WR terminus at Windermere via Keswick, but there were no funds, even for the authorised line as far as Keswick, so the plan was dropped[4]. The C&WR continued its independent existence, although in 1857 its shareholders, already dissatisfied with the line's direction and management, were precipitated into a state of overt dispute with their board over concessions made in tolls to the Fletchers of Clifton Colliery. The Fletchers featured prominently on the C&WR board and persuaded Lord Lonsdale, the owner of the mining royalty, to back them by threatening to build his own tramway from Clifton to Workington, if the C&WR did not reduce its tolls. The rank and file C&WR shareholders then demanded that

Lonsdale, in the guise of the WJR, might as well run their railway at a fixed income and suggested a modest 3½%, rising to 4½% over seven years[5], but Lonsdale turned down what must have been the gift of the decade.

By 1858 the rapid expansion of the hematite trade was beginning and, on 9th April, Furness hematite interests, led by Henry Schneider, attended, as shareholders, a meeting of the South Durham & Lancashire Union Railway (SD&LUR). The purpose of the meeting was to promote a branch from Kirkby Stephen, along the Eden Valley, to Clifton near Penrith, a line intended to be the first stage in an approach to West Cumberland via Keswick. In spite of the most vigorous opposition by the Furness interests, the project was promoted and subsequently authorised by Parliament[6].

Centre left is Workington Bridge station c.1930. The Cockermouth & Workington signalbox near the centre of the photograph controlled the link between the C&W line and the Cleator & Workington curve from Cloffocks Junction. (Sankey archive: 6176)

The link westward from Penrith was promoted by a separate company, the Cockermouth Keswick and Penrith Railway (CK&PR), authorised, in 1861, to run from a junction with the Lancaster & Carlisle line at Penrith, to the C&WR at Cockermouth[7].

By this time the SD&LUR had been absorbed by the Stockton & Darlington Railway (S&DR) and the L&CR by the London & North Western Railway (LNWR)[8], which put the LNWR in a strong position to gain the Furness and West Cumberland iron ore traffic. It was already handling the bulk of the southbound trade from Carnforth and would carry the Durham to Furness coke traffic which started, on 4th July 1861, between the SD&LUR junction at Tebay and the FR at Carnforth. Now it would have control over this new link at Penrith. But it was not only the hematite traffic which the LNWR cornered as, at this time, it was exercising a stranglehold over the Scottish traffic of the Midland Railway by virtue of its control of the MR leased 'Little' North Western Railway at both of the latter's Lancaster and Ingleton outlets[9].

When the CK&PR found itself in difficulties over capital, it was not surprising that the S&DR and the LNWR were prepared to come to its aid. An agreement, dated 11th September 1862, allowed the LNWR to work, with full running powers, the passenger and goods traffic of the CK&PR and, in return for £25,000 capital, to fix rates. Two board members were to be nominated by the LNWR, but the most significant clause came near the end:

'It is agreed that it would be to the interest of the Keswick Company and of all other parties and of the Public ... if the Cockermouth (and Workington) Company would enter into general working arrangements with the LNWR for

facilitating the full and free interchange of traffic over their line to and from Workington and the Keswick Company undertake to use their best exertions to secure such an arrangement.'

With a similar working agreement for mineral trade, the CK&PR received a further £25,000 from the S&DR, these agreements being confirmed by the CK&PR Act of 1863, which appears to have passed unopposed[10].

As noted in Chapter Six, the West Cumberland coast line's other important feeder, the WC&ER had, in 1863, obtained powers to extend its Frizington branch northwards to a junction with the C&W at Marron Foot[11], providing a direct outlet from the ore field to the LNWR and the S&DR. Its significance was enhanced by the publication of plans, by the Maryport & Carlisle Company, for a branch from Bullgill to the Cockermouth & Workington line at Brigham, their Derwent branch.

The Derwent branch of the Maryport and Carlisle Railway

The Maryport & Carlisle Railway was the oldest of the West Cumberland lines. It had, with the Newcastle and Carlisle Railway, provided the original route between the Cumberland coast and the north-east coast and, after the opening of the Caledonian Railway, also provided a link with Scotland. After a difficult start due to management problems, it had built a solid commercial reputation and thrived on the traffic of the coal and iron fields[12]. With the development of the hematite trade, there was a build-up of coke traffic from the Newcastle district and of ore and pig-iron to the Lanark area. The M&CR therefore viewed the nascent CK&PR with some anxiety as it would, undoubtedly, abstract a significant part of the traffic from Durham.

FR 2-4-2 tank engine No. 70 and crew wait for their next turn of duty in the platform at Siddick Junction. (CRA Shilcock collection)

The M&CR had successfully fended off an attempt by its northern rival, the North British Railway (NBR), to penetrate the Cumberland coalfield and, in 1853, powers had been obtained to build a railway over the moribund Carlisle canal – this line being opened, to Port Carlisle, in 1854. In the same year, further powers were obtained to make an extension from the Port Carlisle line at Drumburgh, to Silloth Bay, where a harbour was to be built. This extension opened in 1856 and the harbour at Silloth was completed in 1859[13].

In 1861, the Carlisle and Silloth Bay Railway and Dock Company tried to get powers for a line to Bolton, in the northernmost part of the coalfield. Having been repulsed by the M&CR, in June 1862, the Silloth company amalgamated with the North British Railway. At this time the M&CR obtained an Act for two branches into the area, to Mealsgate and to Bolton, despite opposition from the Silloth company.

A more ambitious project appeared in 1863. The Dumfriesshire & Cumberland Junction Railway, planned to tap the iron trade traffic between West Cumberland and Lanark, was promoted by the now familiar iron-trade interests and railway builders, the Brogdens. Having survived the exigencies of the Ulverstone and Lancaster Railway construction, the Brogden company were bought out by the Furness Railway in 1862, and had acquired the Ogmore coalfield in South Wales where they were improving the railway facilities[14]. Alexander Brogden, one of John's sons, had taken a special interest in the family's northern assets and was chairman of what became known as the Solway Junction Railway (SJR), of which James Dees, the West Cumberland engineer, was a board member.

As the SJR reckoned to cut the rate for ore to Scotland by 1/- a ton, the M&CR opposed the scheme in Parliament, but the SJR obtained its Act in 1864. The line was to commence from the Caledonian Railway at Kirtlebridge and, after a connection with the Glasgow & South Western at Annan, would cross the Solway on a long viaduct, to a junction with the M&CR at Brayton. A proposed curve to the North British Railway at Abbey Holme, on the Silloth line, was later replaced by using a three-mile section of the Silloth line between Kirkbride and Abbey Holme[15].

Thus three mainline Scottish companies were now on the M&CR's doorstep. However, the M&CR, in common with the FR and the Whitehaven companies, had its own man of action in John Addison, who realised that the SJR and the WC&ER formed a potential new through route, requiring only the completion of six short miles between Bullgill and the Cockermouth & Workington line at Brigham. It was his intention that the M&CR should step into that gap, thereby consolidating its position. The result was the M&CR's Derwent Branch Bill of 1863-64.

By 1864, the Cockermouth & Workington line had become the strategic focus in West Cumberland. The LNWR, whose intentions were already clear, made the first attempt through the Cockermouth Joint Station Committee (C&WR/CK&PR), which informed the C&WR board, on 2nd February 1864, that the LNWR would be prepared to work the C&WR on the same terms as those agreed with the CK&PR.

The C&WR, now becoming conscious of its position, politely declined, as an:

'arrangement under which the working company had entire control of the rates complete with general running powers would prejudice the interests of this company.' [16]

The S&DR made a similar offer, on 22nd March 1864, but by this time Lord Lonsdale had stepped in with his initial offer of 8%, or equal terms[17], for a lease to the WJR. The C&WR spurned the S&DR and, intoxicated by its newly gained popularity, turned down Lonsdale as well.

The C&WR chairman, John Steel, MP for Cockermouth, wrote to Lonsdale personally, on 23rd March 1864, demanding a guaranteed 10% in perpetuity[18]. Keen as he was, this was too much for Lonsdale to stomach and, after exchanging formalities, the

WJR closed the negotiations[19]. Almost immediately the CK&PR stepped in with its own ploy. Its line was not yet finished, so the suggestion was made that the C&WR should defer a decision until the real value of the line, as judged by the volume of through traffic, was known. The C&WR should, it claimed, be *'identified with the CK&P by lease or otherwise'*. [20]

Lord Lonsdale now turned his attention, unsuccessfully, to the acquisition of the WC&ER[21], his alternative strategic course. The M&CR were the next in line to approach the C&WR, they did not offer amalgamation but instead asked politely for a guarantee of full traffic facilities between the junction of its proposed Derwent branch and Cockermouth, and the WC&ER at Marron. John Addison's letter continued, that the M&CR would be:

'glad to avoid the alternative of extending their survey ... so as to form an independent junction with the Cleator and Keswick lines.' [22]

The C&WR appointed yet another committee to examine the M&CR offer and, after exchange of letters and a meeting at Maryport, this committee reported that the M&CR board was *'so fair and liberally disposed towards this company'* that terms had been agreed[23.] The formal agreement between the M&CR and the C&WR was sealed on 4th October 1864.

This agreement did not escape Lord Lonsdale's notice however, and on 11th October the WJR made a new offer of 10% for the C&WR[24], which was accepted on 18th October. The dismay of the M&CR on hearing of this can be imagined. The two miles of line between Marron and Brigham, which was so vital to them, was now in Lonsdale's hands. On 1st January 1865 the WJR

took possession of the C&WR, anticipating the statutory Parliamentary approval.

The story was not quite concluded however, as the Cockermouth and Workington & Whitehaven Junction Lease Bill had to pass the committee and was scheduled for examination by Group Seven, House of Commons, along with the M&CR Derwent Branch Bill. Lonsdale could not have been surprised by petitions against the lease bill, from both the M&CR and the WC&ER.

But the M&CR took the whole of West Cumberland by surprise by its next move – a Bill to amalgamate all the railways in West Cumberland. John Addison wrote to all the other railway boards inviting them to send two representatives to a meeting at Maryport on 28th November 1864[25, 26, 27], but all declined to attend, making various feeble excuses. The M&CR pressed on and approached the other companies for traffic statistics to accompany the Bill, again without success. The Bill was withdrawn, but the M&CR had made its point.

The *Railway Times* commented with uncanny foresight on the West Cumberland lines:

'These disjointed associations are now almost hemmed in by closely compacted and united systems and they must either adhere in self protection or fall a prey, one by one, to the snare of the fowler.' [28]

The situation was rendered even more explosive by the publication of the half year reports and accounts. The dividends for the half year to 31st December 1864 were: M&CR 11%pa; W&FJR 8%pa; WC&ER 12%pa and an unprecedented 18%pa from the WJR – according to the *Railway Times* the highest rate of dividend ever paid by a railway company in the United Kingdom[29].

On the left is the double line into Cockermouth Goods, formerly the terminus of the Cockermouth & Workington Railway. In the centre is the single line from Cockermouth Junction to the Cockermouth, Keswick & Penrith Railway's Cockermouth station. View taken in the mid-1930s. (CRA: Pattinson collection)

An east-bound passenger train for Penrith runs into Cockermouth station, c.1920, hauled by a LNWR 'Cauliflower' 0-6-0. (Sankey archive: 6736)

The Parliamentary battle of 1865

Now the time arrived for the Parliamentary Committee hearings. The Committee on Group Seven decided to hear the evidence relating to the M&CR Derwent branch and the Cockermouth lease bills together, starting on 7th March 1865[30].

Against the Derwent branch were the petitions of the C&WR (now repudiating its agreement with the M&CR), the Solway Junction Railway, the CK&PR, the WJR/W&FJR group and, for good measure, Lord Lonsdale in his own right. John Addison was the first to give evidence. He tried, with more than a little success, to build a picture of the M&CR as an injured innocent, claiming only what was its right, and the C&WR/WJR agreement of 18th October 1864 was ample evidence of the latter company's perfidy. He then went on to discuss his company's attempts to promote rationalisation of railway management in the area, which could only be in the public interest, claiming that there were 53 directors for 102 miles of railway in West Cumberland! The Lonsdale camp tried to prove that the Derwent branch and M&CR running powers to the WC&ER, would rob the WJR of one third of its traffic, although that case was somewhat diminished by the Committee's knowledge of the 18% dividend declared by the WJR. In any case, the point of equal distance for traffic from the Cleator line to the north, was at Frizington, north of the main part of the ironfield, so the shortest route was still via the W&FJR, the Whitehaven tunnel and the WJR. Henry Cook, of the Whitehaven joint companies, tried, rather rashly, to claim that the C&WR single line, with all

its colliery sidings, was far too dangerous to safely permit running powers to other companies.

Towards the end of the evidence a surprise visitor appeared on the Lonsdale side in the person of James Allport of the Midland Railway. Allport maintained that the M&CR line would be *'almost destructive of the Whitehaven and Maryport Railway'*. His appearance however, was too good an opportunity to be missed by the M&CR, whose Counsel took pleasure in reminding Allport that the Midland had been known to take running powers and even to build competing lines, at the expense of their rivals' traffic. He went on:

"Counsel	'Are you particular friends with the Whitehaven Company and is it to be your route in competing with the LNWR to the north?'
Allport	'Nothing of the kind. We have had relations with that district for many years and so have the LNWR.'
Counsel	'Are you seeking to make an independent line of your own from Lancaster to Carlisle?'
Allport	'No'.
Counsel	Have you not threatened to do it?
Allport	'Yes, for many years. The LNWR saw clearly that an independent line would be made. The line has been surveyed. The LNWR offered to give us running powers.' "

This exchange is the probable source of the rumours, circulating at this time, of a Midland plan to use the Furness line as part of a route to Scotland, which would be completed by the SJR and improved by the use of the W&FJR Duddon viaduct. It is clear that the Midland had remained confident that it would obtain full running powers over the Lancaster & Carlisle line, its final decision to build the Settle & Carlisle line not coming until after the breakdown of the L&CR negotiations on 1st February 1865.

Finally, T.S. Dodgson, Manager of the WC&ER, appeared and told of the delays to traffic at Whitehaven, the 'turnpike gate' of West Cumberland. The hearing lasted three days, at the end of which the Committee found for the Derwent branch and against the Cockermouth lease bill. The C&WR, represented by John Steel, MP for Cockermouth, and Lonsdale, were determined to have the Bill recommitted and proposed to oppose the Derwent branch bill in the Lords.

Reporting back to Edward Waugh, the C&WR solicitor, Steel wrote in despair:

'Sir H Willoughby, the gentleman I had requested to negotiate this with the Committee was found dead in bed this morning and that's an end to his assistance in this matter. I shall try myself this evening and night in the House and report progress.' [31]

The cause proved to be lost however, and soon the C&WR was abandoned, to be dealt with summarily in the mopping up operations. The Solway Junction Railway was opened for goods and mineral traffic on 1st September 1869 and for passengers on 8th July 1870.

The Duddon Crossing

The final act of the West Cumberland drama of 1865 began on 13th March, in the same Committee that had thrown out the Cockermouth and Workington Lease Bill[32]. Again, the Committee decided to examine both the W&FJR and the rival FR Duddon Crossing Bills together. The W&FJ scheme was almost a replica of George Stephenson's original plan, which had been authorised in the W&FJR Act 1845, but was subsequently abandoned during the financial crisis of 1848, where the matter had rested during the early and unprofitable years of the W&FJR's existence.

In 1863 the question had again been raised, as the CK&PR was then under construction and would offer an alternative route from West Cumberland to the south, by way of Penrith. Further a massive deposit of hematite ore had been discovered at Hodbarrow, on the north shore of the Duddon estuary, and the mine was now in production. Thus, on 22nd September 1863, the W&FJR board requested Thomas Drane, its engineer, to examine the possibility of crossing the Duddon. On 6th October Drane reported that, in his opinion, the traffic did not at that time justify the expense, but by 7th March 1864 the W&FJR was again examining the matter, doubtless spurred on following a meeting of managers at Furness Abbey, on 23rd September, when it was agreed that on the opening of the CK&PR traffic would be forwarded by the shortest route[33], an agreement most significant in relation to traffic taking the Midland route into Yorkshire. Even allowing for the shortening of the Furness route by the proposed F&M Joint Railway, the point of equal distance from the Midland Railway's Clapham Junction, where the Penrith and Whitehaven routes joined, was between Whitehaven and Workington. Hence traffic from the Workington area, via the

C&WR and the northern part of the WC&ER, would be lost by the W&FJR.

On 10th October 1864 the W&FJR engaged the engineer James Brunlees, who had successfully built the U&LR, to draw up detailed plans for crossing the Duddon and also for a new southern exit for Cleator traffic from Egremont to near Sellafield. At its meeting on 28th October, the FR board was informed that J.R. McClean, the FR's engineer, had met Lord Lonsdale, informing him that the FR considered any shortening of the Whitehaven line not to be immediately necessary, but that it would be willing to co-operate.

However, he added:

'The question of communication with the Barrow Docks is one of great importance and must be borne in mind in laying out any line for the above purpose.'

McClean was instructed to prepare plans for a FR Duddon crossing scheme to be used in the event of the W&FJR's plans proceeding. Proceed they did. On 31st October, the FR board ordered that a Bill be prepared. The W&FJR offered to co-operate with the FR, if the latter built a new line from the former's viaduct at Ireleth to Lindal, but the FR declined to make the Ireleth – Lindal line [34] and went ahead with its own Bill for a crossing from Hodbarrow to Barrow. Battle was joined at the Parliamentary Committee on 13th March 1865.

The rival projects differed in several fundamental ways. The W&FJR's plan was coupled with powers to double the main line from Whitehaven and was for a double-line viaduct, whereas the FR's scheme was for a single line. The W&FJR's viaduct ran upstream from the little shipping place above Crab Marsh Point, known as Borwick Rails, and needed no opening span, but the FR's viaduct had an opening span, as it would otherwise have blocked navigation in the Duddon.

The FR scheme, however, had the advantage of distance, as it reduced the overall length of the route by more than 1½ miles over the rival plan.

The FR opened its case with its professional 'neutral' Henry Schneider, now a veteran of the F&MR Bill Committee. Schneider enjoyed his work and lived up to his reputation for colourful remarks by stating, of the W&FJR's suggestion that the FR should build a line from Ireleth to Lindal:

'I have heard of some mad schemes in my life and I think this is about the maddest I ever did hear of.'

He attempted to play down the significance of Lord Lonsdale's Borwick Rails as a port, by alleging that he had forbidden the masters of his ships from going there because the navigation was dangerous. The Duke of Devonshire appeared next, with his characteristically cautious and reserved manner, followed by James Ramsden and J.R. McClean. Their message was simple. The W&FJR line had little through traffic, the primary function of the proposed line being the connection of Hodbarrow mine with Barrow docks, while, at the same time, creating an alternative route between Schneider's Park mine and his ironworks at Barrow, avoiding the congested Barrow station goods yard.

Some interesting details were given concerning contemporary traffic flows. Schneider had tried to make out that there would be a large traffic in coal from Cumberland to Barrow, but he was forced to admit that the Cumberland coal was no use for smelting and that, for the West Cumberland furnaces, Durham coke had to be imported. Some 20,000 tons of pig iron went from Barrow to

Scotland, but it went via Carnforth. On passenger traffic, Ramsden claimed that the three trains a day on the Whitehaven line carried an average of only four or five passengers. Henry Cook gave figures of 57,000 tons of ore and pig iron and 17,000 tons of general goods carried southwards by the W&FJR, as against 470,000 tons of ore and pig iron exported via Whitehaven harbour. In contrast, the figures for the FR in 1864 were: ore shipped to Barrow: 224,730 tons; ore conveyed to Hindpool: 239,954 tons; and ore sent south via Ulverston: 223,432 tons.

McClean, who was introduced as President of the Institution of Civil Engineers, told how he had carefully investigated the proposal for a line from Ireleth to Lindal, but that it would cost £80,000 and have a gradient of 1:75 in a tunnel. He had strongly advised the FR against it.

While the FR scheme can be seen to have had many advantages, especially for Barrow, it had all the characteristics of a plan conceived for political purposes, but the W&FJR had powers granted previously, in 1845, for its proposal. The W&FJR

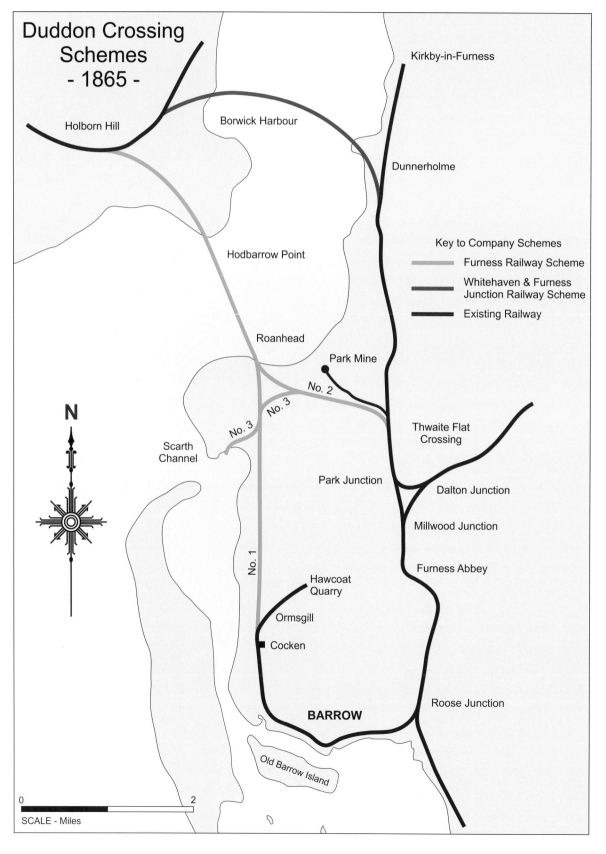

Duddon Crossing Schemes - 1865 -

Key to Company Schemes
Furness Railway Scheme
Whitehaven & Furness Junction Railway Scheme
Existing Railway

The Harbour at Millom, known as Borwick Rails, was a Duddon port of antiquity. It was developed by the Hodbarrow Mining Co. for the export of iron ore by coastal vessels, this being a cheaper option than rail. (Ken Norman collection)

Counsel, realising the advantages, concentrated his case on the free navigation of Borwick harbour so that the port could compete with Barrow on its merits. It was claimed that the FR was intent on destroying the port to capture its increasing traffic, 82 vessels carrying 8,254 tons of ore in 1862, which, by 1864, had increased to 580 vessels carrying 55,825 tons. Nathaniel Caine, one of the Hodbarrow Company proprietors, confirmed that if the ore was shipped at Barrow, instead of Borwick, it would cost his company 1s per ton more, at the provisionally quoted FR rates of 1/6d rail rate plus 2½d dock dues. James Dees represented the Solway Junction Company and said that, while preferring the W&FJR scheme, his company

supported any means of shortening the coast route so that the Scottish traffic could be attracted. He claimed that if the Duddon Crossing was made, the distance between Staffordshire and Annan would be equal by both routes. Finally the Committee heard the opinion of the famous engineer, John Hawkshaw, who had been called in, presumably by Lonsdale, to examine both schemes. He was, of course, in favour of the 'green line' of the W&FJR and said:

'By making the green line the FR would get all the traffic which they would get from making their red line and save themselves all the money.'

73

There could have been little surprise at the Committee's verdict, the W&FJR scheme was approved, but the FR line between Hindpool and Park was also agreed.

Devonshire noted on 18th March 1865:

'The decision will no doubt be inconvenient to us but I hope it will not be a very serious injury.'

At first sight, this appeared to be a resounding Lonsdale victory, but it was, in reality, the final episode in the Lonsdale saga. The C&WR was already lost and now the FR was alienated. Only two days elapsed before the FR offered terms for amalgamation with the W&FJR, and, at the same time, took steps to oppose the W&FJR Bill in the Lords. Lonsdale still pinned his hopes on stopping the Derwent branch in the Lords and was prepared to assume a somewhat shaky position of strength in his dealings with the FR. He saw James Ramsden late in April and, on 2nd May 1865, Ramsden reported to the FR board that Lonsdale would agree to sell the W&FJR to the Furness only if it took the WJR as well, a reasonable point of view as these two lines were managed by a joint committee. A figure of 7% for the W&FJR was mentioned. The Duke of Devonshire noted on 9th May:

'Currey, Ramsden and myself had a long interview this morning with Lord Lonsdale and Mr Furness, the vice-chairman of the Whitehaven & Furness Railway. We have agreed on certain conditions to withdraw all further opposition to their Bill. We referred very slightly to a proposal for leasing their line as it appears some negotiation is going on, on the same subject with the London & North Western and they appear disposed to act fairly towards us.'

It is significant that, at this time, the FR had made an agreement with the LNWR which, although ostensibly to do with the Arnside to Hincaster line, promoted by the Furness & Yorkshire Union Railway and taken over by the FR, was in fact a territorial agreement of 'spheres of influence'. This agreement was dated 16th May 1865 and gave the FR running powers to the NER at Tebay and the LNWR similar powers to Arnside. The spheres of influence , although recorded in the board minutes, remained secret and did not appear in the agreement.

Two days later, on 18th May, Devonshire noted:

'This morning Currey, Ramsden and I had an interview with Mr Moon and Mr Cawkwell on behalf of the L&NWR Co. which proved satisfactory. It was mainly with reference to the purchase of the Whitehaven & Furness Company and apparently this will be accomplished without material difficulties.'

The circumstances were finally clarified on 30th May 1865 when Lonsdale summoned both the W&FJR and WJR boards to his London home at Carlton Terrace and announced that the LNWR had offered 10% for the WJR and the FR 8% for the W&FJR. The boards dutifully concurred and the Furness suddenly became the proprietors of a rather dilapidated single line, with little traffic, at a price described as 'preposterous' by W.B. Kendall[35]. However, it should be noted that the W&FJR was paying an 8% dividend.

The C&WR, for so long in a strong position, was now defenceless and went, cap in hand, to meet the strong men of the LNWR, Richard Moon, James Bancroft and William Cawkwell at Rigg's Hotel, Windermere, on 28th July 1865, having been promised 10%, which was cut down to 7% rising to 10% over four years.

Thus the LNWR had gained control of the eastern route into West Cumberland via Cockermouth and had, together with the FR, pinned down the Cleator line. If in fact the MR ever had any intention of using the West Cumberland route as a means of reaching Scotland that could now be forgotten.

The *Railway Times* remarked:

'The great companies appear to have come to an understanding ... and have divided the (West Cumberland) interests among themselves. The M&C will probably fall to the NER and the WJ has accepted amalgamation with the LNWR, which company will no doubt absorb the CK&P and C&W. The W&FJ has consented to go over to the Midland interest, which already includes the Furness and the Ulverstone, at 8%.' [36]

This can now be seen as a considerable oversimplification as, judged by its lack of active participation in the F&M Joint Line Committee, the MR was showing little interest in Furness affairs. The important result of the activities of 1864-65 was the change in character of the FR, which now included West Cumberland in its territory and could therefore be regarded as a significant main line company.

The agreements of 1865 were informal and Bills were deposited, late in 1865, to legalise the arrangements. Acts for the purchase of the C&WR and WJR by the LNWR, and of the W&FJR by the FR, all received Royal Assent on 16th July 1866[37].

CHAPTER 7 REFERENCES

1   Simmons J. *Op. cit.* p.25.
2   *Victoria County History of Cumberland* Vol.2 (1905).
3   9.10 Vic C342.
4   C&WR DM, 11th Mar. 1847.
5   C&WR SM, 31st Jan. 1858.
6   24.25 Vic C14 21.5.1858.
7   24.25 Vic C.203 1.8.1861.
8   LNWR Agreement, 10th Sep. 1859.
9   Baughan P. *Op. cit.*
10 26.27 Vic. C108 29.6.1863.
11 26.27 Vic. C64 8.6.1863.
12 Simmons J. *Op. cit.* passim.
13 *Bradshaw's Railway Manual 1880.*
14 Richardson J, 1880. *Furness Past and Present.*
15 Solway Junction Railway, LMS file.
16 C&WR DM, 2nd Feb. 1864.
17 WJR DM, 1st Apr. 1864.
18 C&WR DM, 5th Apr. 1864.
19 WJR DM, 15th May 1864.
20 C&WR DM, 5th Apr. 1864.
21 WJR DM, 1st Aug. 1864.
22 C&WR DM, 28th June 1864.
23 C&WR DM, 9th Aug. 1864.
24 WJR DM, 14th Oct. 1864.
25 W&FJR DM, 28th Nov. 1864.
26 WJR DM, 25th Nov. 1864.
27 C&WR DM, 15th Nov. 1864.
28 *Railway Times*, 25th Feb. 1865. p.239.
29 Ibid, p. 203.
30 PRO: BTHR PYB 1/303. Minutes of Evidence.
31 C&WR DM, 28th Mar. 1865.
32 HLRO: Minutes of Evidence, W&FJR & FR bills.
33 WJR DM, 30th Sep. 1864.
34 FRDM, 14th Nov. 1864.
35 Melville J & Hobbs J L. *Op. cit.* p.56.
36 *Railway Times* 1865 p.870.
37 *Bradshaw's Railway Manual 1880.*

THE ULVERSTONE & LANCASTER RAILWAY

As has been shown in Chapter Two, the various schemes to connect the Furness Railway with the trunk route of the Lancaster & Carlisle Railway and the connection with Yorkshire provided by the *'Little'* North Western Railway, all failed during the Railway Mania Parliamentary session of 1845-46.

Burlington noted, on 12th November 1846:

'I went over to Ulverston this morning to meet Mr W. Currey and Mr Robert Stephenson who has now become the engineer of the Whitehaven and Furness Company. He seems disposed to adopt the plans of his father in most respects and to cross the estuary from the Ulverston side to Old Park on piles diverting the river. I do not quite like this plan and hope the Admiralty will force them to a more circuitous route by Greenodd. I walked over the sands with him and Mr Longridge that they might see the course that the river is now inclined to take and what measures be adopted to check it.'

Burlington was, however, sufficiently public spirited and commercially shrewd not to oppose such a line. As Burlington observed, Robert Stephenson had replaced his father George as consulting engineer to the Whitehaven & Furness Junction Railway. George Stephenson was now in semi-retirement and

died on 12th August 1848[1]. It seems that Robert Stephenson was in the process of preparing a new Bill to replace that of the Whitehaven & Furness Junction Lancashire Extension Railway, which had failed to comply with the Standing Orders of Parliament in the previous session, because of errors in the deposited plans and book of reference. However, 1847 saw the beginning of the financial crisis which followed the Railway Mania in which the W&FJR suffered badly from non-payment of calls on shares and quickly abandoned its plans to build the Ulverston to Carnforth link. The Furness Railway was also suffering from financial problems and work on its Ulverston extension, authorised in 1846, was temporarily abandoned. Burlington noted, on 29th January 1847:

'Mr Wm Currey called here this morning having been in Furness on railway matters. Nothing seems to be doing respecting the line by this place, though it probably will hereafter be made.'

By 1850 the Whitehaven & Furness Junction Railway was nearing completion, on its altered route, to a junction with the Furness Railway at Foxfield, which opened on 1st November 1850. The Furness Railway was, by this time, becoming profitable and was pressing on with its Ulverston Extension. The time was therefore ripe for a reconsideration of a line, from the Furness

The fine tower of the 1874 Ulverston station, designed by architects Paley & Austin, is seen in this view of 1910. In the right foreground is Ulverston East signalbox. The island platform served both sides of the down main line facilitating cross-platform interchange between down trains and Lakeside branch services. (Original postcard. Geoff Holme collection: N953)

Railway at Ulverston, to the Lancaster & Carlisle line at Carnforth.

In fact, plans for such a line were now being formulated by J.R. McClean, the consulting engineer to the FR, and John Brogden, railway contractor of Sale near Manchester, who had already shown an interest in Furness and West Cumberland. He had tendered, unsuccessfully, for the building of the original Furness line in 1845 and in the same year had, together with his eldest son, John Brogden Jnr, featured prominently in the Subscription Contract of the Whitehaven & Furness Junction Railway. They had, in fact, subscribed £41,000 compared with Lord Lonsdale's £10,000. However, the Brogdens did not feature in the ballot of W&FJR shareholders, held in 1846, and did not obtain any contracts for the building of that line. It can be assumed therefore that had they sold their 'scrip' shares, having failed to obtain any contract. John Brogden did, however, purchase a modest £500 of shares authorised by the Furness Railway Extension Act of 1846.

The Brogdens and McClean were closely associated elsewhere at this time. McClean, together with his partner, F.C. Stileman, had been engineers to the South Staffordshire Railway, which ran from Dudley on the Oxford, Worcester and Wolverhampton Railway via Walsall and Lichfield, to Wichnor Junction on the Midland Railway's Derby to Birmingham line.

On 1st August 1850 the South Staffordshire Railway was leased by McClean and partners and, in his *"Railway Reminiscences"*, G.P. Neele records:

'At the commencement of 1851 some partners of the lease made their appearance at Walsall in the shape of a Mr Brogden, an old contractor from Manchester, and two or three of his sons. Of these Mr Henry Brogden took up the superintendence of the locomotive department; Mr Alexander Brogden turned his attention to bills and expenditure.'

At this juncture, a review of the Brogden family activities is necessary, to place their Furness projects into perspective. John Brogden was born, on 2nd February 1798, at Worston near Clitheroe, Lancashire, the second son of a freehold farmer who subsequently moved to nearby Hookcliffe. (Several sources have suggested that John Brogden was born at Marton, near Lindal in Furness, but these are in error.) He was educated at a village school and later at Clitheroe Grammar School. On the family farm, John Brogden developed an interest in farm produce, horses and livestock. Leaving home in the 1820s for Manchester, a rapidly expanding centre of commerce, he set himself up in business as a trader in horses and livestock and in 1832, obtained a contract for the cleansing and watering of the city, which led to a similar contract with the City of Westminster, where he became associated with the Earl of Lonsdale. This association may well have led to his later West Cumberland aspirations.

John Brogden was now established at Raglan House, Sale and at 10 Sussex Gardens, Hyde Park, London, with his office at 3 Tib Lane, Cross Street, Manchester. In 1838 he successfully tendered for the construction of part of the Manchester & Leeds Railway between Hunts Bank and Miles Platting, his work on this contract attracting the favourable attention of George Stephenson. More contracts followed, including the Manchester & Birmingham Railway at Stockport and the Northampton to Peterborough line of the London & Birmingham Railway[2].

In the south, John Brogden became a shareholder in the South Eastern Railway and was elected to the board on 17th July 1846. On 20th October 1846 contracts for the eastern section of the South Eastern Railway's North Kent line were let to John Brogden Jnr, although his tender was not the lowest. A further contract for the western section of the North Kent Line, was also let to John Brogden Jnr on 2nd February 1847, even though Jay & Paulin had put in lower tenders. Finally, John Brogden Jnr was given the contract for the link between the North Kent East Junction and the Bricklayers Arms Branch. This was all very well, but on 21st September 1848, the South Eastern Railway board recorded that John Brogden Jnr was 'showing insufficient vigour' on his North Kent line contracts.

On 24th October 1848 the South Eastern Railway board resolved that:

'It was not becoming that questions concerning John Brogden Junior's contract should be discussed in the presence of his father.'

Two years later, in 1850, the South Eastern Railway board noted that John Brogden was taking action against the company for non-payment of claims[3], and it seems likely that, at this point, John Brogden sold out of the South Eastern Railway, thus providing capital for the Ulverstone & Lancaster project.

The first inkling of a renewal of interest in the building of a line between Ulverston and the Lancaster & Carlisle line at Carnforth, was recorded by Burlington on 11th May 1850. He noted:

'Mr Ramsden and Mr McClean came over this afternoon with a Mr Park, Traffic Manager of the Lancaster & Carlisle Railway. They are turning their attention to a line from Lancaster to Ulverston, principally with a view to bringing ore in that direction. It would probably be useful to us and at any rate we must not discourage it. McClean thinks it prudent for us to help Wheatcroft (contractor for the FR Ulverston Extension) out of his difficulties.'

As noted, J.R. McClean was about to enter into partnership with the Brogdens (who by this time had adopted the title 'John Brogden & Sons') in the lease of the South Staffordshire Railway. McClean's offer to lease the Furness Railway had been turned down by the FR board on 27th February 1849.

Herapath's *Journal* of 30th November 1850, contained the Ulverstone & Lancaster Railway's Notice of the Bill for their line. The same edition contained a Notice for a revival of the Furness & Windermere Railway, to run from the Kendal & Windermere Railway, to a junction with the Furness Railway at Ulverston, together with a branch from Haverthwaite to the U&LR at Park Head, near Holker. This line, however, does not seem to have been progressed.

The Lancaster & Carlisle company, having expressed an interest in building the Carnforth to Ulverston line in May 1850, petitioned against the U&LR Bill[4], but this may have been only a tactical objection, because, on 26th February 1851, the L&CR board approved a draft agreement with the U&LR.

The Brogdens were now in the process of moving their activities into Furness. When, on 27th December 1850, John Brogden Jnr signed the Subscription Contract of the Ulverstone & Lancaster Railway Bill, he gave his occupation as ironmaster and his address as Millwood, a mansion near Furness Abbey. On 23rd November 1850 the *Whitehaven Herald* reported that the Brogdens had acquired mining rights at Stainton in Furness and the same source also reported, on 28th December, that, on 17th December, the Brogdens had purchased, outright, all the shares

4MT 2-6-0 No. 43004 runs into the down platform at Ulverston with a Barrow-bound stopping train c.1962. Visible in the photograph are the steps which led down from the original high-level FR station to the through U&L platforms and survived the construction of the new station in 1873-4. (Hugh Oliver, Ken Norman collection: ON 23)

in the Ulverston Canal Navigation Company for £18,000. Prior to this deal the canal company had resolved that it would not sell to a railway and had petitioned against the U&LR Bill[5], policies which seem to have been reversed by the Brogden's cash offer.

The Subscription Contract contained the following:

Duke of Buccleuch, Montagu House, London (FR shareholder)	£1,000
Earl of Burlington, Holker Hall, Cartmel (FR chairman)	£2,000
William Gale, Ulverston (local squire)	£2,000
Robert Wheatley Lumley, London (FR director)	£400
Joseph Paxton, Chatsworth	£200
Henry Kennedy, Upper Bedford Square, London (ironmaster)	£400
John Brogden, Sale	£100,000
John Brogden Jnr, Millwood (ironmaster)	£54,000
James Garstang, Manchester (Alexander Brogden's father in law)	£5,000
Alexander Brogden, Pipe Grange, Lichfield	(Subscription not shown)

There was, however, a separate and powerful agency involved in the scrutiny of the U&LR project. The proposed line crossed two navigable rivers, the Leven and Kent, and the Admiralty, under its powers in this respect, convened a local investigation into the railway project. The report, dated 17th February 1851[6], required that *'proper provision be made for the navigation'* and required for the River Leven:

'... that the viaduct afford a clear breadth of waterway not less than 1,400 feet ... that if the railway embankment and

The Leven viaduct seen from Tredlow Point during its widening in 1863. (For more details see the CRA publication "The Ulverstone & Lancaster Railway")

A panoramic view, looking east, at Plumpton Junction, c.1962. Middle left is the junction with the Lakeside branch and in the right foreground the Priory branch curves away. In the middle distance a 2-6-4 tank engine awaits banking duties. (Author: MAA 85/2)

viaduct should render the crossing of the sands, now enjoyed by the public at time of low water, impracticable, some arrangement be made in the Bill by which the public may have use of a footway crossing on payment of a small toll.'

Recommendations were also made for the river Kent, and the Admiralty was destined to be a continuing irritant to the U&LR.

The Parliamentary Committee examining the U&LR Bill, on 13th May 1851, first questioned Lord Burlington. He stated that the current iron ore production of Furness was exported via Barrow Harbour to South Wales and Staffordshire and the proposed line would provide a rail route to Yorkshire. Joseph Paxton, a Cavendish retainer living at Chatsworth and a Midland Railway director, soon to be knighted for his design of the Crystal Palace, drew attention to the hazards of crossing the sands saying that these would be obviated by the proposed line. McClean gave evidence on the engineering problems of the line and their solution. The Bill was passed by the Committee and received Royal Assent on 14th July 1851.

The Ulverstone and Lancaster Railway Act 1851[7], while containing the usual clauses of a Railway Act of this period, was notable for the large Admiralty influence on its contents. Clauses 22 to 33 were all Admiralty inspired and sought to ensure the free tidal flow in the estuaries of the rivers Leven, Winster and Kent, the approval of the designs of the Leven and Kent Viaducts and their opening spans and the provision of signals and navigation lights at these openings. Additionally, the Admiralty required that the U&LR Co. be responsible for the maintenance of the navigable channel between Chapel Island and the entrance to the Ulverston Canal, for the payment of £20 per annum, to the Duchy of Lancaster, towards the cost of main-

taining the post of Oversands Guide and for the provision of a footpath *'on the landward side of the Leven Viaduct'* to allow the public access to the sands at low water. For the latter the Company were authorised to charge a toll of one half penny per person. There is no evidence that this toll was ever levied. On 26th May 1851, the FR Board met to open the tenders for construction of the line between Lindal and Ulverston. Burlington noted:

'Some talk took place about leasing the [FR] line to the Brogdenites. Paxton (I am afraid very injudiciously) gave McClean a statement of the terms he would accept. I think these are scarcely as good as we have a right to expect.'

On 28th May, Boulton's tender was accepted by the Board. McClean put in a proposal for leasing the line:

'After a long discussion they were rejected, Paxton being for them and Mr Walker, Capt Boyle and myself against them. I am afraid Paxton is nettled and disconcerted. He has acted very injudiciously.'

The lease question arose again, at a FR Board meeting, on 13th November 1851 at Ulverston, called to settle the siting of Ulverston station. Burlington noted:

'It soon became evident that our views on the station question could not be brought to an agreement. On the advice of Mr Harrison [the arbitrator] and with Paxton's warm approbation, the question of leasing our line or amalgamating was again broached and we went far towards an arrangement at 3% for 3 years then 4.5% for perpetuity.'

The meeting adjourned until the next day when:

'The terms of yesterday were finally agreed to and signed by Mr Brogden and myself. The lines are to be amalgamated and our dividend is to be a first charge after [payment of] the debenture interest. The terms, I think, scarcely equal to what we might have arrived at but Mr Harrison advises their acceptance so strongly, I did not want to oppose.'

On 10th December 1851, at Compton Place, Eastbourne, Burlington noted:

'I got up to London early and went to Curreys where we had a meeting of the Furness Railway Directors to consider the agreement drawn up last month at Ulverston. All the Directors were present and the main points of the agreement were consented to. Some modifications were introduced and Mr Lumley named to negotiate with the Brogdens. I doubt their sanctioning all our alterations.'

On 26th February 1852 Burlington again noted:

'Nothing more has been heard from Mr Brogden about the proposed agreement.'

Construction

Following the authorisation of the Ulverstone & Lancaster Railway, two meetings were held, on 8th August 1851, at 12 New Spring Gardens, London, the office of Currey, Holland & Currey, solicitors to Burlington and the Furness Railway Company. Only the Brogdens attended the first meeting, and John Brogden was put forward as chairman of the company, with his sons John Jnr, Alexander and Henry, together with James Garstang, as directors. The second meeting on that day was the first formal

meeting of the shareholders of the U&LR at which the chairman and directors were confirmed.

The next day, 9th August 1851, a meeting of the new directors was held at 15 Great Queen Street, London, at which J.R. McClean was appointed engineer, James Ramsden, secretary and William Currey and J. & W. Norris, joint solicitors. John Brogden and John Brogden Jnr were appointed managing directors. The board then moved to Furness and meetings were held at the Sun Inn, Ulverston, on 15th and 16th September 1851.

At these local meetings bank accounts were opened with the Lancaster Banking Company and Dr Henry Kennedy was appointed to act as the company's agent in the purchase of land for the line. It was also agreed that George Boulton, contractor for the building of the FR's Ulverston Extension, should build the U&LR line as far as the Ulverston Canal. This was a sensible move as spoil would be available from the FR Pennington cutting.

The division of costs for this work was to be decided by an arbitrator. The FR agreed to alter its gradient from 1:100 to 1:80 to facilitate a connection between the two railways at Ulverston. The U&LR board also considered the letting of the contract for its line from the Ulverston Canal to Tredlow Point on the River Leven, but this contract did not proceed[8]. The *Whitehaven Herald* of 15th May 1852 recorded *'a great number of Mr Brogden's men had arrived and it was the intention to complete the works in two years.'* This was to prove a far from realistic prediction. In fact, apart from the section from the FR station at Ulverston to the canal, built in connection with the FR extension to Ulverston, work on the U&LR line did not start until mid-1853.

A study, based on the diary of a Brogden retainer, James Stelfox, and other sources[9], relates that in its early years, the U&LR company purchased or leased, not only the land required for the construction of its line, but also a number of estates which were worked for profit, as well as to provide construction

The signalbox at Leven Junction controlled the eastern spur on to the Lakeside branch at Greenodd Junction. The 1pm express passenger service from Barrow, regularly double-headed during the summer timetable, is seen approaching on 4th May 1954. The Leven Junction curve was not used after 1939. (Author: MAC 158)

material, provisions for the horses and accommodation for the workforce. James Stelfox was initially employed as a farm manager, overseeing traditional activities such as ploughing and marketing farm produce. At a later stage, he supervised the reclaimed land in the Kent estuary and its conversion to arable use. His final role was as inspector of works for the construction of the line which, in its later stages, ran into various problems.

Among the estates acquired by the Brogdens was Lightburn House, on the southern edge of Ulverston town, which provided a local residence for the Brogden family and fulfilled the role of the company office. From the opening of the line, in 1857, Holme Island, near Grange, with its mansion, was to become Alexander Brogden's northern base and a number of directors' meetings were held there.

There was, in fact, little incentive for the Brogdens to rush into the construction of their line, as the Furness Railway's Ulverston Extension was proceeding very slowly because of engineering difficulties with the tunnel at Lindal and the deep cutting at Pennington. The FR line was not opened to Ulverston Road, east of Lindal, until 27th May 1853[10]. The FR directors, in their report to the shareholders, at the meeting on 26th August 1853, commented:

> 'The Directors have not thought it necessary to urge the contractor to proceed more rapidly feeling that much of the importance of the extension depends upon the opening of the Ulverstone & Lancaster Railway to Carnforth.'

It was, of course, cheaper for both companies to proceed at a slow pace. However, the FR line to Ulverston was opened for coal traffic from Whitehaven on 4th April 1854 and for passenger traffic on 7th June 1854[11].

The construction of the Ulverstone & Lancaster Railway was fraught with difficulties, as the building of the sea embankments and viaducts were pioneering engineering projects. Nevertheless, the Whitehaven & Furness Junction Railway board viewed the slow progress with displeasure and, on 26th August 1854, the Joint Manager and Secretary, J S Yeats Jnr wrote to John Brogden:

> 'Sir,
> I am directed by the Directors of this Company to say that having reference to the slow progress of the works on the Ulverstone & Lancaster Railway to which your attention has already been drawn... if you fail to complete your line within the time specified by your Act of Parliament thereby rendering a fresh application necessary, they will avail themselves of the opportunity of opposing your application and apply to Parliament to concede the line to themselves or to some other bona fide projector.'

The U&LR directors and shareholders held official meetings, on 26th August 1853, when it was reported[12] that a large portion of the land required for the building of the line had been purchased. The same edition contained a full page report of the Sheriff's Court held at Ulverston on 24th August 1853, to settle the dispute between the U&LR company and the Revd Thomas Tolming, of Coniston, owner of land east of Ulverston station, acquired under the U&LR Act of 1851. The court upheld Tolming's claim of three shillings per square yard, for 2,843 square yards, and he was awarded £150 damages for loss of value of adjacent land.

Evidence of friction between the Brogdens and the FR group

now began to emerge. Burlington noted, on 19th January 1852: 'Our negotiations with the Brogdens seem in an unsatisfactory state.' On 20th January 1852, William Currey resigned as joint solicitor to the U&LR in circumstances 'which the Directors regretted' and, on 25th February 1853, the U&LR board received a letter from McClean and Stileman resigning as engineers, following a complaint by the Brogdens relating to the late provision of plans for parts of the line.

This resignation heralded a new phase in the U&LR project. Although not recorded in the company minutes, James Brunlees (1816-1892), known to the Brogdens for his work as assistant engineer on the Bolton and Preston Railway, was appointed engineer to the company. He had, in spite of many difficulties, successfully completed the sea embankment at Rosse's Bay on the Londonderry & Coleraine Railway and, after his successful completion of the U&LR line, Brunlees was to be associated with the Brogdens on the construction of the Solway Junction Railway with its long sea viaduct. In 1881 he was knighted for his work on the Mersey Railway with its tunnel between Liverpool and Birkenhead.

Brunlees' work on the construction of the sea embankments on the Ulverstone and Lancaster Railway is described in his paper to the Institution of Civil Engineers on 23rd January 1855. He notes that the works were partially commenced in May 1853 but, owing to the scarcity of workmen and the want of accommodation for them in the neighbourhood, it was only in September 1853 that full operation of the work commenced. He describes his solution to the problem of construction of the sea embankments on the various sections of the line which, although of slightly differing dimensions, as dictated by local circumstances, were essentially the same in construction principles:

> 'The sands are composed of calcareous material and form the interior of the Banks. On the sea slopes there is placed a layer 11" thick of well-prepared clay puddle. On top of the puddle is laid a thickness of 18" of small rubble stones termed 'Quarry rid'. On this is laid pitching stones provided by the excavations and quarries in the immediate vicinity of the works. Work could only be carried out at low tide and only 10 to 12 linear yards of embankment could be formed per day or at a rate of a mile in six months.'

Little evidence has survived, from primary sources, on the detail of the construction and the U&LR minutes are sparse. However, a picture of the progress of the works can be obtained from various secondary sources. It appears that the Ulverstone & Lancaster Railway was constructed in ten contracts, some of which were let, and the company, using their own staff or subcontractors, carried out others. These ten contracts are best described individually:

1. Ulverston Station to the Ulverston Canal

This contract was let to George Boulton, contractor for the FR Ulverston Extension, a sensible decision as much spoil would be obtained from the Pennington Cutting. The *Whitehaven Herald* of 31st January 1852 noted:

> 'The Ulverston cutting was worked day and night and the Ulverstone & Lancaster embankment to the Canal made from the spoil.'

However, as has already been noted, 18 months later the FR

The signalbox at Ravensbarrow was built, in the 1870s, to provide a block post between Leven Junction and Cark. A 4F 0-6-0 hauls a down freight c.1954. The lattice post signals were supplied, in the 1880s, by Stevens & Sons. (Author: MAC 178)

board told its shareholders that they were not pressing their contractor because of the slow progress on the U&LR line. By late 1855 this section of line, together with the viaduct over the Ulverston Canal, had been completed[13]. The Canal Viaduct had been commenced in November 1853 and, to compensate for the loss of shipping access to the canal head, a new basin was constructed south of the viaduct[14] which was opened on 31st January 1854[15].

2. Ulverston Canal to Tredlow Point
The original intention was to invite George Boulton, but instead he was only contracted to provide 164,000 cubic feet of spoil[16] as the Brogdens were to build this portion of their line. James Stelfox noted that the embankment at Next Ness was begun in March 1856[17].

3. The Leven Viaduct
Let to W & J Galloway of Knott Mill, Ironworks, Manchester[18], work on this contract commenced on 10th April 1855[19]. On 31st December 1855, Stelfox recorded in his diary that the original method of sinking the piles had been unsuccessful; 'the piles would not stand'. On 21st January 1856 the Galloways employed pressure water jets for sinking the piles into the sand, a method which seems to have been successful. The difficulties in the construction of the Leven Viaduct was the subject of a second paper, by James Brunlees, to the Institution of Civil Engineers on 20th April 1858. Brunlees noted that:

'... experiments were made to test the bearing power of the sand and the size and form of the disc best adapted to a permanent foundation.'

A disc diameter of 30 inches was decided upon and the piles were sunk by forcing water through them to displace the sand. Brunlees concluded his paper by acknowledging the assistance and co-operation of Mr Harry Brogden on the application of hydraulic pressure in sinking the piles, but it is a matter for speculation whether it was James Brunlees or Henry Brogden who thought of the successful procedure. The rails over the Leven Viaduct were completed on 4th July 1857 and the first engine crossed on that date[20].

4. The Capeshead Embankment
Work commenced on this section of the sea embankment in the week beginning 18th April 1853[21]. This was the first work commenced by the Brogdens themselves[22] and nearly four years were to elapse before the sea embankment was completed. The last pitching stone was formally laid by Mrs Alexander Brogden using a mallet handed to her by James Stelfox[23]. The *Lancaster Gazette* of 14th March 1857 recorded:

'The embankment as completed has a massive appearance and looks well able to resist the fury of the elements ... few of our fellow townsmen ever expected to see it completed.'

5. Quarry Flat to Flookburgh
This inland section of the line, two miles in length, was described by Brunlees in his report to the shareholders' meeting, on 20th August 1856, as being *'light and which will be done in the winter months'*. It was started soon after, but Bell, the subcontractor, was dismissed by the Brogdens and, on 3rd December 1856, James Stelfox was put in charge[24]. By the shareholders' meeting on 25th February 1857 *'great progress had been made.'*

The station at Cark & Cartmel was built by the FR, to designs of architects Paley & Austin, after the takeover of the Ulverston to Carnforth line in 1862. (W. Pinch collection)

The Grange-over-Sands station staff pose for the camera c.1900. This elegant station, built by the FR, replaced the shed provided by the Ulverstone & Lancaster Co. in 1857. (George Taylor collection: T205)

A FR 4-6-4 tank engine hauls a short Up train of four carriages on the Kent Viaduct whilst an ex-LNWR 2-4-0 heads along the Down line with a freight train c.1930. The viaduct received a new deck in 2011. (W. Potter: Ken Norman collection N432)

Arnside Station.

Arnside station as built by the FR after the U&LR takeover in 1862, seen here with a Down train c.1910. Arnside was the junction for the branch line to Hincaster Junction on the LNWR west coast main line. (Original postcard, Geoff Holme collection: GH 229.9.3)

Carnforth Joint Station (LNW & FR Joint) c.1900. The Up and Down Furness platform is on the left and the LNWR platforms on the right. (Ken Norman collection: N 761)

6. Grange contract

This contract was let to William Eckersley, contractor for the Carnforth to Arnside line, in 1856 and by the shareholders' meeting of 25th February 1857 the permanent way was being laid. The first engine ran through Grange on 15th July 1857[25].

7. Meathop contract (Kent Viaduct to Grange)

It is not clear when this work was commenced but it was under way by August 1853, possibly by Brogdens' own men, as on 20th August 1853, damage was done to the embankment at Meathop by the high tide and strong wind. However, Stelfox recorded, on 6th August 1856, that 'Mr Hanson's bank broke' suggesting that, by 1856, this sea embankment contract had been let to William Hanson of Whitnell, Lancashire.

8. Kent Viaduct

The contract for this structure was let to James Featherstone in the autumn of 1856 and, at the time of the U&LR shareholders' meeting of 25th February 1857, was noted to be in a forward state. No doubt the techniques developed at the Leven Viaduct were employed. On 4th July 1857 Alexander Brogden instructed James Stelfox to lay the rails on the Kent Viaduct and, on 18th July 1857, Stelfox noted that trucks came over the Kent Viaduct loaded with Alexander Brogden's furniture, destined for his residence on Holme Island.

9. Arnside Embankment

By the time of the U&LR shareholders meeting on 25th February 1857, the only work necessary to complete the railway was the short embankment between the mainland at Arnside and the Kent Viaduct. Although it had been intended to put this work out to contract, it was in fact carried out by the Brogdens' own resources and was due to be completed by May 1857.

10. Carnforth contract

Let to William Eckersley in 1855, the Carnforth contract was well advanced by the shareholders' meeting on 26th February 1856 and the line was completed by the end of 1856 but the directors decided against opening because of the late season of the year[26].

Lt. Col. W Yolland, on behalf of the Board of Trade, inspected the completed Ulverstone & Lancaster Railway on 7th August 1857[27]. He reported that, although land had been purchased for a double line of railway, the line was single with passing places at Cark and Grange stations. The Leven viaduct was provided with a drawbridge of 30 feet span to allow the passing of vessels at, or near, high water, and he gave a detailed description of the method used by Galloways to sink the piles. He found several deficiencies, mainly concerned with incomplete signalling and buildings, which required a further inspection on 22nd August 1857[28], when he noted that the deficiencies had been remedied and that the Furness Railway would work the line, under a seven-year agreement, using 'one engine in steam' regulations on each section.

On 26th August 1857, twenty years after the first proposals for a coastal route and six years after the incorporation of the company, the opening of the U&LR for passenger traffic was celebrated[29]. A special train left Ulverston at one o'clock for Carnforth and, on the return trip, conveyed a large number of guests from the south, but its departure from Carnforth was delayed by the connecting LNWR train running 45 minutes late! An elaborate dinner was provided by Mrs Slaney at the Furness Abbey Hotel, served in a marquee sited in the grounds of Furness Abbey, with John Brogden in the chair. The toast 'success to the Ulverstone & Lancaster Railway' was given by Lord Burlington. He stated that:

'the railway over which they had that day passed did not

at first sight present many difficulties, but those who had been upon the spot and witnessed the progress of the work knew they had difficulties of no ordinary magnitude to contend with ... and credit was due to the contractor for the manner in which he had so satisfactorily completed his work.'

Lord Lonsdale gave a toast to:

'Mr Brogden and the Directors of the U&LR for the completion of a great public work; they were indebted to his friend Mr Brogden.'

The Brogdens' financial problems

The technical problems associated with the construction of the Ulverstone & Lancaster Railway were enough in themselves to blunt the native enthusiasm of the Brogden family. They had, however, more basic problems with which to contend. Disaster struck on 6th November 1855 when, as John Brogden Jnr was preparing to leave Lightburn House to address a Wesleyan meeting at Dalton, he collapsed and died from a brain haemorrhage, depriving the Brogdens of their principal agent in Furness.

Alexander, the second son, at that time in charge of the family's West Midlands interests and no doubt overseeing the youthful James' activities in South Wales, had to be drafted into north Lancashire to oversee the crucial final stages of the Ulverstone & Lancaster Railway.

The accelerated pace of work, together with the increase in interest rates as a consequence of the Crimean War, placed a serious strain on the financial resources of the Brogden family. On 30th September 1856 the U&LR board recorded that the London Joint Stock Bank was prepared to renew the company's £25,750 loan, but required a repayment of £10,000 as a condition. James Garstang, the U&LR director and Alexander's father-in-law, agreed to provide the £10,000. Alexander had been feverishly, but unsuccessfully, attempting to sell debentures to insurance offices in London.

However, the Furness Railway Directors had a vested interest in the completion of the U&LR line and, on 26th August 1856, they had noted *'The Ulverstone & Lancaster require £30,000 to complete their line'*. After an examination of the U&LR accounts, it was agreed that Burlington and Buccleuch would lend the money, as agents of the FR.

Burlington noted, on 10th November 1856:

'I met Mr Brunlees and Mr H Brogden this morning about the drainage which the Ulverstone & Lancaster Company are obliged to provide for me. The great difficulty is the want of money and they want the work postponed until the emergency passes. I will advance the money on their debentures. I am much inclined to do this rather than have the thing indefinitely postponed.'

By the U&LR meeting of 13th December, the requirements had been increased to £50,000 and the Brogdens agreed to provide Burlington and Buccleuch with £150,000 worth of U&LR shares as security. The loan was made on 1st January 1857 at 5½%. James Ramsden was to be given access to the U&LR books and Stephen Eddy of Carleton Grange, Skipton, a FR director, was appointed to the U&LR board. Finally it was agreed that the U&LR should apply to Parliament not only for additional funds to complete and double the line, but also for powers to sell to the Furness Railway.

The Ulverstone & Lancaster Railway's independent years 1857-1862

On 1st September 1857, Burlington noted in his diary:

'Passenger trains have begun running regularly on our new railway today. They have, I am afraid, been very unpunctual.'

The *Ulverston Advertiser* of 3rd September contained the public timetable for September 1857 of trains between Lancaster, Ulverstone and Whitehaven which afforded *"Direct Through Communication between the Lancashire and Yorkshire Districts and the Iron Ore Districts of Ulverstone and Whitehaven."* Furness and West Cumberland had joined the national railway network.

Alexander Brogden was made responsible for finance, construction, maintenance of way and commercial activities with James Ramsden responsible for operation of trains, stations and signals[30].

On 21st October 1857 the U&LR board decided that, in view of the capital over-expenditure and to provide for the doubling of the line, a Bill should be introduced for the creation of

The unique FR lineside sign erected at Plumpton Junction.

£156,000 in capital, together with powers to lease or sell the company to either the Furness or the Lancaster & Carlisle Railways. The Act received Royal Assent on 12th July 1858. The U&LR board had approached the Furness Railway to raise £100,000 for the same purpose. Burlington noted, on 17th November 1857:

'We had a Furness Directors meeting this morning to consider a new application for assistance from the Ulverstone and Lancaster Railway. After a long discussion we agreed to advance the sum required to meet their present liabilities on their covenanting to sell the line at par to be paid for in 4% preference stock. This Alexander Brogden declined at once and the matter is at an end.'

There were further discussions between the FR and the U&LR in which Ramsden and William Currey acted as intermediaries. On 15th December 1857 Burlington noted, with obvious irritation:

'I have been rather annoyed by Currey having renewed negotiations with the Brogdens on his own account. It seems to me that this may have awkward results and I hope he will abandon the matter altogether.'

And on 17th December:

'On the whole I am glad the Brogden negotiations have failed as I am inclined to think the terms we offered were too favourable.'

On a practical level, the new line was having trouble over its two viaducts. The Leven viaduct was built with an opening span to allow the passage of vessels to and from the port of Greenodd but the navigation of such bridges was clearly outside the experience of the mariners of the day. Even before the line was opened the *Sarah Jane* attempted to run through the bridge on a spring tide and struck the viaduct breaking four columns below water[31].

On 7th December 1857, the U&LR board received two letters on the subject of the Leven viaduct bridge, one from a shipping agent complaining of delay to the navigation as a result of the bridge master opening the bridge only half an hour before high tide to half an hour after high tide and the second from the bridge master reporting:

'I beg to inform you that I had two vessels through here today. (1st Feb.1857) The 'Tickler' of Liverpool came sailing right into the bridge before I had got it open and the signal was up. He got crossways to the bridge and broke one of the timbers of the wooden piles.'

The board resolved, that regulations for the opening bridge be prepared at once, submitted to the Admiralty and inserted in local newspapers.

The problems at the Kent viaduct were more serious. The Act for the line had required the provision of an opening bridge but, after an Admiralty Inquiry in 1856-57, this had not been provided because the navigation was insignificant, although the construction provided a channel for the river. In May 1857 the U&LR had sent a memorial to the Admiralty requesting permission (or authorisation) to complete the Kent viaduct without the opening bridge. The line opened in August 1857 but it was not until 2nd December 1857 that the Admiralty replied, giving notice to the company to provide the bridge. James Ramsden, the company secretary, replied on 26th December:

'Sir,
The Directors are not aware of any new or altered circumstances since the visit and inspection of Mr Curtis (the Admiralty inspector) or that any navigation of value has been seriously interrupted and they desire me respectfully to urge upon their Lordships, consideration of the fact that 35,000 passengers and an aggregate tonnage of 32,000 passed along the line in the three months ending November last, making the question of an increased risk as such a second opening bridge would create of no small importance either to the public or the company. The complete reversal of their Lordships' view of 18th June after a lapse of so very short a time, and which was arrived at after public and searching enquiry and an examination of all parties interested in the Navigation, would seem to suggest that their Lordships have decided upon an 'ex-parte' statement only because it contained some extraordinary and new circumstances demanding their immediate interference, and the Directors being entirely unaware of any such, consider that in asking to be furnished with any copies of any such statements and to be allowed to reply to them, they are not making an unreasonable request nor one not in accordance with your letter of 8th September.'

This letter is the earliest recorded example of Ramsden's diplomatic skills. The Admiralty's reply is also a classic of Civil Service bureaucracy. Their letter of 4th January 1858 read:

' ...my Lords agreed not to insist on the opening bridge being used in the first instance with a distinct intimation to the Railway Company that it should be so constructed as to be capable of allowing the passage of vessels on the necessary notice being given by the Admiralty. My Lords received various depositions from various parties interested in the navigation and, in the performance of their duties on the conservation of navigable rivers, they felt it to be their imperative duty to preserve the navigation free from interruption. They therefore apprise the Directors that proceedings will be taken against them unless the viaduct be opened for traffic up the river after the expiration of a period of three months from 2nd December last.'

On 22nd February the U&LR board took the precaution of inviting the contractor, James Featherstone, to tender for the construction of an opening span. The tender was a modest £523 but the potential for the disruption of rail traffic was the main consideration. However, local interests took a more pragmatic course than the Admiralty and petitioned for a station at Arnside. The eventual outcome was that the Admiralty rescinded their order and trains began to stop at Arnside 'by signal' from the beginning of the November 1858 timetable. The final chapter in the saga of the Kent viaduct opening bridge was written in February 1859 when the Kendal Chamber of Commerce agreed that if a wharf was made at Arnside and a road made from Arnside to Milnthorpe, objections to the failure to provide the opening bridge would cease. An agreement in these terms was concluded in July 1860.

By now the contentious character of the Brogdens was increasingly coming to light. W. & J. Galloway, contractors for the

Leven viaduct, wrote to James Brunlees, from Knott Mill Iron Works, Manchester, on 4th September 1857:

'We presume that we are not considered as responsible for any damages which may occur to the Viaduct from want of rid about the piles ... many of the piles have little sand to sustain them. The trains are numerous and pass over without slackening speed.[32]*'*

Difficulties over the Galloways' account lingered on until January 1858 when a final payment of £5,700 was mutually agreed.

A further area of contention was between the company and its engineer, Brunlees, over his remuneration. This was particularly unfortunate in view of the great service he had given, in conjunction with Galloways, in overcoming the viaduct construction problems. At the board meeting on 3rd February 1858 receipt of letters from Brunlees, dated 14th January, 19th January, 28th January and 29th January 1858 were noted. The board replied that *'the Company have placed the matter in their solicitors hands with whom you are requested to communicate'.* However, on 22nd February, an accommodation over the professional fees was reached and Brunlees' account was settled for £5,000 plus expenses.

At the time of the opening of the Ulverstone & Lancaster Railway, temporary stations were provided at Cark, Kents Bank, Grange and Silverdale, with passing loops at Cark and Grange. On 6th January 1858 the board authorised the building of an engine shed at Grange, together with a short siding and £300 was paid to Stevens & Sons for the provision of signals, but poor traffic at Kents Bank station resulted in its closure, on 1st April 1858. In May 1858 a siding at Arnside was authorised and Arnside station first appeared in the timetable for November 1858.

Also, in November of that year, the board agreed that Kents Bank station should be re-opened if there was a prospect of any business being done there and in fact it was re-opened. A permanent station at Grange was now authorised, but this was not completed until well into the Furness Railway era.

The additional capital provided by the 1858 Act had been directed towards the doubling of the line and, in February 1861, doubling between the east end of the Leven viaduct and Flookburgh was authorised, opening on 30th July 1861. The line between Ulverston station and the Leven viaduct had already been doubled and had opened in August 1860.

During the independent existence of the U&LR there were only two attempts at expansion. On 22nd February 1858 the board agreed the payment of £42 17s 6d to James Brunlees for his survey between Greenodd and Newby Bridge, the course of the later Newby Bridge branch and, on 4th December, the board examined a plan for a line from the U&LR at Carnforth, to the North Western Railway at Hornby. This was precipitated by the notice of a Lancaster & Carlisle Railway Bill for a line between Hest Bank and Morecambe. There was, however, no action on the U&LR scheme, which would have provided the line subsequently authorised as the Furness & Midland Joint Railway.

The financial results of the Ulverstone & Lancaster Railway became increasingly promising, not surprising in view of the strategic importance of the line. The dividends paid for the half years were as follows:

1858 2nd	1½%
1859 1st	2½%
1859 2nd	2½%
1860 1st	4%
1860 2nd	5%
1861 1st	5%

Devonshire had a meeting with Ramsden and the engineer, Stileman, in Ulverston on 19th September 1861. He notes:

'Ramsden has had some conversation with Mr A Brogden about obtaining their line and had some talk about the terms. I am not at all convinced of the propriety of doing anything and feel no terms could be arranged which would not be very onerous on us.'

However, on 15th October, he reported having had a Furness Railway directors' meeting where:

'after a long discussion we decided on making a proposal to the Brogdens for leasing their railway. I cannot say I am quite convinced that the step was a prudent one but I do not believe there is much risk and as the other directors as well as Mr McClean were favourable, I did not think it right to object.'

At a U&LR board meeting at John Brogden's home, Raglan House, Sale on 31st October 1861, a lease to the FR, at 6%, was considered. On 13th November, at Manchester, James Ramsden and Alexander Brogden agreed that the U&LR would be leased to the FR at 5% for two years and at 6% for 1,000 years. However, the FR subsequently offered the U&LR outright purchase at par, for 6% non-voting stock from 1st January 1862. This was accepted by the Brogdens and the FR capital accounts show the sum of £422,939 14s 4d for the purchase of the Ulverstone & Lancaster Railway, and £22,004 15s 0d for the purchase of the Ulverston Canal. However, only £298,000 of 6% U&LR preference stock was issued.

To conclude the story of the Ulverstone and Lancaster Railway some account of the subsequent activities of the Brogdens is necessary. Following the death of John Jnr, John senior continued as chairman of the U&LR, until its sale to the FR, after which he appears to have retired to his home at Sale, where he died in 1869.

The northern activities of the family fell increasingly into the hands of Alexander, who resided for a time at Holme Island near Grange-over-Sands and afterwards settled at Lightburn House in Ulverston. Following the sale of the U&LR, he became interested in the Solway Junction scheme in association with James Brunlees. The Solway Junction Railway Company was authorised in June 1864 with Alexander as chairman.

In addition to his northern interests, Alexander retained his south Staffordshire connections and was elected, in 1867, the first MP for Wednesbury. He was a member of the Lancaster Local Committee and the Carlisle Citadel Station Committee of the LNWR and was one of that company's representatives on the board of the Cockermouth, Keswick & Penrith Railway[33]. In 1873-74 he became interested in the iron ore deposits in Ennerdale and in the proposed Rowrah & Kelton Fell (Mineral) Railway (authorised in July 1874). These deposits proved disappointing and Alexander sold out, but retained his Furness mining interests, as a partner in the Ulverston Mining Company's Lindal Cote mine[34].

The Brogdens' principal activities became concentrated in South Wales, where they operated coal mines, iron mines and the Tondu Ironworks. In connection with these activities they built railways and developed the port of Porthcawl. These were authorised by the Llynvi and Ogmore Railway Act of June 1864 and further Acts.

In 1871 a massive railway building programme by the Government of New Zealand attracted the interest of the Brogdens, and James Brogden went out there with a large number of operatives. The results, however, were disappointing and, by 1872, they were forming the Llynvi, Tondu & Ogmore Coal & Iron Company, with a capital of £550,000 and Alexander as chairman. This company enjoyed the prosperous times of 1872-74 with the Bessemer process in the ascendant but, in common with the iron industries of Furness and West Cumberland, it went into recession towards the end of the decade as a result of new technology and the importation of cheap Spanish ore.

The Llynvi company went into receivership in 1877. The Brogdens became involved in a legal dispute with the Metropolitan Railway, to whom they were contracted for the supply of locomotive coal. The legal wrangling ran from 1873 to 1877, ending in the House of Lords and resulting in the loss of the case with massive legal expenses for the family.

Finally, demonstrating their propensity for dispute, the Brogdens turned against themselves. On 12th January 1880 Alexander commenced an action against his brothers Henry and James, as a result of which the firm of John Brogden and Sons was dissolved on 26th July 1880.

On 5th January 1884 Alexander and Henry Brogden petitioned separately for bankruptcy in the High Court in London[35] and it is thought that their total indebtedness amounted to some one million pounds, but details of creditors have not been found. In 1886 there were further family difficulties over the terms of the will of John Brogden senior[36], nevertheless, Alexander was able to maintain an affluent life style until his death on 26th November 1892.

The Ulverstone & Lancaster line in Furness Railway ownership

From the beginning of 1862 the Furness Railway took over the U&LR line, by which time the Barrow Ironworks was in full production and the steelworks was being planned. Plans were also well advanced for docks at Barrow and for the Furness & Midland Joint Line between Carnforth and Wennington, on the Midland main line to Lancaster and Morecambe. The Ulverstone & Lancaster line had, as a consequence of these plans, become a potential main line.

The Ulverstone & Lancaster Railway Act of 12th July 1858 had authorised the borrowing of £150,000 to discharge the liabilities of the company and to double the line, powers inherited by the Furness Railway. The U&LR had already doubled the line between Ulverston station and the Leven viaduct[37], and between the east end of the Leven viaduct and Cark station, on 31st July 1861[38]. The engineer's estimate for completion of the double line on the Ulverstone to Lancaster section, was received by the FR board on 25th February 1863:

Carnforth – Silverdale	£6,429
Silverdale – Arnside	£3,373
Kent viaduct	£6,811
Arnside – Grange	£2,561
Grange – Kents Bank	£2,845
Kents Bank – Cark	£4,296
Leven viaduct	£7,832

On 31st January 1863 the FR board considered the building of a line from Plumpton to the shipping quays at Greenodd, provided the merchants agreed to abandon the navigation to Greenodd and to dispense with the opening bridge in the Leven viaduct. The letting of tenders for the widening of the U&LR line, to Messrs Roscoe Allen of Preston for £16,408, and for the widening of the Kent and Leven viaducts, to Messrs Galloway for £16,500, was noted by the FR board on 5th August. Admiralty permission was obtained for the permanent closure of the opening span in the Kent viaduct, but, it was not until the passing of the Furness Railway Act, on 16th July 1866, authorising the branch from Plumpton to the foot of Windermere, that the closure of the opening span in the Leven viaduct was sanctioned.

The double line on the Ulverstone & Lancaster section of the Furness Railway was opened as follows:

Carnforth to Grange	4th September 1863
Kent viaduct	6th October 1863
Grange to Cark	1st October 1863
Leven viaduct	circa November 1863

From the opening of the Ulverstone & Lancaster Railway, in 1857, the terminal station of the Furness Railway at Ulverston remained in use. However, in 1860 new platforms were provided on the through line and, in 1860, the original station became dedicated to goods traffic.

CHAPTER 8 REFERENCES

1   W&FJR SM, 25th Feb. 1847.
2   Richardson J. *Op. cit.* Vol. 1 p.22 et seq.
3   Dr E. Course, personal communication.
4   L&CR DM, 17th Dec. 1850.
5   L R Gilpin, personal communication.
6   State Papers 1851. Vol. XXIX, p.123.
7   14-15 Vic C 102.
8   PRO: Rail 700/1&2.
9   Gooderson P. J., 1971. "Railway Construction in Mid-Nineteenth Century North Lancashire" *Transactions of the Historic Society of Lancashire & Cheshire* Vol. 122. pp 137-151.
10 *Whitehaven Herald*, 29th May 1853.
11 *Cumberland Pacquet*, 11th Apr. & 6th June 1854.
12 *Ulverston Advertiser*, 1st Sep. 1853.
13 *Westmorland Gazette*, Dec. 1855.
14 *Ulverston Advertiser*, 10th Nov. 1853.
15 *Cumberland Pacquet*, 7th Feb. 1854.
16 U&LR DM, 2nd June 1852.
17 Gooderson P. J. *Op. cit.*
18 U&LR DM, 17th Aug. 1855.

19 Gooderson P .J. *Op. cit.* p.144.
20 Ibid. p.147.
21 *Ulverston Advertiser*, 21st Apr. 1853.
22 *Manchester Examiner*, 1855.
23 *Ulverston Advertiser*, 12th Mar. 1857.
24 Gooderson P. J. *Op. cit.* p.145.
25 Gooderson P .J. *Op. cit.* p.147.
26 U&LR SM, 25th Feb. 1857.
27 PRO: MT29/18 p.288.
28 PRO: MT6/14/115.
29 *Ulverston Advertiser*, 27th Aug. 1857.
30 U&LR DM, 7th Dec. 1857.
31 Stelfox Diary, Lancaster University.
32 Marshall J.D. *Op. cit.* p.217.
33 LNWR Special Committee Minutes, passim.
34 L.R. Gilpin, personal communication, passim.
35 *London Gazette*, 11th Jan. 1884.
36 D. Budgett, personal communication.
37 PRO: MT29.22.1856.
38 PRO: MT29.22.1862.

THE FURNESS IRON TRADE
AND THE DEVELOPMENT OF BARROW

The opening of the Ulverstone & Lancaster Railway, in 1857, heralded a period in the history of the Furness Railway, which was the most significant in its 77 years of independent existence. Prior to 1857 it was a local line restricted to the Furness district, but, by 1867, not only was it a trunk route connecting the industrial areas of West Cumberland and Furness with the main railway system of the country, it was also the proprietor of the Barrow docks and an operator of shipping services to the Isle of Man and Northern Ireland.

This progress was based largely on the development of the Furness iron trade. Although the Furness hematite ore was rich and pure, too often the deposits were small and unpredictable, but their output had been stimulated by the improved transport provided by the Furness Railway. Henry Schneider had started his mining and prospecting activities in Furness, in 1839, with only limited prospecting success but with modest success in mining in the established royalties. He had made a trial boring in a promising area on the Earl of Burlington's Park Farm, at an early date, without result but returned again to this site in 1850.

He was on the point of giving up when his men, being so sure of the ground, agreed to continue working without pay and, towards the end of October 1850, ore was struck, revealing the largest hematite deposit discovered so far in the United Kingdom. Park Mine was destined to yield 9 million tons of ore in its long lifetime[1]. An even larger sister deposit was discovered in 1860, some two miles away, at Hodbarrow, across the Duddon estuary in south Cumberland[2].

Concurrently with the development of the Furness ironfield, significant progress was being made in the technology of the iron industry[3]. In 1854, Henry Bessemer, more by accident than design, had carried out his first 'blow', in which a current of hot gas was passed through molten pig iron, burning out the carbon and creating the new product, steel. Compared with cast iron, steel had superior qualities and immediately attempts were made to reproduce the process on a commercial scale. The first attempts were a failure, which led Bessemer into protracted research, involving him in an association with the Oldside Ironworks at Workington[4]. His detective work on the materials used at the Oldside works revealed that the presence of phosphorus, introduced by the use of cinder from Staffordshire as flux, prevented the success of his process. Furness and West Cumberland hematite ore contained no phosphorus and once phosphoric contamination was eliminated from iron ores, his steelmaking process proved successful. Bessemer started his own steelworks at Sheffield in 1858, other works soon followed and, overnight, hematite pig iron became the essential material for the new Bessemer steel industry. The demand for Bessemer steel led to the establishment of an increasing traffic in hematite

Barrow Hematite Iron & Steel Works.(K. Norman collection)

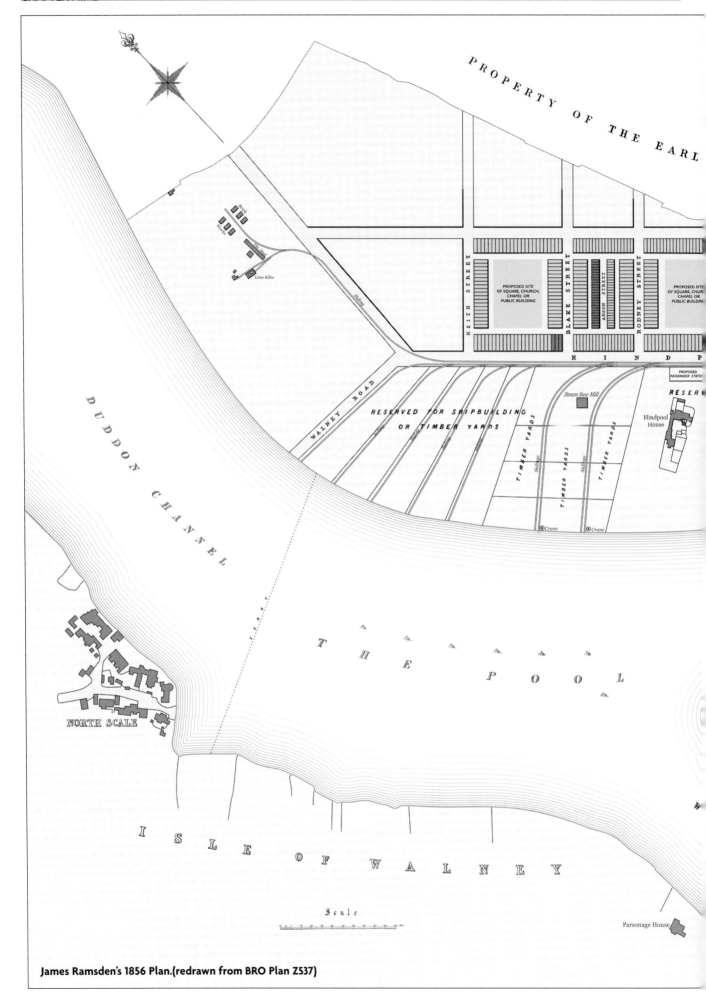

James Ramsden's 1856 Plan. (redrawn from BRO Plan Z537)

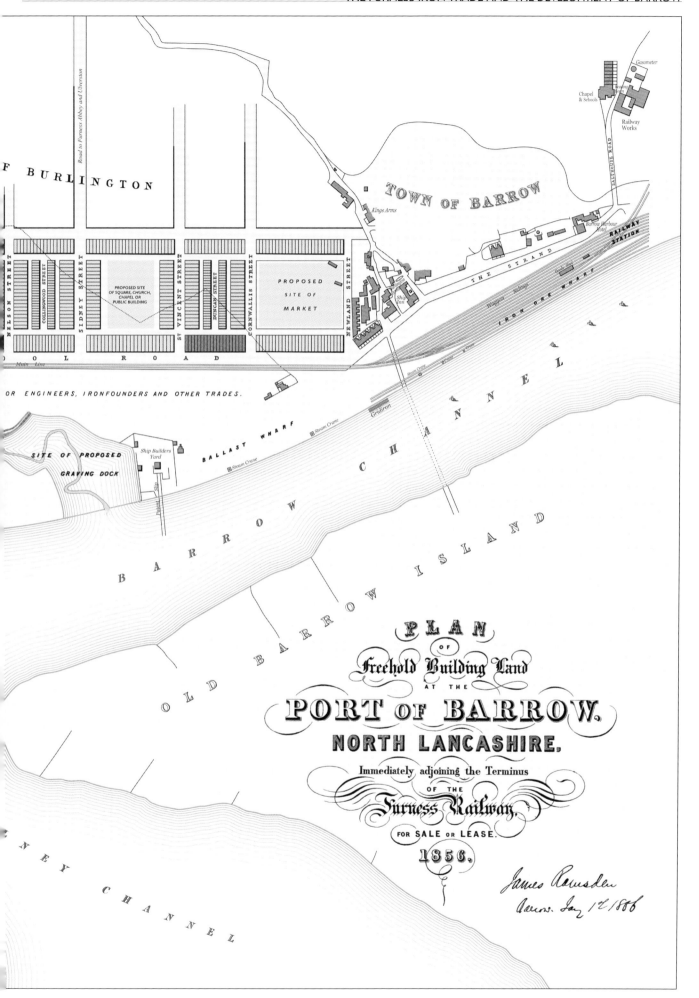

PLAN
OF
Freehold Building Land
AT THE
PORT OF BARROW,
NORTH LANCASHIRE,
Immediately adjoining the Terminus
OF THE
Furness Railway,
FOR SALE OR LEASE.
1856.

James Ramsden
Barrow Jany 1st 1856

ore between West Cumberland and Furness and the iron making centres of South Wales, South Staffordshire and Yorkshire.

Against this background of advancing technology, Schneider was no longer content to remain an iron ore merchant and, together with a new partner Robert Hannay, a Scottish landowner looking for an increased return on his capital, he began, in 1858, to plan an ironworks at Barrow. A site on the Hindpool estate at Barrow, acquired by James Ramsden on behalf of the Furness Railway, was chosen and a tramway from the Furness Railway's Barrow Pier was constructed. The first furnaces were blown in on 17th October 1859[5].

A measure of the success of the Ulverston Hematite Iron Works, as it was known at first, is given by the following figures:

Furness Ore Production		Converted to iron at Hindpool
1857	454,853 tons	Nil
1864	692,420 tons	293,523 tons[6]

The Hindpool works originally consisted of three furnaces, and in January 1860, *'no less than 3,491 tons of superior hematite iron were produced.'* [7] In late 1862, M. Sampson Jordan, a French metallurgist, reported:

'Six furnaces are at present in blast producing about 2,500 of pig metal per week ... on average upward of 60 tons per furnace in 24 hours, a production hitherto unparalleled in the metallurgy of iron. [8]

A railway event of great significance to the Barrow Ironworks was the opening of the South Durham & Lancashire Union Railway (SD&LUR) for mineral traffic, on 4th July 1861. This provided a more direct route for Durham coke to Barrow, via Tebay and Carnforth, at a rate of 9s per ton[9]. Passenger traffic on this new line commenced on 8th August 1861 and it was absorbed by the Stockton & Darlington Railway, on 1st January 1863, before becoming part of the North Eastern Railway system later the same year[10].

The possibility of establishing a steelworks at Barrow was discussed by Devonshire and Ramsden towards the end of 1863[11] and in January 1864 this was agreed. The capital would be

£120,000 to which Devonshire would contribute £10,000 and Schneider and Hannay, of Barrow Ironworks, £40,000. Others connected with the district were to be invited to subscribe[12] and Lord Frederick Cavendish was to be the first chairman. The first general meeting of the Barrow Hematite Steel Company Limited was held on 29th March 1865[13]. The report of the directors noted:

'They are able to report satisfactorily on the progress of the works, notwithstanding delays which had arisen from the difficulties in obtaining labour and other circumstances.'

In May 1864 experiments had been conducted with a small Bessemer converter by Josiah Smith, who had been recruited by Schneider and Hannay, in 1858, as their consultant engineer for the design of the ironworks. Josiah Timmis Smith (1823-1906) was born at Chesterfield and educated at Mill Hill School. After apprenticeship at the Dundyran Ironworks in Scotland he attended the School of Mines in Paris, thereafter working at the Le Creuset Ironworks, one of the most advanced in the world at that time, from which he moved to Dudley, Staffordshire[14].

The Barrow Hematite Steel Company's Bessemer shop was completed in April 1865[15] The directors' report continued:

'The Directors anticipate that by the month of May the manufacture of ingots may be commenced and by the end of June they expect that one of the rail mills will be in operation. The Directors propose to proceed immediately with the building of a second mill for the construction of ships plates, boilerplates and tyres.'

At the second annual general meeting, on 1st March 1866, the directors stated:

'The transfer of the mines and furnaces lately the property of Messrs Schneider, Hannay & Co. has recently been effected in pursuance of the resolution passed at the Special General Meeting held on 15th November last.'

Devonshire was elected chairman, Robert Hannay retired, at

The imposing General Office of Barrow Steelworks faced on to Walney Road and perished on the closure of the works. Steel-making on the site outlived iron smelting but complete closure came in 1983, revealing for the first time the huge tract of land that lay under the iron and steel plants. (Author: MAA729)

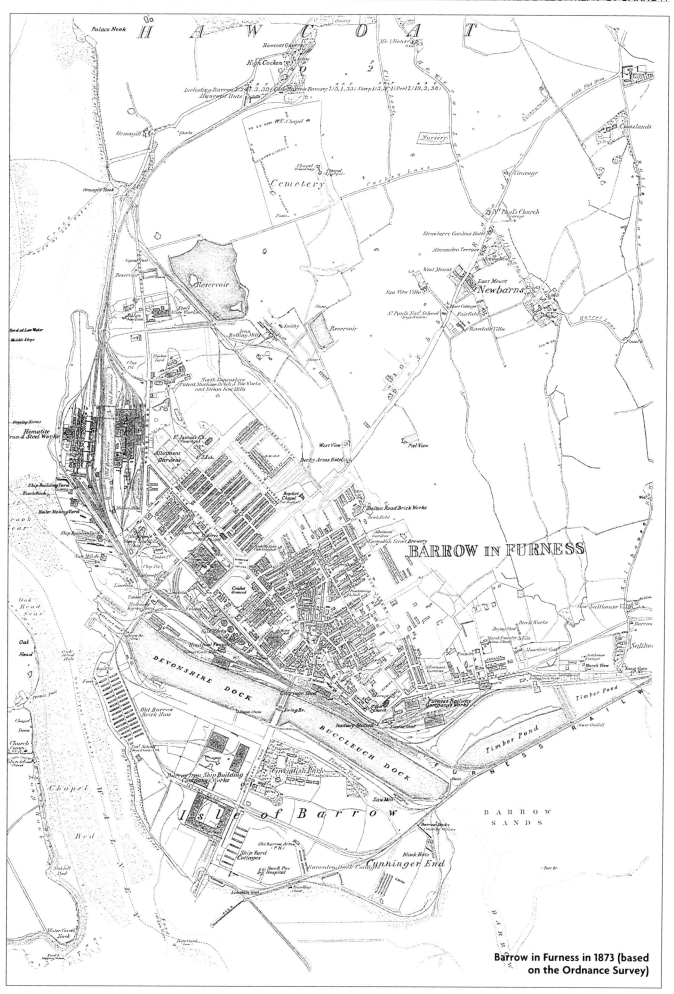

Barrow in Furness in 1873 (based on the Ordnance Survey)

his own request, and John Fell, of Flan How, Ulverston, was elected in his place. Devonshire was able to report that the manufacture of ingots had commenced in July 1865 and that the rail mill had been in operation since the beginning of October. A dividend of 5% on a capital of £90,000 was declared. The balance sheet, dated 31st December 1866, showed total assets amounting to £920,483.

The shareholders of the new company included Thomas Brassey (contractor for the Barrow docks) with £44,000; H.S. Thompson, chairman of the North Eastern Railway; W.E. Hutchinson, Chairman of the Midland Railway; and James Allport, the Midland Railway General Manager[16].

The directors report and accounts for 1867 were presented to the fourth annual general meeting of the Barrow Hematite Steel Company Limited on 20th March 1868. The board contained a predominance of FR interests, including the Duke of Devonshire, chairman; Lord Frederick Cavendish MP (Devonshire's second son); Henry William Schneider; William Currey (Devonshire's legal adviser); Frederick Iltid Nicholl (Buccleuch's principal agent); James Ramsden, managing director of the Furness Railway; and John Fell, Furness ironmaster.

Of the capital of £1million in shares of £100, only £50 had been called, to which had been added £4, in addition to dividends. The results for 1867 allowed the payment of a dividend of 11%, together with a further £4 per share in capital. It was noted that the working of the company, up to the end of 1867, had allowed the payment of £58 on each £100 share. This was a truly remarkable result, attributed to the technological success of the Barrow works and the provision of iron ore from the company's own mine at Park from which, in 1867, 280,000 tons of ore were raised.

The development of the Town and Port of Barrow to 1867

The opening of the Furness Railway in 1846 and the building of a railway station, engineering shop, engine house and pier at Barrow, while significant in railway terms, added little to the village of Barrow. The railway colony consisted only of a school, a *'reading room and two terraces of cottages'* on the Salthouse Road, the most westerly being occupied by James Ramsden as an office[17].

However, the expansion of the ore traffic, facilitated by the railway, led quickly to first steps being taken to improve the harbour and, in 1847, a Barrow Harbour Improvement Bill was introduced by a group of promoters, among which FR proprietors featured prominently. Although the limits of the proposed Harbour Authority did not include Piel Pier, it is not surprising, in view of the distinctly strained relations between the FR and Abel Smith, the owner of the Piel works, that the Bill was opposed by Smith and the opponents appeared before a Select Committee of the House of Commons on 18th April 1848[18]. In his evidence, the Barrow harbour master admitted that he was an employee of the Furness Railway Company and he described the increasing difficulties of navigation between Piel and Barrow. Dredging operations had already been necessary and matters were not improved by the habit of ships masters discharging ballast between Piel Pier and Barrow. The Committee came to the conclusion that the regulation of Barrow Harbour was necessary and an agreement was reached whereby Abel Smith was to appoint one of the proposed Commissioners.

The Barrow Harbour Act 1848[19] received Royal Assent on 30th June 1848 and allowed a toll of 3d per ton to be charged towards the upkeep of the harbour. The Harbour Commissioners, ten in number, included the Lord of the Manor (the Duke of Buccleuch, a FR shareholder), the chairman of the FR (Lord Burlington), Thomas Michaelson, the owner of Old Barrow Island, together with ironmasters, railway directors and an Admiralty representative. James Ramsden was appointed Clerk to the Commissioners at £40 per annum. The Act empowered the FR to lend £5,000 to the Commissioners. Their first meeting was held at Furness Abbey Hotel on 13th December 1848[20] and thereafter, apart from one or two meetings with their consulting engineers, McClean and Stileman in London, the meetings were an annual event in Barrow.

Montague Ainslie, an ironmaster, attended only the first meeting after which the Commissioners became a FR monopoly, except for Michaelson who attended regularly until prevented by illness in 1855. In 1863 the FR bought Old Barrow Island from his estate.

In the 1848 session of Parliament, the Furness Railway had its own Bill. The preamble stated that the purpose of the Bill was:

'To raise a further sum of money for the completion of the undertaking ... and whereas it would be of great public advantage if the said Company were authorised to apply certain portions of their funds in the purchase of one or more steam vessels for the purpose of facilitating communication between Barrow, Piel Pier and Fleetwood.'

The application of railway company funds to the working of steamers was a source of great debate. In 1840, the Steam Ship Owners Association had been formed to protect the interests of existing operators against railway companies, with their advantage of limited liability and massive capital resources, which could lead to a monopoly. The practice of the Board of Trade was to deny such powers unless the service was clearly part of the railway system. The 1848 FR Bill was one of four which put this to the test and, as the Furness Railway was dependent on the Piel – Fleetwood steamer to maintain a contact with the main railway system, the powers were granted, putting the FR in a pioneering position. This was after a Commons Committee, at which the FR's plans were opposed by the Steamship Owners Association, together with the Bristol Steam Navigation Company; the Carlisle & Liverpool Steam Navigation Company; the Steamboat Owners of Glasgow; W. H. & James Hutchinson of Newry; the City of Dublin Steam Packet Company, and the General Steam Navigation Company. The evidence[21] included that of the FR engineer, McClean, who stated that the Piel – Fleetwood service was run at a loss and that he did not think any private operator would wish to take over the service. As a result of this Committee decision, the FR was among the first railway companies legally to own steamers. However, the matter was to be raised again, in 1863, in connection with the proposed services from Barrow to Belfast and the Isle of Man.

By 1854 the £5,000 loan from the FR had been expended and a Barrow Harbour (Amendment) Act 1855[22] increased the borrowing powers of the Commissioners to £35,000. The FR provided a steam tug at 5% interest, which was met out of the tolls, as was the cost of the dredging machine, also obtained in 1854. McClean and Stileman supported a scheme, promoted by Ramsden in 1854, by which the northern approach to Barrow Harbour was to be improved to allow incoming vessels to use this route, thereby tripling the harbour's capacity. In six months, in 1856, 23,000 cubic yards were excavated from the north channel and deposited to form a northern extension to the railway pier. Slowly the sandy Barrow shore, or strand, disap-

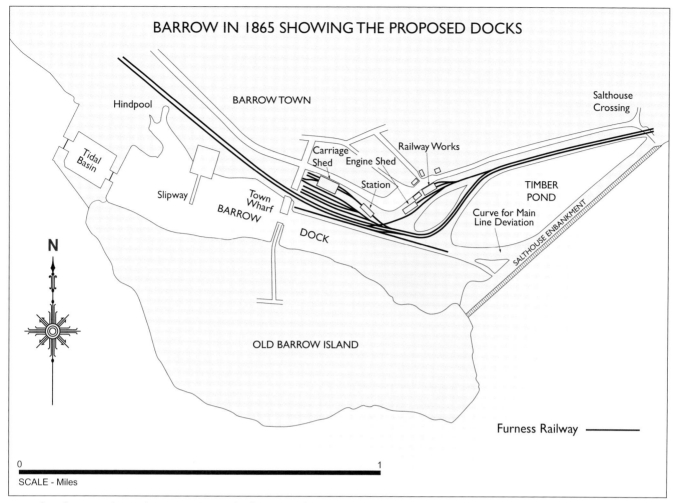

BARROW IN 1865 SHOWING THE PROPOSED DOCKS

peared as the extending railway pier approached Barrow village and the channel was completely cleared, from north to south, by August 1857[23].

Abel Smith's pier and causeway, together with the FR embankments on the Rampside and Barrow branches, had been severely damaged by a storm on 27th December 1852 and, in 1853, Piel Pier was rebuilt by its new owners, the Furness Railway, the railway embankment to Barrow widened and a double line to Barrow station opened[24].

In 1854 the FR purchased the Hindpool estate, a large tract of land north of Barrow village, at a modest cost of some £7,000. This provided scope for the expansion of railway facilities and also industrial development encouraged by the FR. A gasworks was soon constructed and a water supply laid on[25]. The FR erected twelve shops on the estate near the village, a useful, though technically illegal, investment[26]. The original wooden railway pier was rebuilt in local sandstone and the wood from this, together with that from the old jetties of the ironmasters, was used for locomotive fuel. Richard Roper of the Newland Company referred to the end of his company's pier:

'The last shriek of the last stage was heard on the breeze near the mouth of the tunnel south of Dalton not long since, and I hope it did not quite agree with No.3 (Bury 0-4-0 No.3, later preserved) for I have observed it puffing and blowing desperately lately and towards night it gets very red in the face – serves it right, the cannibal.' [27]

The purchase of the Hindpool estate led to the first exercise in town planning. Job Bintley, engineer of the original tramway project, produced a plan for the development of Barrow:

'... laid out in lots suitable for building sites in streets and detached villa including a site for a church and ornamental pleasure ground.'

However, James Ramsden had his own ideas and his plan for urban and industrial development is dated 1st January 1856[28]. This plan took into account the needs of industrial and residential building as well as those of the railway company, the residential and industrial estates being separated by a road, designated Hindpool Road, an extension of the Strand.

In contrast, the streets east of the Strand and on Salthouse Marsh, laid out by a non-railway enterprise, were, and remain, mean and narrow. The main thoroughfares of the present town, Duke Street and Abbey Road, were the direct result of James Ramsden's Hindpool Estate development.

The Barrow Ironworks was reached by a tramway forming an extension of the FR Barrow branch, built using old FR rails and without Parliamentary sanction[29]. This line was extended to Hawcoat sandstone quarry, under powers conferred by the Furness Railway Act 1862, and acted as a spinal route, from which sidings served the industrial establishments springing up in Barrow. William Gradwell had moved from Lowick to Roose in 1844 and set up a joinery business, which had expanded with the railway, so that in 1855 he was able to open the Hindpool Sawmills. William Ashburner had formed a shipbuilding yard, at Hindpool, as early as 1847. The iron foundry of Westray and Forster was also established on the Hindpool estate and this too was served by the railway.

All this activity attracted increasing numbers of craftsmen, small businessmen and labourers to Barrow. In keeping with the times, the leaders of this new community gave first prior-

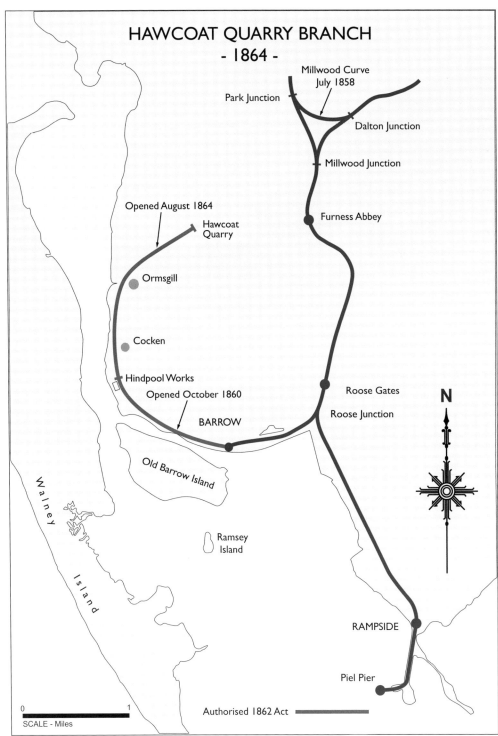

HAWCOAT QUARRY BRANCH
- 1864 -

Millwood Curve
July 1858

Park Junction

Dalton Junction

Millwood Junction

Furness Abbey

Opened August 1864

Hawcoat
Quarry

Ormsgill

Cocken

Hindpool Works
Opened October 1860

Roose Gates

Roose Junction

BARROW

N

Old Barrow Island

Walney Island

Ramsey
Island

RAMPSIDE

Piel Pier

0   1

SCALE - Miles

Authorised 1862 Act ▬▬▬▬▬

Figures from the 1861 Census can be seen opposite.

The plans for a dock at Barrow, drawn up in 1861 by J. R. McClean, the FR Engineer, were regarded with some diffidence by the cautious Duke of Devonshire. He noted, on 7th August 1861, *'This is a serious question requiring much consideration'*. McClean's plan was to close the Barrow Channel, at its southern end, by means of an embankment running from Salthouse to Barrow Island and to build an entrance lock at the north end, giving access from the channel. Powers for this work were not sought in the 1861-62 Bill. Devonshire noted on 15th October 1861:

'We thought of going to Parliament next session for powers to construct docks at Barrow ... but have thought it more prudent to postpone it for a year.'

The resulting Furness Railway Act 1862[30], as well as authorising the purchase of steam vessels for the Piel – Fleetwood service, sanctioned the building of the branch to the Hawcoat quarry, which was to supply sandstone, not only for the construction of the docks, but also for a number of municipal and private buildings. The 1862 Act also empowered the FR to raise further capital of £200,000, equal to 50% of the existing capital account.

The Devonshire retinue and numerous guests celebrated the opening of the grouse

ity to the spiritual needs of their subordinates and, in 1859, on a site near the railway works and offices, Barrow's first church, St George's, was built to the design of the Lancaster architect Edward Paley. Hitherto in the parish of Dalton, Barrow was created a separate chapelry in 1860. The 1861 census indicates that 514 houses in Barrow were occupied, seven were unoccupied and 59 were under construction. The population was 3,135 compared with the 690 recorded by the previous census of 1851.

The 1861 census included 200 Furness Railway employees and indicated their place of birth and occupation, no fewer than 58% being described as labourers, a majority of whom were of Furness origin. However, among the skilled grades such as guards, policemen, railway clerks and engine drivers, a significant number came from outside Furness and its neighbouring counties.

shooting season, as usual, at Bolton Abbey but on 26th August the Duke went over to Barrow, with Lord Frederick Cavendish, to attend a FR directors meeting:

'Mr Nicholl and Capt Boyle were present and also Currey, McClean and Stileman. We had more important business than usual. We have to raise money to purchase the Ulverston Canal and Barrow Island, the latter with a view to the construction of a Float or Dock at Barrow. We did not finally decide as to these docks but empowered Ramsden to communicate with the Midland Railway on the subject and learn their views with respect to encouraging the scheme ... We shall probably deem it advisable to proceed before long with a short branch to Hawcoat with a view to having a good quarry at our disposal.'

Furness Railway employees resident in Barrow area									
Place of birth	Labourers	Police	Gatemen	Shopmen	Enginemen	Guards	Clerks	Porters	Total
Furness	66	1	1	0	10	2	4	4	88
Lancs	20	0	0	8	3	2	3	0	36
Cumberland	15	0	1	3	1	1	1	2	24
Yorks	5	0	0	0	0	0	1	0	6
Westmorland	7	0	0	0	0	2	1	2	12
Other	3	2	0	5	13	0	6	2	31
Total	116	3	2	16	27	7	16	10	197

On 30th September 1862, Devonshire reported in his diary:

'Freddy (Lord Frederick Cavendish) and I went early this morning to Liverpool with Ramsden to see some of the recently constructed Docks at Birkenhead in order to get a better notion of the works we contemplate at Barrow. We crossed over to Birkenhead by the Woodside Ferry ... We went first to the new graving docks in the process of construction; they are on an enormous scale, the longest 750 feet in length by about 100 in breadth ... We then saw the low tide basin and the half tide basin both of which are making rapid progress ... The cost has been prodigious and Ramsden thought the works were needlessly costly.'

Soon after a meeting between the Midland and Furness directors, on 26th September 1862, a Bill for the construction of Barrow Docks was deposited. Petitions against the Bill were put in by Lord Lonsdale seeking to protect his navigation rights in the Duddon estuary, which included access to the little port of Borwick Rails, later to assume great importance as the Hodbarrow mine was developed, and from the Trustees of the Port of Lancaster, under whose jurisdiction the port of Barrow technically still lay. The Lancaster interests were judged to have no locus standi by the Parliamentary Committee on the Bill, held on 12th March 1863, and Lord Lonsdale was accommodated by a change in the northern limits of the proposed port of Barrow.

Devonshire gave evidence to the effect that the tolls raised by the Barrow Harbour Commissioners were insufficient to meet the costs of improving the port. The estimate for the construction of the dock was £120,000.

The Committee found for the FR and the Furness Railway and Barrow Harbour Act 1863 received Royal Assent on 22nd June 1863. On 8th September, the FR board considered tenders for the dock construction and a reduced tender from Thomas Brassey, of £132,971, was accepted by Devonshire and approved by the board on 20th October.

The Barrow Dock scheme was carried out in two stages, although that was not the original intention. The not unfamiliar problems of weather, labour shortages, disputes, riots and materials shortages, held up the work in the way that so many other great engineering works were delayed. The FR pier was kept open to navigation from the south during the construction of the northerly Devonshire dock and tidal basin, but Thomas Brassey never got any further than the construction of the Devonshire Dock, it being rumoured that he lost some £40,000 on the contract. Once Brassey was established as a contractor he nearly always put a great deal of his own money into schemes presumably to ensure he eventually gained the contract. He was always losing money (£44,000 apparently for Barrow docks and Runcorn Bridge together) and ended up with vast numbers of shares in the lines he built!

The Duke of Devonshire and the FR decided that the opening

A steamer berthed in Devonshire Dock alongside the bonded warehouse used as a store by the adjacent Barrow Steam Corn Mills, established in 1871. Always known locally as Walmsley & Smiths, after 1903, the operation was a satellite unit of Liverpool millers, Edward Hutchinson & Co, and in its latter years was reduced to milling animal feed. Closure came in 1967. (Ken Norman collection)

of this first section of the docks, which coincided with the incorporation of the Borough of Barrow in Furness, should be a spectacular occasion in spite of the declining trade in 1867. Although no mention of the event was made in the board minutes, the ceremony, to which notables were invited from far and wide, had the hallmarks of a major publicity exercise. Water was let into the Devonshire dock on 1st August 1867 and James Ramsden, with his usual sense of occasion, was on hand with a 'small gig' which he sailed down the dock the moment the water was deep enough[31]

The formal opening took place on 19th September. After a parade through the town, the principal guests – who included William Gladstone, leader of the opposition – embarked at Town pier on board the new steamer *Herald*, purchased for the Isle of Man service of the Barrow Steam Navigation Company, which sailed round the south of Barrow Island, up Walney Channel and into the new dock. The official party was then conducted round the Barrow Hematite Steel Company's works. A banquet was held in the FR carriage shed, near Barrow station, in the evening. The guests exceeded 1,100 in number and *The Times* described them as *'perhaps the most completely representative assembly of trading and railway interests.'* The *Illustrated London News* pictured the event with appropriate engravings. The *Barrow Herald* of 21st September contained a full account of the proceedings with descriptions of the dock and other prominent features of the town.

The satirical magazine *Punch* took a less deferential view on 5th October 1867:

'Never did Barrow on furnace make such a blaze as Barrow-in-Furness the other day when its docks were opened by Dukes, Lords, Honourables and Right Honourables, MPs, JPs, Mayors, Magistrates local and municipal – in short by such an assemblage of big and little wigs as it was a triumph to have got together in the dead season. But the occasion was certainly worth a crowd and a crow! A Barrow that has grown, one may say, from a barrow into a coach and four in ten years! A Barrow that has swelled almost within the memory of its youngest inhabitant from the quiet coast nest of some five-score fishermen, into this busy, bustling, blazing, moneymaking, money spending, roaring, tearing, swearing, steaming, sweltering seat of twenty thousand iron workers, and the crime and the culture, the dirt and disease, the hardworking and hard-drinking, the death and life, the money and misery they bring along with them!'

The tidal basin was crossed by an opening bridge which carried a rail line serving the north end of Barrow Island. The southern part of the new dock system was created by the completion of the Salthouse to Barrow Island embankment and the sluices between this new Buccleuch dock and Devonshire dock were opened, to admit water, on 9th September 1868, by the Duke of Devonshire[32]. The Buccleuch dock was, however, not completed until 1873, by which time an 80 foot passageway and swing bridge, carrying the road between Barrow and Barrow Island, 'Michaelson Road' had been constructed.

The Furness and Midland Joint Line was opened to passenger traffic on 6th June 1867 and on 1st July the steamer *Herald* inaugurated the service between Piel Pier and the Isle of Man, the owning company, the Barrow Steam Navigation Company, being a combination of the Midland Railway, the Furness Railway and their managers, James Little and Co. Piel Pier had been rebuilt by the FR after the storm of late December 1852, but McClean and Stileman found it to be inadequate for the proposed Irish and Isle of Man services and, in July 1867, Lander & Mellanby were awarded a contract for rebuilding the pier, with passenger landings on two levels.

A gasworks was constructed at Piel Station and over the next two years £20,000 was spent on Roa Island. Piel Pier became well known for a time as the destination of the Midland Railway's boat trains but, in 1881, it was eclipsed by a new station, built in connection with the Barrow Dock extension of the 1870s. It then fell into disuse and was demolished c.1893.

During the early 1860s James Ramsden appears to have been

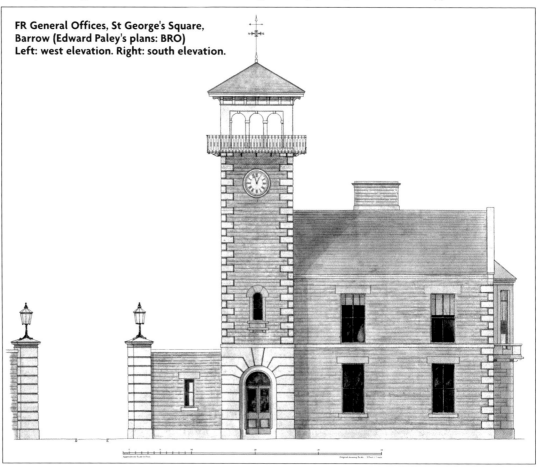

FR General Offices, St George's Square, Barrow (Edward Paley's plans: BRO) Left: west elevation. Right: south elevation.

in a position of supreme power. In 1863 his salary was fixed at £1,000 per annum plus £100 for every 1% net earnings of the FR, at this period running at 8%.[33] He could sign the company's cheques and, in 1861, the FR board had authorised the expenditure of £2,000 on a residence for him on a splendid site overlooking Furness Abbey, with a further £2,233 expended on the mansion, known as *Abbots Wood*, in 1862-64[34], Edward Paley being the architect.

Ramsden, at this time, was responsible for the planning of the expanding town of Barrow-in-Furness and a simple technique was adopted. The FR purchased the land, the streets and drainage were laid out, and the buildings erected, which were subsequently sold.

Such items were recorded in the FR accounts under the heading of 'Barrow Docks, Etc. Examples include:

Forming Hindpool streets and sewering roads	£2,400
Building land in Barrow	£2,307
Roads in Hindpool	£2,189
Forming streets	£2,503
Making streets and sewers	£2,155
Market Hall & Cattle Market	£1,460
Town Hall & Police Court	£3,782

In the accounting year 1868, the Town Hall buildings were sold to the new Corporation (Mayor: James Ramsden) for £15,000, the proceeds of this and other sales being credited to the Docks Capital Account. Some of these activities were subsequently criticised by the FR auditors[35].

In 1866 however, the FR board firmly, if tactfully, brought Ramsden's autocracy to an end. On 8th February they resolved:

'*The recent extensions of the Company (the W&FJ*

Acquisition) and the additional business which will be consequent upon the works now in progress will necessarily increase largely the transactions with other companies and the arrangements in connection with such transactions and with the interchange of traffic will in the opinion of the Board be more conveniently and satisfactorily conducted by a director resident in the district. The Board are of the opinion that Mr Ramsden is the most proper person to undertake these duties which will devolve upon a resident director. The Board are aware that more extensive powers have been hitherto entrusted to Mr Ramsden than is usually the case with General Managers and these powers it is not intended to curtail, but they desire it to be distinctly understood that his appointment as a Director will not confer upon Mr Ramsden the power of making engagements binding the Company with respect to the policies to be pursued towards other Companies nor the power of sanctioning any capital expenditure for the purposes and objects which have not previously received the approval of the board.'

It is difficult to know how much Ramsden had gained personally up to this time, and by what means, but, at the time of his appointment to the board, he was described as one who '*owns a considerable amount of ordinary share capital*'.[36] He was a director of the Barrow Hematite Steel Company, the Barrow Flax and Jute Company and later, the Barrow Shipbuilding Company. An unsuccessful land speculation attempt by him, in 1861, is recorded by Marshall[37], and Ramsden's name appears on a number of title deeds of Barrow property as second owner, although this might have been as a Furness Railway Company nominee, to avoid the problem of the illegality of the Company dealing in land.

Ramsden was instrumental in improving local government, in October 1864, telling a meeting at Ulverston, that he intended to promote the 1858 Local Government Act at Barrow[38]. In 1866, Ramsden, Schneider, Devonshire and William Currey gave evidence to the Privy Council Commissioners on the need for the reform of Barrow's local government. The Charter of Incorporation of the Borough of Barrow-in-Furness was received on 13th June 1867, having been paid for from the FR Dock capital account. James Ramsden was created first Mayor of the Borough, with the aldermen and councillors being nominated by the Duke of Devonshire[39].

The rapid increase in the population of Barrow and the resultant increase in local passenger traffic, consequent upon the development of the steel industry and port, must have taxed the limited passenger facilities of the Furness Railway, because, on 28th February 1862, James Ramsden showed his board a sketch of a proposed enlargement of the railway works at Barrow and of a new passenger station. It can be seen from the FR account books that this station plan was one of several produced for the FR, at that time, by the architect Edward Paley, whose church of St George at Barrow, had been completed. The plan was to build the new station to the

Barrow Shipyard's Devonshire Dock west side, showing, on the right, the floating dock provided in the early 1880s to enable vessels to have minor repairs carried out while in port. The Dock was opened in 1867 in the old channel between Barrow Island and the mainland and was the first section of the major dock system to be completed. The early buildings of the shipyard are shown. (FR 'Port of Barrow' brochure c.1881: Private collection)

landward side of the original railway pier, bypassing the old station by means of a new embankment. The whole of the FR pier and sidings were to be enclosed by a wall along the Strand, into which would be incorporated offices and stables. The tender for these works was let on 16th May 1862 and the new passenger station was opened, on 29th April 1863, at a characteristic ceremony in which Ramsden drove the first train to arrive[40.] This building remains and is easily recognisable although its railway tracks have long gone.

Ramsden clearly intended to take advantage of the dock works to improve the local railway system as, on 20th October 1863, he told the FR board that he:

'required an embankment to be built from the proposed Salthouse embankment to the south end of the railway pier to carry a double line of rails.'

This would have the advantage of carrying the FR main line well away from the existing workshops and, at the same time, reclaim land for their further extension. This work was carried out slowly during the dock construction and formed the later main line from Salthouse Junction, via Buccleuch Junction, to Barrow station yard. The Barrow engine shed was enlarged to accommodate 24 engines in 1864 and, at the same time, the general offices were extended, to plans by Edward Paley, forming an attractive sandstone building with clock tower.

With the completion of the Devonshire Dock, in 1867, it

became possible to close the southern navigation to Barrow pier by the completion of the Salthouse embankment, between Roose and Barrow Island, thus enclosing the proposed Buccleuch Dock and a timber pond. It would appear, from the capital account details, that rails for the line on this embankment were purchased in 1866, but it was not until early 1871 that the passenger traffic was diverted on to this Barrow station approach line. The embankment to Barrow Island afforded a new rail link to serve the south end of the Island, eventually connecting with the north line over the Devonshire Dock basin. A line westward was built towards the Walney channel, where a steamboat pier was constructed, and, later still, the Ramsden Dock station was built south of this pier.

In 1864 the iron ore carried to the Hindpool ironworks amounted to 293,513 tons, much of it originating at the company's own pits at Park. Consequently, plans were made for a direct rail link between Park and Hindpool, which would have the advantage of putting Barrow on a through route to the north. This Park Loop line plan matured at the same time as the FR's Duddon crossing scheme, which had been produced to counter the Whitehaven & Furness Junction Railway's plan of 1864. (see Chapter Seven)

In the 1864-65 Parliamentary session the FR deposited Bills for both the Park Loop and the Duddon Crossing. A junction was to be made with the old line at Park, and the line between Foxfield and Millom to be abandoned – the line to Foxfield being retained as a connection with the Coniston branch. The

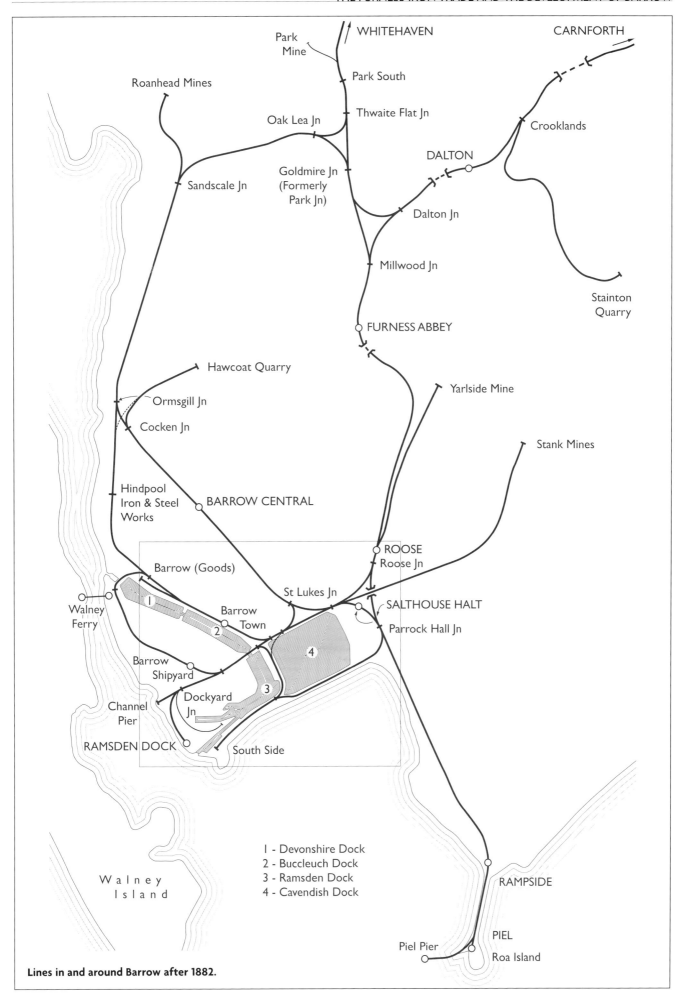

WHITEHAVEN

CARNFORTH

Park Mine

Park South

Roanhead Mines

Thwaite Flat Jn

Crooklands

Oak Lea Jn

DALTON

Sandscale Jn

Goldmire Jn (Formerly Park Jn)

Dalton Jn

Millwood Jn

Stainton Quarry

FURNESS ABBEY

Hawcoat Quarry

Yarlside Mine

Ormsgill Jn

Cocken Jn

Stank Mines

Hindpool Iron & Steel Works

BARROW CENTRAL

ROOSE

Roose Jn

Barrow (Goods)

St Lukes Jn

SALTHOUSE HALT

Walney Ferry

Barrow Town

Parrock Hall Jn

Barrow Shipyard

Channel Pier

Dockyard Jn

RAMSDEN DOCK

South Side

1 - Devonshire Dock
2 - Buccleuch Dock
3 - Ramsden Dock
4 - Cavendish Dock

RAMPSIDE

W a l n e y
I s l a n d

PIEL

Piel Pier

Roa Island

Lines in and around Barrow after 1882.

101

Duddon crossing clauses of the FR Bill of 1865 were struck out in Committee but the Park Loop was sanctioned by the Furness Railway Act 1865[41] for which Royal Assent was granted on 29th June 1865.

Shortly after, the FR purchased the Whitehaven & Furness Junction Railway and inherited the latter's authorised Duddon crossing. However, a depression in trade set in and although a contract for the W&FJR Duddon crossing had been let to P.D. Bennet & Co. for £29,736 in February 1867 and the steelwork for the viaduct had begun to arrive at Ireleth, the reduction in traffic combined with an overspending on capital account, to the tune of £40,000, led the FR to reappraise the crossing plan (see Chapter Twelve). A postponement was ordered which also delayed the Park Loop[42] and this line was not completed until 1882.

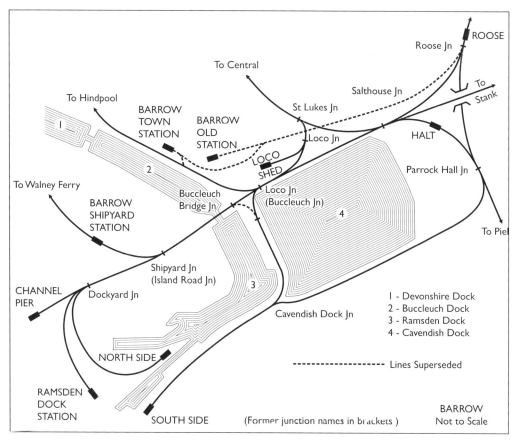

Furness Railway results 1857-1867

During this decade, which was to be the most profitable in the long history of the Furness Railway Company, no less than 85% dividend was paid on the ordinary stock of the company. Moreover the capital account had increased by a factor of nearly five. In 1857 the capital account consisted of:

Consolidated ordinary stock	£240,000
Original 5% preference stock	£100,000
1855 5% preference stock	£59,000
Debentures	£114,877
Total	£513,877

By 1867, with a main line running from Carnforth to Whitehaven, the first stage of the Barrow Docks completed, a branch to the foot of Windermere under construction, a joint line with the Midland finished and the line from Arnside to Hincaster authorised, the capital account now stood at:

Ordinary stock	£1,060,425
U&LR 6%	£298,000
5% stock	£170,000
5% stock	£30,000
2½% stock	£10,000
8% W&FJR preference stock	£227,000
5½% W&FJR preference stock	£50,000
5% W&FJR preference stock	£50,000
4½% W&FJR preference stock	£5,000
Debentures	£494,233
Total	£2,394,568

The receipts for the year 1857 were £68,222; for 1867 they were £286,463[43].

CHAPTER 9 REFERENCES

1   Marshall J.D. *Op. cit.* p.203.
2   Harris A., 1970. *Cumberland Iron* p. 23.
3   Gale W.K.V., 1967. *The British Iron and Steel Industry*.
4   Lancaster J.Y. & Wattleworth D.R. *Op. cit.*
5   Marshall J.D. *Op. cit.* p.221.
6   Richardson J. *Op. cit.* Vol. 2 p.245.
7   *Ulverston Advertiser,* 14th Feb. 1850 & Marshall J.D. *Op. cit.* p.249.
8   *Colliery Guardian,* 23rd May 1863.
9   Marshall J.D. *Op. cit.* p.249.
10 Joy D. *Op. cit.* pp.31.
11 *Devonshire Diaries,* 29th Dec. 1863.
12 *Devonshire Diaries,* 15th Jan. 1864.
13 SRO: Buccleuch muniments, GD 244/144.
14 Richardson J. *Op. cit.* Vol. 2 p.249.
15 *Barrow Herald,* 22nd Apr. 1865 & 27th May 1865.
16 Marshall J.D. *Op. cit.* p.253.
17 Fisher J. *Op. cit.* p.100.
18 Evidence 1847-8 Vol. 7 Commons.
19 11&12 Vic Cap.35.
20 Barrow Harbour Commission Minutes.
21 Evidence Group 5 Vol. 23 11.05.1848.
22 18&19 Vic Cap 170.
23 Barrow Harbour Commissioners, 27th Aug. 1857.
24 FRDM, 26th Aug. 1853.
25 FRDM, 20th Feb. 1855.
26 FRDM, 9th May 1856.
27 *Barrow Herald,* 25th May 1873.
28 BRO: Plan Z537.
29 FRSM, 14th Aug. 1860.
30 25-26 Vic Cap 89.
31 *Barrow Herald,* 3rd Aug. 1867.
32 *Barrow Herald,* 12th Sep. 1868.
33 FRDM, 5th Aug. 1853.
34 BRO: FR Capital Accounts.
35 FRDM, 12th Feb. 1869.
36 *Barrow Herald,* 3rd Mar. 1866.
37 Marshall J.D. *Op. cit.* p.283.
38 Ibid. *Op. cit.* p.293, quoting *Barrow Herald,* 15th Oct. 1864.
39 Ibid. *Op. cit.* p.298.
40 *Barrow Herald,* 2nd May 1863.
41 28-29 Vic Cap 179.
42 FRDM, 13th May 1868.
43 FR Report & Accounts.

NEW ROUTES TO THE EAST

From 1858 onwards, the opening of the Bessemer steel works at Sheffield resulted in an increased traffic flow of hematite ore from Furness to South Yorkshire. On 1st January 1859, the Midland Railway had leased the *'Little'* North Western Railway (NWR) which ran from Skipton to Lancaster, Morecambe and Ingleton, with a connection, at Lancaster, to the LNWR between the Green Area (later known as Green Ayre) and Castle stations. On 10th September 1859, the LNWR leased the Lancaster & Carlisle Railway, thereby finally gaining control of the West Coast route from Euston to Carlisle. By this date, the Ulverstone & Lancaster and Midland systems were separated only by the six miles between Lancaster Castle and Carnforth.

Facilities for the Midland's Scottish traffic had been a sore subject between the NWR and the Lancaster & Carlisle and this problem passed to the Midland and London & North Western Railways. August 24th 1861 saw the LNWR open its line between a junction with the MR at Ingleton, and Low Gill, which, in theory, provided a trunk route for Midland traffic to Scotland. The line from Clapham to Orton, near Low Gill, had been authorised by the original NWR Act of 1846, however, the financial problems of the NWR resulted in the line beyond Ingleton being abandoned, after land had been acquired and some construction work carried out. It was against the background of the dispute over Scottish traffic, between the Midland and the LNWR, that the Furness Railway first became involved in inter-railway politics.

By 1862 the hematite trade was assured of a period of expansion and plans, which had been maturing for some time, went ahead. The shortcomings of the Furness Railway facilities were well recognised by its board. Barrow Harbour, which had been improved considerably by the Barrow Harbour Commissioners since their formation in 1848, was inadequate to deal with the increasing iron ore traffic and any such traffic from Furness to Yorkshire had the obstacle of the short trip, over the LNWR, between Carnforth and Lancaster.

In the 1861-62 session of Parliament, the FR sought powers to operate steam vessels between Barrow, Fleetwood, Douglas and Belfast, in a Bill which came before a Parliamentary Committee on 3rd April 1862[1]. James Ramsden claimed that Barrow had natural advantages over Morecambe and that the opening of the South Durham & Lancashire Union Railway, from Barnard Castle to Tebay, on 4th July 1861, created a new route from the north east to Ireland. Ramsden denied any agreement with either the Midland or LNW Railways.

There were no fewer than 13 petitions against this Bill from shipping companies and ship owner associations, so powers for a service between Barrow and Belfast were struck out of the Bill by the Committee. The FR Act of 1862[2] included a clause empowering the FR to purchase steam vessels, to a total not exceeding £25,000, for a service between Barrow and Fleetwood. As the FR had now been barred from a Belfast service, it had abandoned the idea of a service to the Isle of Man, which, being largely seasonal, would not have been viable

A two coach train from Carnforth passes Wennington Junction signalbox. The coaches will be placed in the up bay to form the rear portion of a Morecambe to Leeds express. (Ken Norman collection)

2P 4-4-0 No. 40409 and Compound 4-4-0 No. 41152 setting off from the bay at Wennington with the 2-46 pm Morecambe-Leeds, having set back into the bay to pick up the portion from Carnforth (dep 2-43) which had arrived earlier behind 2-6-2T No 40011. The date, 27th January 1957. (CRA: Pearsall collection)

in isolation from a Belfast service. It is significant that during the examination of this Bill the Midland Railway remained silent, suggesting that some understanding on the Irish traffic had already been reached between the companies.

On 26th September 1862, a meeting was held in the Furness Abbey Hotel at which a Midland Railway deputation, consisting of Samuel Beale, Chairman, W.E. Hutchinson, Director, and James Allport, General Manager, met the Furness Railway Board. This meeting had resulted from the FR's instruction, of 26th August 1862, to Ramsden, to approach the Midland to 'ascertain their views with respect to the proposed Barrow Docks and the making of a line from Carnforth to Wennington.' By October 1862, the Midland Railway was clearly committed to an alliance with the Furness Railway by which a connecting line would to be made between Wennington, on the Midland's Morecambe line, and Carnforth on the Furness, and the MR Board drew up a provisional agreement, on 1st October, for the formation of a Furness and Midland Joint Committee. This agreement transferred the Midland's Irish traffic from Morecambe to Barrow and defined the spheres of influence in which the Midland was to remain to the east of the Lancaster & Carlisle line and the Furness to the west[3]. It was some years before a permanent agreement was signed, in 1867, by which time the political scene was much altered.

The LNWR opposition

Plans, drawn up by the Midland Company's engineer Crossley and the FR's McClean and Stileman, for the F&M line were deposited late in 1862 and, what at first appeared to be a straight contest between the LNWR and the Midland, had now become complicated by the appearance of a party whose aims were to break the LNWR deadlock on Kendal by means of a line from that town to the FR at Arnside. The Kendal & Ulverstone Junction Railway had the Kendal surveyor Job Bintley, as its engineer, and the line was to run from a terminus near the Kendal basin of the Lancaster Canal to Hincaster, where a trailing connection was to be made with the Lancaster & Carlisle line, before turning westward to Sandside and a junction with the FR at Arnside[4]. The Kendal promoters were interested in an improved route to Ireland, and the line would give them an inde-

pendent access to the Midland system via the F&M. It would also carry the Durham coke traffic. The estimated cost was £99,000.

The LNWR became aware of the Kendal and Ulverstone scheme on 21st November 1862, when its special committee received a letter from Chauncey, one of the officers on the L&C line, describing the project. The outcome was that Ramsden and Stileman met Blenkinsop, the LNWR solicitor, and it was agreed that the FR would examine the Bill to see whether there were grounds for opposition on Standing Orders. That the LNWR was content to let the FR protect it from a scheme that was damaging to the former and valuable to the latter, is significant, suggesting that, in spite of the differences between the two over the F&M Bill, they were essentially on good terms.

The Parliamentary Committee's examination of the F&M Bill commenced, on 11th March 1863[5], with the presentation of the LNWR petition against it. The first witness for the Bill was the Duke of Devonshire (former Earl of Burlington and FR Chairman) who set out the aims of the line and described the difficulties experienced at the present junction between the LNWR and the Midland's 'Little' North Western Line. Mineral traffic was increasing and he hoped for increased passenger traffic between the Midlands and the Lakes. Cross-questioned by the LNWR counsel, he denied any relationship between the FR and the proposed Kendal & Ulverstone Junction Railway, stating that the FR opposed it. He also denied any Midland backing for the Kendal Line. Speaking of the Yorkshire traffic, Devonshire said:

'When the LNW Co get it they carry it down to Preston and send it on that way. The Manager of the Midland Company is my authority for saying that the Midland traffic goes via Preston and the LNWR.'

Henry Schneider, the Furness ironmaster, now appeared on behalf of the Furness iron industry, accusing the LNWR of charging an excessively high rate for the Durham coke traffic for the short journey between Lancaster and Carnforth, when it had come by that route. Schneider was a flamboyant character (destined to gain notoriety in his later political career) and, after enjoying the counsel's eulogy on his success as an ironmaster, he

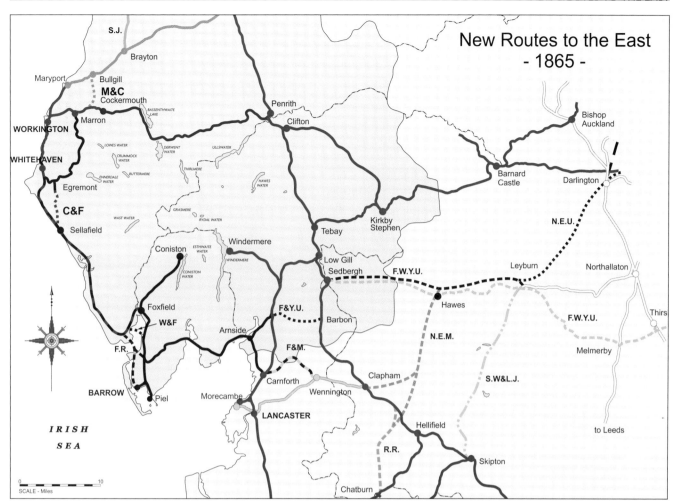

New Routes to the East
- 1865 -

attempted to enlarge on Devonshire's account of the routing of the traffic between Furness and Yorkshire by claiming that the shortest route for Low Moor coal was via Bradford. The LNWR counsel delighted in pointing out that there was, in fact, no connection between the Lancashire and Yorkshire Railway and Midland Railway stations at Bradford. Finally, Schneider described the Kendal and Ulverstone line as *'the most ridiculous and foolish scheme that was ever laid before a Committee of the House.'* This remark indicated the partisan nature of Schneider's evidence, as his traffic in coke, via the SD&LUR, would gain by the Kendal proposal. James Ramsden gave some interesting statistics relating to the Furness iron ore traffic stating that, of the near 600,000 tons carried by the FR in 1862, one third, some 200,000 tons, was carried by the LNWR to south Staffordshire, while only 60,000 tons went to Yorkshire. The importance of the Furness traffic to the LNWR was highlighted, but Ramsden had to admit, on cross-examination, that the shortest route between Furness and Sheffield was via the LNWR and the Manchester, Sheffield and Lincolnshire line. However, he claimed that this was an inconvenient route because of the number of companies it passed over and the indirect connections at Sheffield, whereas the Midland route ran straight to the Park Gate Works at Rotherham. The F&M proposal would make the Midland the shortest, as well as the most convenient, course.

The FR, having attempted to make its case, was followed by the Midland Company's spokesman, their General Manager, James Allport. Allport started by describing the Midland's difficulties in working its Scottish traffic to the north via Ingleton and whilst his argument was not strictly relevant it was ammunition against the LNWR. He went on to claim that the delay at

Lancaster, experienced by passengers travelling between Yorkshire and the Lake District, deterred them from using the Midland route in favour of that via Manchester. He then outlined the Midland's problems at Morecambe, the amount of money expended there by his company and the lack of traffic from the LNWR Morecambe branch to Morecambe Pier, saying that some £100,000 had been spent in anticipation of this traffic, which had amounted to only 1,000 tons. On the following day the significance of Allport's remarks became clear. The LNWR were not sending traffic to Morecambe because they objected to certain clauses in the NWR/LNWR agreement on Morecambe traffic. The conclusion of the Committee proceedings was described, by Frederick Nicholl, in a letter to the Duke of Buccleuch dated 12th March:

'I was at the Committee Room of the House of Commons yesterday and this morning on the Furness Railway Bill now in progress. The Furness and Midland Bill is for a short line of 9 miles between Carnforth and Wennington (on the Little North Western) by which a junction and direct communication will be effected between the Furness and Midland Railways and will be made at the joint expense of the two Companies. This was opposed by the London & North Western for whom Mr Hope Scott appeared and took the entire management. The case was adjourned to this morning when the evidence was completed and Mr Hope Scott commenced his speech for the opponents. When he had about half finished, a whispered communication from his Junior Counsel brought him to a sudden pause and then he announced to the Committee that terms had been arranged between the Companies and that

The signalbox at Carnforth Furness & Midland Junction in June 1967. It controlled the junction between the FR main line, the goods lines and the F & M section to Wennington. Opened in October 1903, it was the final style of FR signalbox. It closed from 7th November 1998 when the direct line to Carnforth East Jct was taken out of use. (Author: MAO2408)

his opposition was withdrawn! So with a few more words the Preamble was declared to be proved. The compromise is in effect that the same running powers and facilities are to be given to both the London & North Western and the Midland over the Furness line. The result is considered very satisfactory by the Furness Company.'

What Nicholl did not know, at the time, was that the Midland had agreed to review the Morecambe agreement if the LNWR opposition to the F&M Bill was withdrawn. This agreement, made in 1859 at the time the Lancaster & Carlisle Bill for its Hest Bank to Morecambe branch was in Parliament, included a clause requiring that traffic from Morecambe to Lancaster and to London be forwarded by the Midland Railway route. The London & North Western wanted the 'shortest route' principle to apply.

Devonshire noted in his diary, on 12th March 1863, that the LNWR facilities *'we gladly acceded to'*. The LNWR noted the arrangements at their Special Committee on 20th March 1863. The Barrow Docks Bill was then examined by the Committee and approved.

Finally the Committee considered the Kendal & Ulverstone Junction Bill. The LNWR was again successful in settling by negotiation, the Bill being withdrawn as a result of the LNWR agreeing with the Kendal traders, that if any line were constructed between the L&C line and Arnside, the rates would be such as to develop the traffic.

Devonshire noted, somewhat peevishly:

'We had united with them [LNWR] in opposing it [Kendal & Ulverstone Junction] and were not parties to the arrangement with which we are no means satisfied. However it did not appear that we could interfere.'

The F&M Act received Royal Assent on 22nd June 1863, but by the end of that year relations between the two companies had become cooler, as there was a threat that discussions between the Midland and the LNWR might, if successful, lead to the abandonment of the F&M line. On 26th January 1864, the LNWR agreed to allow the Midland Railway to lease the Lancaster & Carlisle jointly and that the F&M line be abandoned in favour of a curve, at Lancaster, between the two companies lines north of the Lune Bridge. Also in January the LNWR examined the plans for the Solway Junction Railway. Richard Moon, the LNWR

Chairman, visited West Cumberland in January 1864 but was unable to persuade the board of the Cockermouth & Workington Railway to make an agreement with his company[6]. The FR Board viewed the Midland's change of heart with alarm and Devonshire took a strong line with the Midland at the F&M Joint committee meeting on 18th February 1864, noting in his diary:

'The LNWR had suggested to the Midland Company the abandonment of the line in consequence of having come to an arrangement respecting the Lancaster & Carlisle line. We, however, strongly objected and the Midland Directors acquiesced.'

The Midland bowed to the ducal remonstration and, on 3rd March, the LNWR noted that Ramsden had written to say that the F&M line would proceed.

Building the Furness and Midland Joint Line
The tender for the construction of the F&M line was let to William Tredwell, who had built the original Furness line.

On 7th April 1864 Devonshire noted:

'I came up to London today to attend a meeting of the Joint Committee of the Furness & Midland line to receive tenders. The lowest was from Mr W Tredwell for about £104,000, £4,000 under McClean's estimate. We accepted this as he is said to be a respectable man. The highest was £35,000 more.'

However, after the discovery of an error in pricing, Tredwell, increased his quotation by £5,000 and the contract was cancelled. A new contract was let to Benton & Woodiwiss at £102,850 and, by June 1865, the earthworks were three quarters finished, although difficulties with the construction of the tunnel at Melling were being experienced. On 26th October 1865 meetings of the Furness board and the Furness & Midland Joint committee were being held at the Midland station, Derby and it was at these meetings that the decision to proceed with the Newby Bridge branch was made; this evidenced the Midland Railway influence in the construction of the FR line to Windermere. It was not until 10th April 1867 that the F&M line was completed and opened for goods traffic.

The Carnforth East Junction offices seen in 1955. Originally they were the station buildings at F & M Junction opened in 1868 when the road to it was completed. The station closed when the Carnforth Station Junction to Carnforth East Junction curve was opened in 1880. The buildings were then dismantled and re-erected at East Junction. East Junction box closed from 7th November 1998. (Author: MAC289/2)

The new line was inspected by Major C.S. Hutchinson on 17th April 1867[7]. It was found wanting in a number of respects including incomplete station buildings but the most significant problem was the Melling tunnel, which, in a number of places was up to 10 inches narrower than the clearances laid down in a Board of Trade circular. Hutchinson considered this a danger to the public as opening the carriage doors in the tunnel in an emergency would be impaired. Hutchinson re-inspected on 15th May and, although the other matters had been rectified, the Melling tunnel problem remained; he therefore declined to authorise opening for passenger traffic.

This decision prompted a report by McClean & Stileman, engineers to the F&M, dated 24th May, which showed that there was no danger to the public from the tunnel as it stood. This report, forwarded to the Secretary of the Board of Trade, led to the Railway Department having second thoughts about Hutchinson's opinion and it was agreed that the President of the Board of Trade, the Duke of Richmond, would receive a deputation from the Furness & Midland Railway led by the Duke of Devonshire. At the meeting, which took place on 28th May, it was agreed that the F&M line would be passed and the Board of Trade Memorandum on clearances be clarified in respect of tunnels. The line was opened for passenger traffic on 6th June 1867[8]. Devonshire noted, on 8th August 1867:

'We (the FR Board) went over the Furness & Midland line which had been open for some weeks. Mr Thompson [Harry S Thompson – FR Director, Chairman of the North Eastern Railway] thought the stations too expensive.'

The diverted 09.30 Manchester to Glasgow express hauled by D236 (40036) on the Furness & Midland line at Borwick on 23rd April 1965 during electrification work on the WCML. This station closed in September 1960. (CRA: Pearsall collection)

Melling station looking west on 21st April 1953 with lamp standards recently removed from the down platform. (CRA: Pearsall collection)

By the agreement between the Furness and Midland companies, signed on 8th August 1867, the Midland was to work all the traffic on the F&M line, for one third of the gross receipts, plus all local receipts, with the FR to maintain the permanent way at the expense of the joint committee.

The FR timetable for July shows a special train, leaving Carnforth at 12.50 for Piel Pier, to take passengers for the Isle of Man steamer. The *Barrow Herald* recorded:

> *'The Barrow Steam Navigation Co's splendid new paddle steamer Herald arrived at Barrow from the Clyde on 28th June 1867. On Monday last (1st July) she made her first run from Barrow to Douglas in three hours.'*

From 2nd September 1867 the Midland's Morecambe steamers *Roe*, *Talbot* and *Shelburne* were transferred to the Barrow Steam Navigation Company, a partnership of the Furness, Midland and Messrs James Little & Co. and commenced the service between Piel Pier and Belfast[9]. The 'Barrow Route' had been born.

A new station at Carnforth F&M Junction, built for through trains from the Midland Railway, opened on 1st July 1868, the F&M Carnforth station on Wharton Road being closed from this date[10]. The opening of the Devonshire Dock at Barrow and of the Furness & Midland Joint Line, in 1867, coincided with a general fall off in traffic. Receipts for the first half of 1868 were disappointing and capital expenditure was reduced as far as possible. Devonshire attended a meeting of the F&M Joint Committee at the Grange Hotel on 11th August 1868 and recorded in his diary:

> *'The cost of the line has been extremely heavy, greatly exceeding the estimate. The land in particular will in all probability, when all is paid for, come to nearly £50,000, the original estimate having been only £10,000. The traffic is very poor at present and has greatly disappointed us so far.'*

The LNWR exempted the Midland Irish traffic via Barrow from the 'shortest route' rule[11]. However, no running powers over the Furness line were ever negotiated by either the Midland or the LNWR companies, although through carriages from both were operated.

The Furness and Lancaster & Carlisle Union Railway

The Furness Railway's principal inland traffic was iron ore, bound for the iron-making districts of south Staffordshire, 200,000 tons being dispatched during 1862. This traffic was handed over to the LNWR at Carnforth, but with the opening of the South Durham & Lancashire Union Railway (SD&LUR) to Tebay, for mineral traffic on 4th July 1861, and for passengers on 8th August 1861[12], Durham coke was carried, by the LNWR, from Tebay to Carnforth, where it was transferred to the U&LR. The value of the SD&LUR to the Furness ironmasters had induced Henry Schneider, his partner, Robert Hannay, and others with Furness interests, to invest in the SD&LUR[13]. The subscription contract contained the following names:

Alexander Brogden, Ironmaster, Ulverston	£4,000
Henry William Schneider, Ironmaster, 14 Sussex Gardens, London	£3,000
Robert Hannay, Iron Ore Merchant, Ulverston	£2,000
Montague Ainslie, Ironmaster, Hawkshead	£2,000
Benson Harrison, Ironmaster, Ambleside	£2,000
Richard Roper, Ironmaster, Ulverston	£1,000
William Currey, Solicitor, 9 Old Burlington Street, London	£1,000
Frederick Iltid Nicholl, Solicitor, 18 Carey Street, London	£1,000
Bernard Gilpin, Surgeon, Ulverston	£500

These names represented the Brogdens, the Barrow Ironworks, the Newland Company and the Furness Railway.

As noted, in the context of the Furness & Midland Railway, the FR and the LNWR had good reason to remain on good terms, as both the Staffordshire and the Durham traffic were of mutual benefit.

Moreover, there had been a lull in the strife between the Midland and the LNWR companies, as the LNWR appeared disposed to admit the Midland to a joint lease of the Lancaster & Carlisle line. There had been rumours, in October 1862, that the Midland had plans to penetrate West Cumberland[14] and that the W&FJR scheme for a Duddon crossing, together with the

Solway Junction Railway, were part of a Midland plan to reach Scotland.

However, there is no evidence in the company records of such a scheme. The first note of the W&FJR intention to build the Duddon crossing was on 22nd September 1863, although a firm decision was not made until 10th October 1864, by which time the Midland were anticipating a joint lease, with the LNWR, of the Lancaster & Carlisle line and not until 1st February 1865 did the LNWR reject the terms of the Midland Railway for the L&CR lease.

The Parliamentary Session of 1864-65 was fateful for Furness and West Cumberland with both the Maryport & Carlisle and the Lonsdale controlled Whitehaven Junction and Whitehaven & Furness Junction Railways having ambitions to take over all the West Cumberland lines, whilst to the south, a potential dispute existed between the Furness and the LNWR companies. A vast area of Yorkshire, bounded by the Ingleton branch, the SD&LUR line, the Leeds Northern line of the North Eastern Railway and the 'Little' North Western remained unexploited by rail. Three schemes appeared in this session for lines through this area. The first two were not of direct interest to the FR. The Skipton, Wharfedale & Leyburn Junction Railway was to run via Grassington and Kettlewell to Leyburn; the North of England Union, from both Clapham and Hellifield via Hawes and Leyburn, to Darlington, with a westward branch to Sedbergh, on the Ingleton branch of the L&CR. The third line was of greater significance. The East & West Yorkshire Union line, with Nimmo & MacNay as engineers, was to start from the North Eastern Railway's Leeds Northern line at Melmerby, south of Northallerton, and run westward, via Hawes and Garsdale, to a triangular junction with the Clapham – Low Gill line south of

Sedbergh. Running powers over the L&C line to Barbon were sought, from where a separate section was to run to Arnside, on the FR, with junctions on the L&C main line near Milnthorpe, to provide for west to north and east to south traffic. Between Leyburn and Sedbergh, the East & West Yorkshire Union Railway and North of England Union Railway were in competition.

These two Bills came before a Parliamentary Committee of the Commons on 27th March 1865, by which time the western portion of the East & West Yorkshire Union Railway had been retitled the Furness & Yorkshire Union Railway, with an estimated cost of £145,000.

When the Committee reported, on 6th April 1865, the North of England Union Railway had been cut back to a line from Settle to Hawes, and the East & West Yorkshire Union Railway to a line from Melmerby to Hawes. Under the latter title it received Royal Assent[15], and was later revived by the NER to become the Melmerby to Masham and the Leyburn to Hawes branches. The Midland Railway, fresh from its break with the LNWR over joint use of the L&CR, took over the Settle to Hawes line of the North of England Union Railway, by an agreement dated 31st March 1865 as a springboard from which to reach Carlisle[16], but the Bill was withdrawn, for improvement of the levels, before submission in the following Parliamentary Session. James Ramsden was aware of the possibilities provided by the western section of the East & West Yorkshire Union Railway between Barbon and Arnside, now the Furness & Yorkshire Union Railway and, on 15th December 1864, he had written to Richard Moon, Chairman of the LNWR, enquiring the views of the LNWR on the topic[17]. The reply is not recorded, but Ramsden would no doubt have been advised of the LNWR petitions against the Furness & Yorkshire Union Railway Bill. The LNWR were, at this time, beginning to

Arkholme, the F & M station for Kirkby Lonsdale. A PW team is trying to do its best with some dubious looking ballast. (Ken Norman collection WM028)

A panoramic view of the Arnside to Hincaster line north-east of Sandside station, showing the attractive Bela Viaduct which sadly was demolished when the line went out of use, to fulfil a condition imposed by the owners of the Dallam Estate when it was erected. (Ken Norman collection NW759)

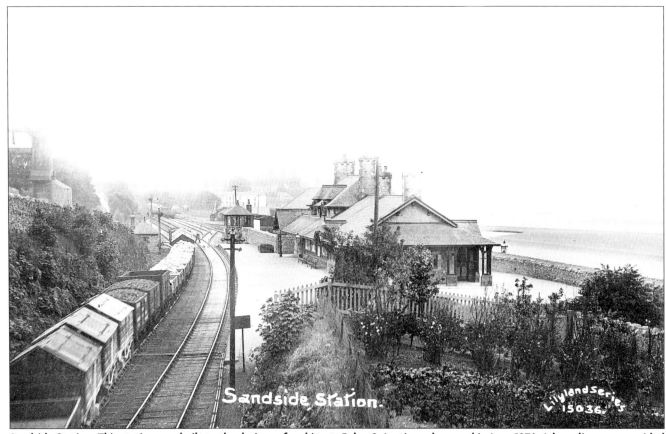

Sandside Station This station was built to the designs of architects Paley & Austin and opened in June 1876. A loop line was provided in 1908 to facilitate the movement of traffic to and from the adjacent quarry. In this postcard scene a trip train is moving from the loop into the sidings c.1920. (G. Holme collection GH456-5-4)

have doubts on the proposed joint lease, with the MR, of the Lancaster & Carlisle line, and on 1st December 1864 had noted *'Mr Allport has put forward claims which render it doubtful if the negotiations could proceed.'* The LNWR was also watching, from its vantage point on the Cockermouth, Keswick & Penrith Joint Committee, the rivalries in West Cumberland and learned, on 16th December, that the M&C Bill to amalgamate the West Cumberland lines would not proceed. It would be aware of the strong position of Lord Lonsdale in West Cumberland and of his dispute with the FR over the rival Duddon Crossing schemes. These complex West Cumberland rivalries are discussed in Chapter Seven.

However, nothing happened until March 1865 when events began to move swiftly. On 9th March, Lord Lonsdale suffered the defeat of his Bill for the lease, by the Whitehaven Junction Railway, of the Cockermouth and Workington line, and on 17th March the Furness Railway was beaten by the W&FJR over the rival Duddon Crossing schemes. On the same day the LNWR learned that the FR had decided to support the Furness & Yorkshire Union line:

'The Furness Company have changed their view with regard to it and are proposing to construct the line themselves, refusing to admit the LNWR to a share in the ownership.'

The FR board sanctioned the payment of £1,800 to the promoters of the F&YUR, on 23rd March 1865, and, on 6th April, the LNWR decided to offer the FR running powers to Tebay in return for similar powers over the proposed line, plus an agreement limiting the FR from promoting any lines east of the L&CR, for northbound traffic.

Devonshire had noted, on 23rd March:

'...came up to London yesterday afternoon. We had a meeting of the Furness Directors this morning to consider what course we should pursue in view of the failure of our Bill for crossing the Duddon ... We have also found it necessary to hold up another Bill introduced in this Session for a line from Arnside to Milnthorpe, The LNWR wish to have a share in it and may perhaps oppose us.'

On 4th May 1865 the LNWR Special Committee noted that the Furness Railway was to make the Furness & Yorkshire Union line, with the LNWR having running powers over it, in exchange for FR running powers to Tebay, an agreement with the FR to this effect being signed on 16th May.

The Furness and Yorkshire Union line went forward under the new title of the Furness & Lancaster & Carlisle Union Railway, and the FR/LNWR agreement of 1865 verified the abandonment of the line beyond Milnthorpe. The 1863 agreement with the Kendal traders, which had followed the Kendal & Ulverstone Railway proposal of 1863, was ratified, the Act receiving Royal Assent on 5th July 1865[18]. The LNWR now set about consolidating its friendship with the FR and invited James Ramsden to become a member of its Lancaster Local Committee, which, from 1866, managed both the L&CR, and the West Cumberland lines of the LNWR[19]. The LNWR and the FR then remained on good terms until the dispute over the WC&ER lease, in 1876.

After playing a significant role in the railway politics of Furness and West Cumberland, the Milnthorpe to Arnside line lapsed into relative obscurity, and, by 1869, during a period of depressed trade, which had led the FR to cut back on capital expenditure, its abandonment was proposed. This, not unexpectedly, led to opposition by the Kendal traders and an extension of time for completion of the line was granted. The FR had taken up its option to alter the route of the line, and, in 1867, had obtained powers to divert to the route of the Kendal & Ulverstone Junction Railway, between Hincaster and Arnside, as set out by Job Bintley.

On 1st May 1867, at Devonshire House, London, the Duke of Devonshire noted in his diary:

'We had a Wharncliffe Meeting of the Furness Railway this morning for the shareholders' approval of a bill vesting in the Company a short line from Arnside to Milnthorpe. It was in fact a matter of course and no opposition was offered from the few shareholders who attended.'

The FR Act 1867, of 20th June 1867[20], abandoned and dissolved the Furness & Lancaster & Carlisle Union Railway, authorising instead the Arnside to Hincaster Junction 'Kendal branch'.

The construction of the line was beset with difficulty. Soon after the contract had been let to Thomas Nelson of 89 Micklegate, York[21] the FR was in dispute, over the purchase of

Another postcard scene showing the single-platform station at Heversham with the approach path from the bridge carrying the A6, on which a single vehicle can be seen travelling towards Milnthorpe. Note the signal post carrying both up and down signal arms. (G. Holme collection GH229-7-4)

Heversham Party. The elaborate embellishments cast into the overbridge girder complement the smart FR No. 1 Saloon coach as it is about to be boarded by a group of distinguished travellers. (K. Norman collection N1435)

land, with George Edward Wilson of Dallam Tower, Milnthorpe (a noted antagonist of railways, who had petitioned against the NWR Milnthorpe branch). This dispute dragged through the courts delaying work on parts of the line. This, in the boom years of 1872-73, allowed costs to rise and, on 10th August 1875, the FR board allowed an increase of £5,000 in the contract price. Construction of the line was finally completed in 1876.

On 31st May 1876 Lt Col W. Yolland reported on his inspection of the new line[22] which described the line as single throughout but with sidings at the two extremes (Arnside and Hincaster Junction). A station was provided at Sandside. As the junction with the LNWR at Hincaster had not been completed, he had to re-inspect and his second report, dated 21st June 1876, sanctioned the opening of the line. Traffic commenced on 26th June 1876, but only a passenger service between Grange and Kendal and the local goods train, used the line, the coke traffic from the North Eastern Railway at Tebay continuing to run via Carnforth, a situation that was to continue until the First World War.

Devonshire, after a visit to the line on 26th September 1876, noted:

'This afternoon Frederick Howard (FR Director), Freddy and I met Ramsden at Grange and went over the newly opened Arnside Branch. The trains run between Grange and Kendal four each way daily. The traffic is rather better than we expected but of little importance. At present we have not arranged for the minerals from the North East to run over the line.'

On 10th February 1877 the FR board received a letter from the unfortunate contractor, Thomas Nelson, stating that he had lost £17,000 on the line and commenting that *'the hostility of the landowners was such as I have never met with in any contract'*. The board agreed to pay Nelson a further £8,000.

CHAPTER 10 REFERENCES

1   Lords Evidence Vol.36 F&G 1862.
2   25-6 Vic Cap 89.
3   FRDM, 9th Oct. 1862.
4   Parliamentary plan K1-1863.
5   Commons Evidence 1863 Vol.15 E2/F.
6   LNWR Special Committee 14751, 7th Mar. 1867.
7   PRO: MT29/28.
8   Greville M.D., 1953. "Chronological List of the Railways of Lancashire" in *Transactions of the Historic Society of Lancashire & Cheshire*, reprinted by R&CHS.
9   *Barrow Herald*, 24th Aug. 1867.
10   Meadows R. *MR Distance Diagram*.
11   LNWR Special Committee 14751, 7th Mar. 1867.
12   Baughan P. *Op. cit.*
13   PRO: Rail 1163/12.
14   LNWR Special Committee, 17th Oct. 1862.
15   28-29 Vic Cap 244.
16   Baughan P. *Op. cit.* p.138.
17   LNWR Special Committee, Minute 9674.
18   28-29 Vic Cap 329.
19   LNWR Special Committee, Minute 10679, 19th May 1865.
20   30&31 Vic C 104.
21   FRDM, 24th June 1871.
22   PRO: MT29/37.

LINES INTO LAKELAND

The Broughton extension of the Furness Railway opened in February 1848 to a terminal station in this small Furness town. The Whitehaven & Furness Junction Railway had abandoned its authorised line by way of a viaduct across the Duddon estuary and, by its 1848 Act, was empowered to deviate its main line to a junction with the Broughton extension at Foxfield, one mile from Broughton. By an agreement between the two companies, Broughton became a joint station.

The copper mining and slate quarrying area of Coniston was only eight miles to the north-east. These industries were of considerable antiquity. The Company of Mines Royal had mined copper ore in the sixteenth and seventeenth centuries and, from 1830 onwards, this industry had been revived by John Barrett. By 1849 his firm was employing 400 men, more than any Furness iron mine of the period[1].

The slate quarries of Coniston were of equal importance, with 10,000 tons of slate being shipped at the Ulverston Canal alone in 1828[2]. The copper and slate were transported by boat down Coniston Water, then by road, either to the port of Greenodd, to the Ulverston Canal, or directly to Angerton, near Foxfield, for shipment. On 12th December 1848 the FR agreed to carry copper ore for not more than 3s 6d per ton and to spend £500 on improving the road between Coniston and Foxfield.

In 1849, John Barraclough Fell, of Spark Bridge on the River Crake, who had a timber yard at Greenodd, proposed a 3' 3" narrow gauge tramway from Coniston to Broughton. The FR, having discharged Fell from his contract to build the Ulverston

extension was, due to the financial crisis of 1848, not in any position to consider such a proposal. However Lord Burlington, the FR Chairman, referred the matter to the company's consulting engineer, J.R. McClean, who recommended a standard gauge line at an estimated cost of £25,000. Burlington noted, on 8th November 1849, *'I fear it will not go on for want of funds.'*[3]

By 1856 trade had improved and, with it, the financial position of the Furness Railway. McClean and Stileman made a new survey for a line between Broughton and Coniston, their estimate of cost being £45,000. The FR considered that the Coniston merchants should make a significant contribution to such a line and, in consequence, the Coniston Railway was promoted as a separate concern. Dame Anne le Fleming, Lady of the Manor of Coniston and owner of the mineral rights, subscribed £4,000 and John Barratt's Coniston Mining Company £6,000. The Coniston Railway Act 1857[4] received Royal Assent on 10th August 1857 and provided for a fixed dividend of 2½% to the local promoters. The Furness Railway, through nominees Buccleuch, Burlington, James Walker, John lltid Nicholl, Stephen Eddy, William Currey and James Ramsden, provided the balance of the capital.

At a shareholders' meeting, held at the Waterhead Inn, Coniston on 27th August 1857[5], in the presence of Lord Burlington, Messrs Nicholl and Eddy (FR directors), James Ramsden and J.R. McClean, Ramsden was appointed secretary and McClean and Stileman engineers. On 7th November, at 9 Old Burlington Street, London, after a FR board meeting, the directors considered a number of tenders for construction of

The FR Rail Motor approaches the main (up) platform at Broughton c.1905. In the centre foreground is the down loop provided in 1903 to allow trains to cross without shunting into the Broughton sidings. (G. Holme collection)

A 1930s view of Woodland station looking towards Coniston. For many years the building on the left served as a post office to this scattered farming community. (CRA: Pattinson collection)

the Coniston line. The engineer had estimated £23,370 and the contract was let to Child & Pickles of Bradford, at a cost of £20,907, for completion by March 1859. The late 1850s saw a depression in trade and Child & Pickles were bankrupted, the line being completed by local contractors, amongst whom was William Gradwell, the Barrow timber merchant.

The original Furness Railway station at Broughton was sited on the level in what was later to become the goods yard. In connection with the building of the Coniston Railway, a new platform was constructed, on a rising gradient, to the north of the existing platform, on which a station building was constructed, designed by James Ramsden's brother John.

The line climbed on a gradient of 1 in 59, which steepened to 1 in 49 at the crossing of the Ulverston road. After 2¼ miles

Woodland Station was reached and the summit occurred near the Dalton road level crossing, some half a mile short of Torver Station. Thereafter the line fell to reach Coniston station, situated high above the village and lake.

At Broughton two roads were to be crossed on the level and certain Broughton residents, who objected to these level crossings, petitioned against them. However, another group, anxious that such objections might jeopardise the construction of the line, counter-petitioned and Lt Col. Yolland was sent to Broughton to look into the matter. His report, dated 14th April 1858[6], favoured the level crossings as authorised by the Act.

The Coniston Railway Company gave notice to the Board of Trade of its intention to open the line in May 1859 and Lt Col. Yolland inspected the line on 25th May. He found a single line of 8 miles 60 chains, laid with 60lb rails secured by inside keys. The signalling arrangements at Broughton were found wanting, the handles for the three signals not being concentrated together. A further inspection was carried out on 14th June and, on the understanding that the line would be worked by one engine in steam, with three block sections, opening for passenger traffic

A panoramic view of Coniston station looking east in the 1930s. A train of LMSR corridor stock stands in Platform 1. (Ken Norman collection N434)

Steam yacht Gondola was said to be designed by James Ramsden and was built at Liverpool by Jones, Quiggin & Co. Delivered to Coniston in sections, she was launched in October 1859. Gondola, in a rebuilt form, still sails on Coniston Water under the auspices of the National Trust. (Ken Norman collection N1362)

was sanctioned[7]. Yolland also noted that temporary stations had been erected and that tank engines would be employed, pending the construction of turntables.

The Coniston Railway opened on 18th June 1859 and was worked by the FR under a five-year agreement[8]. James Ramsden was appointed Manager at a salary of £50 per annum. On 30th July 1859 the Duke of Devonshire (former Lord Burlington) wrote in his diary:

'I went over our new Coniston line with Ramsden this morning. It has been open a few weeks for passengers and so far has answered our expectations. The views from the line are very beautiful.'

Devonshire returned to Coniston on 8th February 1860:

'We went up to Coniston and had a meeting with Mr Barratt to make arrangements respecting the copper ore about which he has been rather troublesome.'

On 8th August he was able to report:
'We had a beautiful afternoon for a sail in the Gondola at Coniston. The Coniston Railway is doing fairly.'

At the FR shareholders' meeting, on 18th August 1860, it was reported that the copper ore traffic had not yet started and that the FR had approved a loan of £10,000 to the Coniston Company at 4%, as the original estimates had been considerably exceeded.

The FR Act of 1862 included powers to raise £30,000 for the liquidation of the debts of the Coniston Company. At the same meeting at Chatsworth, which had agreed the purchase of the Ulverstone & Lancaster Company, the former Earl of Burlington, now 7th Duke of Devonshire, also agreed to the purchase of the Coniston Company and the terms that would be offered to the local shareholders[9]. The Furness & Coniston Amalgamation Act[10] received Royal Assent on 7th July 1862. The special 2% guaranteed shares in the Coniston Company were to receive dividends based on the ordinary share dividends of the Furness Company, 50% for two years, 66% for five years and 100% from 1869. From 1862 the Coniston Railway became part of the Furness Railway system.

The opening of the Ulverstone & Lancaster Railway on 1st October 1857, created a through route between Whitehaven and the LNWR system at Carnforth, but this through route was impaired by reversals necessary at Broughton and at Furness Abbey. In consequence the FR constructed 'expedition curves' at Foxfield and Millwood to allow direct running. These curves, inspected by Captain George Ross for the Board of Trade in June 1858[11], were opened for traffic at Millwood, on 1st July, and Foxfield, on 1st August. A joint W&FJR/FR station was

Loco No 41217 – one of Barrow's two push & pull fitted tank engines for use on the Coniston branch – propels its train out of the Foxfield up platform. Note the dwarf FR branch starter signals on the right. (Author: MAC189)

On 4th May 1963 58116 is ready to leave Greenodd for Haverthwaite with the Lakeside branch trip train. The station building is one of three designed by Paley & Austin for the branch. The signalman carries the tablet loop to hand to the driver. From Greenodd the branch was single-line worked by token. (Author: MAA113)

subsequently built at Foxfield and an agreement for the working of the joint station was signed on 1st January 1861. The north side of the triangle at Foxfield was used for a time for turning engines, but subsequently fell into disuse and was taken up.

The Lakeside branch

During the 1860s the activities of the Furness Railway were mainly directed towards the exploitation of the mineral traffic of the district, however, one line promoted in this period had tourist traffic in mind, foreshadowing a later era in the history of the company. Even so, the motivation for the building of the Lakeside branch had its origins in freight traffic. From the opening of the original Furness Railway in 1846, through coach connections had been provided, between Dalton and the foot of Windermere, to serve an existing steamer service on the lake and allow for the development of tourist traffic.

On 27th April 1847 the FR board recorded:

'Your Directors contemplate the extension of the line from Ulverston to Newby Bridge on Windermere and the establishment ultimately of a connection with Coniston Water.'

However this was before the financial crisis of 1848 and the disenchantment with passenger traffic. The Furness company was not alone in having plans for a line to the southern end of

Windermere, both the Ulverstone, Furness & Lancaster & Carlisle Railway and the Furness & Windermere Railway projects of 1845-46, took this route. The later Ulverstone & Lancaster Railway had also paid its engineer, James Brunlees, to survey a line to Newby Bridge.

It was, in fact, the construction of the Ulverstone & Lancaster line, which was to precipitate the construction of a line from Ulverston to Lakeside. The U&LR was sanctioned by Parliament only after a detailed examination by an Admiralty Court which reported on 17th February 1851[12], that *'an opening or swing bridge be provided'* to secure the navigation of the River Leven to Greenodd. In 1851 this was regarded as entirely reasonable but when the line was completed, in 1857, the opening bridge had become a major embarrassment to the railway (see Chapter Eight). Greenodd was a port with significant shipping traffic and accommodation for the storage of copper and iron ore.

John Barraclough Fell, the contractor who had been paid off the FR's Ulverston extension contract in 1848, had his sawmill at Greenodd. The Newland Company, Messrs Harrison, Ainslie &

Shortly after leaving Greenodd the trip train crosses the confluence of the rivers Crake and Leven on a curving viaduct, since demolished to make way for the A590 realignment. (Author: MAA102)

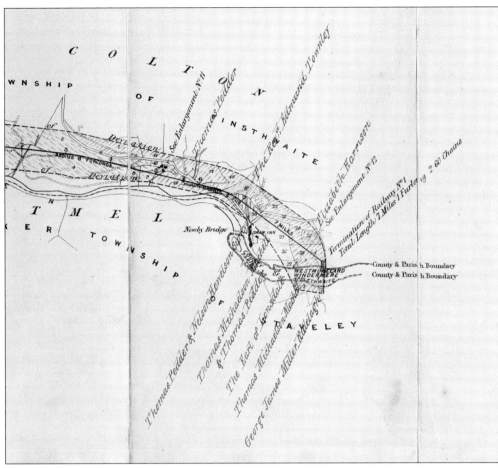

This small section from the 1866 Parliamentary plan for the Lakeside branch shows the original intention was to end the line at the rear of the Swan Hotel where the pier was to be provided for the lake steamers. (Private collection)

'I went to the Board of Trade today with Currey, McClean and Ramsden respecting the navigation of the Leven. The Greenodd people, to force us if possible to give them a railway, are trying to take advantage of a clause in the Ulverstone & Lancaster Act and I fear we may yet have trouble about it, but on the whole the interview was tolerably satisfactory.'

At this time negotiations with the Midland company were proceeding and the Furness & Midland Bill had received Royal Assent on 22nd June. The Midland was interested in access to the Lake District and, by August, the FR was asking McClean to examine the land between Cark and Newby Bridge for a possible new line of railway[13.]

Roper, exported iron ore through the port. Much as the FR would have liked to close the opening span in the Leven Viaduct, there could be no question of doing so without some agreement with the Greenodd traders. At the FR board meeting, on 25th March 1863, the directors sanctioned the doubling of the U&L line and received a report, from McClean & Stileman, on a line, two miles in length, from Plumpton to the shipping quays at Greenodd. McClean estimated the cost of this line at £10,644 and stated that the Greenodd merchants had agreed to the abandonment of the navigation to Greenodd, provided that the line was made.

Devonshire seems to have felt under pressure. He wrote, on 13th May 1863:

Relations with the Midland became cooler and nothing more was heard on the subject of either a branch to Greenodd or towards Windermere until 1865 when the doubling of the line over the Leven Viaduct was planned. In August 1865, the agreements with the LNWR having taken place, the FR once again asked its engineers to survey a line to Windermere and it cannot have been a coincidence that, at this time, Ramsden was instructed to approach the Midland Railway with a view to effecting an agreement for the removal of its Morecambe steamers to Barrow[14]. The next FR board meeting was held at the

Perhaps not a 'line into Lakeland' but the Stainton branch was certainly one into the country! Looking west at Crooklands, east of Dalton in the mid 1930s. On the left is the single line to the limestone quarries at Stainton opened in 1868. Limestone was carried by rail to Barrow Hematite Steelworks. The branch closed in October 1966 along with Dalton Station signalbox. (CRA: Pattinson collection)

The station buildings and veranda refreshment pavilion overlooking the lake steamer landing, seen in May 1963. Following the withdrawal of summer passenger services in 1965 the building was allowed to decay and demolition had taken place before the train services were revived by the Lakeside & Haverthwaite Railway Co. in 1973. (Author: MAA93)

Midland Station, Derby, on 26th October, at which McClean advised that a line should be built from Plumpton to Greenodd and on to Newby Bridge and that access to the Ulverston Canal, for Greenodd traffic, should be improved by the construction of a short branch from Ulverston station to the west side of the canal.

Ramsden and Stileman had seen J.B. Fell on 18th October and it had been agreed that Fell's premises at Greenodd should be bought by the FR, but that his plant should be returned to him. In return, Fell agreed to promote the FR's aims and, in particular, to try to get local agreement to the closure of the navigation to Greenodd so that the opening span of the Leven Viaduct could be eliminated.

The plans for the proposed Newby Bridge branch of the Furness Railway were deposited on 30th November[15]. The line was to run from a junction with the FR, at the west end of the Leven Viaduct, to Newby Bridge, where a pier was to be constructed. A curve was to be made at Plumpton to afford direct running between Barrow, Ulverston and the branch. In addition, a branch line was to leave the FR main line one half mile east of Ulverston station, descending on a gradient of 1 in 52, to reach the west bank of the canal. The estimates for the Bill were: main line and pier, £72,028; Plumpton curve, £4,835; Canal branch £5,470, making a total of £82,333.

The FR Act 1866 received Royal Assent on 16th July 1866[16] and sanctioned the closure of the opening span of the Leven Viaduct, once rail communication had been established between Greenodd and the Ulverston Canal. The capital to be raised was £300,000 plus the usual one third of this amount in loans. This massive sum was to enable the company to carry out a number of improvements in the Barrow area, to divert roads,

make bridges in lieu of level crossings, make a branch to the Stainton Quarry and construct a graving dock alongside the Devonshire Dock Basin at Barrow. By October 1866 the Newby Bridge contract had been let to Benton & Woodiwiss at £69,010 and James Ramsden cut the first sod in December[17.] The mineral branch from Crooklands to Crown Quarry, Stainton was opened on 5th February 1868[18].

By 1866 the economic climate had changed, the boom of 1864-65 had subsided and a period of general depression had set in. It was decided to make the Newby Bridge branch single line, but to extend it beyond the authorised terminus at Newby Bridge for a further 5 furlongs to the steamer landing at Lakeside[19]. By its 1866 Act the Furness Company had been empowered to take £10,000 in Windermere United Steam Yacht Company shares and, in August 1868, the FR ordered a new lake steamer from Seath & Co. of Glasgow[20].

Work commenced on a combined steamer and railway station at the landing, which was now titled Windermere Lakeside, in February 1869: William Gradwell, the Barrow contractor, carrying out the work for the sum of £4,461[21]. The line was opened for coal traffic to Greenodd in March 1869, allowing the FR to abolish the opening span in the Leven Viaduct[22].

On 3rd March 1869 Devonshire wrote:

'Edward (Lord Edward Cavendish) and I rode today to Newby Bridge and on to the landing where our Newby Bridge branch is to terminate. The progress made with the station is not as much as I hoped to see and altogether I am afraid we shall not be able to open the branch as soon as we had hoped.'

Haverthwaite is now the HQ of the Lakeside & Haverthwaite Railway and retains many of the features seen in this 1963 scene where Barrow goods engine 58116 shunts the yard. (Author: MAA114)

brought up a goodly number of passengers and also the indefatigable zealous and courteous Secretary of the FR, H. Cook Esq.'

The opening of Haverthwaite Station was delayed until 1st September.

However, the day after the Directors meeting on 9th August, Devonshire noted:

The contractor's locomotive used on the Lakeside end of the line crossed the Greenodd Viaduct for the first time, on 24th April 1869[23]. Col. C.S. Hutchinson inspected the line on behalf of the Board of Trade on 11th May. At 8 miles 21 chains in length, the line was single throughout, only the two junctions with the main line at Leven and Plumpton being double. Yet again the FR notice to the Board of Trade had been premature, the station buildings were incomplete, there were no clocks and the interlocking at the signalboxes was inadequate. Hutchinson declined to sanction opening for traffic and re-inspected on 2nd June, by which time the shortcomings had been rectified. The official opening had taken place on 1st June 1869 and it was reported in the *Barrow Herald* on 5th June 1869:

'No. 21 engine left Barrow about 7-30 gaily and beautifully decorated with evergreens, flowers, banners ... and from the centre of the engine rose an arch wreathed in flowers and surmounted by the Prince of Wales Feather. The train

'Today the Directors have been over the new line to Newby Bridge and Windermere and then up the lake in the new steamer which we have just built as joint owners in the Windermere Steam Yacht Company. From Ambleside we drove to Coniston and thence back by railway. We went ashore at Bowness and saw Schneider's new house.'

and on 21st March 1870:

'Edward and I went this afternoon up the Newby Bridge line to the Lake Side Station which I wished to see not having been there since the Autumn. It is a large building but perhaps not more than sufficient. It is now nearly finished. There is a very fair traffic on the branch and it seems likely that houses will be built near the station.'

In 1870 the FR doubled the branch as far as Greenodd Station[24].

While the line was under construction a crisis had occurred. In 1866, the year in which the Lakeside branch had been authorised, the Midland Railway obtained powers to build its Settle & Carlisle line, having failed to reach agreement with the LNWR over a joint use of the Lancaster &

The Lakeside branch could be accessed from both the Carnforth (east) direction and from Ulverston (west). The lines, respectively from Leven Junction and Plumpton Junction, formed a triangle which met at Greenodd Junction signalbox. From here to Greenodd station the two miles of the line was double tracked. (CRA: Pattinson collection)

A view of 1963 looking north of the approach to Lakeside station. On the right one of the lake steamers is seen berthed at the quay, showing the easy transfer between train and boat. (Author: MAA101)

Carlisle line. Late in 1867 antagonism to the Settle & Carlisle line was showing itself at the Midland Railway shareholders' meetings[25] and the culmination of this opposition was the formation of a Committee of Shareholders to examine MR capital expenditure. It was against this background that Devonshire wrote to the Midland Chairman, on 29th January 1868:

'It is rumoured that negotiations are in progress between the London & North Western and Midland Companies which it is not improbable may lead to the abandonment of the Settle & Carlisle line and an arrangement for admitting the Midland to the joint use of the Lancaster & Carlisle line including the branch from Kendal to Windermere. Under these circumstances it does not seem premature to remind you that the Furness Company is at considerable inconvenience constructing a branch to Newby Bridge mainly with a view to providing good access to the Lakes from the Midland District. There is certainly not any actual agreement between the Companies on the subject but there can be no doubt we have undertaken the line on such an honourable undertaking with you as justifies me in expressing a confident hope that our interests will not be disregarded but will be fairly protected in any arrangement you may make with the London & North Western Railway.'[26]

Hutchinson, the Midland Chairman, replied (using the Quaker convention for dates):

'Leicester 1st.Mo.31,1868 (31st January 1868)
'...at present there are no negotiations pending between the Directors of the two companies on the subject but Your Grace is probably aware that the Committee of Consultation appointed by the share holders at the Special General Meeting held on the 15th have had an interview with the Chairman and Deputy Chairman of the L&NWR at which a desire has been expressed on both sides for more amicable relations between the Companies. It is

impossible for me to say what may be the result of these communications between the parties, but I beg to assure Your Grace that any honourable undertaking which exists between the Furness and Midland Companies with regard to the Newby Bridge Branch will be respected by the Directors and its interests fairly protected should they enter into any negotiation with the London & North Western Company.'[27]

In the event, the abandonment of the Settle & Carlisle line was thrown out by Parliament and the building of the line went ahead. The Midland took advantage of its connection with the FR and ran services to Windermere Lakeside for many years.

CHAPTER 11 REFERENCES

1   Marshall J D. Op. cit. p.223.
2   Ibid p.46.
3   Ibid. p. 191.
4   20/21 Vic Cap 110.
5   PRO: Rail 129/1.
6   PRO: MT6/16/56.
7   PRO: MT6/19/56.
8   Melville J. & Hobbs J.L. Op. cit. p.50.
9   FRDM, 13th Nov. 1861.
10 25-26 Vic Cap 133.
11 PRO: MT29/19.
12 Parliamentary Papers 1851 Vol 29.
13 FRDM, 5th Aug. 1863.
14 FRDM, 10th Aug. 1865.
15 HLRO: Parliamentary Plan F4-1866.
16 29-30 Vic Cap 1172.
17 Barrow Times, 17th Dec. 1866.
18 Barrow Herald, 27th Oct. 1868.
19 FRDM, 7th Nov. 1867.
20 FRDM, 10th Aug. & 27th Oct. 1868.
21 FRDM, 12th Feb. 1869.
22 Barrow Herald, 27th Mar. 1869.
23 Barrow Herald, 1st May 1869.
24 FRDM, 25th May 1870.
25 Baughan P. Op. cit. p.154.
26 FRDM, 4th Feb. 1868.
27 Ibid.

FURNESS RAILWAY ROUTE DEVELOPMENTS 1868-1895

Approaching Salthouse Junction from Barrow Yard c.1966, a BR 9F 2-10-0 opens up to take the 2pm Carnforth freight up Lindal bank. (Author: MAO2808)

At 30th June 1868 the Furness Railway capital account stood at £2,397,158. Twenty years later it stood at £6,245,216 and was destined to increase to only £7,030,597 during the final 35 years of the company's independence. There was, however, very little expansion of the Furness Railway system during these years. In fact, in the early part of the period, traffic had fallen off (see Chapter Fifteen) and on 13th May 1868 the board reviewed its capital account liabilities. The engineers were requested to review particularly the company's liabilities in connection with the Duddon Crossing scheme, authorised by the Whitehaven & Furness Junction Act of 1865 and inherited by the Furness as a result of its take-over of the former company in 1866.

The engineers, McClean and Stileman, reported to the FR board on 27th October 1868, noting that £12,000 had already been expended on the Duddon Crossing and that a further £9,000-worth of material was on site. The total estimate was £75,000. They also noted that the doubling of the old route, via Foxfield, would cost £42,000 but this was not recommended as there was spare capacity on the existing single line. Traffic on the existing line was 30,000 ton miles of which 18,000 ton miles was Coniston traffic, leaving only 12,000 ton miles of Whitehaven traffic to be carried on the proposed viaduct.

Further, the reduction in mileage by 6½ miles would reduce the receipts by £5,500 per annum. The engineers summarised their findings as follows:

5% on cost	£4,250
Loss on mileage	£5,500
Additional maintenance	£650
Total	£10,400
Less saving on working expenses	£750
Net loss on viaduct	£9,650 per annum

This was a compelling case for the abandonment of the Duddon Crossing, but it did not relieve the Furness Company of its legal obligation to build the viaduct. The additional traffic needed to make the viaduct financially viable was estimated at 150,000 tons per annum and the prospect of this was highly questionable in view of the competition from coastal shipping plying out of Whitehaven and Borwick Rails. There was nothing for it but to seek Parliamentary sanction for the abandonment of the Duddon Crossing and the Park Loop. Therefore, late in 1868, a Bill was introduced for this purpose, which came before a Committee of the House of Lords on 7th May 1869. This situation was not without irony as the protagonists of the rival 1865

Bills for the Duddon Crossings – James Ramsden and Henry Cook – were now on the same side.

Petitioners against the Duddon Crossing Abandonment Bill were the Whitehaven, Cleator and Egremont Railway, the Furness Iron and Steel Company of Askam Ironworks and several local merchants. The Duke of Devonshire claimed that the FR had put forward their Duddon Crossing scheme with great reluctance, primarily as opposition to the plans of the Whitehaven & Furness Junction Railway, which were considered unsuitable by the Furness Railway. He further stated that the anticipated rail traffic in iron ore from the Hodbarrow Mine had not materialised as better arrangements had been made for the shipping of ore from Borwick Rails harbour. Further, the expected traffic southwards from the Cleator ironfield had not developed, as it had proved impossible to compete with the sea rates from Whitehaven harbour; only 6% of the Cleator iron ore traffic coming south by rail. Henry Cook stated that he had been convinced, in 1865, that it would be possible to reduce the through rates by 8d per ton to compete with the coastal shipping rates, but all that had happened was that the shipping rates had been brought down by the same amount.

The party with the most valid objection to the abandonment of the Duddon Crossing was the Furness Iron & Steel Company of Askam. E.T. Wakefield, for the Board of Directors, explained that his company had difficulty in obtaining iron ore in Furness, as nearly all the mines were the property of their rival, the Barrow Hematite Steel Company, therefore it was essential for them to obtain ore from Cumberland and, in particular, from the Hodbarrow mine. It was Wakefield's opinion that the Duddon viaduct would, without doubt, have reduced the cost of ore to his company. In the end the Committee made the FR agree to a rate of 1d per ton/mile for ore by the old route between Hodbarrow and Askam. Also, passengers would be charged rates as though the Crossing had been built. The Committee also conceded that the increase in siding accommodation at Barrow rendered the Park Loop line no longer necessary. The Bill which, in addition, contained powers to extend the Lakeside Branch from Newby Bridge to a steamer landing at Lakeside, received Royal Assent on 9th August 1869[1].

Another project, considered for abandonment, was the Arnside – Hincaster line, authorised by the FR Act 1867 and a Bill for this was drafted for the 1870 session of Parliament. However the *Barrow Herald* of 23rd April 1870 reported that the FR had withdrawn its Bill, having obtained an undertaking from the Cleveland ironmasters that they would support an application for an extension of time to construct the line.

In its policy of retrenchment, the Furness Railway was not alone. The Midland Railway board, as a result of pressure from a committee of shareholders, anxious to reduce capital expenditure following the cost of the London extension to St Pancras, had renewed discussion with the London & North Western Railway regarding the use, by the Midland, of the Lancaster & Carlisle line between Ingleton and Carlisle. However, the Settle & Carlisle Abandonment Bill was thrown out by Parliament in 1869, mainly as a result of the determined opposition of the Lancashire & Yorkshire and North British Railways, who regarded the Settle and Carlisle line as their independent route between England and Scotland[2].

However, the climate was soon to change for the better as, by the middle of 1869, business was beginning to pick up and, on 9th August 1869, Devonshire wrote in his diary:

'We had a meeting of the Furness Directors at Barrow

today. Fewer of the Directors were present than usual, only Mr Nicholl, Ramsden and myself , Currey, Stileman and McClean were also at the meeting. The revenue has increased considerably during the half year and the expenditure, except on permanent way, has somewhat diminished. We are not, however, able to have a better dividend than last half year as some further capital has come in for dividend and we have also cleared off considerable arrears of interest on the overdrawn balance of the Furness & Midland line. The Belfast Steamers are still a loss but they are improving and we have wiped off out of revenue a large part of the loss hitherto incurred. The Newby Bridge line and the Cleator & Furness are both open but not long enough to have much effect on the receipts. We nearly settled to go to Parliament this Session for powers to abandon the Arnside-Hincaster branch. ... There are a considerable number of vessels, some of them very large ones, in the dock and the warehouses are better filled than I had seen them before, chiefly with flour and Indian corn.'

At the FR shareholders' meeting in February 1870, Devonshire was able to report a considerable increase in traffic in the second half of 1869 and various capital projects were authorised, including the completion of the Buccleuch Dock. The first part of this project was the construction of a sea embankment between Salthouse and the south end of Barrow Island. Nearing completion towards the end of 1870 this was laid with rails to provide a new approach to Barrow station and give access to a steamboat pier in Walney Channel, with the ultimate view of superseding Piel Pier.

The new line, opened early in 1871, also provided a link with the Barrow Island lines, which had been built following the opening of the Devonshire Dock in 1867, thus giving rail access to the shipbuilding company's works and the sawmills of Price, Potter & Walker at the south end of the Buccleuch Dock.

But this was only the beginning of the expansion of rail facilities at Barrow. As early as November 1867, with the Devonshire Dock just open and the Buccleuch Dock not yet begun, Devonshire noted, on 7th November:

'McClean made a report to us on the subject of the approaches to Barrow and has a great scheme which he says would make Barrow the best harbour in England and would render it accessible at all times of the tide. The cost he estimates at £140,000. Of course we were not prepared at once to decide on so important a proposal.'

However, due to the depressed state of trade and the consequent reduction in capital expenditure, nothing was done until better times returned.

On the 8th August 1870 the Duke of Devonshire entertained fellow FR Directors; the Duke of Buccleuch and Mr Harry Thompson, chairman of the North Eastern Railway Company, at Holker. In the afternoon James Ramsden and William Currey joined the party for *'preliminary talk on business matters'*. The next day was described by Devonshire:

'We went over to Barrow this morning and had a meeting of Directors. Our earnings for the last half year have been good and would have enabled us to have a dividend of 10% but we thought it better to place £5,000 in a reserve fund and to increase the balance for the current half year. We therefore decided on a dividend of only 8%. We had not

much other railway business but we had a good deal of talk of starting a Shipbuilding Company and also a Company for building and owning a line of transatlantic steamers from Barrow.'

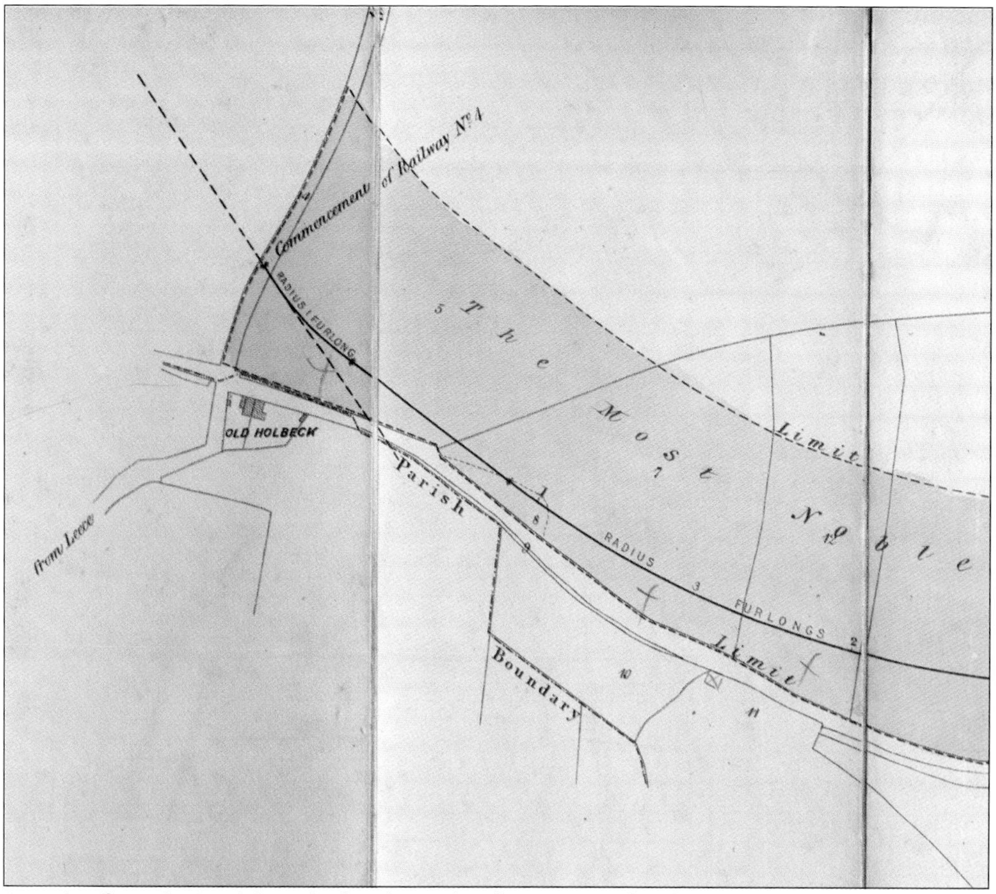

A section from the Stank branch plan shows the Gleaston Loop line (as the dotted line) bearing away from the branch, immediately after the bridge over Leece Lane at Old Holbeck, to climb at a gradient of 1 in 100 and pass north of Leece and south of Dendron.

The Barrow, Park and Gleaston Loops

At the shareholders' meeting in February 1871 it was announced that yet another dock was to be built at Barrow, the Ramsden Dock, which would be enclosed by an outer sea embankment running between Parrock Hall, on the original Piel branch, and Ramsey Island, south of Barrow Island[3]. The same meeting announced a much more significant railway project – the Barrow Loop line which was to run north-west from Salthouse Junction to a junction with the Hawcoat branch at Cocken. In connection with the Barrow Loop line a new main line, the Gleaston Loop, was to be constructed between Lindal and Salthouse, to relieve pressure on the old main line through Dalton. A branch from this line was to be made to the new iron mine at Stank[4].

A Bill for these purposes was introduced late in 1871. It was unopposed and included the following works and estimates:

Railway No. 1 Barrow Loop line (2m 1 furlong)	£36,000
Railway No. 2 Gleaston Loop line (6m 5 furlongs)	£89,007
Railway No. 3 Gill Brow Branch (Lindal) (9 chains)	£2,536
Railway No. 4 Stank Branch (6 furlongs)	£5,907
Railway No. 5 Whitriggs Branch (Lindal) (7 furlongs)	£5,900
Dock and Tidal Basin (Ramsden Dock)	£14,705[5]

However, the Gleaston Loop was removed from the Bill, except for that part of it as far as the Stank branch junction and the Stank branch itself. The truncated Bill received Royal Assent on 18th July 1872[6].

The exclusion of the Gleaston Loop was explained to FR shareholders at their February meeting in 1872. The *Ulverston Mirror* of 2nd March 1872 reported Devonshire as saying:

'The Directors had determined to apply to Parliament for a line between Barrow and Lindal but that would only partly meet the difficulty. They had another project under consideration which would relieve the traffic between Barrow and Ulverston.'

This new project generated misgivings in Ulverston relating to the loss of their main line status and possible interference with the Ulverston Canal. One week previously the *Ulverston Mirror,* reflecting the increasing feeling in the town that Ulverston's former dominant position in Furness was being usurped by Barrow, stated in its editorial of 14th February 1872:

'One of the Barrow papers, the Journal which owes its origins to the Furness Railway Company and is to be recognised by its close adhesion to any policy which the Company approves. ... The people of Ulverston are described as the slaves of antiquated prejudices who refuse to recognise the changes wrought by time and circumstance. We are accused of torturing into a grievance the plan for a single line tramway from Barrow via the South Furness coast through Bardsea to join the main line at Treadlow. For our part we see no effort whatsoever required to torture this matter into grievance. To those who believe in the motto 'Let Barrow flourish at the expense of everybody else' there will be no great wrong in carrying out such a project. If it was necessary to sweep Ulverston off the face of the earth because Barrow required some additional accommodation there would be no grievance at all from the Barrow point of view. The aspect as regarded by an Ulverstonian might be very different. It is pleaded that because the Furness Railway Company have more business than they know very well what to do with, it would be a sound measure of policy to construct a line on the route we have indicated ... Our reply is that as far as the town of Ulverston is concerned the construction of the proposed line would be utter ruination . . . Barrow may laugh at the suggestion that Ulverston may ever again become a port of any consequence but Ulverston must take care that whatever the future may bring forth. Barrow shall do nothing to cripple its chance.'

Devonshire, in his diary account of the FR Directors meeting on 7th November 1872, noted:

'We discussed several Furness Railway matters during the morning. We settled not to apply next session for a coast line from Ulverston to Barrow or for a loop line from Barrow to Park, both of which Ramsden thinks very desirable but we have too much on hand to engage in new undertakings.'

Nevertheless, the plan for a new main line, not a single line tramway, continued to mature.

In 1874 the Conishead Priory Estate was in the process of being sold off in lots for various purposes. William Gradwell, the Barrow building contractor, bought the Gascow limestone quarry and its Saltcoats tramway, connecting with the Ulverston Canal sidings. But of greater significance was a plan for a housing development which showed the *'proposed new line (Plumpton to Barrow)'* as a double line, with a station at Conishead Priory[7]. In the earlier scheme of 1872 work on the branch to Stank Mines was nearing completion in March 1873[8]. That the intention was to continue with the construction of a main line was strengthened by the fact that the road bridge over the line on the main road between Salthouse and Rampside, was built to double line dimensions.

The *Barrow Herald* of 27th November 1873 reported that a new passenger station for Barrow was to be built on the Barrow Loop line where it crossed the Abbey Road. Further, the Barrow Loop was to be extended to a triangular junction with the old main line at Park, a revival of the Park Loop line scheme of 1865-66. Plans also included a branch from Plumpton to Bardsea which:

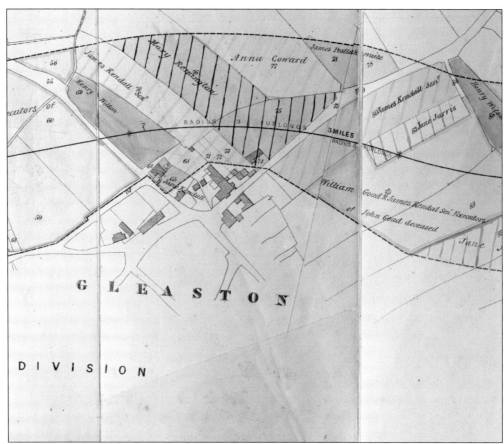

Gleaston village is passed quite closely to the north on a section of level track before the line began another ascent at 1 in 100 as it passes to the north of Gleaston Castle.

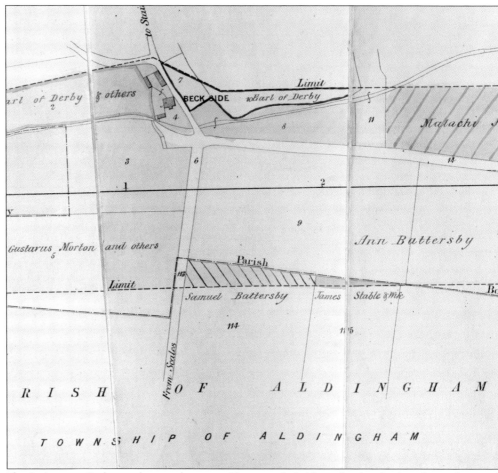

The Stainton to Scales road was to be crossed by an underbridge a few hundred yards south-east of the Beckside crossroads, before the line crossed all the burgage plots on the east side of Little Urswick to turn north and pass Great Urswick on the west side.

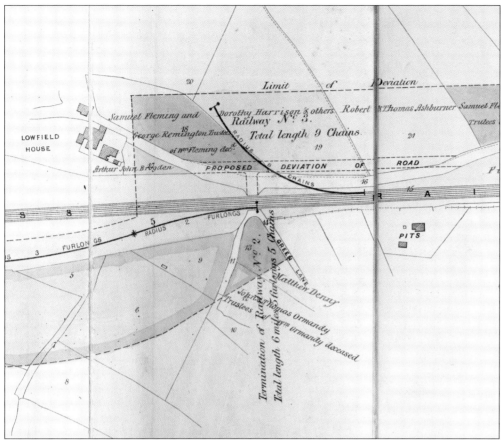

The proposed Loop line was to reconnect with the existing FR main line at Lowfield Bridge, east of the Lindal Ore Sidings. This would have taken the proposed line straight over the mine workings that later caused the collapse of the main line in September 1892. (Private collection)

the extreme south end of the Priory estate on or before 30th June 1875 and make available a station for goods before 30th June 1875. ... On the opening of the loop line from Plumpton to Barrow to provide accommodation for passengers and to stop all ordinary trains to take up and put down passengers at the station.'

Also to be provided under the agreement was a junction with William Gradwell's Saltcoats tramway and the provision of facilities at the junction. No charge was to be made on traffic passing from the tramway to the North Lonsdale Ironworks. This agreement was never signed, but was endorsed with dates two years later. Some later agreement must have agreed the sale of the land as the line was built to the south end of the Priory Estate, a station built at the Priory and a connection made with Gradwell's tramway from Gascow limestone quarry.

'is expected to be the nucleus of a new coast line to Barrow for the purpose of obviating the heavy gradients which are such an obstacle to the mineral traffic between Ulverston and Barrow.'

A Bill was introduced, late in 1875, but it only included a line from Plumpton Junction to a point some half a mile south of the proposed Priory station. A draft agreement of 1874, between John Poole of Ulverston and William Gradwell of Barrow (the vendors) and the FR Company was headed 'New Loop Line Plumpton to Barrow'.

In this agreement the FR undertook:

'...to complete the portion of the new loop line from the existing branch railway to the North Lonsdale Ironworks to

The Barrow Loop line, commenced in 1870, two years before Parliamentary sanction was obtained, was started at its north end with a junction with the FR Hawcoat Quarry branch. It served the new industries which were springing up in the area, including the new ironworks[9]. The decision to build a new passenger station on the Barrow Loop was made by the FR board on 8th August 1872.

A worsening financial climate led to a ruling, on 8th May 1874, that all work would be suspended. However, on 5th June 1877, a contract was let to William Gradwell for the building of the Salthouse Viaduct, which would carry the Barrow Loop over the Salthouse Road to reach its junction with the old main line at Salthouse Junction. On 23rd November 1878 the *Barrow Herald*

Barrow Central station, designed by Paley & Austin, opened on 1st June 1882. It replaced the Barrow station in the Strand, known latterly as Barrow Town. Left of centre is the ornate glass pavilion displaying the preserved 0-4-0 FR No. 3 "Coppernob". A train is leaving for Carnforth c.1912. (G. Holme collection GH452-7-5)

LOCAL RAILWAY TIME TABLE, FROM JULY 1, 1876.

UP.	WEEK DAYS.											SUNDAYS.					
	a.m.	a.m.	a.m.	a.m.	p.m.	noon	p.m.	p.m.	p.m.	p.m	p.m.	a.m.	a.m	p.m	p.m.		
Whitehaven (dep)	....	....	6 45	9 40	....	12 0	....	....	....	4 0	6 0	....	....	....	....	....	....
Millom (Holborn Hill)	....	....	8 10	1055	....	1 13	....	2 10	....	5 18	7 22	....	8 33	....	6 43	....	....
Foxfield Junction arr	....	....	8 27	1110	....	1 24	....	2 20	....	5 28	7 35	....	8 45	....	6 55	....	....
Coniston Lake (depart)	....	....	8 0	1040	....	1250	....	....	2 5	4 50	7 0	....	8 15	....	6 25	....	....
Foxfield Junction ,,	....	....	8 35	1115	....	1 29	....	2 20	....	5 30	7 38	....	8 50	....	7 0	....	....
Kirkby	....	....	8 41	1121	....	1 35	....	2 25	....	5 36	7 43	....	8 55	....	7 5	....	....
Askam	....	....	8 49	1129	....	1 43	....	2 35	....	5 44	7 52	....	9 8	....	7 18	....	....
Dalton	....	....	9 0	1140	....	1 53	....	2 50	....	5 55	8 3	....	9 18	....	7 28	....	....
Barrow Branch.																	
Furness Ab. arr.	....	....	9 25	1150	....	2 5	....	2 55	2 55	6 5	8 15	....	9 25	....	7 35	....	....
Roose ...... ,,	....		9 30	12 0	....	2 15	....	3 5	3 5	6 15	8 25	....	9 35	....	7 45	....	....
Barrow .... ,,	....	....	9 35	12 5	....	2 20	....	3 10	3 10	6 20	8 30	....	9 40	....	7 50	....	....
	am.	a.m	a.m.	a.m.	p.m.	p.m.		p.m.	p.m.	p.m.	p.m.	a.m.	a.m	p.m.	p.m.		....
Barrow ..depart	6 0	6 15	8 45	1125	1 15	1 40	2 50		4 30	5 45	7 50	6 45	9 0	4 45	7 10	....	....
Roose .... ,,	6 5	....	8 50	1130	1 20	....	2 55		....	5 50	7 55	6 50	9 5	4 50	7 15	....	....
Furness Abbey ,,	6 10	6 23	8 55	1135	1 25	1 48	3 0		4 38	5 55	8 0	6 55	9 10	4 55	7 20	....	....
Dalton .... ,,	6 15	6 28	9 10	1145	1 30	1 58	3 5		....	6 0	8 8	7 5	9 20	5 0	7 30		....
Lindal .... ,,	6 20	....	9 15	1150	1 35	....	3 10		....	6 5	8 13	7 10	9 25	5 5	7 35	....	....
Ulverston ....arrive	6 30	6 40	9 25	12 0	1 45	2 10	3 20		4 50	6 15	8 23	7 20	9 35	5 15	7 50	....	....
Windermere Branch.																	
Ulverston depart	....	....	9 30	1210	1 55	3 25	3 25		4 55	6 45	8 35	....	9 45	5 20	....	....	....
Greenodd	....	....	9 36	1216	2 1	3 31	3 31		5 1	6 51	8 41	....	9 51	5 26	....	....	....
Haverthwaite	....	....	9 42	1222	2 7	3 37	3 37		5 7	6 57	8 47	....	9 58	5 32	....	....	....
Lake Side, arrive	....	....	9 55	1235	2 20	3 50	3 50		5 20	7 10	9 0	....	1010	5 45	....	....	....
Bowness ,,	....	....	1050	3 15	3 15	5 0	5 0		6 15	8 0	....	....	....	....	....	....	....
Ambleside ,,	....	....	1120	3 45	3 45	5 30	5 30		6 45	8 30	....	....	....	....	....	....	....
Ambleside, dep	....	....	....	10 0	1140	1140	1 10		1 10	3 50	6 30	....	....	....	....	....	....
Bowness ,,	....	....	....	1030	1210	1210	1 40		1 40	4 20	6 50	....	....	....	....	....	....
Lake Side ,,	....	....	8 35	1130	1 15	1 15	2 50		4 10	5 25	7 55	....	....	4 45	....	....	....
Haverthwaite ,,	....	....	8 42	1137	1 22	1 22	2 57		4 17	5 32	8 2	....	....	4 52	....	....	....
Greenodd ,,	....	....	8 50	1145	1 30	1 30	3 5		4 25	5 40	8 10	....	....	5 0	....	....	....
Ulverston, arrive	....	....	9 0	1155	1 40	1 40	3 15		4 35	5 50	8 20	....	....	5 10	....	....	....
Ulverston depart	6 43		9 39	12 5	1 30	2 13	3 25		4 53	6 18	8 25	7 20	9 40	5 15	....	....	....
Cark and Cartmel ,,	6 58		9 45	1220	2 5	....	3 40		....	6 30	8 38	7 35	9 55	5 30	....	....	....
Kents Bank.... ,,	7 5		9 52	1227	2 12	....	3 47		....	6 35	8 44	7 42	10 2	5 37	....	....	....
Grange-over-Sands	7 10		9 57	1235	2 20	2 35	3 52		5 15	6 40	8 50	7 47	1010	5 45	....	....	....
Arnside........ ,,	7 17		10 4	1242	2 27	....	4 0		....	6 47	8 56	7 54	1017	5 52	....	....	....
Silverdale.. ...	7 25		1012	1250	2 35	....	4 8		....	6 55	9 4	8 2	1025	6 0	....	....	....
Carnforth, (F &M.) arr	7 35		1025	....	2 45	3 0	....		....	....	....	8 10	....	6 13	....	....	....
,, (L. & N.W.) ,,	7 40		1030	1 6	2 50	3 5	4 25		6 40	7 10	9 20	8 15	1010	6 15	....	....	....
Preston ......Arrive	8 35		1133	2 40	....	4 10	6 5		6 45	8 20	1020	....	....	8 15	....	....	....
Manchester L&Y ,,	10 0		....	5 5	....	5 20	8 0		8 30	1015	1130	....	....	10 0	....	....	....
,, L&NW,,	1015		1 0	....	....	6 5	8 5		8 5	9 50	1130	....	....	1248	....	....	....
L'pool, Lime-st ,,	1030		1 5	5 35	....	5 35	8 10		8 10	9 50	1145	....	....	1145	....	....	..
,, Exchange-st ,,	1010		1255	4 40	....	5 15	7 45		9 15	10 0	....	....	....	1010	....	....	....
Birmingham.... ,,	1230		3 40	6 25	....	8 27	1110		1110	2 30	2 30	....	....	2 30	....	....	....
London, Euston ,,	3 0		5 40	8 30	....	9 45	....		....	5 30	5 30	....	....	5 30	....	....	....

DOWN	WEEK DAYS.												SUNDAYS.				
	p.m.	a.m	a.m.	a.m.	a.m.	a.m	a.m.	a m	a.m.	a.m.	a m	a.m.	p.m.	a.m.	a.m.	p.m.	a.m.
London, Euston..dep.	9 0	....	....	....	....	5 15	7 15	7 15	9 0	1010	11 0	12 0	9 0	....	....	....	10 0
Birmingham .... ,,	1030	....	....	....	...	7 25	8 50	8 50	11 0	1140	1220	2 10	1030	....	....	....	1 5
Liverpool Lime-st ,	1235	....	....	....	6 0	9 30	1050	....	1 30	2 0	3 50	4 25	1235	....	....	....	3 45
,, Exchange-st ,,	....	....	....	....	6 25	9 0	1030	1030	1 25	2 45	4 10	4 15	....	....	....	....	1 0
Manchester L & Y ,	....	....	....	....	6 10	9 50	11 0	11 0	1 25	2 35	4 25	4 50	....	....	....	....	1 0
,, L & N W ,	1 0	....	....	....	6 0	9 25	11 0	11 0	1 30	2 0	3 55	4 20	1 0	....	....	....	...
Preston .... ,,	2 35	....	....	6 0	8 5	11 5	1230	1245	2 55	3 50	5 15	6 10	2 35	....	8 20	....	5 55
	a.m	a.m.	a.m.	a.m.	a.m.	a m.	p.m.	p.m.	p.m.	p.m.	p.m.	p.m.	a.m.	a.m.	a.m.	p.m.	p.m
Carnforth .. Depart	4 40	....	8 10	9 50	12 0	1230	1 30	2 30	4 0	5 0	6 5	7 30	4 40	....	9 45	....	7 30
(F. & M. Junct.) ,,	....	....	....	9 53	....	1235	....	....	....	5 5	....	....	....	....	9 47	....	7 32
Silverdale........ ,,	....	....	8 30	10 0	....	....	...	2 40	....	5 12	....	7 40	....	....	9 55	....	7 40
Arnside .... ,,	....	....	8 27	10 7	....	....	....	2 47	....	5 19	....	7 47	...	....	10 2	....	7 47
Grange over-Sands ,,	5 0	....	8 35	1015	1220	1255	1 50	2 55	4 25	5 25	6 20	7 5	5 0	....	1010	....	7 55
Kents Bank .. ... ,,	....	...	8 42	1020	....	....	....	3 2	....	5 32	....	8 6	....	....	1017	....	8 0
Cark and Cartmel..	....	....	8 51	1030	....	....	....	3 10	....	5 40	....	8 5	....	....	1025	....	8 10
Ulverston .. Arrive	5 21	....	9 5	1015	1240	1 15	2 10	3 25	4 45	5 55	6 40	8 20	5 20	....	1040	....	8 30
Windermere Branch.																	
Ulverston Depart	....	....	9 30	1055		1 55		3 25	4 55		6 45	8 35	....	....	1050	....	....
Greenodd .... ,,	....	....	9 36	11 1		2 1		3 31	5 1		6 51	8 41	....	....	1056	....	....
Haverthwaite ,,	....	....	9 42	11 7		2 7		3 37	5 7		6 57	8 47	....	....	11 2	....	....
Lake Side, W. Arr.	....	....	9 55	1120		2 20		3 50	5 20		7 10	9 0	....	..	1115	....	....
Bowness .. ,,	....	....	1050	1230		3 15		5 0	6 15		8 0	....	....	....	....	....	....
Ambleside ,,	....	....	1120	1 0		3 45		5 30	6 45		8 30	....	....	....	....	....	....
Ambleside Dep	....	....	....	8 20	10 0		1140	1 10	1 10	3 50	....	6 30	....	....	....	....	....
Bowness .. ,,	....	....	....	9 0	1030		1210	1 40	1 40	4 20	....	6 50	....	....	....	....	....
Lake Side, W. ,,	....	....	8 35	1010	1130		1 15	2 50	4 10	5 25	....	7 55	....	....	1015	6 0	...
Haverthwaite ,,	....	....	8 42	1017	1137		1 22	2 57	4 17	5 32	....	8 2	....	....	1022	6 7	....
Greenodd .... ,,	....	....	8 50	1025	1145		1 30	3 5	4 25	5 40	....	8 10	....	....	1030	6 15	....
Ulverston	....	....	9 0	1035	1155		1 40	3 15	4 35	5 50	....	8 20	....	....	1040	6 25	....
Ulverston .. Depart	5 20	7 0	9 5	1050	1243	1 18	2 13	3 25	4 50	6 0	6 40	8 25	5 20	8 20	1040	6 25	8 30
Lindal .... ,,	....	7 10	9 15	11 0	....	....	....	3 35	....	6 10	....	8 35	....	8 30	1050	6 35	8 40
Dalton ....Arr	5 35	7 15	9 20	11 5	....	....	2 20	3 40	5 2	6 15	....	8 40	5 35	8 35	1055	6 4[illegible]	8 45
Barrow Branch																	
Furness Ab'y ,,	5 45	7 20	9 25	1115	1255	1 35	2 25	3 45	5 10	6 20	7 0	8 45	5 45	8 40	11 0	6 5[illegible]	8 50
Roose ...... ,,	....	7 30	9 30	1125	....	....	....	3 55	....	6 25	....	8 55	....	8 45	11 5	6 5[illegible]	8 55
Barrow .... ,,	5 55	7 35	9 35	1130	1 10	2 20	2 40	4 0	5 20	6 30	7 15	9 0	5 55	8 50	1110	7 0	9 0
Barrow Depart	5 20	7 0	....	1045	1250	....	2 50	....	4 45	6 50		....	5 20	8 20	....	6 25	....
Roose ...... ,,	....	7 5	....	1050	....	....	2 25	....	....	6 55		....	....	8 25	....	6 30	....
Furness Ab'y Dep.	....	7 10	....	1055	1 0	....	3 10	....	4 53	7 5		....	....	8 30	....	6 3[illegible]	....
Dalton	5 35	7 20	....	1110	1 5	....	....	....	5 6	....		....	5 35	8 3[illegible]	....	6 40	....
Askam .... ,,	....	7 30	....	1120	1 15	....	3 20	....	5 18	7 15		....	....	8 4[illegible]	....	[illegible]	....
Kirkby .. .. ,,	....	7 38	....	1128	1 23	....	....	....	5 26	7 23		....	....	8 55	....	7 5	....
Foxfield Junction Arr.	5 55	7 41	....	1134	1 30	....	....	....	5 32	7 20		....	5 55	9 0	....	7 15	....
Coniston Lake ..Arr	....	9 15	....	1215	1 55	....	4 0	....	6 5	8 10		....	....	9 30	....	7 50	....
Coniston Lake ..Dep	....	....	....	1010	1250	....	....	....	4 50	7 0		....	....	8 15	....	6 25	....
Foxfield Junct.	5 55	7 45	....	1139	1 30	....	....	....	5 37	7 29		....	5 55	9 5	....	7 20	....
Millom (Holborn Hill)	6 5	7 57	....	1150	1 40	....	....	....	5 47	7 40		....	6 5	9 17	....	7 32	....
Whitehaven	7 15	9 20	....	1 10	....	....	....	....	7 0	9 0		....	....	....	....	....	....

Passenger services prior to the opening of the Barrow loop line.

reported that the FR had commenced the construction of a short loop from Salthouse Bridge to the new locomotive shed and onwards to the docks. On 10th July 1880 it reported that the curve between the Salthouse Viaduct and Salthouse Junction had been commenced, a curve from which a branch into the wagon works of S.J. Claye was constructed, running under the line to the locomotive shed.

The Furness Railway Act 1876[10] authorised an extension of time for the construction of the Arnside to Hincaster line, which had been seriously delayed because of the continued opposition of George Edward Wilson of Dallam Tower, Milnthorpe, who had first come to notice by his opposition to the Milnthorpe branch of the North Western Railway in 1845. The Act also authorised the following lines:

Railway No. 1 (2 miles 7 furlongs) from the Hawcoat Branch to the old main line north of Thwaite Flat (a renewal of the powers of the Park Loop line of 1865)
Railway No. 2 (5 furlongs) from No. 1 at Oak Lea to the Millwood Curve.
Railway No. 3 (2 furlongs 4 chains) a new curve between No. 1 and No. 2 at Thwaite Flat.
Railway No. 4 (2 miles 3 furlongs 9 chains) from Plumpton Junction to Bardsea via Conishead Priory.
Capital of £1,000,000 was authorised.

The Furness Railway shareholders' meeting, in August 1876, was told that there had been no revival in trade, that work on the Barrow Loop line had been restricted to earthworks and the Ramsden Dock construction slowed down. Towards the end of 1878 things were so bad in Barrow that soup kitchens were introduced to obviate the distress[11]. The depression continued, but the Furness Railway was able to maintain respectable dividends, on its increasing capital account, until 1879.

At the February 1879 meeting of shareholders, Devonshire painted a gloomy picture. The local iron industry was in an unprecedented state of depression and, to cap it all, the hard won joint ownership of the formerly prosperous Whitehaven, Cleator and Egremont Railway had proved to be running at a loss. This was the result of the need to expend capital on the line and the pressure to reduce rates because of the distressed state of the local iron industry[12].

At Salthouse Junction on 19th June 1957 Black Five 4-6-0 45295 heads an express on to the Barrow Loop line bound for Barrow Central. The Loop line opened in 1882. (Author: MAC22)

schemes as authorised in 1872 and 1876. At Carnforth, a 2 furlong curve was required to provide a much needed direct access from the Furness & Midland Joint Line into the LNWR & Furness Joint station. This curve was opened on 2nd August 1880 and allowed the closure of the inconvenient Furness & Midland Junction station at Carnforth[13].

Finally, the curve between Salthouse Junction and the original Piel branch at Parrock Hall Junction, to allow direct running to Piel from Barrow, which had been built without Parliamentary authority on Furness company land several years earlier in 1873, was formally authorised.

The original main line between Roose Junction and Parrock Hall had fallen into disuse and, on 27th March 1882, became the first part of the original line to close[14]. The 1881 FR Act authorised a further cut back in expenditure on the Park Loop line where, instead of the new curves authorised in 1876, a simple triangle was to be

The Furness Railway had a Bill in Parliament, in the 1879 Session, which contained three modest proposals for new lines. A small spur of 2 furlongs, between the Barrow Loop and the Park Loop at Cocken, was technically necessary to join the two

An up stopping train from Whitehaven hauled by 2P 4-4-0 40654 of Barrow (11B) shed coasts past the brick base of the former Cocken Jct signalbox c.1954. In the background is the massive slag bank of the Barrow Hematite Steel Co. (Author: MAC107)

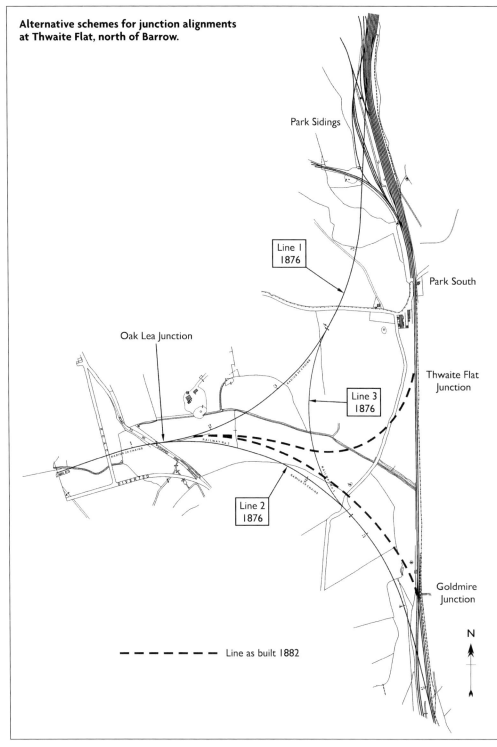

Alternative schemes for junction alignments at Thwaite Flat, north of Barrow.

Park Sidings

Line 1
1876

Park South

Oak Lea Junction

Thwaite Flat
Junction

Line 3
1876

Line 2
1876

Goldmire
Junction

N

– – – – – Line as built 1882

elected MP for the Northern Division of the West Riding of Yorkshire, a seat he held until his death. In 1864 he married Lady Lucy Lyttelton, related by marriage to William Gladstone, whose Private Parliamentary Secretary he became, in July 1872. From the post of First Secretary to the Treasury he was appointed Chief Secretary for Ireland, in May 1882, and it was only an hour or two after being sworn in that he was killed while walking in Phoenix Park, Dublin, with Thomas Burke, the Under Secretary for Ireland. Burke was the intended victim and Cavendish perished in an attempt to protect him.

Lord Frederick Cavendish was not a statesman or orator on the level of his elder brother Lord Hartington, but he was universally liked and trusted. His statue, the first to be erected opposite Barrow's new Town Hall, was moved to the Hindpool Road round-about outside Craven Park where he looked, appropriately, towards the latter-day Devonshire Dock Hall of BAE Systems, current owner of the Barrow shipbuilding works, the last survivor of the Cavendish/Furness Railway promoted industries[16]. He has now been returned to the Town Hall Gardens on the opposite side of the Town Hall from the original site.

Lord Frederick Cavendish was succeeded on the FR Board by his younger brother Lord Edward, whose son, Victor Cavendish, was to become 9th Duke of Devonshire and Chairman of the FR Company on the death, in 1908, of Spencer Cavendish, 8th Duke and former Lord Hartington.

constructed between the old main line at Goldmire and Thwaite Flat junctions. The contract was let to R Ward & Co for £18,983.

The opening of the Barrow and Park Loop lines and Barrow Central station was scheduled for 1st June 1882 and the appropriate notices were given to the Board of Trade. However, fate dealt the Furness Railway and Barrow a terrible blow when, on 6th May 1882, Lord Frederick Cavendish, Devonshire's intended successor to the Cavendish interests in Furness, was assassinated in Dublin[15]. The Furness district was plunged into gloom and the opening took place without formalities.

Frederick Charles Cavendish (1836-1882), the second son of William Cavendish, 2nd Earl of Burlington and 7th Duke of Devonshire, had been a director of the Furness Railway Company since 1863 and of the Barrow Hematite Steel Company and Barrow Shipbuilding Company since their formation. He was

The *Barrow Herald* of 27th May 1882 contained a full description of the new Central station, which put Barrow on a through line between Carnforth and Whitehaven. The '*changing and waiting at Dalton, which for so long has been such a nuisance to passengers .... will be done away with.*'

Major General C.S. Hutchinson inspected the new line, also on 27th May, on behalf of the Board of Trade[17]. He described a line of 5 miles 17 chains commencing at a junction with the existing main line at Salthouse and terminating at Thwaite Flat Junction near Park, with a double line curve of 27 chains connecting the new line with the Dock line, near Salthouse. He noted that a double line curve of 35½ chains, the Goldmire

THE FURNESS RAILWAY.

For several Trains not given in the Columns, see the statements at the bottom of the Columns.

UP	1	2	3	4	5	6	7	8	9 10	11 12	13	14	15	16	17	18	19	1	2	3-4	5

WEEK DAYS. — SUNDAYS

(Timetable data columns for stations from Carlisle to London, including Cockerm'th, Workington, Whiteha'n a, Whiteha'n, Corkickle, St. Bees, Nethertown, Braystones, Moor Rowde, Egremont, Sellafield, Seascale, Drigg, Ravenglass, Eskmeals, Bootle, Silecroft, Millom, Green Road, Foxfield, Broughton, Woodland, Torver, Conist'n La'e, Coniston L'd, Kirkby, Askam, Barrow C.S., Ram Dockar, Roose, Furness Ab, Dalton, Lindal, Ulverston, Greenodd, Haverthw'te, Lake Side, Bowness, Ambleside, Cark & Car'l, Kent Bank, Grange, Arnside, Silverdale, Carnforth, Kendal, Carlisle, Wennington, Skipton, Bradford, Leeds, Sheffield, Derby, London S P, Morecambe, Lancaster, Preston, Man. V., Liverpool Ex, Man. Ex., Liv. Lime St, Crewe, Birmingham, London Eu.)

☞ ON SATURDAYS ONLY a train leaves Barrow C.S. at 10·45 p.m.: Dalton, 10·55; Lindal, 11·0; arriving at Ulverston, 11·8.

Passengers services following the opening of Barrow Central in 1882.

curve, between the new line at Oak Lea Junction and the original line at Goldmire, had not yet been completed, but should be ready for traffic at the end of the month. He also reported that new signal cabins had been provided at Salthouse Junction, St Luke's Junction, Locomotive Junction, Buccleuch Dock Junction, Barrow Central Station East and West, Ormsgill Junction, Thwaite Flat Junction and Goldmire Junction. He recommended a number of minor alterations to the interlocking at these cabins, but stated that the line was safe for opening to the public.

The line duly opened on 1st June 1882 and in connection with this the Furness Railway produced a 'Description of New Signals etc on the new Line through Barrow'. [18] This document refers to Buccleuch Bridge Junction and Central Station South and North cabins, suggesting that, in his report, Hutchinson may have been confused by the lack of signalbox name boards.

On 22nd June Major General Hutchinson inspected the improvements at Park sidings where two new signalboxes – Park South and Park North – had been provided.

Frank Stileman, son of FR Engineer F.C. Stileman, reported to his father, on 10th October 1882:

'Henry Cook (FR Traffic Manager) and myself had accompanied Major General Hutchinson on a number of inspections and re-inspections. The Oaklea Curve was found to be satisfactory.' [19]

The Bardsea branch

The final line built by the Furness Railway, during this period, was the branch from Plumpton Junction to Conishead Priory. An account has already been given of the intentions of the Furness Railway, for a new main line between Plumpton and Barrow, but the FR Act 1876 authorised only the 2 miles 3 furlongs from Plumpton Junction to Bardsea.

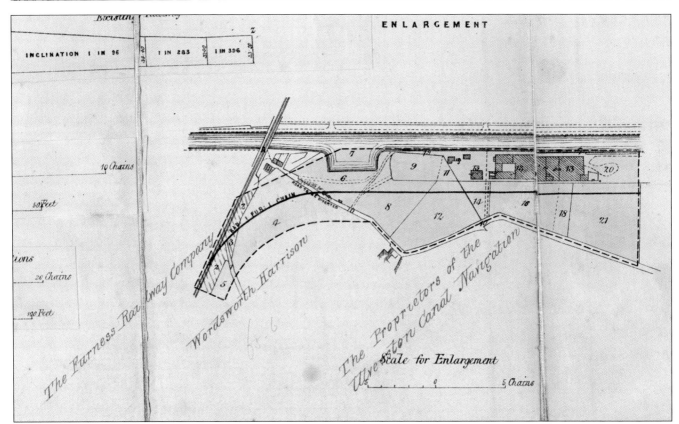

A Parliamentary plan, dated in 1866, shows the alignment of the steeply graded spur from the main line on to the west side of Ulverston Canal, which was eventually constructed in 1872. (Private collection)

The Ulverston Canal was already served by a branch from Ulverston, authorised by the FR Act 1866, a steeply graded line with a maximum gradient of 1 in 50, running from a trailing junction with the Furness down main line, east of Ulverston Station, to the west bank of the canal. The contract drawings[20] suggest that this line was constructed as late as 1870.

While the original purpose of this line had been to provide a rail route between Greenodd and the Ulverston Canal to facilitate the abolition of the opening span in the Leven Viaduct which would block the navigation to the port of Greenodd, its principal purpose had become a rail access to the various industries which had sprung up near the canal, the most important of these was to be the North Lonsdale Iron & Steel Company. This works was under construction in September 1874[21].

The main line ambitions of the Furness Company resulted in the Bardsea branch being constructed as a double line only to Priory, the most notable feature of which was the hydraulically operated, double line, rolling bridge over the Ulverston Canal, designed

by Westray & Copeland of Barrow. The engine house and accumulator tower, which survives, were designed by the FR architects, Paley & Austin, and built by the contractor for the line, William Gradwell[22].

The Bardsea branch, completed only to Priory Station for reasons of cost, was inspected by Major General Hutchinson and his report of 22nd June 1883[23] contains two interesting observations. First he states:

'This railway ... has been partially constructed and has been used as a mineral line for some years.'

However, Westray & Copeland's invoice to the contractor for

Priory station buildings remained intact when photographed in 1955 although the passenger service had ceased in 1916. The giant-sized PRIORY nameboard remains in situ. In more recent times the premises have been converted into an attractive residence. (Author: MAC155-1)

The SLS/MLS Furness Railtour on 27th August 1961 hauled by ex-MR 3F 0-6-0 43282 crosses the rolling bridge over the Ulverston Canal. This bridge was operated hydraulically from the opening of the Priory branch in 1883 but was secured in its closed position when navigation on the canal ceased c.1916. Traffic over the bridge ceased when the branch from Plumpton Jct to the Glaxo chemical works was closed completely on 18th March 2000. (Author: MAA95)

the ironwork of the canal bridge, is dated December 1880[24] and the FR capital accounts[25] indicate that very little was spent on the Bardsea branch until 1880. Hutchinson was, no doubt, referring to that part of the Bardsea branch between the west bank of the Ulverston canal and North Lonsdale crossing, which was built, in 1870, as the original Canal branch.

The second Interesting comment made by Hutchinson was that land had been acquired for four tracks, further evidence of the continuing intention of the Furness Railway to divert its main line via Bardsea, with a marshalling yard at Plumpton Junction. Boundary stones in the fields south of the line at Plumpton still stand as memorials to this abortive scheme. Hutchinson noted that there was only one station, that at Priory, with signalboxes at Canal Bridge, North Lonsdale Ironworks and Priory Station. He approved the opening for passenger traffic and finally reported that arrangements had been made at Plumpton Junction for the passenger train engine to run round its train. He agreed with the FR engineer that certain bridges needed strengthening before the heaviest freight locomotives could use the line. The line was opened for passenger traffic on 27th June 1883[26]. The *Barrow Herald's* FR timetable showed that two round trips per day were all that was offered to the public. Always under-used and with its passenger service reduced to one train daily, the section of the branch between the North Lonsdale ironworks and Priory Station was closed on 6th March 1916. The station building at Conishead still survives, in private ownership.

Latterly, the remainder of the branch was used for freight traffic between Plumpton Junction and the Glaxo Works, which was built on the ironworks site in 1948. The branch, together with the signalbox at Plumpton Junction, where it joined the main line, was formally closed on 19th March 2000, the last freight train having left Glaxo on 27th April 1994[27].

The Whitehaven line

The early part of the period under discussion saw the gradual extension of the double line from Ireleth to Sellafield, the junction between the Furness Railway and the Cleator and Furness line.

Devonshire wrote, on 14th March 1874:

'Freddy and I made and expedition up to Whitehaven today. A good deal has been done on the line since I was last over this part of it. It is now double line from the Abbey to Sellafield except for a short distance near Bootle and that will be completed very soon. A new station at Whitehaven is making progress and several new stations have been built at other places. The original ones were very poor.'

In his Report on the first half of 1874, the Engineer, F.C. Stileman, stated that the double line had been completed between Carnforth and Sellafield Junction[28].

W.B. Kendall, in his manuscript history of the Furness Railway and Barrow Harbour, gives the following dates for the opening of the sections of double line:

Seascale – Bootle	April 1872
Ireleth – Foxfield	December 1872
Foxfield – Millom	March 1873
Millom – Bootle	December 1873
Seascale – Sellafield	July 1874[29]

Station improvements

The period 1868-1895 saw a significant amount of station rebuilding, particularly on the Ulverstone and Lancaster and Whitehaven and Furness sections, where the originals had been somewhat rudimentary. Addressing the FR shareholders' meeting in February 1875, the Duke of Devonshire remarked:

'A good deal of expense has been on the old part of the line and in the improvement of the stations. Several of these

Askam station seen in 1974. The development of iron mines and an ironworks led to the emergence of a small town here in the early 1870s. An inadequate 'Halt' at Ireleth Gates was replaced in 1874 by this fine Paley & Austin building, now listed. (K. Norman collection)

stations, until lately, were in a condition of which the public had a right to complain .... On the White-haven line, especially, some of the stations were of a most inferior description.' [30]

The *Ulverston Mirror* had long campaigned to have such improvements made. In a leading article, on 18th September 1872, while accepting that the arrangements at Ulverston, Dalton and Furness Abbey were satisfactory, Ireleth and Millom came in for particular criticism.

There had been little at Ireleth but a level crossing until the Askam Ironworks was opened in 1865, after which an industrial colony developed. A public meeting, on 1st January 1868, petitioned the FR board for a station to serve the village's 2,000 inhabitants[31] and a platform was subsequently built. The *Ulverston Mirror* talked about Ireleth:

'It is the case that trains are sometimes so long that it is with great difficulty that travellers alight. Only the other day we saw two noble lords well known in the district performing the perilous feat of getting out of a first class carriage on to the bank.'

It went on, about Millom:

'It is, however, at Millom where the grievance is greatest. It is no uncommon thing for a crowd of passengers to be kept waiting in the wind and rain with no shelter other than a small wooden hut usually odiferous of tarry rope ends, oil cans and tobacco smoke. We would think it a blessing to the community if a squall from the sea or a sudden gust of wind down the Duddon Valley would sweep this execrable erection from its present position.'

Even the fine terminal station, built by the Furness Railway at Ulverston in 1854, became inconvenient after the opening of the Ulverstone and Lancaster Railway in 1857. The FR architects produced a splendid design for a new station at Ulverston, which retained the 1854 classical structure as a goods station. Work commenced in May 1873[32] and was completed the next year.

Prior to this, new stations had been built at Arnside (1862), Grange (1863-64) and Furness Abbey (1864-65). Until 1873 the division of trains, into Barrow and Whitehaven portions and vice

One leg of the original Furness system terminated at Dalton. Here the station is seen in the 1960s in the form that followed its rebuilding in the 1870s to enable it to cater for the exchange of traffic with the Whitehaven line, previously carried out at Furness Abbey. A down loop and an up bay were provided, the former serving also as access to the Stainton branch at Crooklands. (Author: MAO2701)

The down platform at Seascale opened directly on to the foreshore making this a popular destination for family outings and Sunday School trips by train. This Sankey image from LMS days shows the compact shopping facilities on the seaward side of the railway which supported the later residential developments promoted by the Furness Railway Co. inland of the station. (Sankey archive: D51)

versa, had been carried out at Furness Abbey station with its down loop and up bay.

In 1873 the platforms and track arrangement at Dalton station were reconstructed on the Furness Abbey pattern and, from 1st May, Dalton became the junction for Whitehaven. The terminal station at Ramsden Dock was extended, in 1885, and a new signalbox provided[33].

One further plan from this period should be recorded. This was for a new seaside resort at Seascale.

On 10th August 1870, the day after they had discussed a ship-building company at Barrow, the FR Directors went to Seascale for a meeting with some directors of the Whitehaven, Cleator & Egremont Railway:

'After luncheon we walked over some of the adjoining land which had been secured with a view to some building on a small scale. There is good bathing and a fine open sea and I think it not unlikely a moderate number of lodging houses may answer. Probably also some Leeds people and others may be induced to build there.'

The upper plan (BRO) shows the scheme for a substantial residential development at Seascale drawn up for the FR by Kemp of Birkenhead in 1879. The lower plan, included in a sale prospectus for the Scawfell Hotel, shows how little had been achieved by 1898.

After a FR directors meeting at Barrow on 12th February 1878 Devonshire reported:

'After our business was over we went up to Seascale where we have at last got possession of some land on which we have long proposed to encourage building operations. We have reason to believe that several persons are desirous to

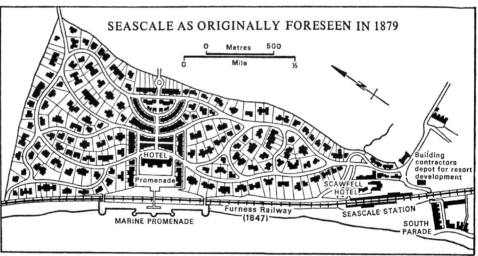

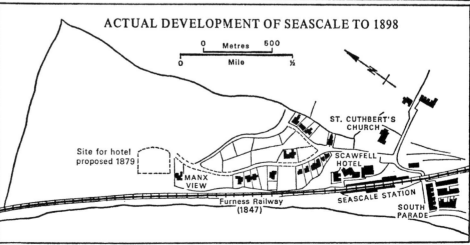

build there and there seems a fair probability that the thing will answer. It does not seem to me to be a very attractive place but it is probably the best on this part of the coast.'

The Furness Railway purchased the Seascale Estate, in 1878, for £4,000[34]. A plan, dated 20th December 1878, shows the proposed residential development, the building of an hotel, a

marine promenade and a pier. This proposal was slow to develop and, it was not until 1914 that a refreshment room was added to the down side building at Seascale station. Hopes that Seascale would develop, as had the Cavendish investment at Eastbourne, were never fulfilled.

Seascale Station Master Atkinson. (G. Holme collection)

CHAPTER 12 REFERENCES

1   32-33 Vic Cap 154.
2   Williams F S. *Op. cit.* p. 184.
3   *Barrow Herald*, 25th Feb. 1871.
4   Ibid.
5   HLRO.
6   35-36 Vic C.99.
7   BRO: Andrews Collection, Plan BD/MA242.
8   *Barrow Herald*, 8th March 1873.
9   FRDM, 25th May 1870.
10 39-40 Vic C. 47; Royal Assent, 27th June 1876.
11 *Barrow Herald*, 22nd Nov. 1878.
12 *Barrow Herald*, 1st Mar. 1879.
13 PRO: MT6 255/4 and 1195/3.
14 FR Signalling Notice.
15 *Barrow Herald*, 9th May 1882.
16 *Dictionary of National Biography*.
17 PRO: MT29 43/187.
18 Geoff Holme collection.
19 PRO: Rail 214/73.
20 BRO: Plans E163, E261 & E263.
21 *Ulverston Mirror*, 5th Sep. 1874.
22 BRO: Plans E348 & E171.
23 PRO: MT6 359/5.
24 Author's collection.
25 FR Capital Accounts (BRO).
26 FR Report, Aug. 1883.
27 CRA Journal, Vol.6 No.16.
28 *Barrow Herald*, 22nd Aug. 1874.
29 *Kendall MSS*. Ref ZK133.
30 *Ulverston Mirror*, 6th Mar. 1875.
31 *Barrow Herald*, 4th Jan. 1868.
32 *Ulverston Mirror*, 16th May 1873.
33 PRO: MT6 387/4 3.6.1885.
34 FRDM, 12th Feb. 1878.

Several members of the Seascale station staff stand outside the booking office and waiting rooms on the up platform as a goods train heads north on the down line in the early 1900s. (G. Holme collection)

The photographer was standing more or less above the arch through which the road passes and shows the station, looking north, with the platform buildings and footbridge in place. On the right is the Scawfell Hotel. The signal is one of the Furness Railway lower quadrant type. The short siding on the up side would be for the loading and unloading of parcel vans. (G. Holme collection)

The photo below shows some of the facilities for handling goods traffic. Vans could be propelling into the goods shed for loading and unloading to a raised platform on the right. A hand operated crane was available to lift heavy objects and space was left for transfer of materials from rail to road vehicles. While the goods shed and water tower survive, the Scawfell Hotel, station buildings, original Vicarage and the cricket pavilion are now all memories. (G. Holme collection)

THE FURNESS RAILWAY AND BARROW INDUSTRY

The Furness Railway directors and their associates had played a dominant role in the creation of the Barrow Hematite Steel Company and, by 1868, no fewer than five of its seven directors were from the Cavendish/FR group (see Chapter Nine). The boom in the iron trade, which started late in 1869 and the huge profits which resulted, led this group to extend its ambitions to include further industrial development at Barrow.

As early as 14th March 1868, the *Barrow Herald,* with its uncanny knack of foretelling the future, was hinting at the possible construction of a shipbuilding works. In November 1869 it was forecasting a jute mill and construction of this commenced in May 1870.

However, it was not until early 1871 that the foundation of the Barrow Shipbuilding Company was effected. Devonshire wrote, on 22nd March 1870:

'The proposed Jute and Flour Mills will be commenced very shortly and there seems no doubt that a shipbuilding works will follow. We walked over Barrow Island and Ramsden explained his ideas as to the site of the shipbuilding yard and also as to that of a better class of houses which seem to be much required.'

(The latter became Cavendish Park.)

On 9th August he reported:

'At a FR Directors Meeting we had a good deal of talk about starting a Shipbuilding Company and also a company for building and owning a line of transatlantic steamers from Barrow. Mr Little and a Mr Duncan, a shipbuilder on the Clyde, have a favourable opinion of the proposal.'

The first provisional meeting of the Barrow Shipbuilding Company was held at Ramsden's residence, *Abbot's Wood,* on 28th January 1871[1]. The Duke noted:

'Frank (Francis Egerton – his son-in-law) and I have been at Ramsden's today to attend the first meeting of the Directors of the Shipbuilding Company just established there. It was attended by Mr Duncan, who is to be Managing Director, Mr Little and Mr Robertson, the General Manager. All the arrangements for proceeding at once are pretty nearly completed and there are already a good many men at work levelling the site. The outlay at present ... is about £92,000, £42,000 of which is for machinery of various kinds and £40,000 for buildings. After the meeting all of us except Ramsden who is confined to the house went to Barrow Island to inspect the site.'

Even before that meeting, on 31st December 1870, the *Barrow Herald* noted that Mr Stewart Robertson had been the subject of a presentation, by the staff of Caird's engine works, on his departure to be managing director of the Barrow Shipbuilding Company. This company was registered on 18th February 1871 with a capital of £100,000[2].

Thus, as early as the beginning of 1870, consideration was being given to the needs of both the commercial and shipbuilding facilities provided by the Barrow Docks. The tonnage of the vessels, which the Barrow Shipbuilding Company proposed to build, was indicated by its contracts with the Eastern Steamship Company:

Duke of Devonshire	3,001 tons
Duke of Buccleuch	3,005 tons
Duke of Lancaster	3,010 tons
Duke of Argyle	3,013 tons
Duke of Sutherland	3,012 tons[3]

By comparison, the cross-channel boats built at Barrow were smaller:

Duke of Connaught (LYR/LNWR)	1,082 tons
Ben-my-Chree (IOMSPCo.)	1,031 tons

This view, looking north at Hindpool South signalbox c.1959, shows Barrow ironworks and the west side of the steelworks. Centre is the double line of track leading to Hindpool North. (Author: MAA48)

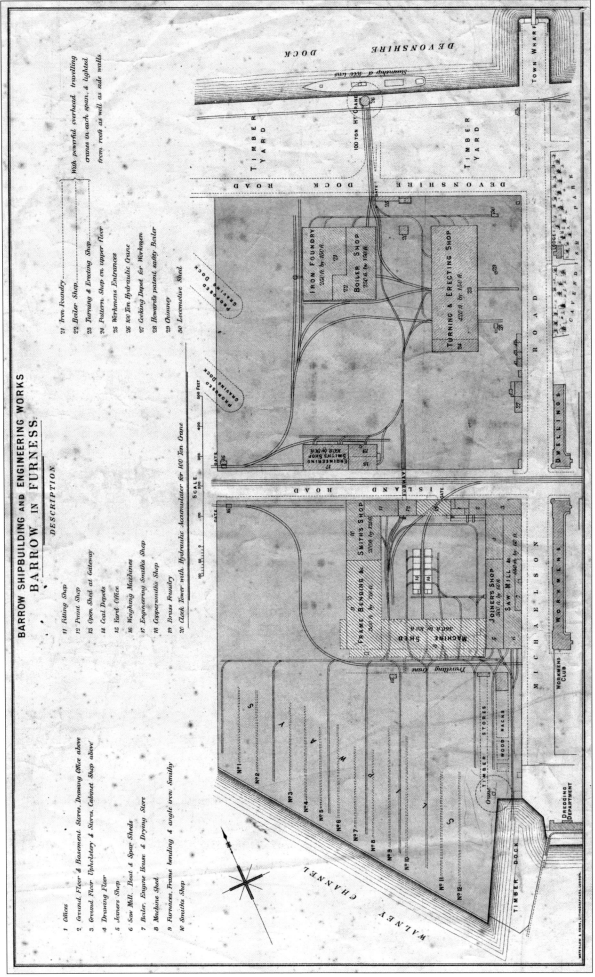

BARROW SHIPBUILDING AND ENGINEERING WORKS
BARROW IN FURNESS.
DESCRIPTION.

1 Offices
2 Ground Floor & Basement Stores, Drawing Office above
3 Ground Floor Upholstery & Stores, Cabinet Shop above
4 Drawing Floor
5 Joiners Shop
6 Saw Mill, Boat & Spar Sheds
7 Boiler, Engine House & Drying Store
8 Machine Shed
9 Furnaces, Frame bending & angle iron Smithy
10 Smiths Shop

11 Fitting Shop
12 Paint Shop
13 Open Shed at Gateway
14 Coal Depots
15 Yard Office
16 Weighing Machines
17 Engineering Smiths Shop
18 Coppersmiths Shop
19 Brass Foundry
20 Clock Tower with Hydraulic Accumulator for 100 Ton Crane

21 Iron Foundry
22 Boiler Shop
23 Turning & Erecting Shop
24 Pattern Shop on upper floor
25 Workmens Entrances
26 100 Ton Hydraulic Crane
27 Coking Depot for Workmen
28 Howards patent safety Boiler
29 Chimney
30 Locomotive Shed

With powerful overhead travelling cranes in each span. & lighted from roofs as well as side walls.

An early ground plan of the Barrow Shipbuilding Company's works. The slipways and the cranage access to the fitting out berths in Devonshire Dock is still very similar today in spite of the construction of the submarine build hall which now occupies the north-west end of the Dock.

On the goods lines north of Barrow Yard was Cornmill Crossing signalbox, seen here in 1954. On the left is Barrow Steam Cornmill built in 1874 with capital provided largely by the FR directors. (Author: MAC46)

The Barrow Companies' finances and the Duke of Devonshire

The Eastern Steamship Company was itself a new venture with a capital of £500,000 of which Devonshire subscribed £25,000. Its purpose was to trade between Barrow, India and China by way of the Suez Canal and no doubt the proposed jute mills were seen as a major contributor to its traffic[4].

The next year, a plan to take over the Allen Line, then trading between Liverpool and Canada, was not successful but, in 1872, the Ocean Steamship Company was formed, to trade between Barrow and America, with a capital of £1m, of which Devonshire subscribed £100,000 and Lord Frederick Cavendish £25,000. The newly knighted Sir James Ramsden, now well established as a capitalist, subscribed £10,000. The rest of the capital came from established shipowners, including Thomas Henderson of Glasgow, who had already been approached to take space in the projected new Ramsden Dock for his Anchor Line[5].

The year 1873 saw Barrow and the Furness Railway at the zenith of their prosperity with the iron trade in a vigorous state and ore and iron prices at unprecedented levels. Bessemer pig iron had more than doubled in price, from 83/- per ton in 1870, to 195/- per ton in mid-1873. Wages and prices were generally inflated, which added to the cost of both capital projects and operations. Towards the end of 1873 some unease was being expressed in the iron trade and by the end of 1874 the price of iron had reverted to 90/- per ton. In June 1874 Sir James Ramsden warned the Furness board that traffic was falling off and that the dividend would be affected. In fact 6¾% was paid. In March 1875 the FR board, having carried out an examination of the company's capital liabilities, resolved that:

> 'No Capital expenditure be hereafter undertaken without a careful estimate having been previously prepared and submitted to the Managing Director who will submit this to the Board.'

As a result, capital projects were slowed down.

The decline in the iron trade, with its inevitable impact on both the Furness Railway company and the various enterprises of the railway/steelworks syndicate, was causing alarm bells to ring. William Currey wrote a letter to the Duke of Devonshire, on 13th June 1876 which included the following:

> 'The financial position of the Barrow companies ... is a question which requires very serious consideration, affecting as it does an amount of property belonging to Your Grace which has of late years arrived at such proportions as to make the security and protection of it of the greatest importance.

> 'Your Grace's investments in Barrow may be roughly stated as:

The Furness Railway	£450,000
The Steel Company	£525,000
The Shipbuilding Company	£225,000
The Jute Company	£61,000
The Steamship Company	£185,000
altogether say a million and a half.	

In 1857, the Directors of the Railway, in appreciation of James Ramsden's services, decided to provide him with a residence worthy of his position. The mansion, Abbot's Wood, complete with home farm and lodges was sited on a wooded hillside overlooking the ruins of Furness Abbey. Built of the local red sandstone and roofed with Kirkby slate, the total outlay by the Company was "not to exceed £2,000." The main house was demolished in the 1960s. (K. Norman collection N959)

'The accounts of all these Companies, except the Steamship Company, are very largely overdrawn as follows:

The Furness Railway	£100,000
The Steel Company	£170,000
The Shipbuilding Company	£170,000
The Jute Company	£120,000
in all some £600,000.	

In providing the requirements of these Companies, Your Grace has borrowed £240,000 from the London and Westminster Bank. You have, on my advice, borrowed a further £180,000 from the Equitable Society and I should prefer that the latter be used to reduce the former so you would be in a position to approach the London and Westminster in the event of any emergency.

'Unless the tendency of looking to Your Grace to meet every emergency which may arise in Barrow is checked and the financial arrangements are placed on a sounder basis, it is certainly possible that misfortune might occur. I would ask you therefore ... to insist on a more systematic regulation of the financial arrangements of the Barrow Companies.

'I have already protested against the system which has been followed. There should be a strict limit to each Company's overdraft which should not be exceeded without your authority.

'I am inclined, after full consideration, to withdraw the recommendation I made to Your Grace last year about the sale of the Railway. Unless some Barrow Companies could be taken over with the Railway, which I doubt is possible, I would advise you to retain control of the Railway.'

It did not take Devonshire long to concentrate his mind. He wrote to Ramsden from Devonshire House, Piccadilly on 19th June 1876:

'My dear Sir,
The financial position of the various Barrow Companies is such as to give me a good deal of anxiety. Their accounts with the Banks are largely overdrawn and as I know from past experience, that generally leads to my having a large sum of money to provide. It is clear that sufficient attention has not been given to the question of finance, which from the magnitude of the Companies is of serious importance. I am advising therefore that meetings of the Directors should be held at Barrow every three months at least and that there should be given special attention to the financial position of each Company.

'A strict limit must be fixed from time to time on the amount to which the bank account may be overdrawn; this limit must not be exceeded without authority from me or someone authorised by me to give such permission. Lord Frederick will make a point of being present on occasions when I do not myself attend.' [6]

This correspondence indicates the massive personal financial involvement of the Duke of Devonshire in the Furness Railway and the Barrow Companies. It also provides further evidence on the little documented possibility of a sale of the Furness Railway to the Midland Company.

The Barrow Companies struggled on as the depression in trade continued, but the problems of the Shipbuilding Company were more than could be attributed to the state of trade. Devonshire noted on 10th August 1875:

'I have been to Barrow again today with Freddy and Edward. We had a meeting of the Shipbuilding Company. The Accounts for the last half year have been made up and are very unsatisfactory. There has been a loss on every ship and also on Howard's boilers. Mr Howard was there and spoke out strongly about the mismanagement of the concern under Robertson. As we have got rid of him I hope matters will now improve but I am not very sanguine. Freddy made some strong remarks on Duncan's neglect in allowing such mismanagement and he had little to say in the way of excuse. Ramsden also is, in my opinion, by no means free from blame. We saw our new general manager, Mr Humphry. He seems to understand what he has to do.'

The shipbuilding company had to raise a further £200,000 in March 1877 and Devonshire took this up in total. He noted, on 12th March 1877:

'The Works have done better this year but we are still in a very anxious position and it will clearly be necessary for me to find a great deal more money to prevent a smash.'

In 1878 the Barrow Shipbuilding Company wrote its £25 shares down to £10, but there were, surprisingly, no catastrophic company failures or personal bankruptcies.

The FR dividend for the second half of 1878 had been 5%, the lowest since 1857, but worse was to come. Receipts for the first half of 1879 were £34,868 less than for the corresponding period in 1878 and the dividend was declared at 3%, harking back to the long-forgotten days of the late 1840s. The *Preston Herald* [7] had some harsh words to say:

'A portion no doubt of the diminution of the divisible funds of the Directors is fairly attributable to the depression in trade but something is also due to the extraordinary policy pursued by the Directors. We have on several occasions pointed out what we believe to be errors in management and predicted that sooner or later the Company would feel the effects of the mistakes which have been made ... it is a matter of notoriety that the energy and attention of the management has been concentrated towards Barrow to the neglect of other places on the line where traffic needed development.'

The Iron and Steel Industry

The position of the Furness iron trade in the late 1870s was set out in a joint letter, dated 17th August 1878, from the Cumberland Iron Mining & Smelting Co. Ltd, Millom, the Furness Iron & Steel Company Ltd, Askam, the Carnforth Hematite Iron Co. Ltd and the North Lonsdale Iron & Steel Co. Ltd, Ulverston. The letter, signed by Thomas Massicks, William Crossley, Edward Barton and E.G. Tosh, on behalf of those companies was addressed to Henry Cook at the Furness Railway, Barrow-in-Furness:

'At a meeting of the undersigned representing the various

Vickers' shipyard 0-4-0 saddle tank *"Jupiter"* approaches Walney Ferry signalbox with a train of empty ship plate wagons c.1960. (Author: MAA41-1)

urgently called for in the interests of both local smelters and the railway companies, we think, on the following grounds sufficiently evident:

In Cleveland and South Wales where hitherto the market for hematites have been almost in the hands of West Coast makers, the introduction of Spanish ores at very low prices have enabled these districts to not only supply their own needs but to oppose us directly in other steelmaking centres and indirectly by themselves in manufacturing steel rails the raw material for which was previously drawn wholly from the West Coast.

The recent heavy reduction of iron ore rates in the Whitehaven District have had the effect of placing that district in many respects superior to our own. With generally better shipping facilities, easier rates on coke and cheaper ores in addition to the above mentioned relief granted on ore rates by railway companies they are able as far as foreign trade is concerned to leave us far behind . . .

In asking for these concessions we believe that a liberal policy on your part will not only greatly relieve us but will be found to react to your benefit.' [8]

ironmaking firms held on 2nd. inst. It was resolved that in view of the present depressed state of their industry, application be made to the Directors of the Furness Railway Company for a reduction of 10% on all iron ore rates, such reduction to date from the 1st July last. That important modifications of these and other rates (as affording the only direction in which further economies are possible) are

The FR board minutes record no response to this plea, but a 10% reduction in rates seems to have been made. However, on 20th May 1879, J.T. Smith attended the FR meeting for the purpose of urging, on the Directors, the claims of the ironmasters for a further reduction in rates. Smith had written to Sir James Ramsden from Barrow Ironworks on 12th May:

'A concession of 10% was made in 1878. We are compelled to approach you again for further reductions. The price of pig iron has steadily gone down and has for some time been entirely unremunerative. The depression of the trade

An aerial view of Barrow iron and steel works c. 1930. The ironworks, in the foreground, was opened in 1859 and the steelworks added in 1864. In that year the ironworks, steelworks and Park iron mines were amalgamated as the **Barrow Hematite Steel Company.** (K. Norman collection T407)

The signalbox at Hindpool North controlled the sidings at the north end of the iron and steel works. Seen in 1955, an ironworks locomotive is propelling a short train of slag tippers to the top of the slagbank. (Author: MAC75)

fate of thousands of immigrants to the booming town whose suffering gave the greatest cause for concern. The *Barrow Herald* of 23rd November 1878 noted that the Mayor, Edward Wadham, the civil engineer and agent for the mines of the Duke of Buccleuch, had called a meeting:

and the more perfect development of the Spanish ore mines admit Welsh and East Coast country ports importing at a price which enables the iron smelters of these places, they have good coke on the spot, to produce pig iron for steelmaking purposes and also steel itself under conditions which threaten to reduce materially the West Coast hematite trade and has already closed several important steelworks at Sheffield and elsewhere who were hitherto supplied from this district ... All business now offering is at a rate which entails a loss.'

Smith concluded by referring to the new process for converting Cleveland pig iron into steel which threatened the hematite trade with severe competition.

The board deputed Ramsden and Cook to investigate the cost of a further concession on rates and this was, in fact, agreed retrospectively on the ironmasters' accounts for 1878 at a cost to the FR of £25,000 loss of revenue, of which no less than £15,000 was from the Barrow Hematite Steel Company, whose shareholders were largely those of the Furness Railway itself.

As if to prove the point, the Furness Iron & Steel Co., of Askam Ironworks, went into liquidation in August 1879 owing the FR £13,000. However, an upturn in trade came to the rescue. The FR shareholders' meeting in February 1880 was advised of this and a 4% per annum dividend was approved which was increased to 6½% at the August 1880 meeting. The short-lived boom of the early 1880s led to a final flush of capital expenditure, mainly directed towards the Barrow Docks.

Taking the wider historical view of the late 1870s, it was the

'...to consider what steps should be taken to establish a soup kitchen or adopt other means to relieve the present distress in the town.'

The employees of the Furness Railway reluctantly agreed to accept a 5% reduction in wages.

On the other hand some slight sympathy must be entertained for the position of Sir James Ramsden. Having started out on his course to create a new town, an expanding source of employment and a fortune for himself, he was forced to keep the evolutionary process going in spite of the cyclical fortunes of the iron trade. Further, having embarked on the creation of Barrow as a port and later a centre of the shipbuilding industry, he became caught up in the inexorable progress of shipbuilding technology where the tonnage of both naval and merchant vessels was increasing. To continue to be viable, Barrow docks had to be adapted to deal with these increasing tonnages.

The Cavendish/FR interest in the Barrow companies withered slowly. Paradoxically, the constantly ailing Jute Company was not disposed of by Cavendish interests until 1897, but the Barrow Shipbuilding Company was re-constituted, in 1888, as the Naval Construction and Armaments Company and sold to Vickers, Son and Maxim in 1897, whilst the Barrow Hematite Steel Company passed gradually into east coast interests. A full account of the role of the 7th Duke of Devonshire in the financing of the Barrow companies can be found in Sidney Pollard's paper *'Barrow-in-Furness and the Seventh Duke of Devonshire'*. [9]

The line over Barrow Island, from Devonshire Bridge to Shipyard Junction on the Dock line, provided access to the various workshops of the Barrow Shipbuilding Company. Formed in 1871, the shipyard's founders were mainly FR board members. A BR diesel shunter passes Walney Ferry signalbox with a trip train to the modern Vickers shipyard on 11th October 1973. (Author: MAO3806)

CHAPTER 13 REFERENCES

1 Marshall J D. *Op. cit.* p.343.
2 Ibid. p. 344.
3 Harris N., 1989. *Portrait of a Shipbuilder: Barrow-Built Vessels from 1873* p.197.
4 Marshall J.D. *Op. cit.* p.344.
5 *Barrow Herald*, 13th July 1872.
6 L.R. Gilpin, personal communication.
7 Quoted in *Barrow Herald*, 16th Aug. 1879.
8 FRDM, 24th Sep. 1878.
9 Pollard S., "Barrow-in-Furness and the Seventh Duke of Devonshire" *Economic History Review*, Dec. 1955.

CHAPTER FOURTEEN

BARROW DOCKS AND FURNESS RAILWAY SHIPPING SERVICES

Barrow Pier c.1862 before the enclosure of the Devonshire and Buccleuch Docks. Far right is the recently completed St George's Church. (G. Holme collection N1425)

The Barrow Docks, as authorised by the Furness Railway and Barrow Harbour Act 1863[1], comprised the enclosure of the Barrow Channel between the mainland and Old Barrow Island, from Hindpool in the north to an embankment running from Salthouse to the south end of the Island. However, at the time of the formal opening of the docks on 19th September 1867, only the Devonshire Dock, between the tidal basin at Hindpool and the Low Level Bridge at Barrow Town pier, had been completed. South of this point, the Barrow railway pier remained open to the tide and to shipping until the Buccleuch Dock was created by the completion of the Salthouse embankment.

The Duke of Devonshire opened the sluices between the Devonshire and Buccleuch docks on 9th September 1868[2].

Meanwhile James Ramsden, in the chair at the FR shareholders' meeting in August 1867, reported that the Devonshire Dock was opening at a time when the shipping trade was in a very depressed state[3], and a further problem was reported by the FR engineer:

'The present structure of Piel Pier is unfit for carrying out the Irish and Isle of Man steamboat traffic.'

A tender by Lander & Mellanby for £10,354 was accepted for the necessary improvements at Piel. The *Lancaster Guardian* of Saturday 28th March 1868 contained an editorial on Piel Pier:

'The many disadvantages under which Piel laboured as a place of departure for the Irish Steamers are being gradually removed. A small time since, a small gas-works was built on the island and this enabled the Furness Railway Co. to light the pier with gas which was much needed. Another great inconvenience was that the train could not convey the passengers close to the vessel. This is now remedied by the new pier which runs parallel with the old one and is of the same level throughout. It is constructed entirely of wood

with the exception of about 100 yards near the shore and that is formed of slag and other refuse from the ironworks making a solid embankment. A station and waiting room are attached to the extremity so that every convenience is now afforded to the numerous passengers who avail themselves of the facilities offered by the short sea route.'

The Duke of Devonshire observed, on 10th August 1868:

'Piel Pier is now nearly finished and the arrangements seem very good.'

Early in 1870 consideration was being given to a further dock extension at Barrow. The Furness Railway consultant engineer drew up plans for an extension of the docks from Buccleuch Dock to a basin east of Roa Island which had the advantage of reducing the dredging requirements in the Barrow Channel. However, an alternative scheme was for the enclosure of a large tract of sand by the building of an embankment between Roose and Barrow Ramsey Island at a cost of £26,000[4]. This latter plan was adopted.

The Duke of Devonshire noted, on 31st May 1870:

'We decided on ordering a new and more powerful dredger to deepen the approaches to the docks from Piel and afterwards dredge the bar. We also propose to deposit the material between Barrow and Ramsey Islands with a view to forming an additional dock. It will be necessary to lay down a line of rails from Salthouse to bring stone and pitch to the bank.'

The Furness Railway Director's meeting on 8th February 1871 referred to this plan as the Ramsden Dock. The cost included:

Basin at Ramsey Island	£65,000
New steamboat quay	£17,000

Dredging	£28,000
Total including extras	£166,750

The same meeting authorised the sale of 50 acres of land on Barrow Island to the newly-formed Barrow Shipbuilding Company on deferred terms.

The contract for building the Ramsden Dock basin was let to William Hanson who had successfully completed the difficult Meathop contract on the Ulverstone and Lancaster Railway some years before[5].

On 12th June 1871, with traffic rising, the board authorised the expenditure of £16,644 for the completion of the Buccleuch Dock. The *Barrow Herald* of 22nd July 1871 recorded:

'Our docks are being extended and completed with the utmost despatch. The graving dock is in the course of construction at the western end of the harbour, Buccleuch

Dock is undergoing an extensive improvement employing 150 men and two locomotives.'

In August 1871, the FR engineer reported to the shareholders' meeting:

'About one quarter of the excavation has been removed to form the Buccleuch Dock and the timber wharves are well advanced. The contract for the Ramsden Dock Basin has made satisfactory progress.' [6]

However, it was not until towards the end of the year that the FR deposited its Bill for the dock works: F.C. Stileman's official estimate, dated 30th December 1871, was for £323,500. The same Bill also included the Barrow loop line, the mineral line from Salthouse to Stank, two short branches at Lindal and the replacement of several level crossings by bridges and new roads. The

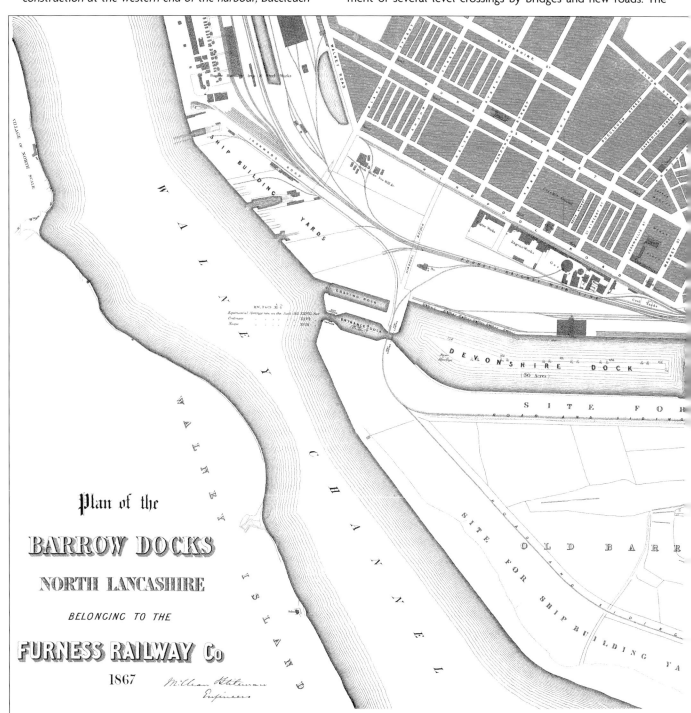

Furness Railway Act 1872[7] received Royal Assent on 18th July 1872 and authorised new capital of £1m, plus £333,000 in loans. The graving dock was opened on 1st August 1872.

Work on the Buccleuch Dock continued and, in August 1872, the FR shareholders were informed that the south side wharves had been completed. Covering an area of 33 acres, the Buccleuch Dock was formally opened on 14th February 1873. The *Barrow Herald* of 15th February reported:

'The caisson was removed from the communication between the Devonshire and Buccleuch Docks about noon and a short time afterwards the 'Dione' steamed through having on board His Grace the Duke of Devonshire, Lord Frederick Cavendish, Sir James Ramsden, Mr William Currey and Mr Stileman and others. After steaming the whole length of the Dock the party disembarked at Messrs. Price, Potter and Walker's new sawmills at the south end where

the special train was waiting for them. The new dock will have a communication with the Ramsden Dock now in course of construction by an entrance basin 100 ft. wide.'

On 18th June 1873 the steamship *Duke of Devonshire* was launched from the yard of the Barrow Shipbuilding Company, the first of the steamers for the Eastern Steamship Company. The *Barrow Herald* of 21st June reported:

'These ships are to constitute what will be known as the 'Ducal Line' to trade between London, Barrow and Calcutta. The ship is of 3,050 tons displacement.'

The FR contracted the Barrow Shipbuilding Company, on 10th August 1874, to build the Ramsden Dock gates for £44,644 and, by 1st December 1876, the FR board was predicting the completion of the Ramsden Dock by the autumn of 1878, with £150,000 being

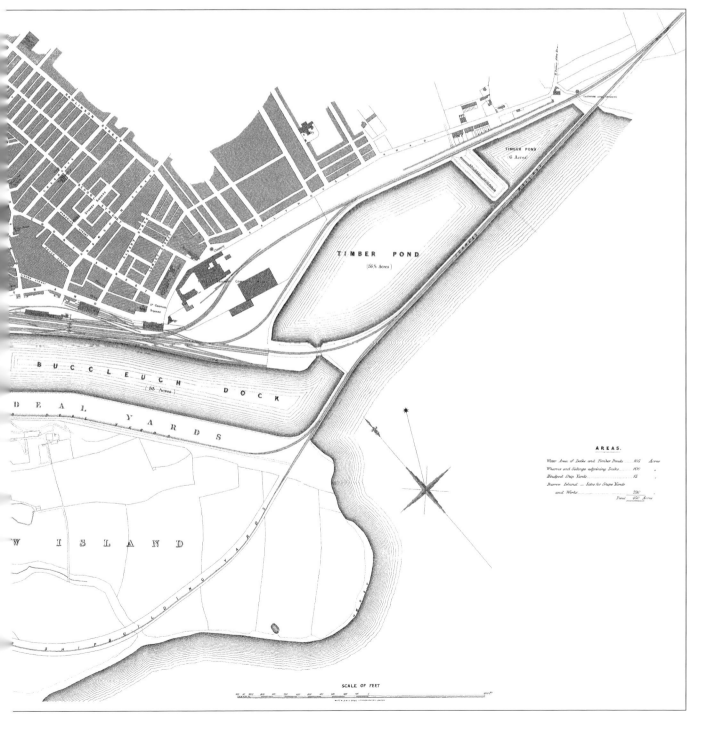

SCALE OF FEET

143

Loco Junction at Barrow on 9th July 1954. A trip train hauled by 2F 0-6-0 58156 (LMS 22977) is signalled into Barrow Yard. The higher signal arm on the post is for Shipyard Junction and Ramsden Dock sidings via the Buccleuch Dock bascule bridge. (Author: MAC32)

enclosing the Cavendish Dock was completed about the same time[10].

The *Barrow Herald* of 29th March 1879 recorded that:

'On Monday morning the 24th March the new Ramsden Dock entrance basin was formally opened by Messrs Little and Co's steamer Ariadne.'

This auspicious occasion was marred by the gloomy financial position of the Furness Railway Company, as related to its shareholders' meeting, by the Duke of Devonshire, in February 1879:

'The principal branch of industry in the district upon which ... the prosperity of the railway depended was in a state of unexampled depression.' [11]

Water levels were equalised in the Ramsden, Buccleuch and Devonshire Docks on 27th May 1879 and the first ship entered Ramsden Dock on the morning of 24th November 1879 when the Anchor Line's vessel *Scotia* arrived from New York, after a passage of 18 days, to berth at the North American Quay (the Anchor Line Basin).

According to the *Barrow Herald* of 29th November 1879 the inauguration of the new dock attracted a considerable number of people.

Fortunately, as the Barrow Docks were nearing completion, there was an upturn in trade. The *Barrow Herald* of 15th May 1880 enthused:

'The greatest activity is everywhere apparent in the docks at Barrow there being large shipments of metal to America and elsewhere. The passageway between the Devonshire and Buccleuch Docks has been closed by the pile-driver ... Mr

estimated for the remaining work, including £11,000 on the opening bridge between the Buccleuch and Ramsden Docks. However, as early as August 1875, the FR board reported to the shareholders that the docks works were proceeding slowly because of the continuing depression in trade and the *Barrow Herald* of 24th June 1876 noted:

'Very little progress is being made on the Barrow Docks.'

Although not recorded in the company minutes, William Hanson was employed only on the construction of the Ramsden Dock basin, the Furness Railway employing its own labour to complete the dock works. The report of the directors to the shareholders' meeting in August 1876 recorded that:

'The earthworks in connection with the Ramsden Dock Basin are nearly completed.'

Devonshire told the meeting:

'The Docks already completed ... had brought a very large amount of traffic to the railway. The Dock dues themselves had paid a very fair return being 2% on the cost of the docks ... They were in fact getting more ships than they could accommodate and this was one reason which induced them to extend the docks.'

Work had commenced in widening the passageway between the Devonshire and Buccleuch Docks together with the building of a high level bridge over this passageway[8]. The tide was admitted to the Ramsden Dock on 12th June 1878[9] and the embankment

The 1863 Barrow station in the Strand c.1973. The station was built alongside Barrow Pier. At the centre is the building that housed the Barrow Control Office from its introduction in 1918. (Author: MAA1010)

Gradwell is making every effort to complete the widening of the passageway as early as possible. The traffic to and from the Barrow Docks is now worked from the Ramsden Dock.'

At the FR shareholders' meeting, held on 31st August 1881, it was announced that the widening of the passageway between the Devonshire and Buccleuch Docks had been completed and that the Ramsden Dock Station and steamboat quay had been opened on 1st July 1881, with the transfer of the Isle of Man service from Piel Pier[12].

The new high level road bridge across the passageway between the Buccleuch and Devonshire Docks was completed in 1882. It was a hydraulic 'lift and roll' structure, and a second parallel span was completed in 1886.

By this time the Barrow Docks capital account stood at a staggering £1,652,799[13]. The traffic figures in tons for the Barrow Docks for the period 1883-1896 were:

1883	685,309	1890	734,181
1884	521,076	1891	640,061
1885	651,961	1892	602,816
1886	751,859	1893	592,256
1887	726,267	1894	534,706
1888	646,282	1895	447,310
1889	733,197	1896	695,292

Furness Railway Shipping Services 1867-1895

Following the opening of the Ulverstone & Lancaster Railway in 1857, the Piel-Fleetwood service, no longer the FR's link with the outside world, had reverted to seasonal running, and the year 1868 saw the departure, from Barrow, of the old Fleetwood steamer *Helvellyn* which had been purchased by the FR as long before as 1848. Nevertheless the FR decided to purchase a replacement vessel of 282 tons built new by McNab & Co. of Greenock. The *Walney* arrived at Barrow on 8th May 1868 and commenced the Fleetwood service on 1st June[14]. She had been designed to double as a tug for the Barrow Docks and as the dock traffic increased she was used more and more on this duty. At the end of the 1869 season it was decided to abandon the Fleetwood service altogether[15].

By the time the FR was opened for passenger traffic, in August 1846, the Windermere Steam Yacht Company was operating two steamers on Windermere, the *Lady of the Lake* and *Lord of the Isles* and in connection with these, omnibuses were run between the FR terminus at Dalton and the steamer landing at Newby Bridge, for the rest of the season. In 1849, a rival concern, the Windermere Iron Steamboat Company, introduced its *Firefly* and *Dragonfly* and, in 1858, the two companies amalgamated to form the Windermere United Steam Yacht Company.

When the FR Act 1866 authorised the building of the branch to the south end of Windermere, powers were also granted for the FR to take shares in the United Company. The FR Act 1869, which authorised the extension to 'Lake Side', also ratified an agreement between the FR and the United Steam Yacht Company, dated 12th March 1869, by which a new steamer, the *Swan* was to be provided. Built by Seath & Co. of Rutherglen, she was launched at Lakeside on 5th June 1869, five days after the FR branch opened for passenger traffic[16].

On Coniston Water, the steamer *Gondola,* which had been launched on 1st December 1859, continued to operate seasonally during the period under review and long after. The position of the Furness Railway on Windermere was settled by the Furness Railway (Steamboats) Act 1872[17], which confirmed the agreement

of 12th March 1869 between the FR and the Windermere United Steam Yacht Company and noted that the FR held £6,665 of the yacht company's stock from a total capital of £14,988. It also confirmed an agreement, dated 28th April 1871, by which the yacht company sold its undertaking to the FR.

In 1878, the steamers *Cygnet* and *Teal* were built for the Furness Railway, by the Barrow Shipbuilding Company, to replace the veteran *Firefly* and *Dragonfly*, which were both scrapped at Lakeside in July 1880[18]. The last of the old United vessels, the *Rothay,* was replaced in 1891 by the FR's *Tern* built by Forrest & Co. of Wivenhoe, Essex, at a cost of £4,800[19]. *Rothay* was scrapped at Lakeside in July 1892[20].

The most modest of the Furness Railway's shipping activities was the Walney Ferry. The boom period of the early 1870s led to a serious lack of residential accommodation in Barrow and, while the formal colonisation of Walney Island was not to take place until the Vickers Company began to build their 'Vickerstown' after the turn of the century, some cottage property was built on the island in the early 1870s. The west shore, with its fine sandy beaches, had become a place of recreation for the increasing population of the town. At this time, access to Walney Island was by a ford from Hindpool, at low tide, augmented by a variety of small boats. The *Barrow Herald* of 16th December 1876 contained the first reference to the possibility of a ferry between Barrow and Walney, but it was not until 2nd June 1877 that it was able to announce the FR's intention to provide a steam ferry. The FR placed an order with the Barrow Shipbuilding Company for construction of the Walney Ferry. Build No. 53, *'Steam Ferry No. I'* was laid down in August 1877[21] and was launched on 5th January 1878[22]. It took some time to complete the terminal facilities and it was not until 1st July 1878 that Henry Cook, the FR Secretary and Traffic Manager, formally opened the service.

From a national viewpoint, the most important of the shipping services associated with the Furness Railway were those from Barrow to Belfast and, during the summer season, to Douglas, Isle of Man. The opening of these services, in 1867, was described in Chapter Ten. The steamer *Herald* arrived from the Clyde on 28th June and made her first run to Douglas, in three hours, on 1st July. From 2nd September the three steamers *Roe*, *Talbot* and *Shelburne*, operating the Midland Railway service between Morecambe and Belfast, began to sail from Piel Pier, the Midland Railway diverting its boat trains to Barrow over the newly opened Furness & Midland Joint line.

Neither the Midland nor the Furness Railway had powers to own and operate steamers to Douglas and Belfast and, although the title 'Barrow Steam Navigation Company' was used from 1st July 1867, the four steamers remained in the ownership of the Glasgow partnership of James Little & Company. An agreement dated 1st May 1868, but retrospective to 1st September 1867, created the Little/Midland/Furness partnership and in December 1868 the *Barrow Register of Shipping* noted the ownership of the *Roe, Talbot, Shelburne* and *Herald* as:

Robert Little & James Morton, Greenock (Littles)	16/64 share
James Ramsden & Lord F. C. Cavendish (FR)	24/64 share
James Allport & W. E. Hutchinson (MR)	24/64 share

The capital of the new partnership was set at £57,000 and the agreement was renewed in 1873, 1883 and 1894, on this last occasion for three years only, by which time the MR had obtained powers for its new harbour at Heysham and the Barrow route was under serious threat[23].

Buccleuch Dock c.1920. In the foreground is the Michaelson Road high level bridge, with a lift-and-roll hydraulic operation, built above the passage between the Devonshire and Buccleuch Docks, and affording road access to Barrow Island. (Sankey archive: 8318)

In common with other railway shipping services, set up primarily to bring traffic to the railway, the Barrow route at first ran at a loss and matters were not helped by the depression in trade during the late 1860s. Devonshire reported to the 1869 spring meeting of FR shareholders:

'The Belfast Service, at its commencement, was not of a paying kind ... but is now decidedly improving.' [24]

By the end of 1869 the loss had been written off.

However, 1870 brought about increasing prosperity, which led to the partnership's decision to purchase another steamer, the *Antrim* (900 tons), launched from the Port Glasgow yard of Robert Duncan & Co. in December 1870 and was registered at Barrow on 2nd January 1871. She was renamed *Manxman* on 27th May 1880[25].

Of the three original Morecambe steamers, the *Roe* lasted, unchanged, until scrapped in 1887, the *Talbot* was renamed

Armagh in March 1873 and the *Shelburne*, renamed *Tyrone* was sold to a Calcutta company, Roxburgh Spence, in 1883. However, it seems possible that the *Armagh* and *Tyrone* were taken off the Barrow route, because, shortly after the opening of the new Ramsden Dock Station and steamboat quay, for the Isle of Man service on 1st June 1881 and for the Belfast service on 1st October 1881[26], it was announced that the new steamer *Donegal*, of the Barrow Steam Navigation Company, had arrived at Ramsden Dock pier on 30th December 1881 and that her sister ship, the *Londonderry*, was nearing completion[27.] This suggested that these paddle steamers were new, but they were in fact built in 1866 and bought from the Burns Line, having been their *Camel* and *Buffalo*. [28]

On 26th January 1883 the paddle steamer *Duchess of Edinburgh* was registered at Barrow, having been built in 1880 for the South Eastern Railway's Dover – Calais service. After alterations at Barrow, she was renamed *Manx Queen* in June 1883 and entered the Isle of Man service. The Barrow Steam Navigation Company purchased its last paddle steamer, the *Rouen*, from the London, Brighton & South Coast Railway, in 1882 and renamed her *Duchess of Buccleuch*.

Towards the end of the period the first of two screw steamers, the *City of Belfast*, was built for the partnership by Laird Bros of Birkenhead at a cost of £40,000 and the FR board noted on 28th April 1893, that her trial trip had been successful. The second steamer the *Duchess of Devonshire*, was built at Barrow and launched on 21st January 1897.

CHAPTER 14 REFERENCES

1   26-27m Vic C.84.
2   *Barrow Herald*, 12th Sep. 1868.
3   *Barrow Herald*, 31st Aug. 1867.
4   FRDM, 12th June 1871.
5   FRDM, 28th Feb. 1871.
6   *Barrow Herald*, 19th Aug. 1871.
7   35-36 Vic C.99.
8   *Barrow Herald*, 9th Mar. 1878.
9   *Barrow Herald*, 7th Sep. 1878.
10   *Barrow Herald*, 10th Aug. 1878.
11   *Barrow Herald*, 1st Mar. 1879.
12   *Barrow Herald*, 30th Aug. 1871.
13   FRDM, 12th Mar. 1885.
14   *Barrow Herald*, 9th & 16th May 1868.
15   *Barrow Herald*, 7th May 1870.
16   Davies K., 1984. *English Lakeland Steamers.*
17   35-36 Vic C.83 18.7.1872.
18   PRO: Rail 214/50. FR Managing Director's Minute Book.
19   FRDM, 27th Nov. 1890.
20   PRO: Rail 214.50 op. cit.
21   *Barrow Herald*, 1st Sep. 1877.
22   Harris N. *Op. cit.*
23   BRO: DT/DH 20/2.
24   *Barrow Herald*, 6th Mar. 1869.
25   Barrow Register of Shipping.
26   *Barrow Herald*, 20th Aug. & 17th Sep. 1881.
27   *Barrow Herald*, 3rd December 1881.
28   McNeill D.B., 1960. *Coastal Steamers & Inland Navigation of the North of Ireland* Vol.1 p.78.

Ferry No. 1, introduced 1878, shown at the Walney terminal c. 1900. (G. Holme collection)

THE FURNESS RAILWAY: RESULTS AND CRITICISM 1868-1896

This middle period in the history of the Furness Railway, running from the opening of the first dock, at Barrow, in 1867, to the end of James Ramsden's working life in 1896, can be considered in two parts. The first part opened with the depression of the late 1860s. The results of this were keenly felt by board members, officers and shareholders alike, as the depression followed a period of buoyancy in which the Barrow Docks were authorised and started, agreements were made with both the London & North Western and Midland Railways, the Whitehaven & Furness Junction Railway was acquired and the Barrow Hematite Steel Company's works opened.

However, when trade improved, from the middle of 1869, the relief felt by all led to an unprecedented capital spending spree, further fuelled by the country-wide trade boom of the early 1870s. As has been shown in Chapters Twelve and Thirteen, there seemed to be no limit to the capital being poured into Barrow. The inevitable downturn in the iron trade, when it duly came in 1874, was even more painful than that of the late 1860s. However, by 1880 things began to improve again – as it turned out, for the last time.

The FR dividends for the period 1868 to 1882 were:

1868	7%	1876	6¼%
1869	6½%	1877	8%
1870	8½%	1878	6%
1871	10%	1879	3½%
1872	10%	1880	6¾%
1873	9½%	1881	6¼%
1874	6¾%	1882	7%
1875	6½%		

Apart from the 3½% paid in 1879 (the lowest FR dividend since 1852) these were quite good results – better in fact than those of the LNWR and the Midland[1].

Considering this first half of the FR's middle period in more detail, the *Barrow Herald* of 8th June 1867 was already warning of a downturn, pointing out that employment in the local building trade had dropped to one quarter of what it had been at the beginning of the year. As noted, the FR report to its shareholders, for the first half of 1867, stated that the docks were opening at a time when the shipping trade was in a very depressed state. The FR revenue for the second half of 1867 was £148,276, but for the corresponding period in 1868 it was £132,250. This downturn led, understandably, to the FR's shareholders taking a greater interest in the affairs of the company.

At the shareholders' meeting held at Westminster in February 1868, the chairman, the Duke of Devonshire, remarked:

'I am glad that we have a larger meeting of shareholders than usual. We have sometimes had but one or two other than the Directors. Indeed on some occasions we have had none ... I may attribute the presence of those here today to a desire to inform themselves as far as they possibly can of the present position and prospects of the Company.'

William Cavendish, 7th Duke of Devonshire and 2nd Earl of Burlington (1808-1891), was chairman of the Furness Railway Company from 1848 to 1888 and a major investor in Barrow industry. (Carte-de-visite)

A Mr Head, describing himself as a shareholder of the Taff Vale Railway, called for a check on capital expenditure and for a limitation of passenger facilities which, he argued, were provided in excess of need, as indicated by the passenger receipts. This was, no doubt, George Head of Rickerby House, Carlisle, also a director of the Lancaster & Carlisle Railway. A year later Head belaboured the FR directors on the expenditure on the Barrow Docks, a matter which was to become a favourite topic in later years. He also objected to the appointment of J. R. McClean to the Furness board:

'I have nothing to say against him, but having been so long mixed up with the transactions of the Company, he is not the sort of man I want to have represent our views.' [2]

An interesting episode marked the end of the decade and was typical of the much greater concern with finance engendered by the depression. On 10th February 1869 the Furness Railway Company auditors, Henry Beloe and Frederick Currey, wrote to the board qualifying their approval of the accounts in the following respects:

1. £3,500 credited to the Barrow Steel Company for their

London office.
2. Alterations to the Furness Abbey Hotel had been charged to the station revenue account.
3. £4,609 credited to the Barrow Hematite Steel Company had not been paid for four years.
4. £11,336, shown as paid to the Duke of Devonshire for land at Hindpool, referred to a purchase made many years previously.
5. The Barrow Steam Navigation Company suspense account showed only a debit of £2,000 on the traffic whereas this should be £5,086 to 30th June 1868.
6. The Midland Railway Company had failed to render accounts for the working of the Furness & Midland Joint line.
7. On the subject of the agreement with James Little & Co., the managers of the Barrow Steam Navigation Company: "It seems to us that by these arrangements, if legal, as to which we offer no opinion, Messrs Little & Co. could pledge the credit of the Furness Company to an unlimited extent."
8. The contribution by the Furness Company of £1,000 to the building of St James' Church, Barrow, was not approved by a special resolution of the shareholders.'

James Ramsden admitted that the purchase of the Hindpool estate (on which much of the industrial development at Barrow had taken place, including the Barrow Hematite Steel Company's works) had exceeded the company's legal powers, but that this matter was not the auditors' concern.

Nevertheless, some of these matters were subsequently regularised.

The report does, however, highlight the cavalier methods of James Ramsden, but how much these methods were directed to his personal gain can only be the subject of speculation. The evidence of his investment in Barrow industry indicated that he had, by one means or another, accumulated considerable wealth. The very first vessel to be launched from the works of the Barrow Shipbuilding Company was the steam yacht *Aries* of 145 tons, for Sir James Ramsden[3].

As noted in Chapter Nine, resulting from the efforts of James Ramsden, Barrow-in-Furness received its Charter of Incorporation as a Borough on 13th June 1867. This was an essential move as the growing town had totally outstripped the resources of the various public services, which were based at Dalton and Ulverston. To avoid the delay which would have resulted from the nomination and election of aldermen and councillors, the Duke of Devonshire was invited to nominate these appointments in the first instance, after which a democratic process would be instituted. Characteristically, Devonshire chose well, nominating men of proven capability. The aldermen were H.W. Schneider and Robert Hannay, the promoters of the Barrow Ironworks, Myles Kennedy of the Ulverston Mining Company and James Ramsden. The councillors included Josiah Smith, manager of the steel works; Edward Wadham, the Duke of Buccleuch's agent; James Fisher, Barrow shipping agent, and William Gradwell, the timber merchant and building contractor. Ramsden was created the first Mayor and the council meetings were held for a time in the Furness Railway's offices at Barrow. Other than Kennedy and Hannay who retired, the council was confirmed by the subsequent elections[4].

It was inevitable, however, that this Cavendish/FR/Steelworks-based council would engender opposition, which soon manifested itself as the Ratepayers Protective Association,

Sir James Ramsden, in later life. Ramsden (1822-1896) joined the Furness Railway as Locomotive Superintendent on 29th January 1846, was knighted by the Queen in 1872 and retired as General Manager in 1895. (Carte-de-visite)

a group of builders and land agents, described by Joseph Richardson, editor of the *Barrow Times*, at that time supportive of the Ramsden regime, as the 'Cabal'.

The subject of complaint was the proposed sale of the municipal buildings which had been constructed, without legal powers, by the Furness Railway. However, the FR was only asking the original cost of £15,000 and this was, after acrimonious exchanges, agreed[5].

The prosperous times, which commenced in 1870, understandably led to the FR shareholders' meetings being conspicuous for the lack of shareholders' complaints, but, at the meeting in August 1875, by which time trade had fallen off, there was again a call for the closure of the capital account. The chairman replied that the company had:

'no choice but to provide for the trade or let others come and do so.'

At the meeting of shareholders in February 1876 there were more vociferous complaints. A Revd Mr Sanderson said that the Board was not providing sufficient train accommodation at small stations where traffic was to be obtained and he objected to further expenditure on the docks *'which had never paid and would never pay'*. A Mr Baldwin objected to the raising of £800,000 in capital and proposed that this should be raised by debentures. He noted that £1,500,000 had been spent on the docks and objected to more being spent.

As the decade wore on matters continued to deteriorate. A

A splendidly behatted gathering of FR employees, including shunters, foremen and guards, photographed in the early 1900s, probably at Whitehaven. (Courtesy of Mr & Mrs D Webb)

barometer of West Cumberland trade was the traffic on the Cockermouth, Keswick & Penrith Railway, the direct line to the north east. Isaac Fletcher, the chairman, told the shareholders at their meeting in August 1878 that iron ore traffic had fallen from 41,000 tons in the first half of 1877, to 19,000 tons for the corresponding period in 1878. Sadly, Fletcher became so depressed by the state of West Cumberland trade that he committed suicide early in 1879[6].

As noted, towards the end of 1878 the Mayor of Barrow, Edward Wadham, was organising the provision of soup kitchens to relieve distress in the town[7].

The half-year meeting of shareholders of the Furness Railway, held in February 1879, was a gloomy occasion. The chairman said it was a matter of great regret to the directors that they had to present such an unsatisfactory report and the Duke referred particularly to West Cumberland where the Furness Railway had, on 1st July 1878, become joint owners, with the LNWR, of the Whitehaven, Cleator & Egremont Railway. Such was the distress in that district that there had been a serious fall in traffic and it had been necessary to reduce rates. The result was that the joint line had operated at a loss[8].

Matters continued to deteriorate further, the FR dividend for the first half of 1879 was 3%, the lowest since 1851 and the directors' report noted that it had been necessary to reduce rates still further. The new Ramsden Dock, on which so much capital had been spent, had opened at a most inauspicious time.

However, what proved to be the last rally in the iron trade was beginning. Throughout Furness and West Cumberland the furnaces which had stood idle, were blown in. The Askam Ironworks reopened on 13th January 1880 and, by February the price of hematite iron had increased from 45s. per ton, in August 1879, to 140s. per ton[9].

This upturn in trade allowed the FR dividends to return to their customary high levels, at a time when the company was completing a number of expensive capital projects. The Belfast and Isle of Man steamer services were transferred from Piel Pier to the new Ramsden Dock Station in 1881, the Barrow and Park loops, together with the new Barrow Central Station, were opened in 1882, and the branch to Conishead Priory, which served the North Lonsdale Ironworks, opened in 1883.

The report to the shareholders' meeting in August 1883, which recorded the opening of the Bardsea branch for passenger traffic on 27th June 1883, also blamed a falling off in traffic on a depression in the iron and steel trade.

This middle period, covering the years 1883 to 1896 was one of unmitigated gloom and despondency and coincided with the disappearance from the scene of the pioneering personalities. This 'middle period' is best illustrated by the details of the results from 1883 to 1895, giving the first half year figures:

	First half year Receipts	Expenditure	Operating Ratio	Dividend for year
1883	£272,913	£126,937	46½%	4¾%
1884	£250,269	£119,751	48%	3¼%
1885	£233,216	£108,145	46¼%	2½%
1886	£216,894	£99,362	45¾%	2%
1887	£219,054	£99,789	45½%	2¼%
1888	£227,776	£101,868	44¾%	2¾%
1889	£244,286	£105,803	43¼%	4¼%
1890	£262,018	£115,611	42½%	3¾%
1891	£248,204	£121,211	48¾%	2¾%
1892	£209,005	£113,279	54%	1½%
1893	£221,339	£111,121	50%	1¼%
1894	£218,544	£109,603	50%	1½%
1895	£198,385	£102,565	51½%	½%

The average dividend on the ordinary stock for this second period was 2½% compared with 6½% for the years 1873-1882. However, bearing in mind the costs associated with the Regulation of Railways Act 1889, which required the interlocking of points and signals and the application of continuous brakes on passenger coaches, the operating ratio showed that the Furness Railway was operated efficiently.

It must be pointed out that the Furness Railway capital account consisted of a larger proportion of guaranteed and preference stock than most railway companies. In 1881 the debenture, guaranteed, and preference stock, of the Furness Railway had been consolidated into 4% stock and, in 1894, this totalled £3,720,857, compared with £2,642,000 of ordinary stock. Consequently, whilst the profitability of the Furness company can be judged only in part by its ordinary stock dividend, it never failed to pay the dividend on its guaranteed preference stock. Put another way, the voting shareholders in the Furness Railway were a minority interest and furthermore, a significant number of these were the directors themselves. From the incomplete records of ordinary stock shareholders[10] it can be seen that Cavendish interests accounted for some £350,000 and Buccleuch interests some £100,000 of the company's ordinary stock. Ramsden himself held a 'significant' amount of the ordinary stock[11], allowing his appointment as managing director.

During these last 14 years only essential new works were carried out. The dredging of the Piel and Barrow channels, to maintain the navigation to Barrow docks, was an ongoing commitment. The original Ulverstone & Lancaster Railway viaducts over the Kent and Leven were no longer capable of carrying the heavy loads of the 1880s and in June 1885 the FR let a contract to Handyside & Henderson of Derby for their reconstruction, the price being £19,811. The High Level bridge at Barrow, which provided the essential communication with the various works on Barrow Island, was doubled at a cost of £15,000, accommodation at Ramsden Dock Station was increased by the provision of a second berth and platform and new signalling, in 1885, at a cost of £2,800. On the other hand, the proposal for a branch line to Walney Island, to serve the increasing residential development and the salt works at the south end of the Island, was declined by the FR board in 1889.

The Furness Railway was under continuing pressure to improve its passenger accommodation as the population of Furness expanded and, in 1890, the board sought tenders for some thirty 3rd class carriages to meet Its requirements.

The Furness iron industry was also going through difficult times. The special position of Furness and West Cumberland hematite ore and pig iron had been eclipsed by the development of the Gilchrist-Thomas basic steel-making process which allowed the use of phosphorus bearing ores from the Midlands and North-East. On 22nd March 1892 Henry Cook, Secretary and Traffic Manager, stated that he had received:

'Urgent application from the three railway companies interested in the carriage of coke from Durham for a reduction in rates on the plea of severe competition to which the blast furnaces in the Furness District were exposed by the introduction of Spanish ore to Middlesbrough and other iron making centres.'

This was a further blow to the west coast iron trade.

Cook pointed out that if the Durham coke traffic was to be transferred to the shortest route, via Hincaster Junction and Arnside (instead of Carnforth), the Furness Railway proportion of the proposed reduction of 1/- per ton would be only one halfpenny per ton. The LNWR was not to be appeased and its arrangement to conduct the Durham coke traffic via Carnforth was to continue. Nevertheless, the FR found it necessary to concede 1d per ton on its coke rates from 1st January 1892.

In 1892 the FR shareholders resumed their criticism of the Barrow docks revenue and expenditure, demanding separate accounts. Henry Cook reported that it was not practicable to meet this request on the grounds that the capital expenditure included both the docks and the railway and that working expenses also included the docks and the railway. He supported his view by stating that other dock-owning railways did not keep separate accounts:

'An indication of what we can positively state as to the value of the docks' contribution to the traffic received by the Company is that, for the 12 months ending 31st December 1891, it was £102,000. This only represented the direct traffic of the docks but they also had to be credited with a proportion of traffic which they have been the means of bringing to the railway by leading to the establishment of nearly all the industrial works in Barrow.'

Cook quoted a figure of £102,000 for the docks traffic for 1891. Given that the docks' capital expenditure, quoted in 1885, was £1,652,779, this represented a 6% return on capital and a profit of 3%, giving an operation ratio of 50%.

The Furness Railway received a serious setback in 1892 when mining under the main line at Lindal led to a subsidence, on 22nd September, in which locomotive No. 115, a Sharp Stewart 0-6-0, was lost. This led to an interruption to traffic at Lindal for several months. Harrison, Ainslie and Company, proprietors of the Lindal Moor Mines, sought an agreement with the Furness Railway for a reduction in iron ore rates to compensate the company for the abandonment of working under the railway, but this was declined[12]. The subsidence problems led to further consideration of a new main line between Plumpton and Salthouse and a survey for such a line was ordered by the FR board on 27th September 1894. Plans were resurrected for a junction station and marshalling yard at Plumpton, but the work was never carried out.

These final years of the Ramsden era saw the departure from the scene of all the pioneering personalities. Lord Frederick Cavendish had been assassinated in 1882, his younger brother, Lord Edward, had died of natural causes and was replaced on the FR board by his son Victor who became the 9th Duke of Devonshire in 1908. The Duke of Buccleuch and Queensberry died in May 1884 and was replaced on the board by Edward Wadham, his mineral agent. The other Buccleuch representative, Frederick lltid Nicholl, who had been a director since 1853, retired in December 1889 and was replaced by Lord Muncaster. The 7th Duke of Devonshire resigned on 26th May 1887 and was replaced by his eldest son, the Marquis of Hartington who was elected chairman. The 7th Duke died on 21st December 1891 and his effigy in bronze was not erected in Furness, but in his other empire at Eastbourne, where he looks out from the Grand Parade across the English Channel.

Sir James Ramsden suffered a serious illness in 1875 and for the latter part of that year – in which the take-over of the Whitehaven, Cleator & Egremont Railway by the LNWR had been under consideration – was convalescing in Egypt. He had returned to work in time to take a full part in the formulation of the tripartite agreement for the working of the Cleator & Workington Junction Railway.

During the final years of his office, Ramsden came under increasing attack from shareholders. At the meeting held on 19th February 1887, with Ramsden in the chair, a Manchester shareholder, Mr Stephen Scott, remarked that:

'As Sir James' time was so taken up by other undertakings and his official position at Barrow, the interests of shareholders would be better conserved by the appointment of a General Manager.'

He went on to say that:

'Other undertakings greater than their own contented themselves with one Secretary but the Furness Railway had two, one being the son of the Managing Director.'

Sir James replied:

'That a general manager should be appointed in place of himself was a matter which should be left in the hands of the shareholders. As to the charge of "Jobbery" in connection with his son acting as Assistant Secretary, he might mention that the sum paid to him was £200 per annum.'

Scott went on to attack Ramsden at the shareholders' meeting in August 1887, at which the Marquis of Hartington, the

The high level bridge, viewed from the side of Buccleuch Dock looking towards Devonshire Dock, is shown having been opened to allow the passage of a coaster. (G. Holme collection 452-4-3)

new chairman, presided. Scott proposed that Ramsden be pensioned off at £1,000 per annum and be replaced by a general manager.

Owing to diabetes, Ramsden's health continued to deteriorate and he retired as Managing Director on 21st May 1895, his retirement coinciding with a low point in the fortunes of the Furness Railway. No dividend was paid on the ordinary stock of the company for the first half of 1895 and during that year the price of the FR ordinary stock fell to 71½d, the lowest on record[13].

Sir James Ramsden died on 19th October 1896, his estate amounting to £69,402[14], which included his shareholding in the Furness Railway, and this passed to his only son, Frederic James Ramsden. Frederic Ramsden, who had been assistant secretary under Henry Cook, was appointed superintendent of the line on 29th December 1896. Cook continued as company secretary until the end of 1896 when, together with Richard Mason, the locomotive superintendent, he retired. Frederic Ramsden became a FR director in November 1908 in place of Sir John Hibbert and he was appointed chairman of the FR board on 13th April 1917, on the death of Lord Muncaster[15].

Furness and Midland amalgamation proposals

The early relations between the Furness and Midland companies are set out in Chapter Ten. After the passing of the Furness & Midland Joint Line Act in 1863, with its associated schemes for the transfer of the Midland's Belfast and Isle of Man steamer services from Morecambe to Barrow, there were suggestions that the Midland company was interested in a Cumberland west coast route to Scotland via the Furness, the Whitehaven & Furness Junction, the Whitehaven Junction and Solway Junction Railways. It was suggested that the Whitehaven & Furness Junction's scheme for a Duddon Crossing, formulated in 1864, was to shorten the west coast route for the Midland. However, by this date the Midland Railway was anticipating a joint use of the Lancaster & Carlisle Railway between Ingleton and Carlisle. It was only after the W&FJR had obtained the Act for the Duddon Crossing, in 1865, that negotiations between the LNWR and the Midland companies broke down and the Midland introduced its Bill for the Settle and Carlisle line, authorised by the Act of 16th July 1866.

Following the 1865 agreement, the LNWR purchased the Cockermouth & Workington and Whitehaven Junction Railways in 1866 and the Furness acquired the Whitehaven & Furness Junction Railway.

From 1866 a period of depression of the Cumberland and Furness iron trade set in, but this was followed by a boom in the years 1870-1873, leading to a period of unprecedented inflation in prices and wages, which collapsed from 1874. By early 1875 the FR board resolved:

'No capital expenditure to be hereafter undertaken without a careful estimate having been made and submitted to the Managing Director (Sir James Ramsden) for submission to the Board.' [16]

This came at a time when the Ramsden Dock and the Barrow loop line were under construction and it was in 1875 that William Currey warned his noble master of the dangers of his commitments in Furness and recommended the sale of the Furness Railway. Although Ramsden was instructed by the FR to approach the Midland and London & North Western companies with possible amalgamation in mind, nothing seems to have resulted from his approach[17].

On 13th July 1876 William Currey wrote to Devonshire warning him of the dangers of his massive liabilities In the Barrow companies:

'I am inclined, after full consideration, to withdraw the recommendation I made to Your Grace last year about the sale of the railway.'

The possibility of a sale of the Furness Railway to the Midland continued to be recognised. On 18th November 1876 the *Barrow Herald* noted:

'We understand that the Midland Railway are in treaty with the Furness Railway for leasing.'

When the FR complained bitterly to the LNWR over the latter's agreement to purchase the Whitehaven, Cleator & Egremont Railway, Ramsden met William Cawkwell of the LNWR and it was agreed that the Furness would be admitted to joint ownership of the WC&ER:

'Provided that, if the FR amalgamated with the Midland Railway, the MR will not be entitled to any share in the WC&ER.' [18]

Ramsden declined this offer, suggesting that at that time an arrangement with the Midland Railway was still under consideration.

However, on 30th April 1877, the Furness signed the tripartite agreement, with the LNWR and the Cleator & Workington Junction Railway, which was to settle the working of the West Cumberland lines until 1923.

The Midland card was played by the Cleator & Workington

The numbers of employees in the service of the FR can be gauged from the fact that a small wayside station such at Woodend on the WC&ER had a staff of six men including a Stationmaster. (K. Norman collection)

matters on which he wished to see me. It seems probable that the Midland Railway Company will agree to take over the Furness line.'

On 2nd November he wrote:

Junction Railway in 1879. It had, on 6th June 1879, given notice to its partners in the tripartite agreement, the LNWR and the FR, that it intended to open its line for mineral traffic on 1st July 1879. The LNWR refused to agree. On 11th July the C&WJR board resolved that the secretary be authorised to make any arrangement with the Midland Railway which he considered to be in the interests of the company and would benefit the traders in the district. However, mineral traffic worked by the FR commenced, and nothing further of contact with the Midland is recorded.

The FR timetable from 1st June 1882, on which day the new Barrow Central Station opened, provoked a vitriolic editorial in the *Ulverston Mirror* of 10th June:

'Barrow is playing a most determined and unconscionable game of beggar my neighbour with Ulverston. She has already done her utmost so far as cutting us off by sea; now she is endeavouring to cut us off effectually by land. The alterations that have recently been made ... constitute, one of the most highhanded, audacious and monstrous scheme ever devised by an ambitious and overreaching town to damage a whole district for the express purpose of benefiting itself.'

The complaint related to the fact that the five trains each way, between Whitehaven and Carnforth, now travelled some seven extra miles by serving Barrow Central and further, it encouraged people on the Whitehaven line to attend Barrow market instead of Ulverston's.

In the following October, when rumours started to circulate that the FR was to be taken over by the Midland Railway, the *Ulverston Mirror* commented:

'No better piece of news has reached Ulverston for some time than the announcement that there is a chance and almost to the extent of a probability of the FR being absorbed by the Midland Railway Company ... Ulverston has indeed occasion to be exultant in the hope of emancipation from the clutches and of a domination which has for so long oppressed her.'

On 12th August 1882 Devonshire noted in his diary:

'Ramsden came here this morning having several Barrow

'I attended a meeting of the Furness Railway Directors this morning which had been called to consider the question of disposing of the line to the Midland Railway Company either as exclusive owners or in conjunction with the London & North Western Company. Ramsden had, however, ascertained that they would only offer 5% which we were not at all disposed to accept.'

This was understandable as the FR had paid a dividend of 7½% for the first half of 1882, however, the FR, from 1883, was destined never to reach 5% during the rest of its existence.

Again the negotiation came to nothing but Ulverston and Dalton were placated, to some extent, by the introduction of the 'Local Board trains' which used the old direct route between Dalton and Askam.

Discussion of an amalgamation between the FR and the MR resulted from the MR obtaining powers, in 1896, to build a new harbour at Heysham, south of Morecambe. This heralded the end of the Barrow route to Belfast operated by the Barrow Steam Navigation Company.

Of the many formulae considered by the FR, to protect its interests over the ensuing years, one was amalgamation with the Midland. A figure of 3% was suggested in 1901. However this was rejected by the Midland Board as *'It would be regarded as antagonistic by their LNWR friends.'* [19]

CHAPTER 15 REFERENCES

1   *Bradshaw's Railway Manual 1914.*
2   *Barrow Herald,* 6th Mar. 1869.
3   Harris N. *Op. cit.*
4   Marshall J D. *Op. cit.* p.298.
5   Ibid. p. 301.
6   *Barrow Herald,* 31st Mar. 1878 & 12th Apr. 1879.
7   *Barrow Herald,* 23rd Nov. 1878.
8   *Barrow Herald,* 1st Mar. 1879.
9   *Barrow Herald,* 17th Jan. & 14th Feb. 1880.
10   PRO: Rail 214/52.
11   *Barrow Herald,* 3rd Mar. 1866.
12   FRDM, 27th Jan. 1894.
13   *Bradshaw's Railway Manual 1905.*
14   Kellett J., 1990. *James Ramsden: Barrow's Man of Vision* p.75.
15   FRDM, 13th Apr. 1897.
16   FRDM, 22nd Mar. 1875.
17   *Devonshire Diaries,* 29th Apr. 1875.
18   FRDM, 1st Dec. 1876.
19   FRDM, 26th June 1901.

THE FURNESS RAILWAY
IN WEST CUMBERLAND 1866-1875

A Furness Railway circular, dated 30th June 1866, announced that on 1st July 1866 the FR would take possession of the Whitehaven & Furness Junction Railway and that Henry Cook, manager of the W&FJR, would be appointed Secretary and Traffic Manager of the FR[1]. James Ramsden had already been promoted, from Secretary and General Manager of the FR, to Managing Director.

A series of agreements, based on the results of the Parliamentary session of 1865-66, consolidated the position of the LNWR and the FR in West Cumberland.

1) By the LNWR and FR Agreement of 29th June 1866, the LNWR was to have running powers over the FR between Whitehaven Bransty Station, Corkickle, Preston Street and the tramway between Preston Street and the south side of Whitehaven harbour; the FR would have running powers over the tramway between Bransty and the north side of Whitehaven harbour. The Whitehaven stations were to be jointly operated by the LNWR and the FR under a joint manager, with all traffic from the West Cumberland District to the LNWR beyond Carnforth, south and east, to be sent by Whitehaven, when this was the shortest route.

2) By the LNWR and Maryport & Carlisle Railway Agreement of 2nd April 1866, the M&CR was to provide traffic facilities to Maryport and places north thereof and to the Newcastle and Carlisle Railway; through passenger trains would be operated between Whitehaven and Carlisle; traffic from the WC&ER would be exchanged, one

half at Marron Junction and one half at Maryport; coal from Linefoot to Workington and Maryport to be charged at the same rate for both routes and there would be joint use of Maryport station by M&CR and LNWR.

3) Under the LNWR and WC&ER Agreement of 10th May 1866, through rates were to be provided between Marron Junction, Workington and Cockermouth; there would be running powers to the WC&ER between Marron Junction and the M&C Derwent branch at Brigham; all mineral and pig iron traffic from WC&ER to Scotland would be divided, one half via Whitehaven and Workington and one half via Marron Junction and to be so charged, whether or not so sent.

4) The LNWR and Cockermouth, Keswick & Penrith Railway Agreement 1866 provided that the goods and passenger stations at Cockermouth would be occupied as joint stations, with mineral traffic between CK&PR and Workington, and CK&PR and WC&ER at Marron Foot, charged at the same rate.

These agreements effectively tied down the West Cumberland traders, leading to a short period of railway stability and the links in the second phase of railway building in West Cumberland were also completed. The WC&ER extension to Marron Junction, on the Cockermouth and Workington line, was opened to mineral traffic on 15th January and to passenger traffic on 2nd April 1866. The Maryport & Carlisle Railway

The arrival of the railway largely dictated the location of the ironworks established at Harrington in 1857. Founded by Charles Henry Plevin and Edwin Lewis, the works stood on a plot of land leased by them on the seaward side of the railway, south of Harrington harbour. Initially the works with a single furnace had little success but in 1863, under new owners Messrs Bain, Blair and Paterson, further furnaces were erected and the works prospered. The business expanded with limestone quarries at Distington and their own coal mines. (K. Norman collection)

IRON WORKS, HARRINGTON.   A. DEANS

Derwent branch, from Bullgill to Brigham, opened for goods traffic on 12th April and to passenger traffic on 1st June 1867. The Cleator & Furness Joint line, from Egremont to Sellafield, opened for all traffic on 1st August 1869. The Solway Junction Railway opened for mineral traffic on 13th September 1869 and for passenger traffic on 8th August 1870[2].

The West Cumberland iron trade

The Furness Railway completed the double line from Barrow to Sellafield during July 1874. The opening of the WC&ER for mineral traffic, on 11th January 1856, linked the Cleator iron field with the Whitehaven Junction Railway and provided a stimulus for the construction of several new ironworks on the West Cumberland coast. These included Workington Hematite Iron Company Limited, incorporated on 6th November 1856, which opened its Oldside Works, on the north side of the river Derwent at Workington, in 1859. At Harrington an ironworks had commenced operation in August 1857 and, in 1863, this works was taken over by Bain, Blair & Paterson from Scotland. The company reactivated Harrington harbour, opened up collieries and took over the tramway, constructed by Henry Curwen in 1845-46, from John Pit down to Harrington harbour.

In 1862 a major project was begun, sited north of Workington on the east side of the WJR line. What was to become the West Cumberland Iron & Steel Company Ltd had, by 1871, a rail rolling mill as well as smelting furnaces and steel converters. Just north of Bransty station at Whitehaven, the Lonsdale Iron & Steel Company opened its works in August 1871 and work on the construction of the Lowther Iron Works, alongside the Oldside Works at Workington, commenced in 1872.

The final iron trade development in West Cumberland was the construction of two works south of Workington, between the WJR line and the sea. In July 1872 the Moss Bay works was commenced and, by 1877, was making steel rails. Just to the north, the Derwent Iron works was opened in 1874, having been promoted by Scottish interests[3].

Some idea of the expansion of the West Cumberland iron trade can be obtained from the following production figures:

Year	Iron Ore – tons	Pig Iron – tons
1856	259,167	25,530
1859	400,306	50,079
1862	533,120	103,455
1864	784,174	141,033
1869	848,974	129,107
1873	1,021,690	456,877
1880	1,148,246	790,343
1882	1,725,438	1,001,181[4]

The Whitehaven, Cleator & Egremont Railway's Whitehaven ambitions

During the years 1870 to 1873 the boom in the iron trade led to inflation of prices, wages and railway rates, with the profits of the WC&ER, in this period, leading the LNWR to renew its interest in a take-over. There had, however, been a depression in trade, in the late 1860s, which had induced the FR to seek powers, in 1869, to abandon the Duddon crossing scheme, inherited when it took over the W&FJR in 1866. Both the LNWR and the WC&ER had petitioned against the abandonment Bill on the grounds that the opportunity to shorten the distance between West Cumberland and the iron trade districts of Staffordshire and South Yorkshire was being lost. However, the evidence produced to the Parliamentary Committee revealed that iron ore was still being shipped through Whitehaven Harbour and Borwick Rails, Hodbarrow, at rates with which the railway could not compete. The fact that the FR was prepared to reduce its rates, between Millom and Barrow, to those which would have applied via a Duddon crossing, tipped the balance in favour of the abandonment Bill, which was subsequently passed.

The bulk of WC&ER traffic passed through Whitehaven yielding considerable profit, and the dividends of the WC&ER were 10% in 1869, 12½% in 1870 and 13% in 1871.

The operating expenses of the WC&ER were relatively low. The board of directors consisted largely of local businessmen, who, compared with the highly professional LNWR and patrician FR boards, seemed not a little parochial. It was reluctant to make decisions on capital expenditure, passing the urgent request from its traffic manager, John Russell, for additional siding accommodation and rolling stock, backwards and forwards between the main board and the works committee.

Additionally, there had been internal friction. In April 1870 the ageing Lord Lonsdale and veteran director James Lumb resigned from the board, the latter attempted to convene a Special Meeting of shareholders on 2nd May 1870:

'For the purpose of taking into consideration whether the Board of Directors have the confidence of the shareholders.'

Though this meeting does not seem to have taken place, there was an exodus of directors in May 1870. Lord Lonsdale was replaced by John Norman of Maryport, James Lumb by John Cowans of Carlisle, Sir Robert Brisco by John Tyson of Whitehaven and James Stirling by Thomas Dixon also of Whitehaven.

On 25th August 1870, the new board received a proposal from the LNWR, to purchase its railway at 10% in perpetuity. This proposal led to a meeting in Liverpool on 28th October attended by Richard Moon, Chairman of the LNWR, William Cawkwell, director and former General Manager, James Bancroft, director, James Ramsden, Managing Director of the FR, A.B. Steward, Chairman of the WC&ER and James Dees, director and engineer, now a principal mine owner in West Cumberland. Richard Moon stated that the LNWR had been advised that it could not absorb the Cleator line without the FR joining the lease and therefore he had invited Mr Ramsden to attend. (This was significant in the context of the LNWR take-over of the WC&ER in 1876-77.) Mr Steward stated that the offer of 10% was considered insufficient and James Dees commented that the present WC&ER rates should be continued and should include all terminal charges. The LNWR side found Dees' request 'most objectionable' and the meeting broke up. However it was agreed that the LNWR offer should be put to the WC&ER board, which duly met. Messrs Steward, Head and Dixon voted for the LNWR offer and Messrs Clarke, Tyson, Fisher, Cowans, Norman, Jefferson and Dees voted against the offer. On 17th November the WC&ER noted that the LNWR offer had been withdrawn.

Possibly as a result of this conflict being won by James Dees and the newer generation of directors, A. B. Steward resigned as Chairman, although he remained as a director, to be replaced by Henry Jefferson of Springfield.

The new board then turned its attention to local issues, mainly involving the doubling of various sections of the line and the increasing problem of subsidence, due to iron working under the line. (see Chapter Twenty).

The new benefit of rail transport enabled the development of blast furnaces on the north side of the river Derwent at Workington, between the Whitehaven Junction Railway and the sea. The Oldside Works, on the right in this view, were owned by the Workington Hematite Iron Company, incorporated in November 1856. Four open-topped furnaces began operation late in 1859. In 1877 the entire plant closed to enable the old furnaces to be replaced with six of a more modern closed-top design. The works re opened in 1879 as the Workington Iron & Steel Co. and went on to enjoy a profitable existence until 1930. The Lowther Ironworks, on the left in the photo, started life as the North of England Hematite Company in 1872, on land leased from the Earl of Lonsdale by Scottish promoters. Foundations were laid for two blast furnaces and one went into operation in the following June and the second a year later. The works had a chequered history with its owners being liquidated on two occasions. The business was acquired by the Workington Iron & Steel Co. in 1911 and closed shortly afterwards. (Sankey archive: 6173)

On 12th November 1873, with the hematite boom at its height, the WC&ER board noted that William Baird & Co. proposed a line from Rowrah to its new mines at Kelton Fell. The WC&ER board ordered that plans be made for its own line into Ennerdale and that a petition against the Rowrah & Kelton Fell (Mineral) Railway Bill be prepared. However, the latter Bill was approved and received Royal Assent on 16th July 1874.

At the same time a renewed liaison with the LNWR manifested itself. On 10th June 1874 the WC&ER board noted that negotiations were taking place with Richard Moon *'to secure the coal traffic west of the Marron Extension'.* On 2nd September the WC&ER board noted that:

'...a private firm intends to apply to Parliament for a line from Harrington to Dean Moor to serve anticipated coal traffic from Winscales, Gilgarran and Dean Moor.'

The board immediately requested its engineer, George Boyd, to survey a line:

'...from between Rowrah and Branthwaite and some convenient point on the LNWR between Harrington and Workington.'

For reasons which remained unexplained, the WC&ER Bill, deposited late in 1874, proposed only a branch from the main line at Ullock Junction to the coalfield at Gilgarran.

The 1875 WC&ER's Bill did however include:

'...purchase of land at Mirehouse Junction and running powers if necessary over part of the Furness Railway.'

The Bill came before a Parliamentary Committee of the House of Lords on 24th April 1875. There was no petition against the Gilgarran branch clause, but opposition to the *'land at Mirehouse Junction'* clause was formidable. The seven petitions against this clause were from the Furness Railway Company; the Trustees of the Town and Harbour of Whitehaven; the Earl of Lonsdale (the 3rd Earl had succeeded to the title in 1872); Lord Leconfield (mineral royalty owner); the London and North Western Railway; the Mineral Proprietors and Traders of Whitehaven and John Postlethwaite, occupier of *The Hollins,* a mansion near Mirehouse.

In his opening speech for the Bill, the WC&ER counsel, Sir Edmund Beckett QC, launched a tirade against the petitioners:

'Why it is the case I do not know, but although all the places in that neighbourhood have increased amazingly in population, Whitehaven has not done so. Take Barrow, for example, which a little time ago was nothing, has now a population of 40,000; but Whitehaven has been actually stagnant; the population has absolutely fallen off. Now whether that is owing to the mismanagement of the Trustees, who have a Petition here, or whether it is due to the fact of Lord Lonsdale's refusing to sell land, I cannot say.'

The West Cumberland Hematite Iron Co. was incorporated in November 1860, with a largely local shareholding, to take advantage of the demand for high quality Cumberland iron in the new Bessemer steel converters. Their works were also close to the railway line north of Workington LNWR station. For ten years the company did steady business in the manufacture of pig iron and wrought iron plate but, by 1870, advances were being made into steel production and rail rolling. The Company was reformed in 1872 with additional capital as the West Cumberland Hematite Iron & Steel Co. Within twenty years of its re-formation the entire plant was closed down and, despite a brave attempt in 1899 to resume pig iron production on the site, all trace of the enterprise was removed. (K. Norman collection)

Sir Edmund went on to describe an alternative line, proposed by the petitioners, for the improvement of the access to Whitehaven harbour, pointing out that such a line had been authorised by the W&FJR Act of 1848, but had never been constructed.

T.S. Dodgson, secretary and General Manager of the WC&ER, gave evidence for the Bill.

He reported that 80% of traffic on the line was minerals and only 20% goods and passengers. He agreed that the original agreement with the W&FJR allowed a charge of 8½d per ton between Mirehouse Junction, Bransty and Whitehaven Harbour, but when the 10-year agreement expired, in 1866, the new agreement reduced the toll to 6½d per ton.

Dodgson went on to give some interesting figures for the current mineral traffic, a total of one million tons of iron ore:

Ore for local consumption	667,559 tons
Shipment at Whitehaven	113,191 tons
To Middlesbrough	44,281 tons
South via Carnforth	76,947 tons
North to Scotland	130,691 tons
Traffic through Mirehouse Junction	600,000 tons

He admitted that the additional land sought at Mirehouse was for a new passenger station and that an extension to

Whitehaven had been discussed informally. Wilson Harrison, traffic manager of the WC&ER, stated that:

> '....the principal delay to train traffic was not at the Whitehaven tunnel itself but was the inability of the LNWR to collect traffic from Corkickle Sidings which were inadequate. Our own sidings at Mirehouse would mitigate the problem.'

He had to agree that detention of wagons by the traders was a serious problem. Delays by the Whitehaven Hematite Iron Co., at Cleator Moor, were 5,822 wagon days between June and December 1874 and similar delays occurred at other works.

The Committee considered the evidence and found for the Gilgarran branch and the additional land at Mirehouse. It is a matter for speculation why the WC&ER proposals for Whitehaven elicited such massive opposition, for once, the 'Town' and 'Castle' factions were united. The additional land at Mirehouse was not implemented, being overtaken by the creation of the L&NW & FR Joint line in 1878.

CHAPTER 16 REFERENCES

1   Author's collection.
2   Joy D. *Op. cit.*
3   Lancaster J.Y. & Wattleworth D.R. *Op. cit.*
4   Ibid. pp 161-3.

WEST CUMBERLAND COMPETITION

With the benefit of hindsight, the Parliamentary skirmishing over the 1875 proposals of the WC&ER pale into insignificance, compared with the momentous events of the 1876 Session of Parliament. As is often the case with major competing railway schemes, it is difficult to be certain which scheme came first and which was introduced as opposition. That is what happened in 1876.

As early as 16th September 1874, the WC&ER board had instructed its engineer to survey a line from between Rowrah and Branthwaite to the LNWR Whitehaven Junction Railway near Parton. However, only a line from Ullock Junction into the coalfield at Gilgarran was included in the 1875 Bill. This omission was remedied in the WC&ER 1876 Bill, which also included lines towards Workington.

The proposed lines were:

No. 1 The Mowbray branch – a short line from Frizington to mines near Mowbray.

No. 2 The Moss Bay extension, from the terminus of the authorised Gilgarran branch to the LNWR line at Moss Bay.

No. 3 The Moss Bay branch – a short line from line No. 2 into the Moss Bay ironworks.

No. 4 The Harrington branch – a branch from Moss Bay southwards to Harrington harbour.

No. 5 The Workington extension – a line running parallel to the LNWR from Moss Bay to Workington.

No. 6 The Whitehaven branch – running from the Moss Bay extension, via Distington, to a junction with the LNWR at Parton.

The WC&ER board sanctioned this Bill on 27th October and the Parliamentary Notice was dated 10th November 1875.

However the *West Cumberland Times* of 16th October reported on plans for the building of a new Independent railway in West Cumberland:

'Repeated representations from the freighters of the district around Harrington, Workington and Maryport to the local railway company for a reduction in the present tariff for the transmission of minerals and other goods being fruitless, an influential and well attended meeting of the landed proprietors, iron masters and coal owners was held at the Station Hotel, on Friday to consider the question. It was the general opinion of the meeting that additional railway accommodation was necessary between the Cleator iron district and Harrington, Workington and Maryport and a resolution to that effect was passed unanimously. A Committee was appointed to consider the best route and to report to another general meeting shortly to be held with a view to lodging an application to Parliament in the next Session. The proposed route is from Cleator Moor via Keekle and Distington. From Moss Bay the line will run to Workington … then it will curve to the West Cumberland Ironworks and then along the sea beach to Maryport.'

One week later the *West Cumberland Times* noted that a further meeting had been held on 16th October, with Isaac Fletcher presiding and that it had been decided that the new line would run from Cleator to Workington:

'The ground that such a line will pass through is an entirely new district which at present is not directly served by any existing railway system. In the event of the LNWR declining to reduce their rates between Workington and Maryport the new line will be continued to the last named town over land belonging exclusively to some of the promoters.'

The Bill was duly deposited and the lines proposed in the Cleator & Workington Junction Railway Bill were:

No. 1 A line from the WC&ER at Cleator Moor to a junction with the railway of Lord Lonsdale at Workington dock.

No. 2 A line from line No. 1 to a junction with the LNWR at Siddick.

No. 3 A line from line No. 1 to Harrington.

No. 4 A line from line No. 1 to New Yard, Workington (Moss Bay).

The *West Cumberland Times*, of 6th November 1875, reported that the 3rd Earl of Lonsdale was to be Chairman of the new company and that the vice-chairman would be Henry Fraser Curwen of Workington Hall. The proposed capital was to be £150,000. On 1st January 1876 the promoters were recorded as:

Henry, 3rd Earl of Lonsdale	Land and royalty owner
H.F. Curwen	Land and royalty owner
A.G. Thompson	Land and royalty owner
J.S. Ainsworth	Ore proprietor and iron master
William Fletcher	Shareholder in West Cumberland Iron & Steel Co.
R.A. Robinson	Lord Lonsdale's agent
J.R. Bain	Partner: Harrington Ironworks
T.H. Falcon	
C.J. Valentine	Partner: Moss Bay Ironworks

Victory of the Cleator and Workington Junction Railway

The competing schemes came before a Parliamentary Committee of the House of Commons and the evidence ran for an unprecedented seven days between 15th and 23rd March 1876. The Minutes of Proceedings and evidence totalled some 460 printed pages.

There were five Petitions against the WC&ER Bill, from the Earl of Lonsdale; the Maryport & Carlisle Railway; the London and North Western Railway; the Cleator & Workington Junction Railway and the Furness Railway.

The proposals by the Cleator & Workington Junction

Railway also had five Petitions against them, from the Furness Railway; the Maryport & Carlisle Railway; the London & North Western Railway; the Whitehaven, Cleator & Egremont Railway and the Trustees of Town and Harbour of Whitehaven.

The essentials of the two Bills were set out in the opening speeches of principal counsel. Mr McIntyre, for the WC&ER Bill, outlined the development of the company up to the authorisation of the Gilgarran Branch in the previous session and described the six proposed lines, noting that the Mowbray branch was unopposed.

He made the point that the districts of Ullock, Gilgarran and Dean Moor were rich in iron ore, coal and limestone and that their potential would be increased if there was a direct communication with Whitehaven, Harrington and Workington. Regarding the Petition of the LNWR and the FR, he considered that mutually satisfactory arrangements could be made with those companies.

He had more to say on the Petition of Lord Lonsdale. This was, he said, a Petition by the promoters of the C&WJR and some of their employees, who were occupiers of property on the proposed line.

The principal witnesses for the WC&ER Bill were T.S. Dodgson, Manager; John Monroe Mackenzie of Lanarkshire, a partner in several West Cumberland iron companies and the Gilgarran Coal Company; Jonas L. Burns Lindow, Chairman of the Whitehaven Hematite Iron Company and a director of the WC&ER and George Boyd, resident engineer of the WC&ER. During the evidence it was noted that opposition to the WC&ER Whitehaven Branch (Line No. 6) had been withdrawn.

The opening speech for the C&WJR was made by its principal counsel, Sir Edmund Beckett QC, veteran of the 1875 Bill, in which he had represented the WC&ER. He said that since the cross examination of witnesses on behalf of Lord Lonsdale's Petition, some accommodation had been reached between the LNWR and the WC&ER and that, in effect, those companies were working against the C&WJR Bill as *'the common enemy'*. He pointed out that the dividends paid by the Whitehaven Junction Railway had been high and that the LNWR had purchased it for 10%.

The WC&ER had also paid very high dividends:

'Nothing can be more natural than that those two people should combine against anybody else making a new line of railway through the neighbourhood for the purpose of getting reduced rates. The railway originated from the Meeting in October last ... it was a bona fide movement of the traders in the country, or some of them, all having a direct and simple interest in getting a line of railway made for their ore and mineral purposes.'

Sir Edmund then recalled the evidence given in the 1875 WC&ER Bill proceedings, in which he had represented that company, and that the lack of capacity of the Whitehaven tunnel, as the main route between Cleator and Workington, could not be contradicted.

On the matter of the WC&ER being willing to accommodate the traffic of the district, he pointed out that the Gilgarran branch, authorised in the 1875 Session, had not been started. Further, the Bairds had come in and were making their own line from Rowrah to Kelton Fell. He then turned to the evidence of T.S. Dodgson, that there was no coal between Moor Row and Distington. This was wrong, the coal only needed railway accommodation. The communication

proposed with the Workington docks was better than any that could be offered by the WC&ER and LNWR, with their level crossing north of Workington station. Concerning rates, Sir Edmund pointed out that the WC&ER had the right, under its Act, to charge 3d per mile plus terminal charges, whereas the C&WJR could charge only 1½d per mile and the terminal charges were subject to control by the Board of Trade.

The first witness for the C&WJR Bill was William Fletcher, a former director of the Cockermouth & Workington Railway and the Cockermouth, Keswick & Penrith Railway, a partner in collieries near Workington and Director of the West Cumberland Hematite Iron & Steel Company. Counsel then quoted from a report dated 16th October 1875:

'In addition to the Junction with the WC&ER at Cleator Moor it is proposed to make a Junction with the Egremont Branch a little south of Moor Row Station in order to construct a new railway with the Furness Railway as well as with the system of the Midland Railway which possesses running powers to Egremont over the Furness Railway.'

While it was true that the C&WJR was contemplating lines both south to the FR and north to the M&CR, the Midland element was, as before, without fact. The Midland Railway had no running powers over the Furness line other than their joint ownership of the Furness & Midland Joint railway between Wennington and Carnforth.

Mr Fletcher then commented on the coal seams north of Keekle, which would be served by the proposed C&WJR line. These were the 'yard band' and the 'six quarter' seams which provided coal suitable for making coke, a badly needed commodity in West Cumberland, which currently relied on coke from the Durham coalfield. William Fletcher had to concede that the Midland Railway had no running powers beyond Carnforth but that the FR was considering amalgamation with the Midland. These plans, though in existence, came to nothing.

The second witness for the C&WJR Bill was Henry Fraser Curwen of Workington Hall who confirmed the support for the C&WJR project in Workington. Robert Robinson of South Lodge, Cockermouth, gave evidence as principal agent to Lord Lonsdale and reported that Lord Lonsdale would have given evidence in favour of the C&WJR Bill, but that he had been obliged to return to the north because of failing health.

John Stirling Ainsworth, a partner, with his father and brother, in the Cleator Iron Ore Company, also appeared for the C&WJR Bill. He confirmed that the Petition against the C&WJR was mainly by shareholders in the WC&ER.

Henry Cook, Secretary and Traffic Manager of the Furness Railway, which was petitioning against both Bills, explained the working of the Whitehaven tunnel under block regulations and pilotman. He agreed that the traffic capacity could be increased by the use of more powerful locomotives. William Cawkwell, LNWR Director and former General Manager, described the additional facilities being developed on the Whitehaven Junction line particularly in the area of Workington station, newly built in 1875-76 with many additional lines laid in, which made the proposals unnecessary. The Parliamentary Committee considered the evidence and found the preamble of the C&WJR Bill proved in its entirety but the preamble of the WC&ER Bill proved only regarding the unopposed Whitehaven and Mowbray branches.

News of the success of the Cleator & Workington Junction Railway Bill in the Commons Committee soon reached Workington and was the subject of great rejoicing. The *West Cumberland Times*, of 1st April 1876, reported huge bonfires being lit to celebrate the return to Workington of Charles James Valentine of the Moss Bay Ironworks, who had given evidence for the Bill. Bands paraded the streets led by a banner proclaiming *'Success to the Cleator & Workington Junction Railway'*. There was, however, the technicality of the examination of the two Bills by a Committee of the House of Lords. The same evidence was given, albeit in a more concentrated form, but the outcome was the same[1]. The emasculated WC&ER Bill and the C&WJR Bill both received Royal Assent on 27th June 1876.

Further confrontations

Only a few days after the passing of its Act of Parliament, the C&WJR held its first directors' meeting, at the Station Hotel, Workington, on 11th July 1876. The 3rd Earl of Lonsdale, unable to give evidence to the Commons Committee for the Bill because of ill health, had died and the chairmanship of the company passed to Henry Curwen. The directors included Major Andrew Green Thompson of Bridekirk, Cockermouth, a director of the Caledonian Railway, the Cockermouth, Keswick & Penrith Railway and the Solway Junction Railway; J.S. Ainsworth of the Whitehaven Hematite Ironworks, Cleator Moor; William Fletcher MP of Brigham Hall and J R Bain of Harrington Ironworks. William Fletcher was elected vice-chairman.

On 31st October the C&WJR board requested its engineer, John Wood of Carlisle (who was supported by the Barrow firm of Wadham, Turner & Strongitharm), to prepare plans for a line from Cleator Moor to the Cleator and Furness line south of Egremont and from the northern end of its authorised line to the Maryport & Carlisle's Derwent branch at Dearham. William Fletcher and R.A. Robinson were authorised to meet the Furness Railway, to seek its support for an approach to the WC&ER, regarding running powers to the Cleator and Furness line.

Fletcher, Turner and solicitor Waugh met Sir James Ramsden and Henry Cook at the Furness Abbey Hotel on 3rd November 1876. FR support was sought for the line to the Cleator and Furness south of Egremont or, alternatively, with WC&ER support, a shorter line at Moor Row with running powers to Egremont. The C&WJR representatives also sought an agreement under which the FR would either work its line, lease it, or purchase it. Ramsden agreed to these proposals, provided that the C&WJ did not enter into negotiations with any other company pending the outcome of the Bill.

The C&WJR duly wrote to the WC&ER about the curve at Moor Row. The WC&ER replied, in a letter dated 8th November, *'that the Directors cannot consent to the loop line at Moor Row and running powers to Egremont'*.[2] The C&WJR replied, on 10th November, *'the proposal falls so far short ... of meeting our requirements ... that the Board have declined it'*. The C&WJR board resolved to publish Parliamentary Notices for its proposed Dearham and Egremont branches, which led the WC&ER to agree to seek powers for a loop line at Moor Row.

The WC&ER board had, meanwhile, been entertaining the possibility of opting out of its increasingly difficult position by selling out to the LNWR. On 6th November the WC&ER board received a proposal from the LNWR, offering a lease at 10%.

The board immediately accepted this proposal and two days later, on 8th November, issued a Parliamentary Notice for an amalgamation Bill. An agreement was sealed with the LNWR on 16th November 1876.

This came to the notice of Sir James Ramsden who wrote, the same day, to the LNWR's William Cawkwell:

'I am greatly surprised to learn that you intend to take over the Cleator line without offering half to the Furness Company in accordance with our past undertakings from time to time both with you and Mr Moon when the question has been under discussion. I cannot believe that your Company seriously intends to behave so badly to one of your most faithful allies. We have always kept faith with your Company at times to our great disadvantage. I think you should have asked me to see you before your (Parliamentary) notice was given. It is now too late and you must therefore not be surprised at any steps we may be advised to take to protect our interest.'

At the FR board meeting on 1st December, Ramsden reported that he had met William Cawkwell, who was willing to agree to a joint purchase of the WC&ER provided that, if the Midland Railway took over the Furness, the Midland would not be entitled to a joint share in the WC&ER. Ramsden declined this proviso and the FR took steps to deposit a Bill seeking joint purchase of the WC&ER.

Meanwhile, Henry Cook had, on 20th November 1876, written to the WC&ER expressing surprise at the Cleator company's arrangements with the LNWR. The WC&ER board, on 22nd November, expressed *'astonishment at the content and tenor of such a letter'*.

The WC&ER Secretary replied on 28th November on behalf of the board:

'There is no obligation to communicate their business arrangements. They are not aware of any propositions for a Joint purchase. The clause in your bill is most objectionable and if persisted in may distance the friendly relations which hitherto existed between the Companies. ... It is now seen in the Parliamentary Notices of the C&WJR that the FR has become allied with this opposing Company and is contemplating a further extension of their system into our district with powers to lease, amalgamate and supply capital. My directors consider that you are acting in a hostile and detrimental manner toward their Company.'

Thus, at the beginning of the 1876-77 Session of Parliament, four further Bills had been deposited: the FR Bill seeking joint purchase, with the LNWR, of the WC&ER; the WC&ER Bill seeking powers for a loop, between its lines at Moor Row, to allow direct running to Egremont from the C&WJR line; the WC&ER Bill seeking amalgamation with the LNWR, and the C&WJR Bill seeking powers for the line from Cleator to the Cleator & Furness south of Egremont and from near Seaton to the M&CR Derwent branch at Dearham. This latter Bill also included working by, or lease by, the FR.

It seemed essential that some accommodation should be reached among the various companies to avoid yet another protracted Parliamentary confrontation. Nevertheless, at a meeting at Whitehaven on 5th December, the FR agreed the terms of the C&WJR Bill and agreed to work the C&WJR for five years from the opening, excepting the Moss Bay and Harrington branches, *'on the same terms on which the CK&PR is worked by the LNWR and NER'*. Looking back on these arrangements, when giving evidence to the Select Committee on the Cleator & Workington Junction Railway Bill of 1882, which sought, unsuccessfully, to authorise the 'Northern extension', William Fletcher stated:

'After the working Agreement with the Furness Railway had been signed on 5th December 1876, I was horrified to learn for the first time from Sir James Ramsden that he was using our Working Agreement as a lever to enable him to make terms with the L&NWR Company to be admitted into partnership with them in the leasing of the Whitehaven, Cleator & Egremont Railway. Sir James Ramsden stated in the House of Commons Committee that I had been acquainted with these negotiations from the first. I do not state for a moment that Sir James Ramsden would state anything which he did not believe to be correct ... but in that matter his memory is at fault. ... I may say that, had I known what I know now, that Working Agreement would never have been entered into.'

In the same Committee Sir James Ramsden stated:

'Mr Fletcher was perfectly aware what our policy was at the time and that we were going to fight the London & North Western in the best way we could.'

By the FR board meeting of 23rd February 1877, Ramsden reported a breakthrough in discussions with the LNWR. William Cawkwell had agreed that the FR could enter into a joint purchase of the WC&ER, subject to certain conditions. Negotiations continued and, on 15th May, Ramsden reported that an accommodation had been reached. The LNWR required that the Dearham and Egremont extensions should be deleted from the C&WJR Bill but that the clause relating to

working of that line by the FR should remain. There was no mention of the Midland Railway.

The LNWR undertook to deposit a Bill for the joint vesting of the WC&ER in the next session and it was further agreed that *'very considerable concessions be given (to the traders) regarding rates on the WC&ER system because of the considerable opposition in West Cumberland to the amalgamation proposals.'*

The Cleator & Workington and Furness Railway Agreement of 6th April 1877 contained the following clauses:

1. This Agreement relates to railways Nos. 1 and 2 of the C&WJR Act 1876 i.e. Cleator Moor Junction to Workington Dock and to Siddick Junction.
2. The Agreement excludes Railways Nos. 3, 4 & 5 of the 1876 Act.
3. The C&WJR will make all Junctions, sidings and turntables, station yards, engine sheds ... signals and other works ... sufficient for the working of the railway.
4. The C&WJR to provide such telegraphs to be sufficient in all respects to meet the requirements of the Board of Trade.
5. The Furness Company shall have sole working and use of the railway ... and will use their best endeavours to fully develop all through traffic.
6. A Joint Committee be established to fix rates and charges.
7. Gross receipts to be divided between the two Companies FR 33⅓% on all receipts other than mineral traffic and 35% on mineral traffic.
8. The Furness Railway to have priority in any sale of the C&WJR Company.
9. The C&WJR to end the Agreement if the Furness Railway becomes vested in any other undertaking.

This agreement was confirmed in the C&WJR Act 1877, which received Royal Assent on 28th June 1877.

The traffic arrangements between the LNWR, the FR and the C&WJR, were set out in a separate agreement dated 30th April 1877, which came to be known as the Tripartite

Winder station looking north in the 1930s. (CRA Pattinson collection)

Agreement. Its preamble set out the history of the differences between the participants and the accommodation which had been reached. The principal clauses were:

1. The Workington Company's Bill to be proceeded with only so far as it seeks to authorise the Working Agreement with the FR.
2. The LNWR would not oppose that agreement in Parliament.
3. The LNWR would join with the FR in the working of the C&WJR *as they may find expedient.*
4. Mineral traffic (including coal, coke and pig iron) passing between the WC&ER south or west of Yeathouse and other places competitive between the lines of the Workington Company and the Cumberland lines of the LNWR to be divided equally between the two routes or so accounted for.

This appeared to have settled all disputes. As judged by the dearth of diary entries on the subject, the Duke of Devonshire seems to have left West Cumberland matters to Sir James Ramsden. However, he reported, on 7th August 1877:

'We made an expedition to the Cleator District which the Furness Company will for the future be more closely related than hitherto. We went by Egremont and Marron Junction to Workington whence we got out and went to look at the works which have latterly been commenced on the new Cleator & Workington Junction Railway. We afterwards returned by Whitehaven.'

The LNWR duly deposited the Bill for vesting of the WC&ER, jointly in the LNWR and FR, and this Act received Royal Assent on 17th June 1878.

The LNW&FR Joint line came into being on 1st July 1878[3], after a one year interregnum as part of the LNWR.

However, the C&WJR trader/proprietors had no intention of being marginalized by their powerful neighbours.

Whitehaven, Cleator and Egremont Railway final developments

The table of dividends paid by the WC&ER between its opening in 1856, and its sale In 1877 (see table below) show it to have been a highly profitable railway, achieved by a combination of heavy traffic, high rates, low operating costs and low capital expenditure.

TABLE OF DIVIDENDS			
Whitehaven, Cleator & Egremont Railway			
1856	4%	1867	9½%
1857	5¾%	1868	9½%
1858	7%	1869	10%
1859	8%	1870	12½%
1860	10%	1871	13%
1861	10%	1872	12%
1862	7¾%	1873	11¼%
1863	13½%	1874	8¾%
1864	13½%	1875	9¾%
1865	10%	1876	10½%
1866	9%	1876	10% paid by the LNWR in perpetuity

However, the sheer volume of traffic dictated that parts of the original single line had to be doubled.

One intractable problem remained — the railway served a hematite mining area. Hematite tended to occur in ore bodies, worked in layers until exhausted, at which time the workings were abandoned and very often collapsed, causing a 'sink-hole' to appear on the surface of the ground. The mine proprietors had the right to take ore from under railway lines, the only requirement being that they gave the railway company due notice.

The WC&ER was plagued with actual or threatened subsidence in an area roughly bounded by Egremont, Moor Row and Eskett. In some critical areas the railway paid for the mining voids to be packed with rubble: alternatively the ore under the line was purchased and not extracted. The ultimate solution was the building of a deviation line, as was done in 1864, when a new line through Cleator Moor was constructed and, in 1872, when the Winder deviation was authorised to bypass subsidence north of Eskett. Eskett station was retained as a terminal goods and mineral depot.

On 26th May 1874 Col. F.H. Rich, of the Board of Trade Railway Department, inspected the Winder deviation and a second line of rails onward to Rowrah. He found that a new station, named Yeathouse, had been built on the deviation to replace the old Winder station. He authorised opening for passenger traffic and this took place on 27th May. However, a memorial from local residents led to the WC&ER board reopening Winder for passenger traffic[4].

One of the most worrying and inconvenient threats of subsidence affected the line at an under line road bridge north of Frizington station. Col. Hutchinson, of the Railway Department, required that passengers be detrained at temporary platforms and a footpath be provided between these platforms for the passengers to walk over the threatened section[5], a practice which was to continue until 1888[6].

A Frizington deviation line of 47 chains length reached the point of invitation of tenders but the plan was not carried out during the life of the WC&ER. The meeting of Joint Line officers, at Keswick on 26th June 1878, abandoned the project in favour of lifting or packing under the line as required and the provision of watchmen to be continued.

Capital works, carried out from 1867 to 1877, included the Bigrigg branch, from Bigrigg Junction south of Moor Row on the Egremont line to Bigrigg in 1867[7]; the doubling of the line from Frizington to Eskett in 1871[8]; and from Rowrah to Marron in 1873[9]; also the Winder deviation and double line onwards to Rowrah in 1874[10].

The principal capital scheme of the independent years of the WC&ER was the Ullock Junction to Parton line via Distington, which had a double junction with the C&WJR at Distington.

Authorised as the Gilgarran branch in 1875 and the Whitehaven extension in 1876, the contracts were let to Harrison Hodgson at board meetings on 7th June 1876 (Gilgarran branch) and 3rd January 1877 (Whitehaven extension). The Joint Committee opened the Ullock to Parton line to traffic on 2nd June 1879[11].

Although the WC&ER intended to double the line between Moor Row and Sellafield, no action was taken and it fell to the Joint Committee to authorise the second line of rails between Egremont and Gutterby Junction[12]. Nelson and Company carried out the work and the double line was opened for passenger traffic on 1st June 1881[13]. The Mowbray branch from Frizington, authorised by the WC&ER Act 1876, was opened on 10th January 1880[14].

A view of Yeathouse station looking north. (G. Holme collection GH231-4-4)

CHAPTER 17 REFERENCES

1   *West Cumberland Times,* 27th May 1876.
2   C&WJR DM, 10th Nov. 1876.
3   *West Cumberland Times,* 27th May 1876.
4   WC&ER DM, 3rd Mar. 1875.
5   WC&ER DM, 23rd June 1875.
6   JCM, 19th Jan. 1888.
7   WC&ER SM, 25th Feb. 1868.

8   WC&ER DM, 6th July 1871.
9   Capt Tyler report, 17th Aug. 1873.
10 Col. Rich report, 26th May 1874.
11 JCM, 21st Oct. 1879.
12 JCM, 1st Nov. 1880.
13 JCM, 7th July 1881.
14 JCM, 17th Feb. 1880.

An engine and van at Frizington station c.1910. The locomotive is FR 0-6-0 tank No. 102, formerly WC&ER No. 6 *"Parkside".* (G. Holme collection)

THE CLEATOR & WORKINGTON RAILWAY: EARLY YEARS

The Tripartite Agreement of 30th April 1877 had set down the working arrangements between the FR, the LNWR and the C&WJR.

The Furness Railway had obtained joint ownership of the Whitehaven, Cleator & Egremont Railway with the LNWR, from 1st July 1878. However, unlike the FR, which was tied to its relationship with the LNWR, the C&WJR was a relatively free agent.

Its directors had, on 9th January 1877, considered the various tenders for the construction of the line, including those of William Gradwell of Barrow-in-Furness, Thomas Nelson of Carlisle and Robert Ward of Glasgow. After some negotiation, the tender was let to Robert Ward & Partners for £97,767 14s 7d. The 1877 Act had authorised the working of the C&WJR main line by the Furness Railway and the ownership of shares by the latter.

On 17th January 1877 the FR allocated shares to the following nominees:

Duke of Devonshire	£9,000
Lord Edward Cavendish	£4,000
Francis Egerton	£4,000
Sir James Ramsden	£4,000

The first meeting of the Cleator & Workington & Furness Joint Committee, authorised by the agreement of 6th April 1877, was held at Whitehaven on 26th December at which it was agreed that William Fletcher and R. Alleyne Robinson would represent the C&WJR and Lord Frederick Cavendish and Sir James Ramsden

the FR. Ramsden was appointed a director of the C&WJR on 21st August 1878. In the light of subsequent events, the wisdom of appointing Ramsden might be questioned, but it was normal practice, when one company had powers to take shares in a second, for the first to appoint directors to the second. A local example was that of the Cockermouth, Keswick & Penrith Railway to which board the working companies – NER and LNWR – each appointed two directors. What was not anticipated in 1878, was that later, the ironmaster proprietors of the C&WJR would adopt an aggressive policy on through rates.

It had been agreed that the line would be built as a double line and that, in view of the tripartite agreement, it was no longer necessary to consider a line to the Cleator & Furness south of Egremont.

However, Baird and Company had obtained powers in 1874 to construct the Rowrah & Kelton Fell (Mineral) Railway and the C&WJR had powers to construct a branch to Harrington by its 1876 Act. So, in order to complete the link, the C&WJR sought powers, in the 1877-78 session, to build its Rowrah branch from Distington. This line, of just over six miles, was authorised by the Cleator & Workington Junction Extension Act of 4th July 1878.

Robert Ward was awarded the contract for the construction of the Rowrah branch on 8th November 1878. It was agreed that the Rowrah & Kelton Fell Railway, if sold, would give first refusal to the C&WJR[1]. At the half year shareholders' meeting, on 14th February 1879, it was noted that the Moresby Coal Company was constructing a branch to its Walkmill colliery.

The Cleator Moor station of the C&WJR, seen here in the 1930s, was renamed 'West' by the LMS to distinguish it from the station on the FR/LNWR Joint line which became 'East'. (CRA Pattinson collection)

Moresby Junction, seen in the 1930s, controlled the siding into the Moresby Coal Company's Walkmill pit. At one time a platform was installed here served by workmen's trains. (CRA Pattinson collection)

The company gave notice to the LNWR, that it intended to open its line for mineral traffic on 1st July 1879. The LNWR objected to this, upon which the C&WJR again played the 'Midland card' by authorising its secretary:

'...to make any arrangement with the Midland Railway Company which he may consider for the interests of their Company and the benefit of the traders of the district.'

However, some accommodation must have been reached as the *West Cumberland Times* noted that *'the Main Line was opened for mineral traffic on 1st July 1879.'*

The main line was from a junction with the LNWR & Furness Joint Line near Moor Row (Cleator Moor Junction), to the LNWR's Whitehaven Junction Railway at Siddick Junction, a distance of 11 miles 15 chains and was double throughout. That part of Railway No. 1, (Chapter Seventeen: 'No 2') connecting the main line with the Lonsdale Dock at Workington (27 chains), was to be used for mineral traffic only.

Stations were provided at:

Cleator Moor
(0 miles 15 chains)
Moresby
(2 miles 78 chains)
Distington
(6 miles 8 chains)
High Harrington
(7 miles 34 chains)
Workington
(9 miles 32 chains)

There were connections at Moresby Junction (2 miles 38 chains) with the branch to the Walkmill Colliery; at Rowrah

Moresby station, near the summit of the C&WJR, served the mining community of Moresby Parks. (CRA Pattinson collection)

Junction with the proposed line to Rowrah (6 miles 8 chains) and at Harrington Junction (8 miles 7 chains), with a branch to the Moss Bay Ironworks.

The passenger traffic was to be worked by the Furness Railway Company, off its own system, as far as Workington station where, for the present, it would terminate, although it was intended to erect a station at Siddick Junction and to run trains to this point.

There were over 6½ miles on a gradient of 1 in 70 and signal-boxes were sited at Cleator Moor Junction, Cleator Moor station, Moresby Junction, Moresby station, Rowrah Junction, Distington Junction, High Harrington, Moss Bay Junction at Harrington, Workington station, West Cumberland Junction (Dock Junction) and Siddick Junction.

Major Marindin, the Board of Trade inspector, recommended a number of alterations to the interlocking at the various signal-boxes on the line, but sanctioned the opening of the Cleator & Workington Junction main line for passenger traffic and this took place, between Moor Row and Workington, on 1st October 1879[2].

The junction station on the LNWR line at Siddick was opened on 1st September 1880[3].

At the half year shareholders' meeting, held on 29th August 1879, it was noted that £229,465 had been spent on capital account and that the extra cost was attributed to the doubling of the main line, which had not originally been contemplated. On 12th November the board agreed that its No. 4 railway, from Harrington Junction to Moss Bay, would be worked by the FR on a temporary basis and that its No. 3 railway, from Harrington Junction to Harrington, would be worked by James Bain & Co. of Harrington Ironworks.

The Distington Ironworks branch dispute

A much more serious dispute between the C&WJR and its neighbours arose over the Distington Ironworks. The authorisation of the C&WJR and of the Whitehaven, Cleator & Egremont line from its Gilgarran branch, through Distington to Parton, in 1876, led to the creation of a partnership, in 1878, to build an ironworks at Distington. The Distington Hematite Iron Company had William McCowan, later to become a C&WJR director, as its chairman, with the remaining interests coming from the

Looking north at the Distington Joint station in the 1930s. (CRA Pattinson collection)

Kilmarnock district in Scotland. The works came into operation about the same time as the C&WJR was opened.

The traffic from this works was to create a dispute between the partners in the tripartite agreement. The C&WJR and FR Joint Committee noted, at its meeting in Westminster on 6th November 1879:

> 'The representatives of the Furness Company ... reported that the North Western Company and the Furness Company are willing to consider the Distington Ironworks a competitive station under the Tripartite Agreement provided that the Cleator & Workington Company will undertake not to make a branch line into the works. The representatives of the C&WJR declined to accept this condition.'

The meeting was adjourned and, on the next day, 7th November, the LNWR hosted a meeting at which Sir James Ramsden and Henry Cook represented the FR and William Cawkwell, George Findlay and Richard Roberts (traffic manager) represented the LNWR.

This meeting noted that the C&WJR could put a short line into the works by agreement with the landowners and thus secure the traffic. The owner of the land was Mr Curwen, chairman of the C&WJR. It was agreed that the division of traffic from Distington Ironworks be conceded, but, in the event of any branch being made, the concession would be withdrawn. As it turned out, the ownership of the intervening land was not as the C&WJR believed.

A later view, c.1962, showing Distington Joint signalbox and the Gilgarran branch curving away to the left. (Author: MAA171)

Having returned to Barrow following this meeting, Sir James Ramsden wrote to William Fletcher, on 10th November:

> 'My dear Sir,
>
> 'I have received notice of a Special Meeting of the Cleator & Workington Company to be held at Workington ... to consider ... an application to Parliament for a branch to the Distington Iron Works. I regret that I am unable to be present at this meeting to state my objections to this proposal as I gathered from what passed at our recent meeting in London that you and your colleagues are already determined to make this application to Parliament.
>
> 'I regard the proposal of the Branch as an unnecessary

Harrington Junction, looking north c. 1934, was the hub of the C&WJR system with branches from this point to the Derwent and Moss Bay ironworks at Workington and to Harrington and Lowca. (CRA Pattinson collection)

outlay of Capital, for which no adequate return is possible and coupling this with the general policy which is being pursued by you and your colleagues to which I object as being in my opinion contrary to the true interests of the Shareholders, I feel that I can no longer work harmoniously with the Board of the Cleator & Workington Railway and therefore beg to resign my Seat.'

William Fletcher replied on 12th November:

'Before receiving your letter of the 10th Mr Robinson and myself had resolved to recommend to the Directors not to promote a branch to the Distington Iron Works this year in the hope that an amicable arrangement may yet be effected to secure our Company access to the north upon reasonable terms over the Joint Line.

'I trust therefore you will now be willing to recall your resignation and let me have the pleasure of returning you the letter instead of having to lay it before the Board.

'As regard your complaint against the general policy of the Directors, I can confidentially assert that it has been adopted ... with the single object of securing the utmost possible success of the undertaking by all legitimate means. If the Directors rested content with anything short of this they would fail in their duty to the Company.'

Sir James replied, on 17th November:

'My resolve to withdraw from the Board of the Cleator & Workington Railway was not arrived at suddenly; I have had it in contemplation for some time. The constant demands & threats reiterated at every meeting, a general

policy of aggression being kept steadily in view as well as a desire to reduce rates for the benefit of the traders, while the interests of the shareholders in maintaining the rates were ignored, at last compelled me to withdraw from the disagreeable position in which I felt my self placed.

'The kind of policy pursued by you and your colleagues is one to which I am not accustomed and is so contrary to what I consider should be the guiding principle of a Railway Director that I could no longer sit at a Board where such was the ruling spirit.

'The Cleator & Workington have secured a most exceptionally favourable working agreement and one which must entail a loss upon my Company. You have also obtained, mainly through my intervention, everything which can reasonably be asked for as regards a fair share of the traffic of the district and I am sure it will be more conducive to the interests of the Shareholders of the Cleator & Workington line if a pacific policy be entered upon by your Board. At any rate unless such a policy be adopted I cannot cooperate with you,'

William Fletcher replied from his residence *Brigham Hill* on 19th November:

'Dear Sir,
Your letter of the 17th leaves me no course open but to recommend the Board to accept your resignation. If you had given as reason for resigning that you found the office incompatible with your interest in competing companies the reason would have been intelligible to your colleagues and would had passed unchallenged. But when you attribute the step to their pursuance of an aggressive policy detrimental to the Shareholders and to their desire to reduce rates for the benefit of the Traders, I will not wait

Looking north at Workington Central station on 24th April 1965, showing the signalbox in a dilapidated condition. The line through Workington Central closed on 26th September that year. (Author: MAO0908)

until the next Board Meeting before entering my protest against both of these charges.

'As to the first charge I am willing to leave it to the Shareholders themselves to be the Judges whether the Board consulted their interests or not in refusing to yield to the attempts of the two Companies to deprive this Company of ordinary and reasonable traffic facilities. As to the second charge, if I am right in taking it to mean that some Directors have endeavoured to serve their own purposes as traders at the expense of the Company, the charge is so serious a one that I must call upon you either to substantiate or withdraw it.

'I have always held at the Board with the unanimous support of my colleagues that we sought to exact the full Parliamentary rates unless in cases where competition renders some abatement necessary to secure a fair share of the traffic, and you will find that without any exception the rates upon traffic in which I am personally concerned are in every instance at least as high as the Company have powers to charge.

Yours truly,
W. Fletcher'

At the eighth half yearly general meeting of the shareholders of the C&WJR, held at the Good Templars Hall, Workington on 27th February 1880, the Directors' Report noted that the main line had been opened for general purposes on 1st October 1879 and that the Rowrah branch was making satisfactory progress.

The dispute over through rates continued and a meeting on this subject was held at Barrow on 10th August 1880, at which both the Duke of Devonshire and Sir James Ramsden were present[4].

The C&WJR representatives, led by their chairman, William Fletcher, demanded a through rate from Moor Row to the Maryport Ironworks via the C&WJR. Fortified by the joint ownership of the Whitehaven, Cleator & Egremont line with the LNWR and the tripartite agreement, the FR representatives *'did not consider the application a fair one under all the circumstances and could not concur in it'*. It was agreed to submit the matter to the Standing Arbitrator. The C&WJR representatives retired hurt and it was at this time, no doubt, that they first contemplated a direct line to Maryport.

The branch to Workington Dock left the C&WJR main line at Dock Junction, seen here c.1934. The Dock Jct engine shed, mid-centre, maintained the small stud of the Company's own locomotives required for lines not worked under the agreement with the FR. (K. Norman collection N285)

However, the ninth half yearly meeting was next on the agenda and was held at Workington on 27th October 1880. A first dividend of 3½% was agreed and it was noted that the Whitehaven Hematite Iron Company, at Cleator Moor, was constructing a branch line from their works to the C&WJR main line. The opening of the Moresby Coal Company's Walkmill pit, near the main line, was also recorded.

These were important potential sources of traffic. On a sadder note, the death of the chairman and director, H.F. Curwen, was recorded and that his place on the board had been filled by J.L. Burns Lindow of Irton Hall, Holmrook, ironmaster. William Fletcher was appointed to the chair.

The Maryport extension plan

The C&WJR was now determined to promote a Bill for a line to the Maryport & Carlisle Railway. It had proposed a meeting with the M&CR on 29th September 1890, but this proposal does not seem to have found favour with the M&C board, so preparation of the Bill proceeded. On 15th October the C&WJR board noted that its proposed extension was:

> 'to obviate the obstruction placed by the LNWR in the way of the Company forwarding traffic between Siddick Junction and Maryport.'

The Bill was also to include the controversial branch to the Distington ironworks. The deposited plan, prepared by the company's engineers, John Wood of Carlisle and A.H. Strongitharm of Barrow, together with the other necessary papers, was duly deposited and proposed the following lines:

No. 1 Siddick to north of Maryport Station on the M&CR.
No. 2 A spur from No. 1 to the south end of Maryport station.
No. 3 A branch to the Solway Ironworks at Maryport.
No. 4 A branch to the Maryport Ironworks.
No. 5 A branch from Distington to the Distington Ironworks.
The C&WJR board met at Workington on 11th February 1881.

William Fletcher led the meeting and was accompanied by John Ainsworth of The Flosh, Cleator (Whitehaven Hematite Iron Co.), J.R. Bain of Harrington (the Harrington Ironworks), Robert Alleyn Robinson of South Lodge, Cockermouth, Jonas L. Burns Lindow of Irton Hall (ironmaster) and Major Andrew Green Thompson of Bridekirk, Cockermouth (Director of CK&PR, Solway Junction and Caledonian Railways). Also in attendance were T.S. Dodgson, the General Manager and Secretary, E.L. Waugh, the Solicitor, and John Wood, the Engineer. The meeting considered the various developments.

The Maryport & Carlisle Railway had second thoughts. It realised that the traffic from a potential major source on to its line could not be spurned, but it viewed with distaste the C&WJR proposal, in its Bill, to run branches directly into works on the M&CR system. It wrote on 24th January 1881, that it had considered its Company's Petition against the C&WJR Bill and that if certain clauses were withdrawn the Petition would be reduced to a 'watching petition'.

The outcome was a meeting between the boards of the C&WJR and M&CR, on 8th February, at which it was agreed that the C&WJR would have the same use of the Maryport station as the LNWR held, by the agreement of 1st July 1871. The C&WJR agreed to withdraw the clauses in its Bill relating to the lines to the south end of Maryport station, the branch to the Solway Ironworks and the branch to the Maryport Ironworks. The LNWR noted this agreement and, on 8th February, George Findlay, of the LNWR, wrote, from Euston Station to T.S. Dodgson of the C&WJR:

> 'upon the subject of Capt. Galton's award fixing the rates for iron ore from Cleator Moor to Maryport at 2s 2d per ton ... we are prepared to put the reduced rates in force for all traffic intended to pass from the Cleator District west or south of Yeathouse Station including that station to Maryport by the C&WJR route.'

Findlay wrote again, the next day:

In this scene, c.1964, the main line of the C&WJR is in the foreground. To the rear is Siddick Junction signalbox controlling the connection of the C&WJR with the Whitehaven Junction line. (CRA: White collection)

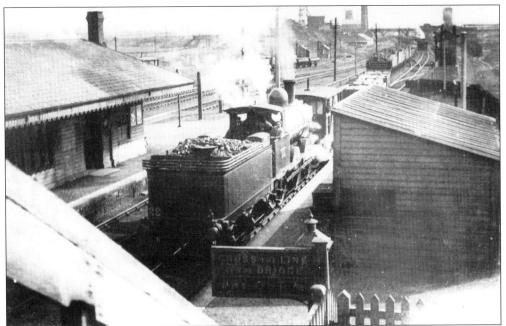

The LNWR works a freight train northbound from Workington into Siddick Junction station. In the left background the C&WJR line can be seen descending on an embankment. St Helen's colliery is just visible, as is the overbridge carrying the C&WJR Docks branch. (K. Norman collection)

'With reference to the conversation which took place in my office when you were here with your Directors on 4th inst. when Mr Fletcher mentioned the coke rate from the Newcastle District ... to the C&WJR line ... I understand that the application of your Company is that these rates shall apply not only to the Whitehaven Hematite Ironworks at Cleator Moor but also to the Harrington & Moss Bay works. As your Company are willing to accept a proportion of 3d per ton terminals and not mileage I have to intimate that my Company is willing to accept that mode of division provided the North Eastern and Maryport & Carlisle Railways also agree to the proposal.'

As a result of this accommodation by the LNWR, the Maryport branch was struck out of the C&WJR Bill of 1881 and only the controversial Distington ironworks branch was authorised.

This branch was to remain an issue and the subject of correspondence between the C&WJR and the Board of Trade. The 1881 Act, which authorised the branch, did not give compulsory powers to purchase the land for the branch, as it was not for public use. Subsequently, the 1883 Act (clause 30) gave running powers over the LNWR and Furness Joint Line Gilgarran branch, to the Distington Ironworks. The C&WJR then sought to avoid its responsibilities to build this line and the penalties for not doing so, on the grounds that the purchase of the necessary land had not been possible by private treaty. It came to light that the owner of an essential parcel of land, one Charles Fisher of Distington Hall, who had been opposed to the construction of the branch, had sold his land to the LNWR and Furness Joint Committee, so ensuring that the line would not be built. The protracted correspondence with the Board of Trade on this matter[5] resulted in the branch being abandoned with Board of Trade approval.

Yet another dispute serves to illustrate the unhappy relationship between the C&WJR and its working partner, the Furness Railway. The subject was the rates applied to traders own wagons. Henry Cook had written from Barrow to his opposite number T.S. Dodgson on 9th March 1881:

'Traders Wagon Hire:
I have reported to our Managing Director what took place

at the meetings held at Great George Street on Monday and Tuesday last and I am instructed to say that while he assents generally to all that Mr Cawkwell (LNWR) said at both those meetings, he protests strongly against the question of the traders wagon hire being again submitted to arbitration.

'The agreement between our two Companies for the working of the Cleator & Workington Junction Railway provides that all questions in dispute shall be submitted to a standing arbitrator. This question of the Traders Wagons hire has been submitted to the Arbitrator and his decision is given and now because that decision is adverse to your Company your Directors seek to set it aside by what we consider unfair proceeding. My Directors protest against this manner of conducting business and if you really mean to act in this way in every case of dispute it will put an end to all amicable working between the Companies.'

William Fletcher replied to Henry Cook, on 11th March:

'At the time the rates were settled by the three Companies (in the Tripartite Agreement) the fact that the tolls upon the railway are the same whether the traffic is carried in Company wagons or in Traders' wagons seems to have been overlooked and a differential rate was agreed to and it is to put the matter right that we have asked your Company and the LNWR either to alter the rates or have the matter settled by arbitration.

'At the time the Working Agreement was entered into, your Company and this were on very friendly terms and were both endeavouring to protect themselves from the obstructive and arbitrary policy of another Railway Company but since the other interests have been separated and some of the Covenants in the Working Agreement unperformed ... my Directors consider that an accusation of unfair dealing not only comes with a bad grace from you but tends to widen the breach which your actions have already caused between the two Companies.'

The basis of this dispute seems to have been the fact that the Tripartite Agreement did not recognise a reduced rate for traffic carried in traders' wagons. At the meeting of the Joint Committee, on 29th June 1880, the C&WJR claimed that the traders should be charged at the gross rate in the Company's wagons and that an allowance be made to the traders for their

On the Rowrah branch at Brownrigg curve an LMS 0-6-0 tank engine hauls limestone empties up the bank in the mid-1930s. CRA Pattinson collection)

Oatlands station on the Rowrah branch in the mid-1930s. Sited away from habitation, the station and sidings existed to serve the Oatlands colliery of the Moresby Coal Co. (CRA Pattinson collection)

own wagon use. The LNWR agreed, but the FR did not. The matter was referred to the Standing Arbitrator, Captain Douglas Galton of the Railway Department, and a meeting was convened at the United Hotel in London on 22nd July 1880. The Furness Railway members of the committee did not turn up. At a meeting, on 6th January 1881 they declined to accept the ruling of the Arbitrator. The dispute dragged on, but disappeared from the minutes of the Joint Committee in subsequent years suggesting that some accommodation had been reached.

The C&WJR resolved, on 15th August 1881, that, as the LNWR had agreed to adopt this company tariff of rates between Workington and Maryport, the Maryport Extension clause in its Bill had been struck out. It also noted that the Rowrah branch should shortly be opened for mineral traffic and would be worked by the Furness Railway.

In 1881 dividends of 3½% p.a. and 4½% p.a. were declared for the two half years, a far from unsatisfactory result for the second complete year of working of what was a new, competitive railway.

On 14th April 1882 it noted that the Rowrah branch would be opened on 1st May, but whilst intended for mineral traffic, the Rowrah branch involved the main line and was, therefore, subject to inspection by the Board of Trade. Major General Hutchinson reported, on 26th April, that the signal arrangements were provided for in the existing raised cabin near Distington Junction and laid down the requirements necessary for the opening to be approved.

He also noted that the company was considering the possibility of using the branch for passenger traffic at some time in the future[6]. It was not until the next December, however, that contracts were let, to Fleming & Murray, for the building of stations at Arlecdon and Oatlands[7]. Opening for passengers took place on 3rd July 1883 with the service being worked by the FR under the terms of the Working Agreement[8].

CHAPTER 18 REFERENCES

1   C&WJR DM, 12th Sep. 1877.
2   C&WJR DM, 12th Sep. 1879.
3   Joy D. Op. cit. p.178.
4   C&WJ & FR, 10th Aug. 1880.
5   PRO: MT6 366/10.
6   Ibid.
7   C&WJR DM, 8th Dec. 1882.
8   C&WJR DM, 13th July 1883

The station at Arlecdon, at the eastern end of the Rowrah branch, in the mid-1930s. The Coal Company ran its own workmen's trains between Arlecdon and Oatlands until the closure of the branch in 1938. (CRA Pattinson collection)

THE CLEATOR & WORKINGTON JUNCTION RAILWAY'S NORTHERN EXTENSION

The Cleator & Workington Junction Railway, having been frustrated in its attempt to break out to the north with its 1881 Bill, by the undertakings given by the LNWR and the M&CR to the Parliamentary Committee, discussed its Northern Extension again at the meeting on 30th September 1881. The C&WJR had the support of the North British Railway (over whose Silloth Branch the Solway Junction Railway's line ran between Abbey Junction and Kirkbride Junction) in its application to Parliament, in the 1882 session, for a line from the C&WJR north of Workington to the Solway Junction Railway at Brayton. Such a line would give the C&WJR an independent route to the

iron industry of the Scottish lowlands, via the Glasgow & South Western and Caledonian systems. There would also be an independent route to Carlisle, giving access to Edinburgh via the North British line and to Newcastle via the North Eastern line, for its coke traffic.

This proposal was, however, clouded by the destruction of parts of the Solway Junction Railway viaduct by ice floes, which had occurred on 29th January 1881[1]. The viaduct was not to reopen until 1st May 1884. The C&WJR resolved to press ahead with its ambitious Bill, which not only sought powers for the northern extension to Brayton, but also a short eastern exten-

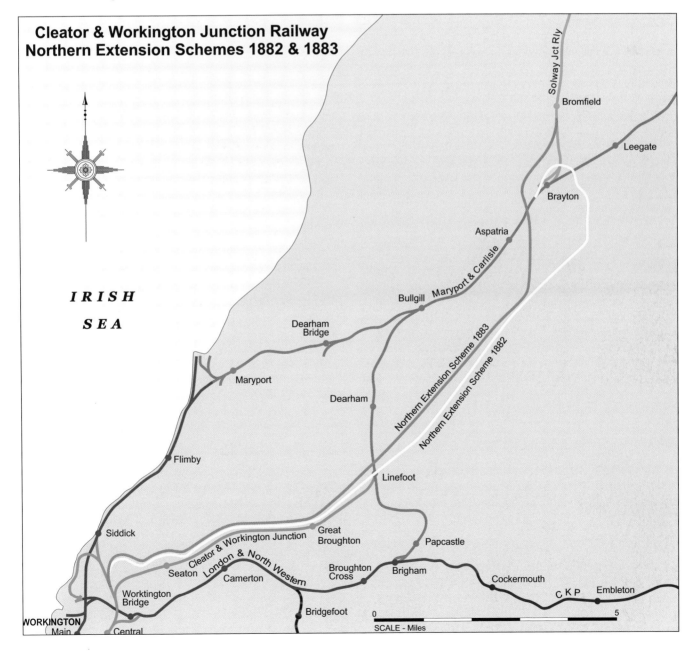

**Cleator & Workington Junction Railway
Northern Extension Schemes 1882 & 1883**

sion from the main line at Cloffocks to the LNWR's Cockermouth and Workington line at Workington Bridge. This would give direct access to the Cockermouth, Keswick & Penrith line and the South Durham coke traffic. A *Gazette* notice was published, dated 15th November 1881, and the Bill was deposited on 31st December 1881[2].

The new railways, proposed by the 1882 Bill were:

No. 1 From the mainline of the C&WJR, 304 yards north of the bridge over the Cockermouth & Workington Railway, to the Solway Junction Railway, 100 yards east of the Brayton Junction signalbox. (The proposed junction with the SJR was unusual in that the line crossed both the M&CR and SJR lines by overbridges and joined the SJR from the north).

No. 2 From line No. 1 to the M&CR Bolton branch at Baggrow.

No. 3 From the main line of the C&WJR to the Cockermouth & Workington line of the LNWR at Workington Bridge.

While confirming the tripartite traffic agreement of 30th April 1877 between the C&WJR, the LNWR and the FR, the Bill sought powers for a new working agreement with either the FR, the M&CR, the Solway Junction Railway, the North British Railway or the Caledonian Railway. Running powers were sought, for the North British Railway, over the whole of the C&WJR system and for the working company, over the NBR. The C&WJR also sought running powers for itself over the Solway Junction Railway to the junction at Abbey Holme and over the NBR from Abbey Holme to both Silloth and Carlisle Canal Junction.

Not surprisingly, these proposals elicited opposition from the FR to protect the working agreement, from the LNWR, the M&CR, who were to be bypassed, and from the Caledonian on the grounds that they objected to any advantage their arch-rival, the North British might gain. The evidence was heard twice, first by a Commons Committee, on 23rd March and secondly by a Lords Committee, on 27th and 28th June 1882.

The principal witness for the Bill was William Fletcher, the chairman of the C&WJR and a partner in the Moresby Coal Company, the output of which was stated as 250,000 tons per annum, all of which was carried over the C&WJR line from Moresby Junction. On the subject of the working agreement, Fletcher stated that he was horrified to learn for the first time, in December 1876, from Sir James Ramsden, that Ramsden was using the agreement as a lever to make terms with the LNWR over the joint purchase of the Whitehaven, Cleator & Egremont Railway; he added that if he had known this, the working agreement would not have been made. Ramsden insisted that Fletcher was aware of his purpose, to use the C&WJR as a 'fighting-line', throughout. Counsel for the FR pointed out that this knowledge had not stopped the C&WJR from extending the working agreement to the Rowrah branch.

The discussion then moved on to the more tangible matter of division of traffic rates. Referring to the tripartite agreement of 1877, Fletcher claimed that it had been understood that the agreement would include traffic going beyond Workington to Maryport, but the LNWR had objected. Fletcher went on:

'a little before the Parliamentary contest of last year (the 1881 Bill) the LNWR agreed to grant a through rate to Newcastle but so soon as our Bill had been thrown out, they withdrew their consent. ... We are still desirous of getting a through route to the north and the east independent of the LNWR Company which has control over us.'

Finally Fletcher turned to the traffic which the proposed line to Brayton would facilitate; he estimated the annual tonnages would be:

Iron ore	1,825,000
Coke	1,100,000
Pig iron	1,000,000
Limestone	400,000

and that there were extensive deposits of limestone on the route, which was in short supply at the furnaces of West Cumberland.

Thomas Steele Dodgson, Secretary & General Manager of the C&WJR – who formerly held the same post with the WC&ER, until its purchase by the LNWR in 1877 – told the Committee that the LNWR received such an exorbitant amount from the through rate for traffic going north and east beyond Maryport, that, in many instances, his company lost money from the mileage, gaining only from the terminal charges. Charles Valentine, a C&WJR director and manager of the Moss Bay Hematite Iron and Steel Company of Workington, confirmed that the access to limestone, provided by the proposed line, would be sufficient for the needs of the West Cumberland trade. George Snelus, of the West Cumberland Ironworks at Siddick, stated that his company was not sending rails through Carlisle to any great extent because of the prohibitive rates. Finally, John Wood, the Civil Engineer to the C&WJR, outlined the engineering aspects of the proposed lines and estimated the cost at £140,000. He admitted that there was a ruling gradient of 1 in 70.

Ramsden stated that a working agreement with the North British Railway would be neither in the interests of the traders nor of his company.

The Commons Committee, while indicating its sympathy with the C&WJR's proposals, expressed the opinion that to grant running powers over the whole of the Company's lines would constitute a serious breach of the 1877 Agreement and it granted running powers only over the proposed line and the old line from the junction to Workington. Only the line from near Siddick to Baggrow was approved, effectively cutting off the proposed link with the SJR and the NBR. The Lords' Committee chairman, after hearing all the evidence, asked the representatives of the LNWR and M&CR to bind themselves not to raise their rates. This undertaking was given, but the Committee ruled that the preamble of the Bill was not proved; thus the C&WJR had failed again.

However, it was not to be deterred and, on 20th October 1882, decided to deposit another Northern Extension Bill for the 1883 Parliamentary Session. It should be remembered that Furness and West Cumberland were enjoying what was to prove no more than a temporary boom in the iron trade.

Success of the 1883 Bill

The Bill for the 1883 session of Parliament went ahead. The *Gazette* notice was dated 14th November 1882 and described two proposed lines. Gone was the inconvenient 'spiral' approach to Brayton of the 1882 Bill. The new Northern Extension swept over both the M&CR Bolton branch and the main line to make an end-on junction, with the Solway Junction Railway, east of Brayton station. A short spur was to connect the northern extension with the M&CR main line west of Brayton. The spur between the C&WJR and the Cockermouth and Workington line, of the LNWR, at Workington Bridge, thrown out of the previous Bill, was reintroduced. Fresh powers were also sought for the

Viewed from the overbridge at Calva Junction c.1934, the main line to Siddick Junction is on the left. At right centre an 0-6-0 tank engine is signalled from the Northern Extension line on to the main line. In the left distance is St Helen's Colliery. (CRA Pattinson collection)

line into Distington ironworks. Finally, comprehensive connections with Harrington harbour and ironworks were proposed. From the original Moss Bay branch, a line was to run down to Harrington harbour, with south and north side branches, and from the Harrington branch, two short branches were to be made into James Bain & Company's Harrington ironworks.

Running powers were to be sought:

1. Over the Solway Junction Railway to its junction with the North British Railway at Abbey Holme Junction;
2. At Brayton station;
3. Over the North British Railway between Silloth and Canal Junction, Carlisle:
4. At Workington Bridge station, on the LNWR Cockermouth and Workington line;
5. Over the junction between the Rowrah & Kelton Fell (Mineral) Railway and the line of the Whitehaven, Cleator & Egremont Railway, at Rowrah.

Running powers for the North British Railway, over the Northern Extension and the main line onwards to Workington station, were also sought.

Finally, powers were sought to allow new agreements for the working of the C&WJR's old and proposed lines with the FR, the M&CR, the Solway Junction and the North British and Caledonian Railways.

The Bill, deposited on 30th November 1882[3], came before the House of Lords Committee on 14th June 1883, and the estimate of cost, made by the company's engineers, John Wood and Augustus Strongitharm, was £202,123. Petitions against the Bill were made by the LNWR, the LNWR & Furness Joint Railway, the Maryport & Carlisle Railway and the Solway Junction Railway. The evidence was heard on 20th, 21st and 22nd June[4]. The essence of the C&WJR case was made by Thomas Steele Dodgson, its Secretary and General Manager, who commented that there had been no difficulty in raising the capital for his railway company in West Cumberland. In fact, it had been necessary to refuse requests for shares. The subscribers were largely the traders of the district. He also said

that the LNWR lines in West Cumberland were an island, separated, by a distance of 31 miles, from the main LNWR system, by an independent company, and continued that the LNWR *'are freebooters and marauders'* in the district. Dodgson stated that an accommodation had been reached, with the LNWR and Furness Joint Railway, about running powers over the controversial branch between Distington Junction and Distington ironworks.

Dodgson continued, that the Northern Extension would tap extensive mineral traffic from the local mines and quarries, but, in addition, it would put the local traders into direct connection with the North British and Caledonian companies, the Glasgow & South Western Company and, at Carlisle, with the North Eastern and Midland companies. While accepting that the proposed line would be competitive, he maintained that there would be no interference with the traffic, over the LNWR, between Workington and Maryport.

In cross-examination by Mr Pope QC, for the LNWR, Mr Dodgson stated that some 6,000 tons of traffic was destined for the C&WJR line and would be carried by the proposed curve at Workington Bridge. To Mr Pember QC, on behalf of the M&CR, Dodgson had to admit that the M&CR route, between Brayton and Workington, was slightly shorter and that the gradients were more favourable, but he maintained that the 'shortest route' principle for charging rates would apply.

Following a protracted discussion of rates by competing routes, the Committee found that the Preamble of the C&WJR was proved. The Act received Royal Assent on 16th July 1883.

At the half yearly Meeting of the C&WJR, on 24th August, a dividend of 3% p.a. was authorised. The Board reported:

'The inability of the Company within their present limits to obtain a share of the through traffic to and from the district has prevented the revenue from keeping pace with the recent increase in capital. This drawback will be removed by the extension authorised by the Act obtained on 16th July 1883.'

Looking north at Calva Junction in the mid-1930s, In the distance, right, is the home signal from the Linefoot Junction to Calva C&WJR's Northern Extension line. (CRA Pattinson collection)

It should be noted that the Act contained no reference to any working agreement other than that with the Furness Railway and no running powers over the C&WJR line by the North British Railway or others. These clauses must have been negotiated out of the original bill during its course through Parliament.

On 11th August the agreement allowing running powers to the C&WJR over the joint line to Distington ironworks was sealed[5] and on 9th November, R.H. Hodgson's tender, for the building of the Workington Bridge curve, was accepted by the board.

The diversion to Linefoot

The now depressed state of the iron trade led to the C&WJR reviewing its capital commitments. The first line to be abandoned was the branch from the Moss Bay line into Harrington harbour, and by 21st December 1883, the C&WJR had decided to limit its purchase of land for the Northern Extension to the point of crossing the M&CR Derwent branch. On 1st February 1884 the C&WJR was in communication with the M&CR to agree a junction with its Northern Extension and the M&CR Derwent branch at Linefoot. On 9th May, the contract for the Northern Extension, as far as the M&CR Derwent branch, was let to R.H. Hodgson for £34,128.

A meeting with the M&CR directors was held at Maryport on 14th April 1885, when William Fletcher, for the C&WJR, stated the terms on which his company would agree to abandon the Northern Extension beyond the M&CR Derwent branch. These were running powers from Linefoot to Brayton; the C&WJR to make its own through rates; running powers to be agreed with the FR, as working company; costs of abandonment to be shared between the two companies; the M&CR to be offered running powers over the C&WJR to Workington but, after due consideration, the M&CR wrote back, the same day, stating that it could not agree to the required running powers over its line from Linefoot to Brayton. Matters rested until a joint meeting of the two boards, on 1st May 1885, at which the C&WJR put forward new proposals. Again there appears to have been no progress because, on 14th November, the C&WJR published the *Gazette* notice for its Parliamentary Bill. This Bill

proposed a short line, from the authorised Northern Extension, to the M&CR's Derwent branch at Linefoot; running powers from Linefoot to Brayton; the M&CR to double its line from Linefoot to Bullgill; working agreements, for operation of the Northern Extension and spur to Linefoot, with the Furness, the Maryport & Carlisle, the Solway Junction, the North British and Caledonian Railway Companies and abandonment of the authorised Northern Extension north of the proposed spur at Linefoot.

William Fletcher headed a C&WJR Parliamentary Committee to monitor the progress of this Bill and he reported to his board, on 22nd March 1886, that there had been lengthy discussions with representatives of the M&CR, which had led to an agreement being signed and sealed. An agreement with the North British Railway, of 7th November 1884, was to be cancelled, powers to run over the M&CR to Brayton were not to be sought and an undertaking was given not to seek powers, in the future, to build the abandoned portion of the Northern Extension from Linefoot to Brayton. Fletcher also reported that the petitions of the Furness and Caledonian Companies had been withdrawn. The Act, which received Royal Assent on 25th June 1886, confirmed the agreement with the M&CR, of 16th March 1886, and abandoned the two short branch lines from the Harrington branch to the Harrington ironworks.

Among the local events at this time, the shareholders' meeting, on 27th February 1885, was notified that the branch to Workington Bridge had been completed and would open immediately, the running powers over the LNWR and FR joint line to Distington ironworks was now in operation and that construction of the Northern Extension was making good progress. Thomas Steele Dodgson had resigned as Secretary and General Manager and had been appointed a director, in which capacity he continued until his death, on 8th January 1891. The branch to Harrington harbour was opened on 19th December 1885[6].

The *West Cumberland Times* of 1st January 1887 reported that on the previous Wednesday (29th December 1886) the first train had run over the Northern Extension. This was not a passenger train but an 'officers special' by which the FR consulting engineer, Frank Stileman; the C&WJR engineer, Mr Strongitharm; Mr Anyon, the company secretary, and others carried out their inspection of the new works. The paper noted that opening as far as Seaton, for mineral and goods traffic, would take place on 1st January 1887. The junction at Calva, as it was on a passenger line, had been inspected by Col. Rich of the Board of Trade on 13th December 1886. The junction with the passenger line of the M&CR at Linefoot was inspected on 24th March 1887 and the file contains a diagram of the signalling arrangements at Linefoot Junction[7]. The Northern Extension was opened throughout for goods and mineral traffic on that date[8].

On 12th September 1887, Anyon, the Company Secretary, wrote to the Board of Trade Railway Department stating that it was the intention of the C&WJR to open its line for passenger traffic, between Calva Junction and Linefoot Junction, one month from that date. The Board decided, on 14th October 1887, that the Northern Extension passenger service would be limited to trains between Workington and Seaton on market days. However, at this time, the Company agreed with the FR, that the latter would work the Northern Extension and the spur to Workington Bridge, under the terms of the Working Agreement, and that *'not more than four trains a day from Moor Row to Linefoot'* would be provided on being given *'three months notice'*.

There must have been some delay as the opening was put back to 1st December 1887 by a further letter from Anyon to the Railway Department[9]. Col. Rich carried out his inspection and reported on 7th December. He noted that there were stations at Seaton and Great Broughton, that the ruling gradient was 1 in 70 and that most of the line utilised 'Kirk's Patent Steel Sleepers' manufactured, from 1885, by the Moss Bay Hematite Iron & Steel Works[10]. Despite only single track being laid, the bridges and earthworks had been built to double line dimensions. He required that, because of the steep gradients between Seaton and Linefoot, this section should be kept clear of trains while a train is approaching Seaton from Workington.

His most significant (and enigmatic) requirement was that, as there were no turntables:

'it will be necessary that the Company shall undertake to stop (terminate) all trains at Seaton unless they are through trains from other parts of their system, which are drawn by engines with their funnels in front.'

Anyon wrote to the Railway Department, on 13th December, acceding to this requirement. On 13th January 1888 the Board noted that the Northern Extension had been opened for passenger traffic on 4th January, but no details of the service was recorded.

The Cleator & Workington Junction Railway 1888-1922

Thus by 1888 the Cleator & Workington Junction Railway had completed its system and for the remainder of its independent existence its fortunes continued to be dictated by the fickle nature of the iron and steel trade. Its capital account in 1895 consisted of the following stock:

3½% Debenture	£13,175
Preference 4½%	£70,000
4% Preference 1882	£40,200
4% Preference 1883	£127,500
Ordinary	£216,010
Total:	£466,885

During the whole of this period it paid its dividends on the debenture and preference stock in full. The dividends on the ordinary stock were:

1880	3¾%	1888	2⅜%
1881	4%	1889	3¼%
1882	4¾%	1890	2⅜%
1883	3%	1891	½%
1884	2½%	1892	0% (coal strike)
1885	2%	1893	¾%
1886	1⅞%	1894	1½%
1887	3½%	1895	2%

However, from 1897 onwards, the directors sought to sell the line to the Furness Railway under the terms of the 1877 agreement, but the FR, with its reduced fortunes, consistently declined these offers.

Consequently the Cleator & Workington Junction Railway remained an independent line until it was absorbed into the London, Midland & Scottish Railway in 1923. By that time all the remaining iron and steel works in West Cumberland had become part of the United Steel Companies Limited and this company owned the large majority of the shares in the Cleator & Workington Junction Railway.

Looking north-east at Seaton station. c.1962. The squat C&WJR signalbox is long closed. (Author: MAC75)

CHAPTER 19 REFERENCES

1   Edgar S & Sinton J M, 1990. *The Solway Junction Railway* p25.
2   HLRO: C18-1882.
3   Parliamentary plan, C33/1883.
4   Lords Evidence Vol.8.
5   C&WJR DM, 11th Aug. 1883.
6   C&WJR DM, 8th Jan. 1886.
7   *CRA Journal*, Vol.4 p.182.
8   C&WJR DM, 14th Apr. 1887.
9   PRO: MT6 450/16.
10 Lancaster J.Y. & Wattleworth DR. *Op. cit.* p68.

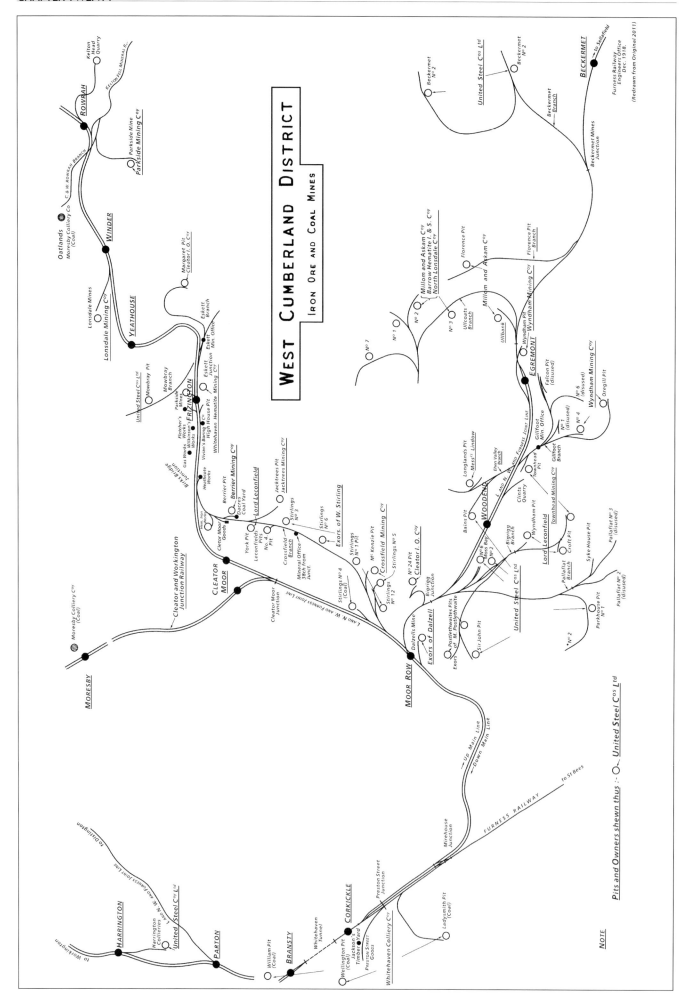

WEST CUMBERLAND DISTRICT

IRON ORE AND COAL MINES

THE LNWR & FURNESS JOINT LINE

The Joint Committee was appointed by the main Board of the two companies and consisted of Richard Moon, the Hon. William Lowther and Miles MacInnes for the LNWR and the Duke of Devonshire, Lord Frederick Cavendish and Sir James Ramsden for the Furness. However, at a preliminary Joint Officers' Meeting, held at Keswick on 27th June 1878, attended by George Findlay, Traffic Manager, G.P. Neale, Superintendent of the Line, S.B. Worthington, District Engineer Manchester, Francis Webb, Mechanical Engineer and B.A. Bedford, District Traffic Superintendent Whitehaven, for the LNWR, and Sir James Ramsden, Managing Director, and Henry Cook, Secretary and Traffic Manager, for the FR, it was agreed that the maintenance of the permanent way north of Birks Bridge Junction would be carried out by the LNWR and the remainder by the FR. The signalling would be the province of the LNWR and the telegraphs that of the FR. It appears that the seventeen WC&ER locomotives had not been taken into LNWR stock and all, except No.16, which was to be sold, went to the Furness, who numbered them from 98 to 113. The locomotive sold, identified by the LNWR as 'E', a small tank engine, was sold for £550, in December 1879, to Messrs Ackers, Whitley & Co. of Leigh[1]. The passenger carriages were divided, but later, the LNWR sold its share to the FR. The side tipping ore-wagons, suited to traffic for shipment, were taken by the FR, the LNWR taking over the chal-

For half a mile north from Sellafield station the FR/LNW Joint line to Egremont, on the right, runs alongside the FR single line towards St Bees, seen curving away to follow the shoreline after crossing the river Ehen. (CRA Pattinson collection)

drons, for local use between the mines and the iron works.

The former Traffic Manager of the WC&ER, Wilson Harrison, was appointed 'Outdoor Inspector' under Bedford and Cook: this post later became 'Joint Superintendent'. The take-over of the workshops and engine shed at Moor Row by the FR was discussed but deferred; they were eventually to become the FR base from which the Joint Line and the C&WJR were worked.

The officers then considered the various new works projects inherited from the WC&ER, the latter's Civil Engineer, George Boyd, being appointed New Works Engineer. It appears that the Gilgarran branch, its extension to Distington and the Whitehaven branch from Distington to Parton were nearing completion and extensive sidings for the Distington Ironworks, then under construction, were approved at a cost of £4,500 together with sidings for Wythemoor Colliery near Gilgarran

An engine shed existed at Moor Row from the opening of the WC&ER in 1856 but appears to have been damaged in a fire the following year and repaired in 1858. In 1878, following the creation of the FR/LNW Joint line agreement, a new four road shed was erected. This survived as BR shed 12E until 1954, closure being accelerated by structural damage due to mining settlement. In August 1939 ex-FR 0-6-0 No. 12494, rebuilt with a Belpaire boiler, and ex-L&Y No. 12110 rest between duties. (K. Norman collection)

Egremont station was rebuilt in this form after the acquisition of the WC&ER jointly by the FR and LNWR in 1878. This small market town was the centre for the local hematite mines. Workmen's, school and excursion trains continued to use the station long after any regular passenger services were provided. (K. Norman collection: H362)

and Bain's Harrington No. 4 pit near Lowca. The new line between Ullock Junction and Parton was opened for traffic on 2nd May 1879[2]. The one mile long Mowbray branch at Eskett, authorised in 1876, had not been commenced and it was agreed that this work would be carried out as soon as possible. A contract was subsequently let, to Stone & Watts of Barrow, and the branch opened for mineral traffic on 10th November 1879[3]. The Frizington deviation, which had been proposed to avoid the subsidence north-east of Frizington station, was postponed and the detraining of passengers at this point, introduced in 1875, was destined to continue until 1888.

The two loop lines at Moor Row, authorised in 1877 as a counter to the C&WJR's threat to build its independent line to Egremont, were considered and it was agreed that a better alignment could be found. The LNWR agreed to include powers for the abandonment of the Moor Row loops, and for the proposed Gillfoot branch at Egremont, in its forthcoming 'Omnibus Bill'. The loops were never built, but the short, 56 chains, Gillfoot branch was opened on 1st March 1880[4].

Finally, the officers considered the Moor Row – Egremont – Sellafield line, which at that time remained single, and it was agreed that the whole section would be doubled. On 1st November 1880 the Joint Committee let a contract to Nelson & Co. for the Egremont – Gutterby section, which was opened on 13th June 1881[5]. The doubling, onwards from Gutterby to Moor Row, was considered at a number of Joint Committee meetings over the years but it was never carried out. In fact when Gutterby Junction was closed in 1894[6] the double line terminated at Woodend.

Financial problems

The Joint Committee held its first meeting at Euston station on 18th July 1878; Moon, Lowther, Cavendish and Ramsden being supported by various officers. The recommendations of the officers' meeting at Keswick were endorsed and the related capital

expenditure agreed. Thereafter the Joint Committee met twice a year until 1889, after which the meetings became annual.

For convenience, matters relating to the joint stations at Carnforth and Whitehaven were included on the agenda, but the Joint Committee acted largely as a 'rubber stamping' body for expenditure. Subjects considered varied from the very large – for example, the rebuilding of the Carnforth Joint Station between 1880 and 1884 – and the very small, such as the replacement of Birks Bridge Junction signalman Kelly's wooden leg![7] The last meeting was held on 15th October 1908, after which the respective main boards carried out the rubber stamping.

During the first world war, Alfred Aslett, the FR General Manager, attempted to convene a Joint Committee meeting, to which the General Manager of the LNWR, Guy Calthrop, replied, on 22nd November 1916:

'I regret neither my Chairman nor myself can agree to a meeting of the LNW&FR Joint Committee being held at the present time. We are far too busy at Euston to give time to meetings of this kind which, after all, would merely be called for the purpose of formally recording matters which have long since been disposed of. As far as I am aware there are no outstanding questions of any importance which render it necessary for a meeting to be called.' [8]

In the early days of the Joint Committee, nothing was recorded in the Minutes relating to the poor financial performance of the Joint Line until 1883. However, on 12th February 1879, Devonshire recorded:

'We had a meeting of the Furness Railway Directors today at Barrow. The traffic has greatly fallen off in the later part of last year and seems likely to become still worse as many furnaces, especially in Cumberland, are out of blast. … The

Mining subsidence necessitated the construction of a deviation at Cleator Moor. A new formation was laid between Moor Row and Birks Bridge, near Bowthorn. The original line was retained for freight services to industrial premises along the route. (CRA Pattinson collection)

Cleator & Egremont which we have now acquired jointly with the London & North Western Company has been very unprofitable to us and has made our accounts decidedly worse than they otherwise would have been. The LNWR consented to very low rates and in addition the traffic has fallen off.'

A warning was given to the FR shareholders, by the Duke of Devonshire, on 27th February 1879 by which time the first half year of joint working had yielded its accounts. After describing the iron trade as being in a state of unexampled depression, he continued:

'Owing to the acquisition of the Whitehaven, Cleator & Egremont undertaking by themselves and the LNWR, the

accounts as presented did not draw as clear comparison as might have been desired between the working of the past half year and the corresponding period of 1877. There had been a loss to the FR. ... This result had been mainly due to the decrease in traffic on the line but it was partly owing to the reduction in tolls, which had to be conceded in consequence of the distressed state in which people connected with the iron industry were placed. ... Expenses had been very large ... there had been a large outlay on repairing the permanent way.' [9]

The Joint Committee minutes for 28th February 1883 contained a set of accounts for the second half of 1882, together with Ramsden's summary of half year losses since the formation of the Joint line. These losses were:

Seen here in the mid-1930s after the closure to passenger traffic in 1931, is what, in LMS days, became the East station at Cleator Moor. This was built on the loop line from Moor Row to Birks Bridge Junction. (CRA Pattinson collection)

A mile south of Corkickle station, Mirehouse Junction marked the northern limit of the WC&ER, seen here as the double track bearing left on a rising gradient towards Moor Row. The single track is the FR main line heading south towards St Bees. (CRA Pattinson collection)

Half year to 12.1878	£22,007
to 6.1879	£17,637
to 12.1879	£18,141
to 6.1880	£7,512
to 12.1880	£14,102
to 6.1881	£16,940
to 12.1881	£11,297
to 6.1882	£11,366
to 12.1882	£10,999

While comparison of the Joint line accounts for the second half of 1882 with those of the last half year of the WC&ER, to 30th June 1877, cannot be valid in any detailed respect, some significant trends are revealed:

	WC&ER Half year to 30.6.1877	LNW&F Joint to 31.12.1882
Receipts	£45,220	£30,600
Expenditure	£14,990	£18,556
Operating ratio	33%	61%
Preferential dividends and interest	£3,146	£23,043
Balance	£27,174	(£10,999) deficit
Capital Account	£447,440	£536,000 + additional sums raised by LNWR
Dividend p.a. for ½ year	11%	Not applicable

The marked fall in receipts can be attributed to three factors. First, there had been a fall in traffic due to the depression in the Furness and West Cumberland iron trade, but by 1882 there had been a revival. In fact that year saw over one million tons of iron produced in West Cumberland, a record not to be broken until 1956[10]. This suggests that the second factor – competition from the Cleator & Workington Junction Railway, opened in 1879, with the associated reduction in rates – was the more important. More problematical is the increase in the cost of operating the railway, something like 100%. This may be partly due to the fall in receipts, although it is not possible to reduce the operational and maintenance costs of a railway in line with receipts in the short term. However, the WC&ER was a basic railway, which the new owners saw fit to bring up to their own standards, one example being that the number of signalling block posts was increased from 12 to 28 during 1879[11]. Finally, the Joint line was crippled by the interest charges, principally at 10%, on an inflated capital base. There must have been a lively discussion at the meeting on 28th February but nothing was recorded.

It was not until some 24 years later, on 21st February 1906, that the Joint line's finances were again formally discussed and this was by the FR main board[12].

The figures given were for the full year of 1905:

Receipts	£55,322
Expenditure	£36,992
Operating ratio	69%
Balance	£16,330
Guaranteed div. + loan interest	£45,950
Deficit	(£29,620)
FR share of loss	£14.870

The circumstances revealed are unchanged from before, except that the guaranteed dividend of 10% was much more seriously out of line. The FR paid $1^{7}/_{8}$ % in 1905. As a postscript to the Joint line results it is worth recording the receipts for 1917, when, because of the war effort, the iron trade was operating at maximum capacity. The receipts, reported by the Joint Superintendent, J. Shaw, was a massive £608,738. However, those profits could not be used to offset the Joint line's accumulated deficit as, under Government control, any railway's profits in excess of those of 1913, had to be paid to the credit of the Railway Executive Committee.

Finally, while considering finance, it is necessary to refer to a matter which caused great concern to all the railway companies, not least the FR and the LNWR – the Railway & Canal Traffic Act 1888. In the 1870s as noted:

'Manufacturers, farmers and traders felt that rail charges should fall in sympathy with the general fall in prices.' [13]

After a Railway Commission had investigated specific complaints, the 1888 Act required each railway company to submit, to the Commission, a revised schedule of rates and charges. The Commission duly held an enquiry into the joint line's proposals and the petitions of various traders groups. The FR Board noted with relief, on 29th April 1892, that the Commissioners had rejected the case of the ironmasters on every point except the Whitehaven Tunnel toll, which had been abolished. The Railway Rates & Charges (Furness Railway etc.) Order No. 7 Confirmation Act 1892 allowed traffic between Mirehouse Junction and Whitehaven Docks to be

The fireman of a Sellafield to Moor Row workmen's train exchanges single line tokens with the signalman at Beckermet Mines Jct on 18th June 1957. The Mines branch and signalbox date from 1906. Both box and signals are of LNWR pattern. (Author: MAC218)

charged as 4 miles and between Mirehouse Junction and Bransty station as 2½ miles. The FR Board considered this result very satisfactory.

Final years

The exhaustion of some of the hematite mines in the traditional orefield lying between Egremont and Eskett, led to new exploration further south, where prospecting, to a much greater

depth revealed some of the largest ore bodies in West Cumberland. The Ullcoats Mine, just south of Egremont, commenced in 1901 and a branch line, which opened on 11th August 1902 was built to it from Ullcoats Junction. Nearby, the Ullbank Mine, of the Millom & Askam Hematite Iron Company, was served by a second branch from Ullcoats Junction and this was opened on 28th September 1903[14]. Further south, the Beckermet Mining Co. Ltd commenced its No. 1 pit in 1903, its No. 2 pit, at Winscales, in 1916 and the Haile Moor pit in 1939, now belonging to the United Steel Company, the owner from 1919 of the remaining West Cumberland iron and steel works[15]. A branch line to No. 1 pit was built, to FR design, at the expense of the mining company by C.W. Hunter, the Barrow building contractor, in 1906, at a cost of £5,681[16], which was extended to the No. 2 Pit in about 1917. The Haile Moor pit was served by an aerial ropeway, a technology used in Furness, which was much cheaper than the conventional railway.

The final mine in the West Cumberland ironfield, found in 1915, was the largest. It was decided that this Florence Pit justified its own branch line and this was built, to FR design, in 1918[17]. The junction with the main Joint line was at Florence Pit Siding, between Ullcoats Junction and Beckermet Mines Junction.

As the ironfield expanded to the south, it contracted in the north. Further, some of the more northerly coal pits were worked out. Also in the north, the Cleator & Workington Junction Railway's Northern Extension to the Maryport & Carlisle Railway's branch at Linefoot Junction, and the connection between Cloffocks Junction and Workington Bridge, on the LNWR's Cockermouth and Workington line, robbed the northern end of the Cleator Joint line of through traffic. The south to east curve between Marron Junction No. 3 and No. 2 boxes was closed on 1st October 1902, and these boxes were abolished[18]. In 1914 the main line between Rowrah and Bridgefoot was converted to single line, worked on the electric train staff system[19].

To conclude the story of the Cleator Joint line, passenger train services should be mentioned, although these were of rela-

Marron Junction, looking east in the mid-1930s, was at the northern end of the Joint line where it joined the LNWR Cockermouth & Workington section. (CRA Pattinson collection)

In the final years of traffic on the Joint line, a Clayton class 17 diesel D8505 waits for its ore wagons to be loaded at Beckermet Mine. (Author: MAA748)

tively small importance compared with the mineral traffic. A passenger train service was introduced on 1st June 1881 between Parton, on the LNWR, and Distington Joint Station[20], but by the meeting on 30th October 1883, it was noted that the earnings had only been £10 per annum, therefore it was decided to discontinue this service from 1st January 1884. A revival of the service, on Thursdays and Saturdays, commenced on 2nd November 1913 but was discontinued on the outbreak of war, in 1914. At a later date the lower part of this line was used by a workmen's train between Parton and a platform serving Harrington No. 4 Pit at Lowca. A platform was provided at Beckermet Mine and a workmen's train service introduced on 15th January 1912[21].

Reflecting the decline of the northern end of the Joint line system, the exchange station at Marron Junction, with its three platforms, was closed on 1st July 1897. Thereafter the joint line passenger service ran between Whitehaven Bransty and Workington, via Moor Row and Rowrah. The Egremont and Sellafield line was served by trains from Bransty[22].

After 44 years as a separate entity, the LNW&F Joint line passed into the ownership of the new London, Midland & Scottish Railway on 1st January 1923, together with its old rival, the C&WJR. Remarkably, both the Joint line and the C&WJR systems remained largely intact throughout the LMS era and well into British Railways' times, becoming a Mecca for the railway enthusiast.

The last revenue-earning traffic from the then northern limit of the WC&ER route was limestone from the quarries at Rowrah. Here the trip train for Moor Row is preparing to depart behind 4MT 2-6-0 No. 43009 on 27th June 1955. (Author: MAC234)

CHAPTER 20 REFERENCES

1   LNWR manuscript notebook of locomotives sold, G. Holme collection.
2   JCM, 21st Oct 1879.
3   JCM, 17th Dec. 1880.
4   Ibid.
5   JCM, 7th July 1881.
6   C.R. Clinker, personal communication.
7   JCM, 15th Oct. 1890.
8   FRDM, 8th Dec. 1916.
9   *Barrow Herald,* 15th Feb. 1879.
10   Lancaster J.Y. & Wattleworth D R. *Op. cit.* p.163.
11   Joint Lines Sectional Appendix, Jan. & Aug. 1879.
12   FRDM Minute 2414.
13   Parris H. *Op. cit.* p. 223-4.
14   JCM, 24th July 1906.
15   Kelly D., 1994. *The Red Hills* p.111.
16   FRDM, 21st Feb. 1906.
17   BRO: Plan E102.
18   JCM, 25th Nov. 1902.
19   C.R. Clinker, personal communication.
20   JCM, 7th July 1881.
21   C.R. Clinker, personal communication.
22   Working Timetable, May 1909.

CHAPTER TWENTY-ONE

THE ASLETT ERA

Sir James Ramsden, old and ill, retired from his post as Managing Director on 21st May 1895. He continued as a Director of the FR until 11th August 1896 and died on 19th October 1896. The Furness Railway needed a new manager and the Directors looked to the Caledonian Railway for advice. Charles Scotter and James Thompson, of that Company, recommended Alfred Aslett, the General Manager of the Cambrian Railways[1]. Aslett (1847-1928), the son of a Great Northern Railway superintendent, who had earlier been personal secretary to George Hudson, the 'Railway King', started his railway career on the Great Northern Railway in 1862. In 1881 he was appointed Chief Accountant of the Eastern & Midlands Railway and, in 1884, became manager of that line, which was to become the Midland & Great Northern Joint line. In 1891 he was appointed General Manager of the Cambrian Railways where he *'developed the passenger traffic to a remarkable extent'.*[2] Aslett took up his post on the FR, in October 1895, at a salary of £1,500.

The veteran Henry Cook, Secretary and Traffic Manager who had served the Whitehaven & Furness Junction Railway for 10 years and the Furness for 31 years, was asked to continue as Secretary. Cook tendered his resignation on 26th December 1896 and was granted a pension of £573 p.a. from 1st July 1897[3] and died in May 1903. After Cook's retirement Alfred Aslett assumed the joint post of Secretary and General Manager, an office he was to hold until he retired in 1918[4].

Another FR stalwart to go at this time was Richard Mason, the Locomotive Superintendent, who retired on 30th June 1897[5]. Mason was, like Ramsden, a former Bury, Curtis & Kennedy employee who had commenced his service with the FR on 1st June 1849[6] after a period with the Preston & Wyre Railway.

The opportunity was taken to replace him by another '5-star' recruit, William Frank Pettigrew, who was appointed Locomotive and Carriage & Wagon Superintendent in February 1897[7]. Pettigrew had learned his trade at the Stratford Works of the Great Eastern Railway, where he rose to the post of Assistant Manager, before transferring to the London & South Western Railway as Manager of their Nine Elms Works[8]. His FR appointment carried a salary of £600pa, which was increased to £700 in 1899. In 1900 he was offered the post of Locomotive Superintendent of the Great Central Railway[9], but when the FR offered him a salary of £1,000 p.a., he decided to stay. In 1899 he published the first edition of his notable work *"A Manual of Locomotive Engineering"* which ran into a number of editions. His first locomotive designs were an 0-6-2T tank engine, of 1898, and, in 1899, an 0-6-0 tender engine, both with 4' 7½" driving wheels and 18" x 26" cylinders.

Other appointments were those of Frederic Ramsden, to the post of Superintendent of the Line, and W. H. Whitworth, to the post of Civil Engineer. Frank Stileman, son of F.C. Stileman of the firm of McClean & Stileman, assumed consultant status. Whitworth resigned in 1908 and was replaced by the 36 years old District Engineer of the Northern Section of the North British Railway, David Rutherford[10]. When Pettigrew resigned on 30th June 1918, Rutherford was appointed to the combined post of Engineer and Locomotive & Wagon Superintendent at a salary of £2,000 p.a. In consequence of this appointment he was credited with the design of the 1919 4-6-4 tank engines[11]. F.J. Ramsden

Alfred Aslett (1847-1928) was appointed FR General Manager in 1895 in succession to Sir James Ramsden, on his retirement. Starting work on the Great Northern Railway, he became Manager of the Eastern & Midlands Railway and then General Manager of the Cambrian Railways before coming to the Furness Railway. He retired in 1918. (K. Norman collection: 586)

resigned on 20th May 1908 and was appointed a Director[12].

His post of Superintendent of the Line was filled by A.A. Haynes, who had served the Traffic Department of the FR for 24 years[13].

This influx of new, young officers during the Aslett era was matched, to an extent, by changes in the Board of Directors. The 7th Duke's eldest son, the Marquis of Hartington, had taken over the Chairmanship of the Furness Company in 1887 and became the 8th Duke on the death of his father in 1891. He was one of the prominent Liberal politicians of the late Victorian era. Victor Cavendish, son of Lord Edward Cavendish, the 7th Duke's third son, was appointed to the Board in 1891 in place of his late father. He became the 9th Duke in 1908 and was appointed Company Chairman in the place of his late uncle.

In 1892 another prominent Liberal politician, Sir John Hibbert, had been appointed to the Board. Hibbert was then 68 years old

John Hibbert (1824-1908) was appointed an FR director in 1892 and later held the position of Deputy Chairman from 1896 until 1908. His public career included service in each Gladstone administration, latterly as Financial Secretary to the Treasury. He was Chairman of Lancashire County Council from its formation until 1908. (G Holme collection)

and had been Parliamentary Secretary to the Treasury under Gladstone. In spite of his age he was a successful Director, chairing many shareholders' meetings, in the absence of the 8th Duke, with flair and skill, which earned him the approbation of the normally antagonistic ordinary shareholders. He died in his 79th year in 1908 and was replaced by Frederic Ramsden[14]. On the resignation of Sir James Ramsden, James Little, partner in James Little & Co., who operated the Irish Sea steamer services of the Barrow Steam Navigation Company, was appointed to the Board[15], but the difficulties over the Midland Railway's Heysham Harbour scheme, which was essentially competitive to the

Barrow route, led to his resignation from the Board on 9th August 1905. He was replaced by William Burnyeat of Moresby, a West Cumberland ironmaster. The veteran Edward Wadham, mineral agent of the Duke of Buccleuch, had replaced the latter on the Board as early as 1884, and when he retired in 1911, was replaced by Sir John Randles, Chairman of the Workington Iron & Steel Go. Ltd. Thus, throughout the Aslett era, the Furness Railway Company was fortunate in having a highly professional and experienced Board of Directors.

Passenger traffic developments

On July 2nd 1895, the Board Meeting which had appointed Aslett, also set up 'Traffic & Works' and 'Finance' Committees. These Committees relieved the senior members of the Board from much routine work.

The Aslett era could be described as the 'romantic' period of the Furness Railway. It was characterised by shiny red locomotives, elegant dark blue and white passenger coaches, attractive stations, which fitted into the Lakeland environment, lake steamers and, with its Circular Tours of the Lakes, a flourishing tourist trade. This era was captured on film by a number of photographers, notably Edward Sankey of Barrow. The Furness Railway issued postcards as part of their advertising campaign and even produced a brochure on their tours, in French, for the Paris Exhibition of June 1910.

By the end of 1912 Aslett had increased the number of passengers by 53% and the passenger income by 44%, compared with 1895[16].

This was a remarkable achievement and was recognised by the FR Board in its 'Reports to Shareholders'. After the Report on the first half-year of 1899, the Financial Times of 19th August 1899, noted that the operating ratio of the Furness Railway was 48.10% and the lowest in the country[17]. It went on to state:

'For the most satisfactory net result and dividend among British railways in the past six months, the palm must be handed to the Furness Company.'

The increase in passengers for 1899, compared with 1896, was 347,495, equivalent to £17,014 in receipts. The Directors noted, at the Meeting of Shareholders for the second half of 1902, that they were giving a:

'...willing testimony to the energy and ability of our

Adjacent to Ramsden Dock Station signalbox, a set of passenger rolling stock painted in the Aslett livery of ultramarine blue and white is in the charge of an 0-6-2 tank engine No. 102 c. 1910. (Sankey print: RS2)

General Manager, Mr. Aslett, and to the manner in which he has administered the Company's affairs ... ever since he came to the Furness Company.'

However, it was later acknowledged that the increase in passenger traffic contributed only a 1¼% dividend on the Ordinary Stock of the Company[18].

It was the case that Aslett's contribution to the fluctuating fortunes of the Furness Railway was mainly in the sphere of reduction of working expenses. A table of operating ratios, freight traffic and dividends for the period 1896 to

A view of the coal and ore handling facilities at Ramsden Dock c. 1916. Grab cranes were first introduced to speed the handling of imported ore for the Furness and West Cumberland furnaces. (CRA Walker collection)

1913 shows how the FR compared with the average of a group of major railway companies; the figure of 48.1% for the first half of 1899 was indeed the lowest of any UK railway. Even so, it was the state of the iron trade, which was the final determinant in the fortunes of the Company. The 8th Duke of Devonshire told the shareholders meeting on 12th February 1902:

'We have carried 57,841 tons less of iron ore, 44,391 tons less of pig iron and 73,105 tons less of coke, coal and other minerals ... The iron and steel business, as you know, is so uncertain a quantity that the directors are always reluctant to put forward any sanguine views as to its future'.

At an earlier meeting on 21st February 1900, a good half year in which a dividend of 4%pa on the Ordinary Stock was approved, he had raised the contentious issue of iron trade railway rates. The recent increase in the price of coal led to consideration being given to an increase in rates, but Devonshire felt such an increase would be prejudicial to the iron and steel trades of the district. He went on, demonstrating his skill as a seasoned politician:

'In regard to this question, it is a somewhat difficult one for me being Chairman of this Company and also of the Barrow Hematite Steel Company, because my interests may to some degree be conflicting. I have sometimes, one day as Chairman of this Company to resist what may be considered as importunate demands of the Steel Company, while on the next, as Chairman of the Steel Company, I may have to protest against what is considered the importunate demand of the Railway Company. ... In these matters I have little more to do than to act as arbitrator and I think you may rest assured that your interests are very well protected by the Deputy Chairman and other members of the Board'.

The ultimate criterion of success, as seen through shareholders' eyes, was the value of the Ordinary Share stock and this depended on the dividends earned. As has been noted, the payment of such a dividend came from the residual profit, after the payment of the various guaranteed, preference and debenture stock dividends.

The Furness Railway carried a heavy burden in this respect:

Guaranteed 4% stock	£779,125
Consolidated Preference 4% stock	£1,300,750
Preference Stock A 4%	£350,000
Preference Stock B 4%	£200,000
Preference Stock 1894 4%	£100,000
Preference Stock 1899 4%	£150,000
Debenture Stock 3%	£2,346,123
WC&ER Vesting Act 1878 LNWR Stock 10% (one half)	£268,000
TOTAL	£5,493,998
Ordinary Stock	£2,625,000
TOTAL CAPITAL EMPLOYED	£8,118,998

These figures were those shown in the accounts for the year 1913. This was a relatively good year, in which the total net income was £279,433. However, after the payment of the guaranteed and preference stock dividend, only £67,749 remained to pay a dividend on the Ordinary Stock, at the rate of 2.5% for the year. The £100 shares had sold for £170 in the boom years of the early 1870s but by 1904, had fallen to £47.

Aslett was beset by further problems, namely those arising from disputes with the railway staff over pay and conditions, which came to a head in the early years of the 20th century.

Hitherto the railway companies had not recognised the railway unions, insisting that their employees should negotiate directly, a position which became progressively untenable.

The FR Directors' Report for the second half of 1907 noted that the Company:

'had concurred in the arrangement which had been come to between the principal railway companies and the Board of Trade for the establishment for a period of seven years of Conciliation Boards composed on the one side of elected members of staff and on the other side of representatives appointed by the directors, to deal with questions of wages and hours of labour of employees ... engaged in the manipulation of traffic.'

Notwithstanding these arrangements, a railway strike took place in 1911 in which one third of FR staff withdrew their labour.

Furness Railway Results 1896-1913 Table of FR Operating Ratios & Dividends

(compared with the average of a number of main line companies where available)

Half year	Operating ratio %	Average %	Goods / Mineral £	Dividend % pa	Notes
1896 1st	50.76	63.50	168,121	1	
1896 2nd	49.00		174,759	2	
1897 1st			175,889	1½	
1897 2nd			182,096	1	
1898 1st	50.56	56.00	185,386	2	
1898 2nd	48.38		194,384	3	
1899 1st	48.10		196,126	3	Lowest in UK
1899 2nd	47.64		209,805	4	
1900 1st	47.78	62.80	210,025	3½	
1900 2nd	49.25		209,805	3½	
1901 1st	51.37	66.20	179,647	2	Depression
1901 2nd	48.90		187,176	3	Depression
1902 1st	50.40		177,312	2	Depression
					Lowest in UK
1902 2nd	48.52		197,942	3½	
1903 1st	52.45	63.90	191,776	2¼	
1903 2nd	49.96	61.15	186,972	2¾	Depression
1904 1st	54.65	63.73	169,281	½	Depression
1904 2nd	52.54	61.00	152,193	1	Depression
1905 1st	53.64		165,560	¾	Depression
1905 2nd	48.84		190,179	3	
1906 1st	50.76	63.50	195,686	2¼	
1906 2nd	49.00	60.00	198,395	3¾	
1907 1st	49.34		209,212	3	
1907 2nd	50.63	62.00	196,531	3	Depression
1908 1st	56.26	66.74	163,114	½	Iron trade depression
1908 2nd	52.44	61.00	155,578	1	Iron trade depression
1909 1st	54.21		157,332	0	Iron trade depression
1909 2nd	52.18		180,320	1¾	
1910 1st	52.41		195,251	1¾	
1910 2nd	51.71		196,007	2½	
1911 1st			186,826	¾	
1911 2nd	53.40		190,757	2	Rail strike
1912 1st	58.24		173,776	0	Coal strike
1912 2nd	54.12		216,191	3	
1913 Year	58.16		411,235	2½	

New annual form of accounts from 1913.

The 1911 strike led to the appointment of a Commission to review the 1907 arrangements, but also, in turn, to the Railway Conference Agreement (Companies & Men) of 11th December 1911. The FR agreed new conditions of service, which were to operate until 31st December 1914, after which the railway Trade Unions were to be admitted to the arrangements.

These concessions to the staff created a load on the profitability of the Companies and the Railway & Canal Traffic Act of 1913 allowed them to increase their rates to compensate for the improved working conditions, but the increase of some 3.5% incurred the displeasure of the traders.

A further drain on railway companies' resources was the National Insurance Act 1911 and the introduction of superannuation schemes for railway employees, to which the companies had to make contributions.

On the outbreak of war in 1914, the British railway companies passed into the control of the Railway Executive Committee and operating conditions became increasingly difficult due to the demands on rolling stock.

Aslett, now 67 years old, tendered his resignation on 2nd March 1918 and was released by the Board on 15th April 1918. He went on to enjoy 10 years of retirement.

CHAPTER 21 REFERENCES

1   FRDM, 26th June 1895.
2   *Railway Magazine*, July 1913 p.20.
3   *Railway News*, 7th Oct. 1897 & FRDM, 29th Dec. 1896.
4   FRDM, 4th Aug. 1897.
5   FRDM, 5th Feb. 1897.
6   PRO: Rail 214/102, FR Salaried Staff Registers.
7   FRDM, 19th Feb. 1897.
8   *Railway Magazine*, July 1913 p.22.
9   FRDM, 27th June 1900.
10 FRDM, 24th Mar. 1909.
11 FRDM, 8th Mar. 1918 & 21st Feb. 1919.
12 FRDM, 20th May 1908.
13 FRDM, 6th Aug. 1908.
14 FRDM, 17th Nov. 1908.
15 FRDM, 11th Aug. 1896.
16 FRSM, 14th Feb. 1913.
17 FRSM, 23rd Aug. 1899, *Chairman's Report*.
18 FRSM, 19th Feb. 1908.

One of the delights of the Aslett era was the attractiveness of the FR's publicity material. The posters for their Lakeland Tours were so popular that a collector's set of six postcards was produced – four feature here and the remaining two form the back cover of the book. (Private collection)

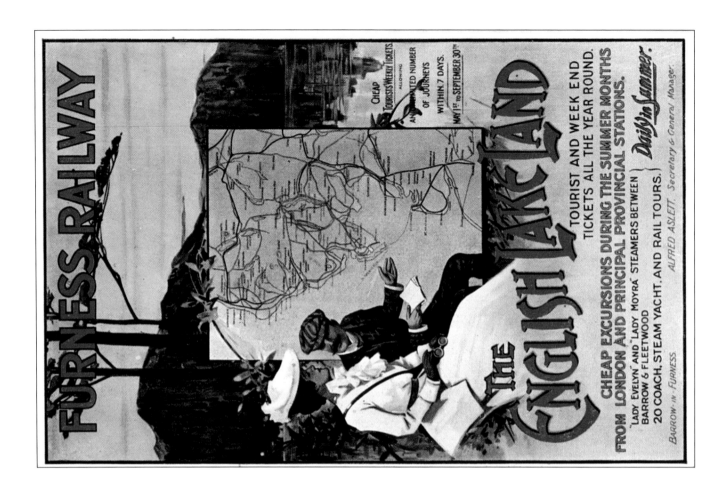

RAIL AND LOCAL STEAMSHIP PASSENGER TRAFFIC DEVELOPMENTS

FR passenger locomotive 4-4-0 No. 128 and her crew. Locos 126 to 129 were a batch of four engines ordered from Sharp, Stewart in 1901. They had larger diameter driving wheels and were more powerful than the 1896 versions. After the grouping, 128 became LMS No. 10145 and continued working until 1930. (CRA Pattinson collection)

By the time Barrow Central Station opened in 1882, the rapid expansion of the population of Barrow had largely come to an end. The most rapid increase had occurred between 1861 and 1881 and the Census of 1891 indicated a population on the Furness peninsula of 95,000, compared with 30,000 at the opening of the Furness Railway, in 1846. These demographic pressures had led to manifest inadequacies in the station accommodation at Barrow, Askam and Millom – the latter two serving iron and steel trade settlements. However, by the time Aslett arrived on the scene, in 1895, the FR stations, where necessary, had been rebuilt with funds provided by the high earnings of the early 1870s.

The rolling stock position was less satisfactory. In 1894 the company owned 381 passenger vehicles, the majority of which were old four-wheelers. The Regulation of Railways Act, 1889 required railway companies to fit continuous brakes to their passenger vehicles and, on 22nd March 1892, James Ramsden advised the Board that:

'...it would be necessary to purchase additional new carriages as the old stock was not sufficiently strong to bear the application of the powerful continuous brakes now required.'

Fifty 3rd class 6-wheelers were ordered, from the Metropolitan Carriage & Wagon Company, Birmingham[1] to augment the growing number of these carriages, purchased since the six 'Cleminson Patent Truck' vehicles were delivered, in 1882.

On 23rd October 1890, James Ramsden advised the Board that the increasing passenger traffic necessitated new engines and that Sharp, Stewart had four on offer at a considerable reduction from cost price. The four new 4-4-0 engines were charged to Capital Account, in the second half of 1890, at a cost of £9,200. They were to replace four 2-4-0s, withdrawn for conversion to 2-4-2 tanks, for branch line working. It is rumoured that the 'Seagulls', Nos 120, 121, 122 & 123, were not highly regarded by Aslett and they were relegated to secondary duties when larger 4-4-0s came along.

Alfred Aslett attended his first Furness Railway Board meeting on 27th November 1895 and it cannot be a coincidence that this particular Board meeting approved the invitation of tenders for three or six new passenger engines, a request made by the veteran locomotive superintendent Richard Mason, at the previous meeting, which had been deferred. The same meeting also decided to invite tenders for the Furness Company's first bogie passenger coaches, 1st/3rd semi-corridor

Barrow Locomotive and Carriage & Wagon works seen from the air c.1920. (G Taylor collection: T403)

At Bowness Pier, two motor omnibuses await the arrival of the steamer. (Sankey print: 9888)

FR No. 3, lovingly remembered as *'Coppernob'* from its domed copper firebox, enjoyed, after withdrawal from service, a celebrity existence in a glass pavilion outside Barrow Central station. In 1924, with chimney temporarily removed, the locomotive is being released from the display case for a visit to the British Empire Exhibition at Wembley. (K. Norman collection: TP256)

composites, with toilets and electric lighting on 'Stone's Patent System'. They also were fitted with a 'communication cord' and were for use on through services to the Midland Railway. At Aslett's second Board meeting, on 9th January 1896, orders were placed for six 'semi-corridor composite coaches with cupboard', and 'six semi-corridor composites with brake'. These first twelve bogie passenger vehicles were built by the Metropolitan Carriage & Wagon Company. However, for the forthcoming season the Board, in a more conservative vein, invited tenders for thirty 3rd Class 6-wheel carriages. Of the thirty 6-wheelers, twenty were built by the Birmingham Carriage & Wagon Company at £585 each, and ten by the Ashbury Carriage Company at £578. In 1899 six composite 6-wheelers were ordered, two with lavatory and luggage compartments, for use on through workings. These were the last of the FR 6-wheelers.

The withdrawal from service in 1899 of FR No. 3 'Coppernob' – one of the original 0-4-0 Bury locomotives of 1846 – led to the creation of what became Barrow's most iconic railway artefact. The FR board took the decision to preserve and restore the locomotive and place it on permanent display in an ornate glass case on the forecourt of Barrow Central station. Here 'Coppernob' remained until, in 1924, she was removed to be shown at the British Empire Exhibition. Another brief outing followed in 1938, with a visit to Birmingham, but wartime bombing in May 1941 finally lost to Barrow its cherished reminder of the town's railway origins. 'Coppernob' now forms part of the national collection of railway heritage at the National Railway Museum at York.

Of great interest was the decision by the Board to accept Aslett's suggestion that the new passenger stock should be painted Ultramarine Blue, with white upper panels, and that existing stock should be similarly painted, and fitted with electric light, as the opportunity offered. The original colour of the FR passenger stock has been variously described, but the *Ulverston Mirror* of 6th March 1880, in recording the rebuilding of certain FR 3rd class carriages with four compartments instead of five, notes that they were *'painted brown externally relieved with vermilion and gold'*.[2] The 'Indian Red' livery of the locomotives was retained.

By 1904 the FR owned 56 bogie carriages and an extension of the Carriage & Wagon shops at Barrow was authorised[3]. Also in 1904, the first corridor coaches with connecting gangways were purchased presumably for through carriage workings to London

(Euston), so that passengers had access to the dining car facilities provided by the London & North Western Railway. Another landmark of 1904 was the scrapping of the last of the old four wheelers[4].

A further important measure was the abolition of the Second Class. At the meeting of FR shareholders, on 11th August 1896, the acting Chairman, Sir John Hibbert, drew attention to a decrease of 236 in Second Class bookings during the first half of 1896, while the Third Class had increased by 63,000 and the First Class by 741. He commented that as the passenger traffic increased, the provision of three classes of accommodation became more difficult, particularly with regard to the marshalling of trains.

The Midland Railway had abolished Second Class in 1876 and the LNWR now ran their Scotch expresses with First and Third compartments only. In spite of grumbling by a minority of shareholders, who saw the end of Second Class as an erosion of middle class railway facilities, the FR abolished Second Class from 1st July 1897.

This change provided Aslett with the opportunity to try a new idea, designed to pacify the middle classes, a 'Reserved Third Class' by which, for the payment of a 'reservation fee', in addition to the 3rd class fare, a compartment could be reserved. The reservation fees ran from 2d for a single journey of up to 10 miles to 1/6d for 61 to 75 miles. Return reservations were 50% higher[5]. Unfortunately the Inland Revenue authorities regarded the reservation fee as an addition to the fare, taking it over 1d per mile and consequently incurring the payment of passenger duty. The FR took this to the Court of Queens Bench but lost their case and the scheme was abandoned in 1899.

Circular Tours and Excursions

Henry Cook, the FR Traffic Manager, had arranged summer season trips to Coniston and a cruise on the steam yacht *Gondola* which, together with the opening of the Windermere Lakeside branch in 1869, and the subsequent FR take-over of the Windermere steamers, provided the opportunity for more ambitious tourist trips, in the form of 'Circular Tours'.

The introduction of these was recorded in the *Barrow Herald* of 18th June 1870. The key to the tours was the employment of subcontractors, to provide the horse-drawn omnibuses between Ambleside and Coniston, and between Lake Bank, at the foot of Coniston Water, and the Lakeside branch station at Greenodd.

At Ambleside Waterhead c. 1910 a horse-drawn omnibus leaves for Coniston with the Outer Circular Tour. (Sankey print: 5195)

On Coniston Water, FR steamer *'Lady of the Lake'* heads south towards Lake Bank Pier c.1910. The popularity of lake cruises aboard the, by now, 50 year-old *'Gondola'* led the FR to order this second vessel for the Coniston service in 1908. (Sankey print: 2291)

A cottage near the FR's Hawcoat quarry had been the childhood home of local artist George Romney. In 1909 the railway company bought and restored the cottage and made it the object of one of their Rail and Coach Tours. (G. Holme collection)

These operators used 'a broad type of open cart, drawn by three horses abreast and having rows of seats for 16 to 20 visitors'.

During the 25 years between the first Circular Tour and the arrival of Aslett only four had been developed:

1. Outer Circular Tour via Lakeside, Windermere steamer, Ambleside, Coniston by omnibus, and thence by train.
2. Inner Circular Tour via Broughton and Coniston, Coniston steamer to Lake Bank, by omnibus to Greenodd and onward by train.
3. Grange Circular Tour: Grange to Kendal and Windermere Town by train, Windermere by lake steamer to Lakeside and Lakeside to Grange via Ulverston by train.
4. Middle Circular Tour: Lakeside by train, Ambleside by steamer, Coniston by omnibus, Lake Bank by Gondola, Greenodd by omnibus and the FR destination by train[6].

Aslett liked the idea, and by 1896 season he had added six more; by the 1898 season there were 20, a number which was to continue up to the First War, (although there were some minor variations).

The original 'Cook's Tours' were as noted:

1. Outer Circular Tour
2. Inner Circular Tour
3. Grange Circular Tour
4. Middle Circular Tour.
Aslett added:
5. Red Bank & Grasmere.
6. Thirlmere & Grasmere.
7. The Four Lakes Tour (Coniston, Grasmere, Rydal and Windermere).
8. Coniston to Coniston via Ambleside.
9. Tarn Hows Tour,
10. Round the Langdales.
11. Ullswater Tour.
12. Derwentwater Tour.
13. The Five Lakes Tour (4 lakes + Derwentwater).
14. Wastwater Tour.
15. The Six Lakes Tour (5 lakes + Ullswater.)
16. Duddon Valley Tour.
17. Eskdale Valley Tour.
18. Cartmel Priory & Newby Bridge Tour.
19. Ennerdale Tour.
20. George Romney's Home, Walney Bridge & Island[7].

NOUVEL ITINÉRAIRE No. 20.

Par la Maison où George Romney passa sa jeunesse, Barrow Docks, Pont et Ile de Walney, et Furness Abbey.

MAISON OÙ GEORGE ROMNEY PASSA SA JEUNESSE.
1742-1755.

VUES MAGNIFIQUES DE ROMNEY'S HOME.

BARROW DOCKS.

VUES SUPERBES DES DOCKS ET DE LA MER.

Déjeûners, Thés, et Rafraîchissements à l'Hotel de l'Abbaye de Furness.

For the Paris Exhibition in 1908 the FR produced a French language version of its Tour brochure. Here the scenic appeal of Romney's home and the docks at Barrow are lauded. (G. Holme collection)

From tickets which have survived, it appears that these Tours could be booked from Blackpool, Fleetwood and any Furness station. The original four (at least) could be travelled in either direction.

The 'Romney's Home Tour' warrants special mention. Perched above the north face of the FR's Hawcoat Quarry was a small cottage where the portrait painter George Romney had lived during his childhood (1742-1755).

By 1906 this had been condemned as unfit for human habita-

The FR Fleetwood paddle steamer *'Lady Margaret'*, introduced in 1903, arrives at Fleetwood c.1905. (G. Holme collection)

tion and allowed to fall into a derelict condition. Initially, the cottage was sold to a local builder, Mr Cox, who was to pay £5 and remove the stone, as the cottage was not considered worth renovating. The press became aware of this work and, after representations from Canon Rawnsley of Keswick, one of the founders of the National Trust, work was stopped and the company agreed to buy back the cottage[8].

The company agreed to lease the cottage from the land owner, Victor Cavendish of Holker Hall, Cark, for the nominal sum of 20/- (£1.00) per annum for 21 years, with a requirement to put the cottage into good repair and maintain it[9]. Aslett's fertile mind came up with the proposition to refurbish this cottage, add an extension over the old joiners shop and make it into a Romney museum. Tenders for the work were invited and considered in 1908[10] but it was not until 1909 that the refurbishment, costing £491[11], was complete. A new 'Circular Tour' was introduced which included Walney Island via the new Walney Bridge opened in 1908[12].

In 1910 a 'Tea Pavilion' was added at Romney's Cottage, the grounds extended and fenced, at a cost of £350 and it was noted that, during the 1909 season, 1,309 people had visited[13].

In addition to the 'Circular Tours' Aslett increased the number of cheap fares on the Furness line. These included, Cheap day return, Weekend return, Weekly return, Fortnight return, Angler, Golfer, Tennis and Pleasure party. A number of Special Excursions were run each season.

By the turn of the century Aslett's reputation was high, the FR dividends had been increasing (1896 1.5%, 1897 1.75%, 1898 2.5%, 1899 3.5%), and at the Shareholders' Meeting on 22nd February 1899, the Duke of Devonshire referred to the very satisfactory increase in passenger traffic, 15% between 1895 and 1898. Sir John Hibbert stated:

'I would like to bear testimony to the very earnest labours of our General Manager on behalf of the interests of the Company.'

On 21st February 1900 the Duke of Devonshire, in announcing a dividend of 4% p.a. for the half-year, referred to:

'Our excellent General Manager to whose ability and exertions the present prosperous condition of the Company is to a very large extent due.'

Fleetwood Steamers

It was early in 1899 that consideration was first given to a re-opening of the Barrow – Fleetwood steamer service. The original service, of 1846, had lost its importance on the opening of the Ulverstone & Lancaster line in 1857, but it continued to utilise the old steamer *Helvellyn* until her withdrawal in May 1868 and replacement by the *Walney*, ordered new by the FR. The *Walney* was designed to act also as a tug in the Barrow Docks. The latter duties increased in importance with the expansion of trade and, on 7th May 1870 the *Barrow Herald* reported that the *Walney* would not be plying to Fleetwood during the forthcoming season, because of the demands on her at Barrow Docks. Aslett judged that a Barrow – Fleetwood service would provide for complementary traffic flows, one from the Lancashire resort of Blackpool, to the Lakes and the other from Furness to Blackpool. Tenders for a steamer were sought and, on 24th March 1899, that of J. Scott & Co. of Kinghorn was accepted for a 15-knot paddle steamer *'similar to one being built for the North British Railway's Clyde services';* the cost was £13,750. At the FR Shareholders' Meeting on 22nd August 1900, Sir John Hibbert reported that the paddle steamer *Lady Evelyn* had been delivered to Barrow the previous week and would run daily, except Sundays. It was a great success; the increase in passengers between the first seven weeks of the 1901 season and the same period of 1902, was 29% and, in 1902, the Barrow Docks steam tug *Furness* was required to provide a relief service[14]. This prompted the decision to seek a second-hand steamer with a passenger capacity of 1,000 and, in February 1903, the FR purchased the paddle steamer *Lady Margaret* from the Bristol Channel firm of P. & A. Campbell, for £14,502. A vessel capable of 17 knots, she had been built in 1895 by Macmillan of Dumbarton. The shareholders were advised, on 19th August 1903, that 'the Blackpool traffic to the Lakes is developing in a remarkable manner' and by the end of the 1903 season the Fleetwood bookings were double those of 1901[15]. Before the 1904 season the Lady Evelyn was lengthened by Vickers, Barrow Yard[16]. A further purchase at this time was the Walney, a passenger tender, the second vessel of this name to be owned by the FR. The first had been sold in 1897[17]. The 1906 season saw 120,115 bookings compared with 28,279 in 1901[18].

Addressing the February 1908 Shareholders' meeting, Lord Muncaster stated:

'It is probable that the two paddle steamers 'Lady Evelyn' and 'Lady Margaret' with the assistance of the small steamer 'Walney' will find it difficult to cope with the rapidly developing business ... In the course of the next few years we have little doubt that it will be necessary to provide a larger steamer.'

On the same day the FR Directors offered the Lady Margaret to the Admiralty at Sheerness for £14,000, virtually what they had paid for her in 1903; this offer was accepted. Attempts to charter a suitable replacement fell through and in 1908 the paddle steamer Philomel was purchased from the General Steam Navigation Company, for £5,250. She was certificated to carry 999 passengers.

After the 1909 season the Board decided that, as the Philomel needed a new boiler, she should be sold and replaced. The Barry Railway offered their Devonia for £22,750 but Pettigrew, the Locomotive Superintendent, advised against the purchase after an inspection. Consideration of a new build ended with the decision to purchase the Barry Railway's Gwalia for £21,750, and this vessel, renamed Lady Moyra, commenced sailings in the 1910

season. Again the number of passengers increased, 127,617 being carried. The Philomel defied all attempts to sell her and she was finally purchased by Thomas Ward, for £1,600 as scrap.

For 1913, the railways accounts began to be made up on an annual basis, as required by the Railway Companies (Accounts & Returns) Act 1911, but as the Fleetwood service was confined to the summer season, the passenger figure for 1913 is comparable and, at 179,000, showed yet another increase. Following the outbreak of the First World War life went on as before for quite a time and the railways planned the usual seasonal tourist services for 1915. However, the war quite quickly affected the maritime world; seafarers became impossible to find for seasonal coastal tourist traffic, as the merchant service was diverted to the war effort and, unable to run, the Lady Evelyn and Lady Moyra were requisitioned by the Admiralty in 1916. The war finally over, the FR Board, on 21st February 1919, considered the future of the Fleetwood service and their two steamers, which were about to be released by the Admiralty.

The Lady Evelyn, which had cost £13,750 new, and valued at £5,831, was sold to W.H. Tucker, of Cardiff, for £20,000. The Lady Moyra, which had cost £21,750 second hand and valued at £15,491 was sold to the same firm for £30,000[19]. These elevated prices no doubt reflected a scarcity of merchant vessels following the ravages of war. The two 'Ladies' eventually became English Channel ferries Brighton Belle and Brighton Queen. Both were lost during the Dunkirk operation early in the Second World War[20].

One final attempt was made to revive the Fleetwood service, when, on 8th August 1922, the steamer Robina was chartered and ran to Fleetwood from the now disused Isle of Man berth at Ramsden Dock Station – the former Fleetwood Pier having been demolished in 1919 after becoming unsafe. Sadly, the operation up to 22nd September 1922 resulted in a loss of £73 and the experiment was discontinued[21].

At Ambleside Waterhead c. 1910, FR steamers 'Tern' and 'Swift' are seen operating the Lakeside – Bowness – Ambleside service. (Sankey print: D629)

A second, larger Walney Ferry was commissioned by the FR and went into service in 1902. It became redundant with the opening of the Walney Toll Bridge in 1908 and went to serve as a ferry across the river Itchen in Hampshire. (G. Holme collection)

Lake Steamers

The Lake steamers had been among the first attempts of the Furness Railway to build up its tourist traffic. As already noted, the *Gondola* had been introduced on Coniston Water in 1859, the year in which the line to Coniston was opened.

On Windermere the FR introduced their first steamer, the *Swan,* in 1869, after the opening of their Windermere Lakeside Branch. The three vessels of the Windermere United Steam Yacht Company, the *Dragon Fly*, the *Fire Fly* and the *Rothay* were taken over together with the Company, by the FR, in 1872.

The first two were replaced by the *Cygnet* and *Teal* in 1879. In the early part of the Aslett era, no doubt to cater for the increasing numbers of 'Circular Tour' passengers, the decision was made to purchase an additional boat and an order was placed with T.B. Seath & Co. of Rutherglen at a price of £9,465[22]. The new vessel, launched early in 1900, was named *Swift*.[23]

In 1897, a private yacht, *Britannia*, was offered to the FR at £1,200 but was declined. However, in 1907, a new offer of £500 was successful and *Britannia* entered the FR fleet to be used for private parties. She was taken out of service in 1915 owing to the war conditions and in May 1918 the FR Board noted: *'It has not been nor is likely to be a source of profit.'* [24] She was subsequently broken up for scrap[25]. The veteran *Gondola* continued to play an important part in the 'Circular Tours' programme, running between Coniston and Lake Bank. On 9th August 1907 the FR Board decided to provide a second boat on Coniston Water and an order was placed, with J & I Thorneycroft of Southampton, for a steamer to carry 379 passengers (*Gondola* carried 228), at a cost of £5,600. The *Lady of the Lake* was launched on 26th May 1908.

The Walney Ferry

Among the Furness Railway's local steamer services the humble Walney Ferry must be included. When first introduced, in 1878, it had been a boon to the small number of residents on Walney and to visitors to the excellent sandy beaches on the west side of the Island. However, the new owners of the Barrow Shipbuilding Works, Vickers, Sons & Maxim, planned an extensive residential colony on the Island for its increasing workforce. In 1899, the Barrow Harbour Master, Admiral Barnett, had visited Southampton to inspect the Itchen Steam Floating Bridge and,

subsequently, Pettigrew submitted plans for a similar floating bridge for Walney Ferry costing £8,000[26]. At the same period the Barrow Corporation proposed to purchase the ferry, as an interim measure, pending their building of a Walney Bridge. However, the FR objected to the bridge proposal as it would restrict access to the Devonshire Dock gates. The outcome was a contract with Vickers to build a new larger ferry, at a cost of £9,150[27], which went into operation early in 1902 providing a 13-minute service[28].

Work had begun on the Vickers' housing on Walney, soon to be named 'Vickerstown', as early as March 1900 and the original plan for 950 houses was completed in 1904[29]. To relieve the situation, which, in spite of the new ferry, remained a problem, Vickers introduced their own small ferryboats with a capacity of 30 in 1902[30]. It was not long before the bridge proposal was revived and a poll, taken in Barrow on 23rd January 1904, resulted in a substantial majority in favour of a bridge. The Barrow Corporation had already deposited a Bill in Parliament for a bridge; the FR petitioned against the Bill.

Most unfortunately, for the FR's case, on 19th June 1904 the Ferry grounded on an ebb tide and remained out of operation for some eight hours. Photographs of this embarrassing episode were handed round during the Parliamentary Committee on the Bridge Bill, and the Bill was passed[31]. This Act allowed for the compensation of the Railway Company, by the Corporation, which was agreed as follows:

Ferryboat	£5,000
Loss of revenue	£25,000
Land required for bridge	£7,525
Total	£37,525

The Walney Toll Bridge was opened, with great celebration, on 18th August 1908.

The Rail Motor

The burgeoning passenger traffic led Aslett to speculate on what could be done to contain the related increase in working expenses. The Liverpool Overhead Railway had opened its first section in 1893 using an electrified third rail, a system also used on the Lancashire & Yorkshire Railway's Liverpool to Southport electrification, opened in 1904. At the Shareholders' Meeting, on 19th August 1902, a Mr Hague raised the issue of the possible electrification of the Windermere Lakeside branch, pointing out that waterpower for the cheap generation of electricity was available. This suggestion was duly noted by Aslett (who attended the Shareholders' Meetings in his capacity as Company

The FR Railmotor, introduced in 1905, worked mainly on the Coniston branch. Here Railmotor and trailer, in FR blue and white passenger livery, are seen at Lakeside. (K. Norman collection: N76)

Secretary) and no doubt discussed at length with William Pettigrew, but it soon became clear that the traffic on the Lakeside branch was insufficient to service the considerable cost of the necessary infrastructure (power station and distribution) and the provision of dedicated rolling stock. Pettigrew's interests lay in a different direction. He was awaiting the outcome of experiments, being carried out on the Great Western Railway's Stroud Valley line involving an integral steam traction unit and passenger coach, known as the 'Rail Motor Car', one example of which had operated on the London & South Western (Pettigrew's old Company) from 1903[32]. In 1903 Pettigrew produced a provisional plan for a Rail Motor Car for the Lakeside and Coniston branches[33].

Early in 1904 the results of the experiments on the GWR were conveyed to the FR board. The operating cost of the rail motor was 5½d per mile compared with 1s 3d for locomotive and four carriages. The Board approved the construction of a steam powered rail motor to carry fifty passengers. It was to be built in the Company's own workshops, at Barrow, at a cost of £2,000 and was to run on either the Lakeside or Coniston branches[34]. The prototype was examined by the Board, in the workshops, on 14th October 1904 and it was decided that the vehicle should work on the Lakeside branch initially. In connection with this project a 'Motor Car Station' was planned for Newby Bridge, between Haverthwaite and Lakeside stations. Aslett wrote to the Board of Trade Railway Department on 25th November 1904[35] explaining the need for such a station and giving details of the 'Motor Car'. The car and its specially built trailer would be 95 feet long and, on occasions, as traffic required, a third vehicle would be added,

A view of the site of the Harrington & Lowca Light Railway station at Lowca, looking south, c.1962. (Author: MAA229)

making a total of 130 feet. Aslett added that it was not intended to stop any ordinary trains at this station and that the service would be so advertised. This decision was to lead to passenger complaints, as Newby Bridge, with its Swan Hotel, was a popular tourist attraction. At the Shareholders' Meeting on 21st February 1905, Sir John Hibbert reported that trials of the Rail Motor had taken place on the Windermere Lakeside branch and that there had been complaints of vibration and the lack of smoking accommodation. Pettigrew attempted to reduce the vibration and 1st class smoking accommodation was provided in the trailer. After a short period of running between Barrow Central and Lakeside in June 1905, the Rail Motor was transferred to the Coniston branch where, with an additional carriage as required, it was planned to operate the whole of the passenger traffic during the winter months. This transfer, which seems to have been permanent, created a problem in respect of the 'Motor Car Platform' at Newby Bridge, which became redundant under the terms agreed with the Board of Trade. Aslett had to write to the Railway Department on 4th October 1905 requesting permission to stop ordinary trains at the platform. The outcome was the lengthening of the platform to 200 feet in November 1905, and to 340 feet in March 1906.

William Barratt of Broughton, a director of the Hodbarrow Mining Company complained of the Railmotor: 'There can be no doubt that the thing is an absolute failure'.[36]

The Railmotor and its trailer soon fell out of use, the boiler being removed, during the war years, for use with the breakdown crane, enabling this to be independent of the few locomotives fitted up with the necessary pipework to provide steam for it. The trailer body was later sold for use inside a bungalow at Kirkby in Furness.

Light Railway proposals

An important development in railway promotion occurred with the passing of the Light Railways Act in 1896[37].

The object of this legislation was to simplify the authorisation and statutory requirements on railways, to serve rural communities, where the capital for a conventional railway could not be raised. These lines were, as their description suggests, lightly built and speeds were low. On 11th August 1896, the FR Board asked the Engineer to report on possible schemes for Light Railways to act as feeders to the main FR system. Nothing

After the purchase of the Barrow Shipyard by Vickers in 1897 a short spur was laid from the FR line into the range, controlled by the Vickers Gun Range Siding signalbox. The box nameboard survives in the Dock Museum at Barrow. (CRA Pattinson collection)

further was reported on this FR initiative, probably because independent schemes started to emerge. These included:

Coniston & Elterwater	1896
Ambleside & Hawkshead	1897
Ambleside & Keswick	1898
Seascale, Gosforth & Santon	1899
Greenodd & Lake Bank	1901
Broughton & Dunnerdale	1903

The most interesting of these abortive schemes was that of the Walney Bridge & Light Railway. This was proposed by landowners on Walney Island who planned to develop Walney as a tourist resort[38] and came at a time when the shortcomings of the FR's Walney Ferry were being highlighted. The line was to run from the FR at Ormsgill and reach Walney by a bridge north of the entrance to the Devonshire Dock. The Barrow engineers, Strongitharm & Pearson, advised Aslett that the cost would be £50,000. The FR declined to be involved and concentrated on defending its Walney Ferry[39].

There was one successful Light Railway project in Furness & West Cumberland but it came much later and involved no new construction. In 1909 the principal iron and steel works in West Cumberland had combined to form the Workington Iron and Steel Company Ltd which, in 1910, sank its Harrington Colliery No. 10 pit at Lowca, where the next year it commissioned a coke and by-products plant.

Lowca was served by the extension of the old Bain's Tramway from Harrington Harbour, which connected with a branch of the C&WJR at Rosehill Junction. Because of the Company's difficulty in getting its men to Lowca, it obtained a Light Railway Order dated 16th May 1913[40]. Stations were provided, by the C&WJR, at Archer Street and Church Road (Harrington), and by the Harrington & Lowca Light Railway, at Copperas Hill, Micklam and Lowca. The trains, worked by the FR, ran either from Workington, or from Seaton on the Northern Extension[41], and had to climb a gradient of 1 in 17, up to Copperas Hill.

Before leaving the subject of 'light railways', mention should be made of the Ravenglass & Eskdale Railway, a narrow gauge tributary of the FR Whitehaven line. Authorised in 1873, it was built to a 3 foot gauge, 7 miles in length, to serve iron mines near Boot, in Eskdale. Opened for goods traffic on 24th May 1875 and for passengers on 20th November 1876[42], it was conspicuously unsuccessful[43]. On 12th October 1910 the FR Board received a proposal, from E.B. Dawson, a director of the R&ER, that the FR might consider reconstructing the line and working it, for 70% of receipts. Lord Muncaster and W.B. Turner were appointed to investigate the matter. However, Dawson wrote to the FR, in May 1911, stating that his line had been leased to the Eskdale Mining Company. This event did not improve matters and the solution was a lease to Narrow Gauge Railways Ltd, in 1915, and conversion to 15-inch gauge. Early in LMS days, a standard gauge line was laid outside the R&ER track from Ravenglass, for 2½ miles, to a granite crusher at Murthwaite. After various ups and downs, the final salvation for the narrow gauge line came in 1960, when the Ravenglass & Eskdale Railway Preservation Society made a successful bid to purchase the line[44].

In the final years of the 19th century there was something of a revival in trunk route proposals. The Manchester, Sheffield & Lincolnshire Railway had obtained its London Extension Act in 1893. In the same year, the Great Western Railway, under the guise of the Fishguard & Rosslare Railways & Harbours, had

A platform was created in 1911 at Wraysholme crossing, west of Kents Bank station, to facilitate the movement of Territorial Army personnel to a rifle range on the mosses. It later found employment when steps were begun to set up an airship servicing base at Flookburgh during World War I. (K. Norman collection)

obtained powers to build new lines in Wales and Ireland, in order to create a new rail-sea route to Waterford and Cork. The FR was also involved in a trunk route scheme, which planned to reduce the mileage between the Durham coalfield and Barrow by 19 miles. The FR Board discussed the plans for the 'Yorkshire Dales Railway' on 15th July 1896, noting that it was to run from their Hincaster branch, via Hawes and Richmond, to Darlington. By August 1898 the plan had been extended to Middlesbrough and was now titled 'Barrow & Middlesbrough Railway', with a proposed capital of £5,000,000[45], but, by November 1901, it was observed that the Bill would not proceed due to lack of funds for the Parliamentary expenses. In its final form, in 1903, it had become the Barrow, Darlington & Sunderland Railway, having abandoned its line to Middlesbrough in favour of Sunderland.

On 2nd October 1905 the FR Board noted that the Sunderland promoters had withdrawn their support and there the matter ended.

Halt Platforms

A final aspect of local passenger services during the period was the provision of Workmen's Trains, Workmen's Platforms and Halt Platforms, for use by the local population or by specific groups of passengers.

Of the workmen's stations, the most significant was that provided, at the request of Vickers, to serve their Barrow Shipyard. As recorded earlier, the Barrow Shipyard had been purchased by Vickers in 1897 and a rapid expansion took place. On 24th March 1899, the FR Board noted a request for a station *'in proximity to the works'* as, in order to man their expanding works, Vickers needed to recruit from a wide area in Furness and South Cumberland and the only practical means of transport, to and from work, for these recruits, was the Furness Railway. A platform was built at Shipyard Junction on the branch from the Ramsden Dock line to Walney Ferry. It opened for use by special workmen's trains on 1st May 1899[46].

Barrow Shipyard Station

Salthouse Halt seen in 1954. It was served by a summer Saturday-only service to and from Piel station in 1920 and 1921, after which this was discontinued. (Author: MAC24)

had to be extended during the First War and a second platform was brought into use on 18th October 1915. Workmen's trains were now running from, and back to, Grange and Millom. The Shipyard Station was destined to last until 1967, only being closed as a result of the failure, owing to corrosion, of the Buccleuch Dock Bridge.

Vickers were associated with another Halt platform. Naval Construction and Armaments Ltd had constructed a gun range near Eskmeals and this was developed by Vickers. A new branch into the gun range was accessed from a signal box at Monk Moors opened on 6th December 1897, about this time, a platform was built at the junction[47].

A Halt had already been provided at Wraysholme (between Cark and Kents Bank), in 1911, for the West Lancashire Territorials rifle range[48]. Late in the First World War a branch was provided at Wraysholme, to serve a military establishment at Flookburgh, associated with Vickers' airship programme which utilised the Halt, the signal box was opened on 26th March 1917[49].

Another Halt, of distinctly non-military origin, was St Bees Golf Halt, at which a signal for down trains 'to be held at 'Danger' by passengers when required', was provided on 7th April 1914[50].

One of the most interesting of the Furness Railway halts was that provided on the Piel Branch adjacent to Salthouse Junction, which came into operation on Saturday 22nd May 1920[51]. A notice, dated Saturday, 5th June 1920, indicated eight trains each way between the Halt and Piel Station, Saturdays only, from that date. It will be remembered that Piel station was situated on Roa Island and access to Piel Island proper, with its pub and ruined castle, was by ferry. Rampside, with its beaches, was also popular and Salthouse Halt was within five minutes walk from the Barrow Tramway's Roose service. A modified service was provided in the summer of 1921[52], the Halt trains alternating with the normal service trains, which ran from the Platform 3 Bay at Barrow Central Station.

Further north, the extension of the West Cumberland iron field was in the area south of Egremont and some of these new pits were in remote locations. A LNW & Furness Joint Railway Notice of June 1918 states:

'For the conveyance of Iron Ore Miners residing in the district between Cleator Moor and Rowrah, and at the request of the Ministry of Munitions, Workmen's Trains will be run experimentally as under commencing Monday 17 June 1918.'

Two trains per day were provided, between Rowrah and Beckermet Mines and return; they also called at a Halt at St Thomas Cross, south of Egremont, possibly to provide access to the Ullbank Mine. The Joint Line timetable from 2nd October 1922 shows a Workmen's service between Whitehaven Bransty and a Halt on the Gilgarran branch, near the United Steel Company's No. 4. Pit at Lowca, 20 chains from Parton.

Accidents

Although the Furness Railway had the distinction of having no passenger fatalities in train accidents in its long history, the accident reports of the Board of Trade Railway Department show that the Company was, like other UK railways, vulnerable to movement incidents such as derailments, brake failures, misread signals and misunderstood messages, some of which resulted in death or serious injury.

However, two accidents on the FR were probably unique in British rail history. On 22nd October 1892, just after 8.00am,

Sharp Stewart 0-6-0 FR No. 115 was shunting at the sidings at Lindal East, when a massive hole appeared beneath it. The driver and fireman jumped clear and the tender was uncoupled and saved but No. 115 slowly disappeared into the old iron mine workings under the line and, at 200 feet down, could not be saved. Over the years, often around 1st April, schemes have been proposed to rescue No. 115 but none have matured.

On the early morning of 28th February 1903, the Furness line experienced a severe westerly gale, which brought down the telegraph wires on the Leven Viaduct. At about 5.00am, the down Carnforth – Whitehaven mail train ran into the tangled wires. The vacuum brake pipe was severed on one of the coaches, bringing the train to a stand. A severe gust blew the passenger coaches on to their sides on the up line. Remarkably, only thirty-three passengers suffered minor injuries. After a Board of Trade enquiry, a wind pressure gauge was provided, at the west end of the Leven Viaduct, which sounded a warning in Plumpton Junction signalbox if a set level of wind pressure was exceeded. This remained in operation until the closure of Plumpton Junction box.

CHAPTER 22 REFERENCES

1   FRDM, 24th June 1892.
2   *CRA Journal*, May 1982 p.13.
3   FRDM, 14th Oct. 1904.
4   FRSM, 10th Aug. 1904.
5   *Railway Magazine*, Aug. 1898.
6   Ibid, June 1898.
7   Ibid, July 1913.
8   FRCM, 3rd Apr. 1906.
9   FRDM, 11th July 1906.
10 FRDM, 3rd Apr. & 20th May 1908.
11 BRO: FR Capital Account.
12 FRDM, 27th Apr. 1909.
13 FRDM, 23rd Feb. 1910.
14 FRDM, 9th Oct. 1902.
15 FRSM, 25th Feb. 1904.
16 FRDM, 25th Feb. 1904.
17 FRDM, 18th Mar. 1904.
18 FRSM, 13th Feb. 1907.
19 FRDM, 13th June & 8th Aug. 1919.
20 *CRA Journal*, Vol.5 p.36.
21 FRDM, 13th Oct. 1922.
22 FRDM, 23rd Aug. 1899.
23 FRDM, 21st Feb. 1900.
24 FRDM, 10th May 1918.
25 Davies K. Op. cit.
26 FRDM, 6th Feb. 1901.
27 FRDM, 25th Apr. 1901.
28 FRSM, 19th Aug. 1902.
29 Trescatheric B, 1992. *Building Barrow* p. 35.
30 FRDM, 28th Nov. 1902.
31 FRDM, 22nd June 1904.
32 Ellis H., 1959. *British Railway History 1877-1947* p.279.
33 FRDM, 19th Aug. 1903.
34 FRDM, 25th Feb. 1904.
35 PRO: MT6/1588/7.
36 FRCM, 30th Sep. 1907.
37 Ellis H. Op. cit. p.146.
38 FRDM, 29th Feb. 1897.
39 FRDM, 12th Oct. 1898.
40 Lancaster J.Y. & Wattleworth D.R. Op. cit. p.117.
41 Gradon W. McG, 1952. *The Track of the Ironmasters* p.34.
42 *Bradshaw's Railway Manual*.
43 Joy D. Op. cit. p.220.
44 Ibid. p.221.
45 FRDM, 10th Aug. 1898.
46 FR Signal Notice.
47 Ibid.
48 FRDM, 9th Feb. 1911.
49 FR Signal Notice.
50 Ibid.
51 Ibid.
52 FR Working Timetable, 10th July 1921

BARROW DOCKS FROM 1896

The significance of the Barrow Shipbuilding Company and its successor, from 1888, Naval Construction and Armaments Ltd., regarding the capacity of the Furness Railway's Barrow Docks has been outlined earlier. The Barrow Yard, operated by Naval Construction and Armaments Ltd, from 1888 had, in 1896, successfully completed the 14,200 ton first class cruiser HMS *Powerful* for the Royal Navy.

However, the Sheffield firm of Vickers, Sons & Co. Ltd., successful steelmakers, specialising in armour-plating, were seeking to expand into shipbuilding, fitting out, and arming, at a time when, in light of the Franco-Russian Alliance of 1894 and the establishment of a Russian naval squadron in the Mediterranean, Great Britain's position regarding its naval forces was causing concern.

In the Far East there was the growing sea power of Imperial Japan to which, in fact, the Vickers Barrow Yard was to make a significant contribution in the form of the battleships HIJMS *Mikasa* and HIJMS *Katori* and the battle cruiser HIJMS *Kongo*. The big threat, however, was from the Kaiser's Germany. In 1897 the British Government decided not to renew the Anglo-German Commercial Treaty of 1865, which was perceived by Germany as a threat to German trade and the need for a larger German Navy[1].

The ideal vehicle for Vickers' ambitions, was the Barrow Yard of Naval Construction and Armaments Ltd, with its success record as exemplified by the building of HMS *Powerful*. Vickers purchased the Barrow Company for £425,000 in 1897 and thereby ended the Furness Railway/Barrow Steelworks influence in Barrow shipbuilding. In the same year Vickers purchased the armaments firm, Maxim Nordenfelt for £1,353,000.

This formidable combination became known as Vickers, Sons & Maxim. The first fighting ship to be built under the new regime at Barrow was the battleship HMS *Vengeance*, launched on 25th July 1899 – the first warship to be built, engined, armoured and supplied with gun mountings by a single firm. She was completed in 1901[2].

Given this pedigree, it was not surprising that Vickers attitude to the Furness Railway as owners of the Barrow Docks, was aggressive. They wrote to the FR on the matter of the dimensions of the dock gates on 8th February 1899:

'The matter is of considerable importance in view of the ever growing size of ships and for the little margin of room for the battleship now being built by our firm for the Imperial Japanese Government (the Mikasa). The condition of your dock cills will, as you are aware, make it necessary for us to send the ship into the open in an incomplete condition as regards coals, armaments and stores. It will be necessary to involve additional outlay ... on our part.'[3]

The FR estimated the cost of rebuilding the Ramsden Dock gates at £235,833. However, the scheme was eventually limited to the lowering of the Ramsden Dock No. 4 cill, at an estimated cost of £85,995, of which Vickers agreed to pay one half, provided this did not exceed £50,000[4]. A contract for the work was let to John Aird & Co. *'to provide an additional depth of water of six feet'.* The FR shareholders were told:

'It was absolutely necessary that the work should be put in hand without delay so it might be finished in time to allow HMS Vengeance to undock in the course of next year ... Vickers will contribute, substantially toward the cost of the work.'[5]

The FR were clearly trapped by their obligation to provide adequate dock accommodation to Vickers, but, in the mean time, the traffic of the Docks was on an upward trend (although the tonnages and the profits were not necessarily directly related):

Year	Total Imports & Exports (Tons)
1895	447,310
1896	695,292
1897	742,978
1898	830,331
1899	1,043,417
1900	911,870

The death, in 1896, of Sir James Ramsden, the architect of the capital expenditure on the Barrow Docks, allowed the Furness Railway Board to take a more realistic approach. After years of attempting to justify the enormous expenditure of capital on the Docks as necessary for the traffic of the railway, at the Shareholders' Meeting, on 17th August 1897, the first after the Vickers purchase, the acting Chairman Sir John Hibbert commented:

'Of course we know that our docks are rather a white elephant and the more we find work for these docks the better it will be for the shareholders of the Furness Railway Company.'

He went on to say:

'The dredging of Piel Bar ... is being actively carried out to improve the passage of the Barrow steamers carrying valuable Belfast and Isle of Man traffic.'

At the Shareholders Meeting on 24th August 1898, the acting Chairman, Lord Muncaster, was more forthright:

'The Directors are fully alive to the development of the Docks and it is useless probing the Directorate unduly on this point. You may take it that no stone will be left unturned to induce the shipping industries of the west coast as well as traders to come to the Port of Barrow.'

However, he was able to report that there had been an increase of 62 ships, representing an increased tonnage of 20,000. He went on to refer to the MR's Heysham Scheme:

'A neighbouring company with which they were on perfectly friendly terms and with whom they wished to continue their policy of friendliness had announced their intention of creating a port and harbour at Heysham; they

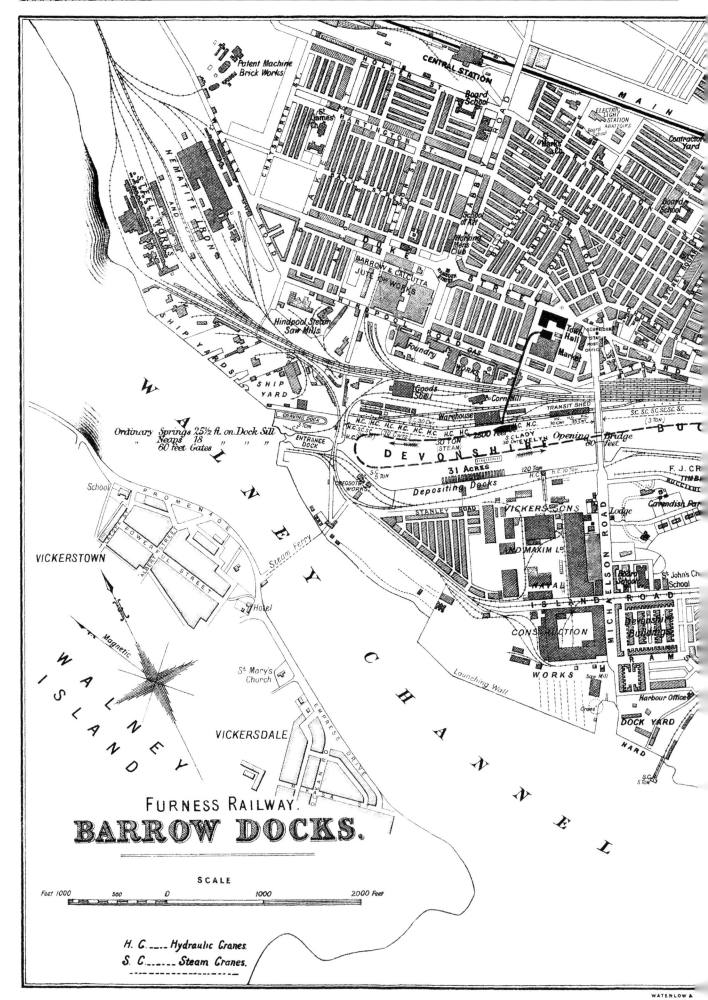

FURNESS RAILWAY.

BARROW DOCKS.

SCALE

Feet 1000   500   0   1000   2000 Feet

H. C. ____ Hydraulic Cranes.
S. C. _____ Steam Cranes.

WATERLOW &

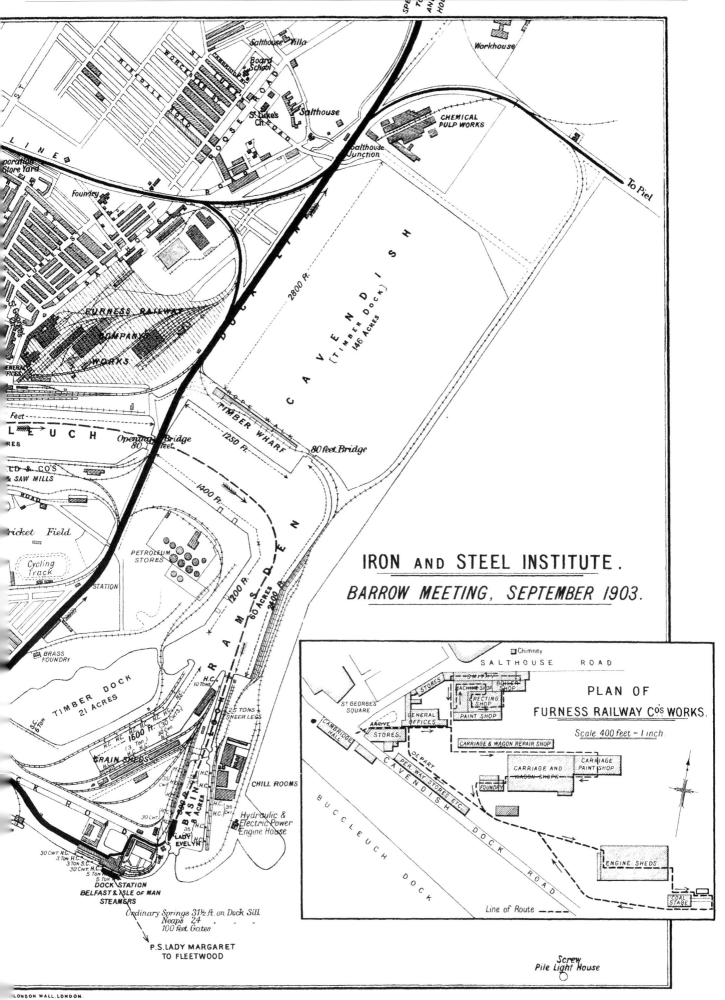

SPECIAL TRAIN TO CARK AND HOLKER HALL

Workhouse

Salthouse Villa

Board School

Salthouse

St. Luke's Ch.

CHEMICAL PULP WORKS

Salthouse Junction

To Piel

KIT DALE

WORCEL

ROOSE ROAD

LINE

Corporation Store Yard

Foundry

FURNESS RAILWAY COMPANY'S WORKS

GENERAL OFFICES

C A V E N D I S H
[TIMBER DOCK]
146 ACRES

2800 Ft.

DUCK LINE

LEUCH

Opening Bridge 80 feet

TIMBER WHARF

ROPE WALK

1250 Ft.

80 feet Bridge

Feet

LD & CO'S & SAW MILLS

ROAD

1400 Ft.

Cricket Field

Cycling Track

PETROLEUM STORES

STATION

1200 Ft.

R A M S D E N

60 ACRES

2400 Ft.

IRON AND STEEL INSTITUTE.

BARROW MEETING, SEPTEMBER 1903.

BRASS FOUNDRY

TIMBER DOCK
21 ACRES

H.C. 10 TONS

S.C. 5 TON

1600 Ft.
(3 Ton)
30 CWT.

25 TONS SHEER LEGS

H.C. H.C.

GRAIN SHEDS

B A S I N 8 ACRES

LADY EVELYN

CHILL ROOMS

Hydraulic & Electric Power Engine House

DOCK ROAD

30 CWT H.C.
3 Ton H.C.
30 CWT. H.C.
5 Ton S.C.

35
H.C.

DOCK STATION
BELFAST & ISLE OF MAN STEAMERS

Ordinary Springs 31½ ft. on Dock Sill
Neaps 24 " "
100 feet Gates " "

P.S. LADY MARGARET
TO FLEETWOOD

Chimney

SALTHOUSE ROAD

St. GEORGES SQUARE

STORES

SMITHY

MACHINE SHOP

BOILER SHOP

ERECTING SHOP

PAINT SHOP

PLAN OF
FURNESS RAILWAY CO'S WORKS.

Scale 400 feet = 1 inch.

CAMBRIDGE HALL

ARRIVE STORES

GENERAL OFFICES

OF PART

PER WAY STORES ETC.

CARRIAGE & WAGON REPAIR SHOP

CARRIAGE AND WAGON SHOPS

FOUNDRY

CARRIAGE PAINT SHOP

BUCCLEUCH DOCK

CAVENDISH DOCK ROAD

ENGINE SHEDS

COAL STAGE

Line of Route

Screw Pile Light House

LONDON WALL, LONDON.

A British Dredging Company vessel is preparing the Deep Water Berth in 1907 to allow Vickers to complete larger ships there without the need to take them into Devonshire Dock. (Sankey print: 530)

have a perfect right to do so. He only hoped it would do them no harm as some people thought. Possibly it might do them some good. He did not, however, see how they could interfere if the Midland Company thought fit to make a dock at Heysham.'

At the Shareholders' Meeting, on 22nd February 1899, the Chairman, the 8th Duke of Devonshire, returned to the matter of Vickers and their requirements:

'The firm of Vickers, Sons & Maxim, which you are aware purchased the Naval Construction Works at Barrow are ... throwing great energy into their shipbuilding business and the Furness Company is doing all in its power to assist them. The firm is now building battleships and cruisers of larger size and consequently requiring greater depth of water and it is not unreasonable to anticipate that in the near future even larger warships will be constructed at Barrow. It is therefore desirable that the Company should be in a position to afford the proper accommodation for vessels of this character.'

Sir John Hibbert commented, to reassure the shareholders:

'The Directors would not agree to ... expenditure (on the docks) unless they could see a prospect of the outlay making a proper return to the Company.'

The lowering of the Ramsden Dock cill was retarded by a subsidence, and, on 20th February 1901, the Duke of Devonshire reported to the shareholders that the work had taken:

'much longer than expected due to the subsidence at the

North Pier Head. The contractor will finish the work in the coming spring.'

Vickers had written to the FR in December 1900:

'The state of the works have caused the Government, in spite of all our endeavours, to refuse to allow us to tender for the last four cruisers given to the trade. Until the cill is completed we are not in a position to deliver the battleship Vengeance which has been waiting delivery since July last, nor to complete the cruiser Hogue or the Japanese battleship Mikasa ... We will look upon you to recoup the very heavy loss we are daily sustaining from the neglect of the Railway Company to finish the lowering of the cill.'

Aslett replied:

'There is no wilful default by the Furness Company.' [6]

At the FR Shareholders' Meeting on 21st August 1901, Sir John Hibbert was able to report that the work on the No. 4 cill at Ramsden Dock had been completed and that HMS Vengeance had been undocked in May, but the dispute between Vickers and the Furness Railway lingered on. The Duke of Devonshire reported to the FR Board, on 25th June 1902, that he had met Albert Vickers at Devonshire House, London, on the subject of the cost of dredging in Walney Channel, for the launching of Hogue, Mikasa and King Alfred; Vickers had agreed to pay the FR £1,718 in lieu of the cost of £2,035. It was also agreed that, in future, there would be agreement between Messrs Vickers and the FR engineer on the cross sections of the channel to be achieved. Devonshire went on to say that Albert Vickers had remarked that:

The 1908 Scherzer bridge is seen half open c.1920. It bridges the passageway between the Buccleuch and Ramsden Docks. (K. Norman collection: N826)

'he felt very sore at having a pistol put to his head in respect of the cost of swinging the battleship Mikasa*'.*

Devonshire had replied to the effect that the FR Co. felt that Messrs Vickers did not treat them generously, that the FR had spent much more money, on behalf of Vickers, than the latter Company's business justified and that the direct benefit to the FR did not equal the interest on the capital cost.

To rub salt into the Furness Railway's wounds Vickers started to dispute the FR's rates for their traffic. The FR Board heard, on 14th October 1903, that Vickers had sent two men into their Barrow Yard with the object of taking particulars of traffic. The Chairman commented that Vickers would not have allowed employees of the FR to enter their works without obtaining permission. The matter of rates was referred to the Court of the Railway & Canal Commissioners.

Vickers' pressure on the FR continued. On 6th November 1903 a letter was received from Vickers to the effect that their contract for building an Atlantic liner, for Cunard, had been turned down because its beam of 80 feet was too wide for the Michaelson and Buccleuch Bridge openings. Vickers went on to say:

'Until the widening can be made it will be necessary to transfer building of larger ships to Clyde Yards.'

The works necessary were:

1. Widening of the Buccleuch and Michaelson
 passageways £160,500
2. Dredging of the Walney Channel £98,641
3. Dredging of the Piel Channel to 9ft below the
 Ramsden Dock cill £58,876

4. Construction of a dry dock £235,000

The FR Consulting Engineer, Frank Stileman, provided the estimates.

Meanwhile, Sir John Hibbert had told the Shareholders' Meeting on 19th August 1902:

'Your dock traffic has been fairly well maintained although, having regard to the large expenditure this property has involved, we have to look forward to a very much increased business before fair return will be obtained for the money invested in constructing the docks and the mechanical appliances connected therewith. In the June half year there was an increase of 34,113 tons & imported ore, timber, petroleum and exported steel rails and pig iron all show a substantial increase.

'We have in the last few years spent £160,000 in making our docks suitable for the large warships which are built by Vickers, Sons & Maxim. This is in addition to the £60,000 subscribed by Vickers to the dock cill work.'

In February 1905 a conference was held, between the FR Board and Vickers, on the subject of the latter's building warships and Atlantic liners of over 80 feet beam. Vickers required a 900-foot frontage on the south side of the Michaelson Bridge and an opening of 100 feet at Buccleuch Bridge, all at FR expense. If an agreement could not be reached, Vickers would transfer shipbuilding to the Beardsmore Yard on the Clyde in which they had a 50% interest.

The FR appears to have agreed to the provision of the berth in the Buccleuch Dock and to the widening of the Buccleuch Dock passageway to 100 feet.

White Star passenger liner 'Scythia' (19,761 tons) being manoeuvred for departure from Buccleuch Dock in December 1920. FR twin-screw tugs 'Furness' and 'Cartmel' and the paddle tug 'Walney' are in attendance. (Sankey print: 1975)

However, Albert Vickers wrote to the FR on 5th March 1906:

'We would point out that (the Buccleuch Bridge widening) should be treated as a burning question as, if the alteration is not completed with the most possible despatch, it will entirely exclude us from obtaining an order for a battleship for the British Government.'

The FR agreed on 30th January 1907 and a tender, for £38,422, was accepted from John Aird & Co. for the widening of the passageway and the replacement of the existing swing bridge by a Scherzer bascule. The new bridge was opened on 12th October 1908[7].

On 9th December 1909 the FR Board were able to report the successful launch and docking of the 19,250 ton HMS *Vanguard*, favourable tides and winds having assisted the manoeuvre. *Vanguard* had a beam of 86 feet and was the first *'Dreadnought'* battleship to be built at Barrow, being completed in February 1910. She had an uneventful war in terms of action, surviving the Battle of Jutland unscathed, but tragically exploded, while berthed at Scapa Flow, on 9th July 1917, as a result of unstable cordite; 804 crew members were killed[8].

The constant friction between Vickers and the Furness Railway Company and between the latter and the Barrow Corporation, led to a proposal that a 'Barrow Docks and Harbour Trust' be formed. This was first discussed by the FR Board on 10th November 1910, but it is not made clear in the Minute as to the origin of this interesting concept, which was based on the example of the Mersey Docks & Harbour Board.

However, the FR Board asked their veteran member, Edward Wadham, to consider and report on the proposal. A copy of his reply, to Alfred Aslett, has survived in the local history collection of Barrow Record Office. Writing from his long-time home, Millwood, near Furness Abbey, on 14th December 1910, Wadham stated:

'Thank you for sending me copies of the Joint Report of the Accountant, Audit Accountant and Mr. Linton, the Goods Manager's Report and the Joint Report of the Solicitor and the General Manager. I have carefully read and considered the above mentioned Reports and entirely concur in the conclusions come to by the Solicitor and the General Manager.

'The Docks were built by and are the property of the Furness Railway Company and are worked in connection with that Company. I am of the opinion that we should be unwise to attempt to make them separate properties, especially if by doing so we took Messrs. Vickers & Co. into partnership in connection with the Docks which would be the equivalent of giving them a 'monopoly' which would be sure to act prejudicially to our interests some day. ... I believe our Engineer and Consulting Engineer are preparing a Report of our exact position and what works are necessary and possible by way of improvement, also an estimate of the cost of the same. I feel sure that if works are recommended they should be carried out by the Furness Railway Co. without any complication of a Trust.'

Another positive development of this period was the lease to Vickers, in 1909, of the 146 acre Cavendish Dock, hitherto totally unused for commercial purposes, for the construction and manoeuvring of airships, an area of activity into which Vickers was moving.

The final docks development of this era was the dredging of a 'Deep Water Berth' in the Walney Channel between the Fleetwood Pier at Ramsden Dock Station and the Harbour Yard Pier. The old Glasgow Pier was demolished in the process, and the dredging of Piel Channel to a greater depth was carried out at the same time[9].

The Buccleuch Dock Bridge fully raised for the passage of Orient liner 'Orsova' (28,790 tons) into Ramsden Dock on her way to sea in 1954. (Author: MAC51)

There was, however, yet another episode of dispute between Vickers and the FR.

The Board Meeting, on 12th November 1912 noted that the battle cruiser HMS *Princess Royal* had been grounded during its undocking. Captain Bissett, the Harbour Master, attributed this to the actions of the pilot but Vickers reacted by insisting on further dredging before the departure of the Japanese battle cruiser *Kongo*.

The Furness Railway position was put clearly in a letter recorded in the Board Minutes of 12th November 1912:

'We are all at times desirous of meeting you in the most liberal manner and in every possible way so far as we can reasonably be asked or expected to do so. There must however come a time when we cannot go on spending money on dredging work, so far as our Capital Account is concerned, unless we can see a fair and proper return for this outlay and which, when incurred, it must be remembered will necessarily involve further expenses year by year in maintenance. Alfred Aslett'

Vickers' reply provides a useful summary of that Company's contribution to work on the improvement of Barrow Docks:

Lowering of the No. 4 Cill Ramsden Dock	£60,000
Widening Buccleuch Dock Bridge	£46,650
Dredging Buccleuch Dock	£10,900
Dredging Walney Channel & Piel Bar & Deep Water Berth	£100,000
Total	£217,550

At the Shareholders' Meeting on 14th February 1913, the Chairman, the 9th Duke of Devonshire, reported that the Deep Water Berth in Walney Channel had been completed and that the improvement in the fairway of Walney Channel and Piel Bar would be completed by the end of the following month. A year later he was able to report that the completion of these works:

'Will now enable the largest battleships and battle cruisers to pass safely in and out of the Barrow Docks.'

This was in February 1914. At midnight on 4-5th August, the Furness Railway, along with all the other major railways, came under Government Control as the result of the outbreak of War.

During the First World War Barrow Docks required two further improvements.

The Ramsden Dock No. 1 cill was lowered, in 1913, by the removal of capping stones to allow the safe undocking of the battleships *Revenge* (31,250 tons) and *Emperor of India* (25,000 tons). The cost was shared between Vickers and the FR.

In January 1916 the FR Consulting Engineers, Palmer, Rendell & Tritton reported that the Devonshire Dock Bridge, between the Devonshire Dock and its tidal basin, and which carried the northern rail connection between Barrow Yard and the north end of Barrow Island, was almost corroded away. The original hydraulically operated lift-and-roll bridge was strengthened by girders as an interim measure, steel for a Scherzer type bridge not being available. Detailed plans for this bridge, based on the standard Scherzer product, were drawn up and can be inspected at Barrow Records Office.

CHAPTER 23 REFERENCES

1   Scott J.D., 1962. *Vickers: A History* p.47.
2   Harris N. *Op. cit.* p.95.
3   FRDM, 1st Feb. 1899.
4   FRDM, 3rd May 1899.
5   FRSM, 23rd Aug. 1899.
6   FRDM, 13th Dec. 1900.
7   FRDM, 14th Oct. 1908.
8   Harris N. *Op. cit.* p.101.
9   FRDM, 13th Nov. 1911.

L. & N. W. & FURNESS RAILWAYS.

THE BARROW ROUTE
TO
BELFAST AND DOUGLAS

JULY, AUGUST,
AND
SEPTEMBER,
1902.

UNLESS CONTRARY
NOTICE IS GIVEN.

One of the first-class Fast Steamers **"Duchess of Devonshire," "City of Belfast,"**
"Manx Queen," or **"Manxman,"** will sail every Week-day as under:—
(Weather permitting and unforeseen circumstances excepted)

BARROW TO BELFAST AT OR AFTER 8-30 P.M.	**BARROW TO DOUGLAS, 2-15 p.m.** UNTIL SEPTEMBER 29TH.
BELFAST TO BARROW AT 8-30 P.M.	**DOUGLAS TO BARROW, 8-30 a.m.** UNTIL SEPTEMBER 30TH.

In connection with the Fast Trains to and from all parts of Cumberland and Westmorland. Trains run alongside Steamer, and
Passengers' Luggage is transferred to and from the Steamers by the Company's Porters, free of charge.
DURING JULY, AUGUST AND SEPTEMBER, the Magnificent Express Steamer

"DUCHESS OF DEVONSHIRE"
Will be placed on the Isle-of-Man Service.

STATIONS.	Fares and Train Times to Belfast.						Fares and Trains Times to Douglas.					
	Last Train for Belfast Steamer leaves at	SINGLE.		RETURN Available to Dec. 31st.			Last Train for Douglas Steamer leaves at	SINGLE.		RETURN Available 2 months. c	
		1st & Saloon	3rd & St'rge	1st & Saloon	3rd & St'rge			1st & Saloon	3rd & St'rge	1st & Saloon	3rd & St'rge
	p.m. s. d.	s. d.	s. d.	s. d.	s. d.			s. d.	s. d.	s. d.	s. d.
PRESTON	6 45	15 9	6 3	25 0	10 6		12A20 p.m.	14 7	6 5	22 6	11 6
LANCASTER, L. & N.W.	6 30	18 0	7 0½	27 6	10 6		12A51 ,,	13 0	6 5½	16 6	11 6
MORECAMBE ,,	5 55	18 0	7 3	27 6	10 6		12A25 ,,	13 3	6 5½	17 0	11 6
WINDERMERE ,,	6 15	20 8	8 6	31 10	14 2		11 45 a.m.	14 2	7 0	23 3	13 6
KENDAL, via Carnforth	6 33	18 11	7 9½	28 10	12 9		12 6 p.m.	12 5	6 3½	19 9	11 6
Do. via Sandside	5 50	18 11	7 9½	28 10	12 9		12 40 ,,	12 5	6 3½	19 9	11 6
CARLISLE, L. & N.W.	4 35	19 6	9 0	32 0	15 0		9 45 a.m.	17 10	9 0	30 0	16 6
PENRITH	5 3	19 6	9 0	32 0	15 0		10 30 ,,	17 10	9 0	29 6	16 0
TEBAY	5 31	19 6	9 0	32 0	15 0		12 25 p.m.	16 6	8 1	26 0	13 6

Passengers holding 3rd class tickets and wishing to travel Saloon,
can do so on payment on board of 10/3 Return ; 7/6 Single.

A—After September 15th, Mondays and Saturdays only. Other
days after September 15th, Preston depart 11-25 a.m., Lancaster
11-57 a.m., and Morecambe 12-5 p.m.

Passengers holding 3rd class tickets and wishing to travel Saloon,
can do so on payment on board of 4/- Return ; 2/6 Single.

C—Tickets issued to Douglas on and after July 30th, are only
available for return up to September 30th.

**Circular Tour and Week End Tickets to Douglas can now be obtained at Carlisle, Penrith, Windermere, Kendal,
Morecambe, and Lancaster.**

The journey may be broken at Grange, Ulverston (for the Lakes), or Furness Abbey both going and returning.
Passengers, Goods, and Live Stock can be BOOKED THROUGH at very Cheap Rates to and from the principal place
Cumberland, Westmorland & Belfast. The Service to and from Douglas is an Express Passenger Service only.
Particulars may be obtained from the Railway Agents, or from JAMES LITTLE & Co., Barrow, from whor
Lists, Guide Books, or any other information may be obtained.

BY ORDER,   **F. HARRISON, L. & N.W.**
ALFRED ASLETT, Furne

JULY, 1902.

The Barrow Printing Company, Printers, &c., Hindpool Road Barrow.

A rare handbill promoting the joint LNW & FR steamer services by the Barrow Route to Belfast and Douglas in the summer of 1902.
(Private collection)

THE FINAL YEARS OF THE BARROW ROUTE TO BELFAST

Alan Pearsall, in his book *"North Irish Channel Services"* [1] highlights the importance of the steam ship in the development of Northern Ireland and, from the opening of the Fleetwood route in 1843, the part played by the railways in the increasing traffic. He points out that, from about 1875, the railways, competing among themselves, *'set a fast pace both in speed and improved facilities'*. The Midland Railway's move from the tidal port of Morecambe to Piel Pier at Barrow, in 1867, led to a relatively fixed boat, train and steamer timetable, thereby improving its competitive position with the London & North Western and Lancashire & Yorkshire joint service from Fleetwood, which served a similar Midlands hinterland. However, by the time the Midland Railway Agreement with the Furness Railway and James Little & Company for the operation of the Barrow Steam Navigation Company's services from Barrow to Belfast and the Isle of Man was renewed in 1894, the Midland was reviewing its Irish traffic facilities, a process which culminated in its purchase, in 1903, of the Belfast & Northern Counties Railway [2]. In June 1892 the MR had obtained powers to build a branch from Morecambe to Heysham, some 3½ miles to the south [3] and at the Midland Railway Shareholders' Meeting in February 1896, the Chairman, Ernest Paget, outlined the Company's plans for a new harbour at Heysham, for their Irish traffic, powers for the construction of which were obtained later that year.

The 'Barrow Route' had become an established feature of the Furness Railway and the Isle of Man was a favourite holiday resort for the more affluent residents of Barrow, therefore it came as a shock when, on 27th February 1896, the recently appointed FR General Manager, Alfred Aslett, had to report the MR's plans to his Board and that he had been in correspondence with Midland Railway director, G.H. Turner.

No doubt after much soul searching, the FR Board decided on a policy of mutual goodwill toward their Midland partners on the Barrow Boats. As evidence of this policy they did not petition against the Heysham Bill.

On 28th April 1896 the FR Board received a suggestion, from James Little & Co., that Piel Pier should be rebuilt for the Belfast passenger traffic, but in the existing atmosphere of doubt, it is not surprising that this suggestion was not pursued. Negotiations between the FR and the MR now continued on a personal basis between the 8th Duke of Devonshire and Sir Ernest Paget [4].

Aslett and Turner met again, on 26th October 1897, and a further meeting was held at the Duke of Devonshire's London home, Devonshire House, on 7th December 1898. The matter dragged on and yet another meeting was held in October 1899 [5]. The essential drift of the Midland's case was that they intended to transfer their Irish traffic to Heysham, but would be prepared to make a lump sum compensation to the Furness Railway and

The tidal berths used by the Belfast and Isle of Man steamers are seen in this view of Ramsden Dock Station from the Walney side of the channel. (K. Norman collection)

Belfast and the North of Ireland.

SHORTEST SEA ROUTE.   ROYAL MAIL SERVICE.

The swift and Powerful First-class Steamships.

"DUCHESS OF DEVONSHIRE,"

"CITY OF BELFAST,"      **"MANX QUEEN," &c.,**

Will sail between BARROW and BELFAST weather permitting) in connection with Through Trains to and from all parts of England, as under :—

From BARROW-IN-FURNESS to BELFAST,

Each Evening (Sundays excepted) at or after 8-30 p.m., as per Monthly Sailing Card, after arrival of Through Trains from all parts of the Midland and Furness Railways.

From BELFAST to BARROW-IN-FURNESS,

Every Evening (Sundays excepted) at 8-30 p.m., arriving in Barrow (weather permitting) in time for the Through Fast Trains to all parts of the Furness and Midland Railways.

Trains arrive at and depart from alongside the Steamers.

Passengers, Goods, and Live Stock are booked through at moderate rates to and from the principal Railway Stations in England and Belfast, and the North of Ireland.

Isle-of-Man.

SHORTEST SEA PASSAGE.   AVERAGE ONLY 3 HOURS.

From about Whitsuntide to end of September inclusive.
The Barrow Steam Navigation Co.'s First-class Favourite Steamers,

"DUCHESS OF DEVONSHIRE,"

"DUCHESS OF BUCCLEUCH."

Or other First-class Steamer, will sail daily (Sunday excepted' between

BARROW and DOUGLAS (Isle-of-Man).

From BARROW to DOUGLAS (As per sailing list.
 ,,   DOUGLAS to BARROW (

Trains arrive and Depart from alongside the Steamers.

N.B.—Passengers' Luggage is conveyed from the Train to the Steamers by the Company's Porters FREE OF CHARGE.

JAMES LITTLE & Co., Barrow-in-Furness.

Berths may be booked at H. W. MACKERETH'S, Ulverston.

A Barrow Steam Navigation Company advertisement in the 'Furness Year Book' for 1906. By this time the Midland Railway had discontinued its Barrow to Douglas service in favour of the Heysham – Isle of Man route. (K. Norman collection)

James Little & Co, an offer declined outright by the FR delegation. On 10th November 1900 the FR received the Midland's latest proposals. These were, in essence, that Little's would be bought out of the Barrow Agreement, enabling them to act as agents for both the Heysham and Barrow routes, and that the MR was prepared to guarantee earnings of not less than £4,000 per annum for the Barrow Route. The FR accepted these terms, but on 16th November 1900, the MR equivocated, stating:

'...it should be clearly understood that no moral obligation is to be inferred regarding the routing of traffic via Barrow.'

An agreement was again deferred.

After the FR's conflict with Vickers over the Ramsden Dock cill, yet another meeting took place at Devonshire House, on 30th January 1901, between the Duke of Devonshire and Sir Ernest Paget who:

'could not see his way ... to give any guarantee that the Midland Railway traffic should be forwarded via Barrow when Heysham Harbour was opened.'

On 26th June 1901, the Chairman reported to the FR Board, that purchase of the Furness Railway by the Midland Railway at 3%, had been discussed. This had not been recommended by the

MR Board as 'it would be regarded as antagonistic by their LNWR friends'. An Agreement was signed, on 17th July 1901[6], the essence of which was that the Barrow Boat Agreement would continue and that the Midland Railway would guarantee gross rail earnings and cross channel traffic receipts of £5,000 per annum.

At the FR Shareholders' Meeting on 21st August 1901, the Chairman, Sir John Hibbert, stated:

'I am pleased to tell you that we have at length come to an agreement with the Midland Company ... in respect of the Barrow boats ... which when the Heysham Harbour works are completed, the terms of a new partnership for seven years has been agreed upon. ... Only by the greatest care and tact has this new agreement ... been brought about.'

Later, in the Parliamentary Session 1901-2, a Bill was presented to authorise the Furness Railway to own and operate steamers between Barrow, Fleetwood, Dublin, Belfast, Larne and Londonderry. The Midland Railway sought similar powers and there were no petitions against the respective Bills by either party.

On 19th August 1902, the FR shareholders were advised that their Steam Vessels Bill had passed, had received Royal Assent and was retrospective. 'Whatever we may have done in the past without Parliamentary sanction has been put right.'

It was noted that the Midland Railway had obtained similar powers by their own Act.

On 9th October 1902, the FR Board noted the significant news that the MR was proposing an amalgamation with the Northern Counties Railway of Ireland.

Regarding Heysham Harbour, the *Railway News* reported:

'The first ordinary train from London to Heysham ... left St. Pancras at 5 o'clock, 1st September (1904) and there were a large number of passengers by it. Four carriages, 1st class and 3rd class dining cars and two composite carriages ran through to Heysham with stoppages at Kettering, Nottingham, Sheffield and Leeds. On the sides of the through carriages were boards bearing the words 'Heysham for Ireland'. [7]

The opening of the Heysham to Belfast service by the Midland Railway, on 1st September 1904, was accompanied by the introduction of four large, brand new, steamers:

TSS *Antrim*	2,100 tons	Clydebank
TSS *Donegal*	2,100 tons	Lairds
TSS *Londonderry*	2,174 tons	Denny Bros.
PS *Manxman*	2,174 tons	Vickers

The Barrow Route continued to be operated by Barrow Steam Navigation Co. steamers:

PS *Manx Queen*	811 tons	1883	ex Littles' Duchess of Edinburgh of 1880
TSS *City of Belfast*	1065 tons	1893	new Lairds
TSS *Duchess of Devonshire*	1265 tons	1897	new Vickers
PS *Duchess of Buccleuch*	785 tons	1903	ex LBSCR *Rouen*[8]

The opening of Heysham had a catastrophic effect on the Barrow Route traffic. On 14th October 1904, the FR board were advised that, during the month of September, there had been a drop in tonnage of 3,554 and, in head of cattle, of 1,654. Even more serious was the allegation, by Alfred Aslett, that the Midland Company were:

'illegally ... instructing James Little & Co. to forward all traffic consigned in Ireland via Barrow by the Heysham route.'

In view of the FR loss of traffic during the month of September 1904, amounting to £6,319, the FR took Counsel's opinion on their position and it was decided to proceed against the MR and James Little & Co. in the Court of Chancery. Devonshire wrote to Sir Ernest Paget, on 2nd January 1905:

'I need hardly add that in view of the amicable relations which have so long existed between the two companies, my colleagues and I would very much regret if litigation should arise between them.'

The MR replied, in a letter from J. Matheson to Aslett:

'If the Furness Company would now agree to give up the proposed partnership and duplicate service which in my view must entail loss on both Companies, I will advise the Midland Board to continue nevertheless the agreed subsidy for the period of the intended Agreement.'

The Court of Chancery gave an interim injunction against the MR and Little & Co. and the MR appealed. Further meetings were held at which two alternatives were considered, a Furness buyout and a Midland buyout. The final outcome was that the Furness would sell their share of the Partnership to the Midland and the Midland would continue to operate the Barrow Route for six years, with a daily boat for two years. At the FR Board meeting on 28th July 1905 the details of the Agreement were noted and that the Partnership had terminated on 30th June 1905. The Agreement was dated 21st July 1905, the Midland giving a guarantee that a portion of the competitive traffic to and from Ireland would be forwarded via Barrow, or its equivalent paid for in cash[9].

The four BSNCo. steamers became Midland Railway property on 1st July 1905 and, from 1st January 1907, the Barrow – Belfast service was reduced to three sailings per week.

The FR hoped that the Midland might relent, regarding the seasonal Isle of Man service, and Alfred Aslett wrote to Guy Granet, on 20th December 1906:

'We had strong hopes that as we had agreed to the tri-weekly service of the Barrow – Belfast steamers coming into operation on 1st January 1907 your Company would see their way to continue the Isle of Man service during the whole of the 1907 season and not curtail it by taking off the Isle of Man boats from 1st July 1907. ... As I have previously reminded you the Barrow – Isle of Man service has been in operation for a period of thirty eight years and its probable destruction, as indicated by your letter, must necessarily be a great blow to my Company in the loss of what we looked upon as a valuable and growing business, particularly in the encouragement of tourist traffic through the Lake District which Heysham does not afford

in connection with the Isle of Man traffic and also in the matter of prestige.'

Aslett's impassioned plea bore fruit; the Midland Isle of Man boat service was run from 18th May to 22nd May and from 1st July to 9th September 1907[10].

That was, however, the end of a much enjoyed Barrow institution, although excursions from Ramsden Dock to Douglas have continued sporadically up to the present day.

The status quo continued until 16th February 1912 when the FR Board discussed a letter from Guy Granet, the Midland General Manager, dated 16th November 1911:

'The agreement of 21st July 1905 and of 14th November 1907 have expired. The obligation to run the Barrow and Belfast boat has ceased to exist. The financial success of the service has not been such as to give this Company any encouragement to continue it. In fact we have lost yearly a considerable amount of revenue.'

The Midland Railway followed up their letter by a statement of the losses on the Barrow – Belfast service:

to 30 June 1908	£13,000
to 30 June 1909	£13,000
to 30 June 1910	£11,000
to 30 June 1911	£10,000

The basis of these losses can be seen, from a manuscript table below, of dock traffic complied in the Barrow Docks Office and preserved in their records. However, it was noted that value of the Belfast – Barrow traffic to the FR was £3,548 in 1911, excluding passenger terminal charges and the Midland guarantee. The FR offered to forego the guarantee of £5,000 per annum and the service continued.

	Exports	Imports	Total
1900	46073	40586	86659
1901	40467	40582	81049
1902	36028	39112	75140
1903	36919	42858	79777
1904	25869	32163	58032
Heysham opened 1.9.1904			
1905	12323	10542	22865
1906	13838	11448	25286
1907	14146	9561	23707
3 sailings per week from 1.1.1907			
1908	7614	8908	16522
1909	5789	8329	14118
1910	11925	8454	20379
1911	8901	7137	16038
1912	6470	8293	14763
1913	10060	10029	20089
1914	5023	8367	11390
Discontinued 29.10.1914			

The railways came under Government Control at midnight on 4-5th August 1914 (see Chapter Twenty Five). On 28th October 1914 the FR Traffic & Works Committee held a meeting, with a long agenda, covering various aspects of the wartime operation of the Furness Railway. During the course of the meeting, Aslett received a telegram, from the General Manager of the Midland Railway, containing the following:

'Admiralty have requisitioned 'City of Belfast' on and from Friday next (30th October). It will be impossible therefore for us to continue sailings between Belfast and Barrow after that date.'

James Little & Co. received a telegram about the same time:

'Government have requisitioned 'City of Belfast' and 'Duchess of Devonshire'. Will advise you tomorrow where they are to be sent. 'City of Belfast' must be in Barrow on Friday morning after which date Belfast – Barrow Service will be permanently discontinued.'

In the discussion, which followed the receipt of this news, Aslett gave the Committee an outline of the history of the Barrow Route and of the various Agreements with the Midland Railway. He stated his intention to write that day to Sir Guy Granet, Midland General Manager suggesting:

'if it is not too late the Admiralty should be asked to consider the desirability of requisitioning one or more of the Isle of Man Steam Packet Company's steamers, five of which were laid up in the Ramsden Dock for the Winter and would be quite suitable for the conveyance of Refugees and German prisoners from Liverpool to the Isle of Man for which purpose I understand the 'City of Belfast' was required by the Admiralty.'

The FR Board noted the position, at its meeting on 12th November 1914, and the fact that unsuccessful attempts had been made to charter another steamer. At the next meeting it was learned that the Railway Executive Committee (member Guy Granet) had given the Admiralty the names of the *City of Belfast* and the *Duchess of Devonshire* as vessels which could be spared. It is matter for speculation whether Granet had used his position and the Admiralty requirements to kill the Barrow Route by offering them his two steamers.

There was, however, a bizarre postscript to the story of the Barrow Route as, on 6th May 1915, James Little and Co. wrote to the FR pointing out that their agreement with the Midland Company as managers, would terminate on 30th June 1915 and that they were considering Barrow or Liverpool as the English port for their services. Rail connections, docks and huge local traffic indicated Liverpool's advantage, but they were reluctant to close their Barrow office and asked whether the Furness Railway could offer advantages at Barrow which would compensate. No harbour dues, passing terminal charges and land rates were suggested. They would be prepared to open the trade with their own vessel *Cottingham*.

The FR Board replied, on 10th June 1915, that a 'no charges' arrangement would create difficulties with other traders; further the *Cottingham* was a non-passenger ship. James Little, the former FR Director, replied:

'The Heysham boats are full every trip and the Midland Company would be the gainers not the losers on having a Barrow service as a secondary feeder.'

Nothing resulted, the war situation grew steadily worse and with it the pressures of traffic on the railway companies. However, on 14th April 1916, the FR Board noted that a meeting had taken place in London with J.W. Little following the closure of the Heysham, Fleetwood and Liverpool services to Belfast. Little pointed out that one of the steamers on the Dundalk & Newry service, the *Dundalk*, was available for £20,000. The FR approached the Midland on this topic; the reply was short and to the point:

'I cannot see any possible chance of the Barrow – Belfast service being renewed.'

After the war, in December 1919, the FR Board were advised that a group of local traders had formed a committee to further the re-opening of a Barrow – Belfast service, but the FR decided that they would not be represented on this committee.[11] The Barrow Route was dead and buried.

After the War the Barrow – Belfast ships were sold to Mediterranean interests[12]. The *Duchess of Devonshire* survived as the *Gibel Dersa* of Gibraltar until 1949.

Chapter 24 References

1   Pearsall A W H, 1962. *North Irish Channel Services.*
2   *Bradshaw's Railway Manual, 1914.*
3   Baughan P. *Op. cit.* p.278.
4   FRDM, 16th Oct. 1896.
5   FRDM, 23rd Nov. 1899.
6   FRDM, 7th Aug. 1901.
7   Baughan P. *Op. cit.* p.300.
8   Barrow Register of Shipping & McNeill D.B. *Op. cit.* Vol.1.
9   FRSM, 9th Aug. 1905.
10 FRDM, 14th Mar. 1907.
11 FRDM, 12th Dec. 1919.
12 McNeill .B. *Op. cit.*

The BSN Co. paddle steamer 'Duchess of Buccleuch' at the Isle of Man berth adjacent to the FR's Ramsden Dock station, seen on the left. (G. Holme collection)

THE FURNESS RAILWAY AND THE FIRST WORLD WAR

The potential value of a railway system in time of war, had been recognised, in France, as early as 1833, but it was the contribution of the railways to the Confederate forces in the American Civil War (1861-1865) and the creation, in 1866, of a Prussian 'Federal Railway Section' which concentrated British minds.

In 1865 the 'Engineer & Railway Voluntary Staff Corps' had been founded:

'for the purpose of directing the application of skilled labour and of railway transport to the purpose of national defence.'

The legislation which was used to set up the Railway Executive Committee was the Regulation of the Forces Act 1871. This provided for the Government taking control of the railways, by an Order in Council, in a national emergency[1].

On 13th March 1911 Sir Edward Grey, the Foreign Secretary, found it necessary to warn the House of Commons that an unprecedented expenditure upon arms and the munitions of war was proceeding[2]. The Royal Navy's orders from the Vickers, Barrow Shipyard, for the period 1904 to 1913, comprised 74 vessels:

Scouts	*Skirmisher & Sentinel*	2
Submarines		64
Cruisers	*Natal, Liverpool & Dartmouth*	3
Battleships	*Vanguard, Emperor of India & Erin*	3
Battle Cruiser	*Princess Royal*	1
Destroyer	*Phoenix*	1[3]

The Railway Executive Committee, formed in November 1912, consisted of a number of railway management notables including;

Sir Frank Ree	General Manager, LNWR (died April 1914)
Herbert Walker	General Manager, L&SWR (Acting Chairman)
Sir Guy Granet	General Manager, Midland Railway
John Aspinall	General Manager, L&YR
Sir Sam Fay	General Manager, Great Central Railway

A huge workload was undertaken, including plans for the mobilisation of the armed forces. A set of 'Instructions' was formulated and sent, in confidence, to the general manager of each railway in January 1914. The Railway Executive Committee took over the railways at midnight on 4-5 August 1914, following the declaration of war against Germany one hour earlier[4].

Management and finance during the War

It was made clear, by the Railway Executive Committee, that the local management of the various railways would continue, as would their financial structure. However, the matter of financial compensation of the railways had already been discussed and decided upon. In the early months of 1914 there was the wide-

---

(S.B.)   (1000)

Furness Railway.

TRAIN ALTERATIONS from SEPT. 1st, 1914.

The following Trains will be discontinued :—

DOWN TRAINS.

1. 11-0 a.m. Barrow to Whitehaven.
2. 12-15 p.m. Carnforth to Whitehaven.

The 12-20 p.m. Carnforth to Barrow will be extended to Whitehaven, leaving Barrow 1-47 p.m., and calling at the same Stations at which the 1-17 p.m. Train from Barrow to Whitehaven is booked to call.

3. 1-10 p.m. Morecambe to Lake Side.
4. The 4-53 p.m. Carnforth to Whitehaven will run to Barrow only, connecting there with the 5-40 p.m. Train Barrow to Whitehaven.

UP TRAINS.

1. 9-17 a.m. Barrow to Carnforth (Mondays only).
2. 8-53 a.m. Whitehaven to Carnforth.
3. 11-40 a.m. Whitehaven to Carnforth.

The 11-25 a.m. Whitehaven to Carnforth will run in the times shown in column 9 (up side) of the Sheet Time Table.

4. 5-25 p.m. Lake Side to Morecambe.

KENDAL BRANCH.

1. 1-55 p.m. Arnside to Kendal.
2. 2-30 p.m. Kendal to Grange.

PIEL BRANCH.

All Trains between Rampside and Piel. 10-45 p.m. Barrow to Rampside, and the 11-6 p.m. Rampside to Barrow (Thursdays and Saturdays only).

CONISTON BRANCH.

The 1-40 p.m. Foxfield to Coniston will run 40 minutes later.

WINDERMERE BRANCH & LAKE.

The Steam Yachts and Branch Trains in connection, shown in the Time Tables to cease running after September 19th, will be discontinued after Aug. 31st.

The 9-10 a.m. Steamer Ambleside to Lake Side and the 10-25 a.m. Train Lake Side to Ulverston will also be discontinued.

ALFRED ASLETT,
Secretary & General Manager.

Barrow-in-Furness,
August 31st, 1914.

To be pasted on the Pocket Time Table issued for July, August and September.

An immediate consequence of the FR coming under Railway Executive Committee control were the amendments issued with the July-September 1914 timetables.

A group of FR officers and board members examine the work to strengthen the Kent viaduct in 1916. From left to right: W Burnyeat (director), F J Ramsden (director), D.L. Rutherford (FR engineer), Lord Muncaster (chairman), A. Aslett (general manager), F Palmer (consulting engineer), and W B Turner (director). (K. Norman collection: N161)

spread view that a war with Germany would be short lived and that victory would be won before Christmas, as a result of the combined might of the British, French and Russian forces. In these circumstances the requirement of the railways to carry naval and military traffic, personnel, armaments, stores and coal, without charge, would lead to a loss, it was therefore agreed that the Government would make up the losses to the level of profits earned in the first half of the year 1913 (or of 1914 if lower). To offset this, any profits made in excess of those agreed, would be pooled. Aslett reported to his Board, on 12th November 1914, that he had written to the Railway Executive Committee pointing out that the first half of 1914 had been a particularly bad result because of a falling off in the iron trade. The Railway Executive Committee was immune to 'special pleading' of this kind but, as it happened, many companies were to be similarly penalised and when they agreed, collectively, to contribute to the payment of increased wages to their staff under the 'War Bonus' arrangements, the '1914' criterion was dropped.

As matters turned out, the war was not 'over by Christmas' and the needs of the war effort increased, dramatically – the traffic arising from the various private contracting firms, in the case of the Furness Railway, the Vickers shipyard and the iron and steel works of Furness and West Cumberland. This effect was shown by the FR results for the first half of 1915, after which, the FR had to pay £36,428 'surplus profits' into the pool. This sum was equivalent to a dividend of 2.75%.

For the full year of 1915, the excess profits amounted to the equivalent of a dividend of 4%. Aslett pointed out this state of affairs to the Railway Executive Committee but Herbert Walker replied:

'If it is any consolation to you, the London & South Western Railway are paying considerably more under the present arrangements.'

The pattern of events continued, and on 3rd November 1916, Aslett wrote again to Herbert Walker stating that the excess profits of the Furness Railway for the months of July and August 1916 were equivalent to a dividend of 10% per annum. He said:

'Is it possible, please, for anything to be done to assist my Company with a view to their obtaining some proportion of this large surplus?'

Herbert Walker replied:

'You are free to write to the President of the Board of Trade but I do not think there is any possibility of any such claim being favourably considered by the Treasury, the members of the Railway Executive Committee are unanimous of the opinion that we must stick to our bargain even though some companies are harder hit than others.'

The Report of the FR Directors for the year 1916 was discussed at the Annual General Meeting held on 16th February 1917 at 14 Great George Street, Westminster. As a result of the illness of the Chairman, Lord Muncaster (who died aged 82 on 30th March 1917 after serving on the Board since 1889), the chair was taken by F.J. Ramsden.

Frederic Ramsden reported that W.B. Turner had died. Turner, who had been a Director since 1894 and who was a West Cumberland ironmaster, was replaced by G. Muir Ritchie, Chairman of the Millom & Askam Hematite Iron Company Ltd (which had just acquired the Ullcoats Mine south of Egremont).

Ramsden made it clear to the shareholders that the published accounts were, by order of the Railway Executive Committee, summaries of the receipts and expenditure, after deduction of the estimated amount of excess profit payable to the Government. What this, in fact, amounted to was a form of censorship; the accounts did not represent the true profit of the Company.

The motives for this deliberate concealment of the true financial position of the British railway companies are unclear; it may have been considered that it was not in the national interest to let the enemy know which lines of railway were of the greatest strategic use in the war effort.

However, one small, but very useful, concession was given to the companies; from 1915 the Government agreed to pay 4% interest on capital expenditure; this provided the FR with £2,991 in 1915. The FR had paid only a 1% dividend for 1914 but, even after the deduction of 'excess profits', 2% was paid for 1915 and 2.25% for 1916.

By the time of the next Annual Meeting, on 21st February 1918, F.J. Ramsden's chairmanship had been confirmed and Col. J.A. Jackson, a director of the Whitehaven Colliery Company, was appointed to the Board in place of the late Lord Muncaster. Ramsden reported that the goods and mineral traffic had been exceedingly heavy, amounting to 5,410,039 tons, the largest on record in the history of the Furness Railway. A dividend, after the deduction of 'excess profit', was agreed at 2¼% for 1917.

The final Furness Railway Shareholders' Meeting of the war period was held at the Furness Abbey Hotel on 21st February 1919 and considered the year 1918. The sense of relief at the cessation of hostilities was manifest. Ramsden paid tribute to the 510 (20%) members of staff who had joined the fighting forces, mentioning particularly the 46 killed or missing and the 67 wounded, to whose relatives he extended the Company's most sincere sympathy. Continuing in the same serious vein, he signalled what was to be the demise of the Furness Railway Company; he announced that Government Control would continue for a further two years.

On the subject of the year 1918, he noted that 6.25 million passengers had been carried, compared with 4.25 million in 1913, the increase being due to the large number of workmen travelling on the workmen's trains provided. The dividend was held at 2.25%. Finally the chairman referred to the retirement of Alfred Aslett from the post of Secretary & General Manager and asked the shareholders to join the directors in wishing him 'a long and happy period of rest'. The appointment of Lionel Speakman from the LNWR, as the new General Manager was noted. The retirement of W.F. Pettigrew from the post of Locomotive & Carriage & Wagon Superintendent had led the board to combine the duties of Engineer with those of Mr Pettigrew under the Engineer, David Rutherford, 'in the interests of the closest co-ordination and economy between two important Departments'.

Wartime operational problems

Many operational problems beset the Railway Executive Committee. While most of these were due to the length of the war, requiring far larger resources than had been planned for, some derived from decisions made at the beginning of hostilities. On coastal shipping services Pratt states:

'none were more remarkable and of more direct influence in disturbing the established order of things than those that effected a complete reversal in circumstances under which so active a competition had been carried out between the railways and the coastal shipping services since almost the advent of the railway era.' [5]

Coastal traffic was regularly landed at 874 places, added to which there were another 2,870 small places available for coastwise traffic to use.

In 1913 the 874 regular ports handled no less than 70 million tons. As has been noted, coastal shipping services frequently had the advantage over the Furness Railway (and many other lines) in terms of rates as the sea, while it presented hazards, was free of the infrastructure costs of the railway: tunnels, bridges and the extensive use of land for stations and yards. Pratt continues:

'With almost overwhelming suddenness a prolonged and varying series of developments led to changes which were revolutionary in their character. When ... coastal sea traffic had to be diverted to rail, the R.E.C. Subcommittee of Goods Managers could consider and approve emergency reduced rail rates; this arrangement came into force on the outbreak of war.' [6]

The causes of the crisis in coastal shipping were several. In the first case many coastal trade ships were requisitioned by the

During the 1914-18 War a butchery was operated at Barrow Central station by the Army Service Corps. It is recorded that the Furness Railway was paid £5 per week for the accommodation requisitioned for the purpose. Here the butchers are seen posing with the Stationmaster, Mr J Marsden. (K. Norman collection)

Admiralty for war purposes, a local example of this being the requisition, on 30th October 1914, of the Midland Railway's Barrow Route boats. This requisition process continued throughout the war, and the FR suffered a final insult in this context with, in 1917, the loss to the Admiralty of the Barrow Docks tugs *Furness* and *Cartmel;* vessels which were an essential part of the Barrow Docks contribution to the war effort. Commander Bissett, the Barrow Harbour Master, commented that the Admiralty proposed replacements; were *'absolutely useless'.*[7]

A second reason for the crisis in coastal shipping was the German submarine fleet. While the German capital ships were largely contained in the Baltic Sea, the U-boats wreaked havoc with Allied shipping, making the coastal trade so hazardous as to become ineffective. A final factor was the diversion of merchant seamen to crucially important international shipping traffic, the success of which, after Lloyd George personally took over the Admiralty, on 30 April 1917, and enforced the 'convoy' system, won the war for the Allies[8]. The coastal shipping crisis placed a massive additional load on the railway system, a load which was a major contribution to an intractable wartime problem, the shortage of wagons. The pre-war railway plans had concentrated on the demands of mobilisation for a short war, and the 'war of attrition' which developed and which led to a massive increase in manufacturing facilities, overwhelmed the wagon supply. As early as February 1915 the Furness Railway, in common with many other railways, was suffering from the hold up of wagons awaiting discharge at Government establishments, the managers of which seemed blind to the transport problems. At this time no less than 10,000 wagons were reported to be so delayed nationally. The Railway Executive Committee, once the problem had been recognised, acted vigorously, and a subcommittee of nine railway superintendents was formed to monitor the wagon position daily. A team of Railway Clearing House inspectors was formed and sent out to report on the position on the ground.

By the middle of 1915 it was accepted that the war was going badly for the Allies. After ill-judged advances by both sides, to Mons, in Belgium, by the British Expeditionary Force, delivered to France with superlative skill, in 1914, by the Railway Executive Committee plan, and by the Germans to within sight of Paris, both armies entrenched on a line from Switzerland to the Belgian coast. On 26th May 1915, Prime Minister Asquith announced the formation of a coalition Government for the more efficient conduct of the war. Lloyd George had already been appointed Minister of Munitions, the first such ministerial designation in British history. In October 1915, a Joint Standing Committee of the Ministry of Munitions, the War Office and the Admiralty was formed, one of whose functions was the introduction of wagon detention statistics.

A 'Traffic Regulation System' was instituted to prevent the despatch of traffic until its acceptance and turnover of wagons was ensured. The statistics for the week ending 6th January 1916 showed the FR in a favourable light with only three wagons detained over 12 days, while by comparison, the Glasgow & South Western had 230 wagons delayed for 2,203 wagon days, but, in spite of its favourable position in the 'league table', the FR was having serious problems with wagon supply. On 15th October 1915 the FR Board received complaints of wagon shortage from the Barrow Hematite Steel Company and the North Lonsdale Iron & Steel Company. At its meeting on 17th December 1915 the FR Board noted a letter from the Barrow Hematite Steel Company:

'The position in regard to wagon supply to these works is

little short of a public scandal as we do not seem to be able to obtain much redress either from you or the Ministry of Munitions.'

As a result of this complaint from their principal customer, Thomas Jackson, the FR Goods Manager, circularised all the railway companies handling FR traffic. The Great Central Railway's reply was typical of the national position:

'You are not alone with regard to the present deplorable position ... We will do the best we can for you.'

A.A. Haynes, reported to the FR Board, at the same meeting:

'Due to the excessive number of wagons we are now receiving, trains are standing on the main line for hours, I suggest two long sidings be provided between Loco. and Salthouse Junctions.'

The Board approved these sidings.

This chronic shortage of wagons impeded the importation of raw materials vital to the war effort, but wagon supply was not the only problem, as illustrated by the FR's difficulties with the Ministry of Munitions, over the importation of iron ore through Barrow Docks. Thomas Jackson, the Goods Manager explained the circumstances in his report of 20th April 1917 to Aslett:

'Mr. J.W. Spiller of the Ministry of Munitions Overseas Transport Department who was here today informed me that he had been going round the various ports in the United Kingdom with a view to hastening the discharge of vessels bringing in foreign iron ore. During our conversation he somewhat surprised me by stating that for the month of March out of 10 principal ports Barrow stood next to the lowest as regards the tonnage discharged per ship per day, but when I got to questioning him I found that no account had been taken of the number of ships which had been dealt with at one time and I told Mr Spiller that no port could be expected to turn out the same tonnage per ship per day from 5 or 6 boats as say from 2 or 3. At the beginning of March we had no fewer of seven cargoes in the docks ... for which of course we had to find wagons and men. Part of one cargo was for Workington and the wagons engaged in that traffic took up a long time in consequence of the longer haulage.'

Jackson went on to explain the use of Barrow Docks, for West Cumberland iron ore traffic, as being the result of the limitations of the harbour at Maryport, in dealing with the larger vessels now engaged on the trade. Suggestions were made respecting the improvement of cranage and of ore storage at Barrow.

The West Cumberland iron ore traffic at Barrow continued to be a problem. The Traffic & Works Committee learned, on 30th May 1917, that there were four ships in the Docks with ore for Workington. It was noted:

'If these were worked day and night as proposed in London, this would require 600 wagons to carry 6,000 tons per day namely 20 trains a day to Workington.'

199,008 tons of iron ore passed through Barrow Docks in the first five months of 1917, of which 46,706 tons was for Workington.

During the 1914-18 War hundreds of additional freight trains were operated to carry fuel and other supplies to Royal Navy vessels based in Scotland. Locomotives and rolling stock had to be pooled among the previously separate railway companies. This Sankey photograph of an LNWR 'DX' class 0-6-0 on a down freight at Seascale may well be one of the so-called Jellico Specials using the Furness route to relieve pressure on the main line over Shap. (Sankey print: 5981)

The coal transport reorganisation scheme

It was typical of the First World War that specific problems were addressed and 'solutions' agreed, by individual government departments, which were counterproductive. Such was the case with coal. In the early months of the war some 250,000 coal miners had enlisted in the armed forces. As a result, coal production in the first 12 months of the war fell by 30,000,000 tons. The Liberal Government continued its traditional 'laissez faire' policy[9]; the price of coal escalated.

In addition, labour troubles, in South Wales, in November 1916 threatened the supply of steam coal to the Grand Fleet, now settled at Scapa Flow, after the inconclusive Battle of Jutland on 31st May 1916. The Government's response was to take over the South Wales mines on 1st December 1916; the rest of the coal industry was 'nationalised' on 1st February 1917[10]. The War Cabinet Report for 1917 noted:

'To find a solution to the problem of providing coal for domestic purposes ... an enquiry was instituted into the whole question of the conveyance of coal, the coalfields from which each market was supplied and the distances over which coal was carried.'

It was found that, in innumerable instances, coal was delivered from distant coalfields to districts which could be equally well be supplied by nearer pits, which would require a shorter railway journey[11].

The 'remedy' was the Coal Transportation Order of 4th July 1917, which divided the United Kingdom into 20 areas. The Barrow district had traditionally obtained its coal from the high quality outputs of pits in the Wigan and Barnsley areas, now they were placed in the West Cumberland coalfield area. This resulted in 6 to 10 special trains each day to and from Whitehaven which put a great strain on the line between Whitehaven and Barrow[12].

The coal traffic was due to a War Office decision, but the imported iron ore traffic at Barrow Docks, destined for Workington, because of pressure from the Ministry of Munitions, was now competing with coal for train pathways. As early as June 1917 Aslett was saying, in a letter to the Director General of Transport:

'...no railway company in the country, as you are aware, is passing through as great an ordeal as the Furness Railway ... we hardly know from day to day how we are going to work the traffic.'

The FR solution for dealing with this increased in traffic was the introduction of a third signalbox at Whitehaven, south of Mirehouse Junction (Corkickle No. 1), thus shortening the single line section to St Bees, together with a block post at Stangrah, to reduce the 5½-mile section between Silecroft and Bootle. The War Office Director of Movements authorised this work and the cost in a letter of 5th September 1918[13]. Stangrah Box was opened on 22nd July 1918 but Corkickle No. 1 was not operational until 9th March 1919[14]

One further improvement in the operation of freight traffic, which should be noted, is that from 4th September 1916, the Durham coke traffic, which hitherto ran via Tebay and Carnforth, was diverted onto the direct Hincaster – Arnside line, with Furness engines working to Tebay and LNWR engines to Lindal and Millom[15].

The introduction, on 1st February 1918, of the FR Control System, operating from a Control Office in St George's Square,

Monk Moors was a halt provided between Bootle and Eskmeals stations for the benefit of workers at the gun testing range. (CRA Kerr collection)

opposite to the General Offices, can only have been beneficial to the utilisation of locomotives and rolling stock.

Passenger services during the First World War

The mobilisation of the armed services and the transportation of the British Expeditionary Force to France by train and boat was carried out to the plan laid down by the Railway Executive Committee (REC) in the months leading up to the outbreak of war. The plan operated with a high level of efficiency. There was, however, a temporary disruption of normal services, but by the middle of September 1914 things were back to normal. In its Instruction No. 71 the REC required that Summer Excursion arrangements be extended to 30th November 1914 excepting destinations in Scotland, including Carlisle and Berwick and Ireland[16]. The Summer Season in 1914 had been a disappointing one for the FR.

Number of Passengers	1913	1914
Windermere Steamers	252,168	190,215
Coniston Water Steamers	308,155	20,157
Fleetwood Steamers	178,831	119,049
Circular Tours	29,982	16,331

The reason for these poor results was not given at the Annual General Meeting for 1914 and it must be speculated that they were due a combination a factors such as the weather, the trade recession and a preoccupation with the political crisis.

Vickers gun range signalbox at Monk Moors. (J Wilkinson)

The Fleetwood steamer service was discontinued from 30th September 1914, the *Lady Moyra* and *Lady Evelyn* being laid up in 1915, due to lack of crew, until they were requisitioned by the Admiralty[17]. The first Admiralty requisitions were of the *City of Belfast* and *Duchess of Devonshire*, the Midland Railway's Barrow – Belfast boats; they were taken on 30th October 1914 for the purpose of transporting refugees and German prisoners to the Isle of Man!

In the Spring of 1915, the 'Business as Usual' frame of mind continued in the civilian population. Plans had to be made by the railway companies for their 1915 Summer Season, but the Furness Railway, with its poor results in 1914, together with the increasing number of workmen's trains, was cautious.

By 1914 the Furness Railway was carrying an increasing and largely unremunerative burden of workmen's trains.

On 5th October 1914, just after the outbreak of war, the Superintendent of the Line, A.A. Haynes, submitted a comprehensive Report on the workmen's trains to the Traffic & Works Committee. Eleven trains were run per day, which utilised three train sets totalling 32 vehicles. These trains ran from Ulverston, Millom and Dalton, to Shipyard Station; in addition one train called at Monk Moors Halt, near Bootle, serving the Vickers Gun Range. Late in 1914 these trains carried 2,000 workmen per day. On top of these dedicated services workmen's coaches were attached to ordinary trains but, as Haynes pointed out:

'We have great difficulty in making workmen confine themselves to these coaches and the Company's workmen are the worst offenders.' [18]

By mid-1915 the workmen's trains had been extended to Grange and, on 23rd July 1915, the Board noted that the Grange service had lost £512, but that Vickers would only pay £250 in compensation.

The onset of winter led, in 1914, to demands for heating in the workmen's carriages and eleven were fitted with heat in December 1914. In turn this created a shortage of locomotives fitted with steam heating apparatus and another eight were so fitted, including three of the 2-4-2T class and three of the Sharp Stewart 0-6-0s. This process of adding heaters to both carriages and locomotives continued throughout the war.

Some idea of the size of the workmen's traffic is given by the figures for the first 12 weeks of 1916 and 1917:

1916	Ordinary passengers 558,385	Workmen 769,735
1917	Ordinary passengers 379,378	Workmen 771,552

It is not a surprise therefore that the 1899-built single platform at Shipyard Station soon became inadequate and a second

On 7th July 1954 the two return Barrow Shipyard workmen's trains await their passengers at the station in Island Road. On the left 4F 44368 heads the train to Grange while on the right one of Barrow's Ivatt 2MT tank locos takes the train to Silecroft. The right-hand platform is the one added in October 1915. (Author: MAC55)

platform with an improved track layout came into use on 18th October 1915[19].

There would be no Sunday steamer service on Windermere, the *Gondola* would not be put into service on Coniston, and only the Middle Circular Tour (No.4) would operate[20].

The first half year results supported the cautious approach. The Lake steamers lost £1,433, the Furness Abbey Hotel £203 and the Refreshment Rooms £142[21]. In the 1916 season the remaining Coniston steamer was suspended.

The 1916 Summer Season was in general very busy. Pratt states:

'Notwithstanding the reduction in train services, the with-drawal of excursion bookings and the almost complete suspension of cheap travel facilities in general, the holiday traffic remained at a high level throughout 1916.' [22]

From Blackpool, it was reported, that in the second week of August 1916:

'all available sleeping accommodation was occupied and that the holiday prospects were surprising, incredible and amazing.' [23]

The year 1916 saw the first closure of a FR branch passenger service. The Conishead Priory branch from Ulverston to Priory, with reversal at Plumpton Junction, had, for many years seen only one mixed (passenger & goods) train each way per day. This was the result of the development of the Conishead Estate, into a major suburb of Ulverston, not having taken place, due to the depression in house building in Furness following the slump of the late 1870s. In 18 weeks only 26 passengers had been booked. The passenger service was closed, on and from 6th March 1916, with the line from North Lonsdale to Priory singled, the lifted

track being used for new sidings, required by the war effort[24]. In later years the line south of North Lonsdale crossing was only used for wagon storage before final abandonment during 1952. The remaining part of the Priory branch, between Plumpton Junction and the Glaxo Works, was formally closed along with the Plumpton Junction signal box where it joined the main line, on 19th March 2000, the last freight train having left the Glaxo works siding on 27th April 1994[25].

On 11th December 1916 the Railway Executive Committee suspended the carriage of passenger luggage and gave notice that:

'Owing to the depleted staff the passenger train services during the Christmas holidays will be greatly reduced ... It is therefore necessary that the public should . ... refrain from travelling except for business purposes between 20.12.1916 and 3.1.1917.'

To curtail non-military railway passenger traffic the Board of Trade ruled that, from 1st January 1917, fares would be increased by 50% and passenger luggage limited to 100 lb per passenger. Railway tickets continued to show the old fare until after the war, when the new fares were printed as 'Actual fare'[26]. The Railway Executive Committee explained their policy in a Circular dated 21st December 1916:

'The increase in fares is not intended as a means of increas-ing the revenue of railways but is put into force solely with the object of curtailing passenger traffic in order to enable the railway companies to comply with urgent demands that have been made upon them by the conveyance of troops, munitions and supplies both in Great Britain and France.' [27]

The Committee also advised the railway companies that, from 1st January 1917, there would be a major curtailment of passenger services. These would include the reduction of branch line services and the deceleration of main line trains.

This resulted in a major review of the Furness Railway passenger timetable, operative from 1st January 1917. For example, as a result of the later running of the 11.45pm train from Euston, the 7.00am train from Carnforth to Whitehaven was cancelled and the 8.15am Carnforth to Barrow was extended to Whitehaven. Details of the changes were contained in the Minutes of the Traffic & Works Committee dated 19th December 1916. After careful consideration the FR decided to withdraw the Windermere steamer service, from 1st January 1917, but it was reinstated, on 2nd April 1917 for the summer season of 1917[28].

Wartime staff shortage

A further problem, facing the railway companies during the First World War, was the enlistment of railway staff in the armed forces. The delusion that the war would be short allowed this process to take place without any restriction, but with the benefit of hindsight it becomes clear that such enlistment of skilled railway employees was totally contrary to the war effort. To offset this drain of essential personnel the Railway Executive Committee encouraged the employment of women. In this context the FR Board commented:

'It would not be suitable to employ women at Barrow as ticket collectors when the collectors frequently have a very rough sort of people to deal with.' [29]

The FR could, however, boast that it employed two ladies as upholsterers in the carriage department! As noted, no less than 20% of the FR staff enlisted during the course of the war, 510 in number. Of these 46 were killed or missing, 67 wounded and six taken prisoner[30].

The chairman, Frederic Ramsden, told the shareholders:

'We look forward to welcoming back in the near future those members of our staff who have … come through their service unscathed.'

Furness Railway locomotives in the First World War

While it is not within the province of this book to deal with the history of the FR locomotives, they did play a vital role and the replacement of locomotives became increasingly difficult as the war dragged on.

The FR were fortunate in this respect as, in 1913, they had taken delivery of the four 4-4-0 passenger engines to Pettigrew's latest – and as turned out last – design (Nos.130-133) also two of his latest mixed traffic 0-6-0s (Nos. 1 & 2).

Before the outbreak of war they had ordered two of his newly designed 4-4-2 tank engines (Nos. 38 & 39) and two standard 0-6-0 tanks (Nos. 51 & 52). These four engines were delivered in March 1915. Before the acute shortage of locomotives, for both the 'home front' and the 'western front' became apparent, the builders were overwhelmed with orders and the Ministry of Munitions took over the control of locomotive building priorities. The FR had managed to order four more 4-4-2 tanks (Nos. 40-43) and two more 0-6-0 tanks (Nos. 53 & 54) which were delivered in 1916.

In 1916 the FR invited tenders for eight more mixed traffic

0-6-0s but were now subject to Ministry of Munitions control; the FR sought to have the Government pay for these engines but this was firmly declined[31]. A joint meeting was held between the FR, the MR and the LNWR at Euston on 11th September 1916. It emerged that the FR still had the policy of allocating one crew to each engine although, in a few instances, 'double manning' had been found necessary. The outcome of this meeting was that the FR agreed to extend 'double manning' and both the MR and the LNWR undertook to work trains over the Furness system with their own locomotives. While there is no record of Midland workings, the LNWR was working coke trains from Tebay to both Lindal and Millom and back, totalling five round trips per day[32]. In addition some of the special coal trains from South Wales to Grangemouth, to serve the fleet at Scapa Flow, ran over the Furness line with LNWR motive power[33].

Early in 1917 the FR managed to get an order accepted by Kitson's for four new mixed traffic 0-6-0s but:

'not on a top priority basis as Kitson's have an order for 12 locomotives for France.' [34]

In December the North British Locomotive Co. accepted an order for a further four of this class, at a cost of £6,450 – the pre-war price for this class of engine had been £3,500[35].

These eight 0-6-0s were delivered in mid-1918, almost too late to be of much help in the war effort, nevertheless, they were a useful addition to the FR locomotive fleet and compensated for thirteen old Sharp Stewart 18 inch 0-6-0s that had failed and were scrapped during the course of the war, repairs not being justified in view of the high cost and shortage of materials[36].

CHAPTER 25 REFERENCES

1   Hamilton J.A.B, 1967. *British Railways in World War I* Ch.1.
2   Pratt E., 1921 *British Railways and the Great War* p.31.
3   Harris N. *Op. cit.* Works list.
4   Hamilton J.A.B. *Op. cit.* pp.23-6.
5   Pratt E. *Op. cit.* p.261.
6   FRDM, 14th June 1917.
7   Taylor A.J.P, 1965. *English History 1914-1945* p.84.
8   Ibid. p.34.
9   Pratt E. *Op. cit.* p.727.
10   Ibid. p. 728.
11   FRDM, 12th Oct. 1917.
12   FRDM, 11th Oct. 1918.
13   FR Signal Notices.
14   *CRA Journal*, Vol.3 p.218.
15   FRCM, 23rd Sep. 1914.
16   FRDM, 27th Dec. 1915 & 11th Aug. 1916.
17   FRCM, 28th Oct. 1914.
18   FR Signal Notice.
19   FRDM, 10th June 1915.
20   FRDM, 11th Aug. 1915.
21   Pratt E. *Op. cit.* p.134.
22   Ibid. p.136.
23   FRDM, 10th Mar. 1916.
24   *CRA Journal*, Vol.6 No.16.
25   *Journal of the Transport Ticket Society*, 1994 p.382.
26   Pratt E. *Op. cit.* p.142.
27   FRDM, 9th Mar. 1917.
28   FRDM, 10th Sep. 1915.
29   FR Annual Report, 21st Feb. 1919.
30   FRDM, 14th July 1916.
31   FRDM, 9th Nov. 1917.
32   Sankey photograph 5981.
33   FRDM, 16th Feb. 1917.
34   FRDM, 6th & 25th June 1912.
35   Ibid.
36   FR loco list.

CHAPTER TWENTY-SIX

THE POST-WAR YEARS 1919-1922

No sooner has the Great War ended than the Army was engaged in guarding strategic parts of the national railway system. Here a detachment of soldiers is standing with bayonets fixed at the entrance to the FR General Offices at St George's Square. Behind them is the canopy with FR cast into the brackets supporting the roof girder of the building on the site of the 1846 Barrow passenger platform. (Sankey print: 7509)

In his address to the Shareholders' Meeting of the Furness Railway, held at the Furness Abbey Hotel on 21st February 1919, Chairman Frederic Ramsden commented:

'Of the future, unfortunately, it is at present difficult to speak. Four years of war have thrown the whole world into the melting pot – socially, commercially and financially – and for the moment it is impossible to say what the ultimate end will be. Personally I am not despondent, for I have the greatest possible faith in the sound common sense of the British nation, which sooner or later must see us through the crisis through which we are now passing. Meanwhile for those who are interested in, and for those who have to operate, the railways of the country, the situation today is not an easy one. We are not absolute masters in our own house. We are controlled by the State and, as I have said, will be so controlled for another two years or possibly more. We have to use every care to see that the interests of our shareholders are properly safeguarded and do not suffer. We have to consider the reasonable claims of the trader and the public; and, lastly and not

least in these days of labour difficulties, we have to try and live in harmony with our staff so that they may give us in the future the same loyal service which I am thankful to say they have done in the past.'

A year later, Ramsden had to tell the shareholders:

'I regret that I am not in a position to make any definite pronouncement with regard to the future of railways.'

He noted the Ministry of Transport Act of 1919 – this transferred the railway responsibilities of the Board of Trade to the new Ministry – and went on:

'...an increase in rates has come into operation on 15th January 1920. It is hoped that the final effect will be to place the railways on a sound financial footing again, but of course during the control period the individual railways as regards their dividend earning powers will obtain no benefit as the increased revenue will in the first place go to the State for purposes of liquidating the present financial loss.'

During the 1919 General Strike volunteers tendered their services to help keep the railways running. Here an assorted group of workers have been applying some elbow grease to FR goods engines Nos 21 and 24 at Barrow shed. (Sankey print: 7513)

For the year 1919 there had been a decrease in receipts of £9,187, but Ramsden pointed out that this figure had been subject to fluctuations in the estimated settlements with the Government. In other words, the Furness Railway continued to be penalised for its success. He stressed that the continuing shortage of wagons made it necessary to divert revenue to 'bring our stock up to a really efficient level.'

Ramsden then turned to the matter of the Capital Account. This was in credit to the tune of £39,000. He attributed this to the sale of surplus land but went on:

'(regarding) the sale of the two steamers 'Lady Moyra' and 'Lady Evelyn', it was with regret that the Board parted with these two boats and deprived Barrow and district of a facility which was, no doubt, appreciated but a short season business of this description is always spec-ulative and the increased charges necessary as regards steamer passage added to the ordinary fares and 50% for rail trips in connection with the steamers would have placed the combined fares at a figure which would have been too high to appeal to holiday makers in great number.'

He noted that, owing to the shortage of ships, the sale was exceptionally favourable, resulting in a credit to the Capital Account. He had to report a decrease in the goods tonnage of 800,000 tons and of passengers of 700,000; these reductions were due to the termination of the war effort. Finally Ramsden referred to the:

'Extensive and complicated negotiations carried on between the Government and the Trade Unions which will entail serious additions to our working expenses.'

He noted:

'The directors deplored the general railway strike which took place early last autumn although they were glad to observe that in regard this company it was carried through without any display of ill feeling and neither do they think that it has left any bitterness behind it.'

The Shareholders' Meeting, held on 25th February 1921, was a gloomy occasion. Frederic Ramsden referred to the coal strike in October 1920. Up to that, point the traffic had been very good; the final results showed an increase of 2.24% in passenger numbers and 9.61% in goods and mineral traffic tonnage. However, he had to say that the trade of the district was bad. In addition they had to contend with high levels of wages and the cost of materials due to the war.

Ramsden went on to say:

'The Government have evidently made up their minds to enforce by legislation some form of grouping and the railway companies themselves recognise that such a step is not inconsistent with the tendency on the part of the different companies to come together which manifested itself before the war. Although, therefore, the Furness Company and others in West Cumberland will be included *in one of the large new groups, the directors feel that a very strong case can be made out for retaining some form of local autonomy ... the West Cumberland and Furness District is somewhat isolated and is to a considerable extent self-contained and we feel very strongly that the local management of railway interests within it should be left to people who thoroughly understand its requirements and are closely connected with the life and trade of the district.'*

Grouping

By the 24th February 1922, on which date the Furness Railway Company held its Annual General Meeting at the Furness Abbey Hotel, chairman Frederic Ramsden was able to confirm that Government Control had ended, as predicted, on 15th August 1921. This made the accounts for 1921 difficult to interpret as the change was mid-year. However, due to the depressed state of trade, there had been a drop in receipts of £82,000, this allowed a dividend of only 1%.

He illustrated the circumstances of this drop by the figures for the production of pig iron. In 1920 this was 8 million tons but in 1921 it was only 2.5 million. In consequence the goods and mineral traffic had decreased by 50%.

The first of two instalments of 'Compensation to Controlled Railways' had been received and amounted to £137,210, but this would be used to offset the deficit.

Passenger traffic had also fallen seriously, due not only to the coal strike, but also to increasing competition from road services. The Board proposed to do everything possible to make good this loss. Fares on the Lake Steamers would be cut, a tourist office in Morecambe re-opened and the line between Leven and Greenodd Junctions, removed during the war, would be reinstated, to allow direct running of trains between Carnforth and Lakeside. Special cheap fares had already been introduced between Barrow, Dalton and Ulverston and much traffic had been regained. Ramsden then referred to the great increase in wages compared with 1913 and that there had been similar increase in Municipal Rates paid; in Barrow this amounted to 136%. These were the factors, he said, which were responsible for the high railway rates on which the present stagnation of trade was blamed. Working expenses had been greatly reduced and that had, unfortunately, led to a very large number of men being dispensed with.

The Chairmen then turned to the matter of the future of the railways. In August 1921 an Act was passed whereby all the railways of Great Britain would, on 1st January 1923, be amalgamated into four groups.

During the years 1920, 1921 and 1922 the FR Board met regularly, but the matters dealt with were largely parochial. For example, on 10th December 1920, it was agreed that the old turntable at Plumpton Junction should be replaced by a triangle for turning engines; in December 1921 the plan to re-locate Moor Row Shed to Corkickle was abandoned and the turntable destined for Corkickle was installed at Millom. The motor bus service, introduced by the FR, between Lakeside and Ambleside, on 1st November 1920 to replace the winter steamer service, halved the losses. After 1921-22, the winter service would be operated by the Lake District Road Traffic Company[1].

The statutory Special General Meeting of the Furness Railway Company was held at the Furness Abbey Hotel on 24th November 1922:

'to consider a scheme for the amalgamation of the London

& North Western Railway, the Midland Railway, the Furness Railway, the Glasgow & South Western Railway and the Highland Railway being constituent Companies in the North Western, Midland and West Scottish Group.'

Frederic Ramsden took the chair and stated that the Railways Act 1921 required the constituent companies to submit schemes of amalgamation before the end of the present year, failing which, compulsory measures would be taken by the end of June 1923. The proposed scheme was made available to the meeting; the new Company will be incorporated under the title of the London, Midland & Scottish Railway Company.

Ramsden pointed out that as all the debentures, guaranteed and preference stock holders in the Furness Railway, would be issued with equivalent paying stock in the new Company, the matter at issue was the Ordinary Stock of the Company. Unfortunately, the dividends on this Stock averaged at only 1.75% for the last 15 years, whereas, for the last three years, the LNWR paid 7.5%. Consequently, the proposal being put to the Meeting was that each £100 of FR Stock be replaced by £30 of the new Stock. On the LNWR record this would give an equivalent dividend of 2.25%.

'In view of these comparisons I think we may congratulate ourselves on the prospect of such an improved income with every reason to believe that it will be maintained, and which we certainly could not have expected to obtain regularly if we had to carry on as a separate undertaking. The negotiators on the other side have, naturally enough, drawn attention to two factors which cannot be ignored. The first is that the earning power of the Furness Company is and has been for many years very variable owing to its dependence upon the prosperity of the iron, steel and shipbuilding trades which, as we all know, are subject to periods of acute depression. Secondly, that the Company has never been prosperous enough to put aside strong reserves to meet heavy renewals or to help the dividend in bad years, ... Your Directors are satisfied that the arrangement proposed is advantageous to the proprietors and we have no hesitation in recommending that you accept it.'

The response of the shareholders at the Meeting was largely sentimental. Col. G.H. Huthwaite said:

'I also testify to the abilities of our general managers Mr A. Aslett and his successor Mr L. Speakman who had always been courteous and ready to assist them where possible. The same applied to the secretaries and to the managers of departments and also to all the employees of the Furness Railway ... no one would be more sorry to say goodbye to the old traditions of the Furness Railway. They could congratulate themselves on the fact that never in the history of the line had there been loss of life through collision or otherwise.'

[This statement needs qualification. A number of staff were killed in movement accidents and several passengers killed at stations but it was true that no passenger was killed in a train accident.]

Another shareholder, M.W. Settle, of Ulverston, pointed out that he had been connected with the FR for almost 60 years; at the beginning of that time the FR shares were worth up to £160 and 10% dividend had been paid. Now they had to accept £30.

This is to Certify that

Mr H. E. Tonge

acted as *Volunteer Engine Cleaner, Patrol & Plate-layer* on the Furness Railway

During the Great Railway Strike of 1919.

He carried out his duties most efficiently.

David J. Rutherford

Engineer and Loco. Superintendent.

A very rare survival is this certificate issued to a Barrovian who volunteered for service on the FR during the 1919 Great Railway Strike. (Private collection)

The auditor, R.F. Miller, said that he had been called into the negotiations, by the Directors. He went on:

> '...it is probably an open secret, that in the first instance, the terms suggested were not nearly as good as those ultimately arranged.'

The vote resulted in 40 shareholders being in favour of the amalgamation terms and only two against.

The London, Midland & Scottish Railway took over the Furness Railway and its two joint lines from 1st January 1923. All that remained was the formality of the last Annual General Meeting. This was held at the Furness Abbey Hotel on 20th February 1923. Frederic Ramsden, the chairman, was now a director of the LMSR.

A final dividend of 2% was approved, for 1922, on the £2,642,000 Ordinary Stock of the Company. The final Capital Account stood at £8,068,034.

The LMSR Report & Accounts for 1935 and 1937[2] give a good idea of how the dividend projections, made in 1922, failed to be met:

Ordinary Stock Dividends:		
	1929	4.5%
	1930	2%
	1931	0.25%
	1932	nil
	1933	nil
	1934	nil
	1935	nil
	1936	1.25%
	1937	1.5%

CHAPTER 26 REFERENCES

1   FRDM, 13th Oct. 1922.
2   BTHR: AC 150 &160.

EPILOGUE

On the 1st January 1923, under the terms of the Railways Act 1921, the London, Midland & Scottish Railway came into being. The largest constituent was the London & North Western, expanded by its absorption, in January 1922, of the Lancashire & Yorkshire Railway. This amalgamation led to organisational problems and, in 1923, the L&Y was operated as a separate LNWR Division. O.S. Nock in his *"A History of the LMS"* states that, at first it was proposed that the Furness and the Maryport & Carlisle companies should become part of the L&Y division, but common sense prevailed and the *FR Magazine* of May 1923 was able to announce that a 'Furness & West Cumberland Section' would be part of the Western Division of the LMS – the old LNWR lines. In the August edition, of what was now the *Furness & West Cumberland Magazine*, was a descriptive article on the F&WC section by the newly appointed Section Superintendent, Arthur Haynes, the former FR Superintendent of the Line. The Section (later called 'District') consisted of the FR lines, the LNWR West Cumberland lines, the Maryport & Carlisle, the Cleator & Workington Junction and a portion of the NBR (now LNER) between Brayton Junction and Abbey Junction on the Silloth branch.

Life at the offices in St George's Square, Barrow went on much as before but, in June 1923, District Engineer, D.L. Rutherford resigned to take up consultancy practice and was replaced by the ex LNWR District Engineer, Birmingham, E.H. Townsend. Also, Edward Sharples, Assistant Locomotive Superintendent at Barrow Works under Rutherford, was promoted to Assistant Mechanical Engineer, Horwich Works (the former L&Y main works) He was to return to Barrow Works, in January 1929, as Mechanical Engineer, Barrow. As the LMS had inherited a number of workshops from the constituent companies, it was inevitable that many of these would have to be closed, in the interests of efficiency. Barrow was one of these, and Sharples had the unhappy task of winding down and closing the Barrow Locomotive and Carriage and Wagon Works of which he had been manager from 1918 to 1923. The LMS Board agreed the closure on 26th February 1931. Ex-LNWR locomotives were to be dealt with at Crewe and the FR engines and others at Horwich. Carriage & Wagon work was to be carried out at Newton Heath, Manchester[1].

A major problem, in the early years of the LMS, resulted from the centralisation of commercial management. By November 1925 the Barrow and Lancaster District Goods departments had been merged. This was symptomatic of what O.S. Nock describes as *'a huge centralised bureaucracy'*. Commercial control came under divisions based on Derby, Manchester and Glasgow. Nock comments:

'Local men who had built up cordial relations and good business with local traders now had to refer to remote centres for authority to arrange deals. There was inevitably delay in getting answers, often hedged around with irrelevant questions and conditions and it was not surprising that the local people began to seek other means of transport when they began to realise that under the new organisation their problems were being handled by far-away people who had no knowledge of local conditions. I became particularly aware of what was happening in the Furness district from which everything had to be referred to Manchester.'

Transport historian, the late Alan Pearsall, used to relate that, at this time, the LMS was known as *'the 'ell of a mess'* !

The organisational difficulties, augmented by significant differences between the Midland and LNWR cultures, not least over locomotive design and practice, led the LMS chairman, Sir Guy Granet (former Midland Railway general manager) to plan a reorganisation of the top management. From 1st January 1926 the general manager organisational was replaced by an 'executive', led by 'President' Sir Josiah Stamp, a leading economist of the day, supported, from 1st January 1927, by four 'Vice Presidents', two of these responsible for operating and commercial policy.

While these organisation convulsions were taking place, a new enemy of the railways had appeared in the form of the motorbus. A good example of what was happening can be found at the north end of the Furness & West Cumberland District. The Cumberland Motor Services had commenced operations, in a small way, in Workington in 1921 with six buses. By 1926 the company had sixty and on 19th March 1926 opened the United Kingdom's first 'Omnibus Station' at Workington. Throughout the UK the versatile bus was making serious inroads into the railway local passenger traffic. During January a deputation from the railway companies visited the Prime Minister, Stanley Baldwin, and highlighted the seriousness of the railways' problem. The ultimate outcome was legislation to allow the four major railway companies to hold shares in bus companies. By 1929, the LMS owned 45% of the Ribble Motor Services and 50% of Cumberland Motor Services[2]. This put the LMS in a strong position regarding the closure of unremunerative passenger lines. A Traffic Committee minute of 30th April 1930 states, regarding the proposed closure of the Glasson Dock branch:

'It was recommended, with the approval of the Executive Committee, that passenger trains be withdrawn from 2nd June next, leaving the passenger transport requirements of the district to be catered for by our associated omnibus undertaking, Ribble Motor Services Ltd.'

A Traffic Committee minute of 25th February 1931 states:

'By reason of the development of competitive road services ... it is recommended that the passenger services between Moor Row and Marron Junction (Joint Line) and between Moor Row and Siddick Junction (C&WJR line) be closed as from 13th April 1931. The area is wholly within the territory of Cumberland Motor Services in which the LMS Company is financially interested.'

The former Joint Line, between Moor Row and Sellafield, continued until 7th January 1935 when it too was closed to passengers. A similar fate befell the Barrow – Piel branch, which was closed to all traffic from 6th July 1936. On 6th May 1946, the LMS restored the Whitehaven – Moor Row – Sellafield service

Barrow experienced air raids in May 1941 and Central Station was badly damaged requiring the removal of the roof over platforms 1 and 2 and of the glass case near the station entrance which held 'Coppernob'. (K. Norman collection)

but it was closed again, due to lack of patronage, from 16th June 1947. This line was, however, used by unadvertised passenger trains. As early as March 1940 a workmen's train was put on between Winder and Drigg; in more recent times it ran between Moor Row and Sellafield for the nuclear plant workers. It was taken off from 6th September 1965. In September 1964 a school train was put on, between Seascale and Egremont and return, in connection with a newly opened Wyndham comprehensive school at Egremont. This service was withdrawn from 10th December 1969[3]. The LNW & Furness Joint Line and the Cleator & Workington Junction line continued to be used for freight, largely mineral, traffic.

A summary of freight closures is made in the following table:

Buckhill Colliery – Linefoot Junction	22nd August 1921
Mowbray branch	21st July 1923
Ullock Junction – Distington Junction	14th February 1929
Distington Junction – No. 4 Pit Siding, Lowca	ditto
Cloffocks Junction – Workington Bridge	26th March 1930
Gillfoot branch	11th February 1931
Dock Junction – Workington Dock	27th July 1936
Distington, Rowrah Branch Junction – Rowrah	8th August 1938
Bigrigg branch	10th September 1951
Rowrah – Marron Junction	6th November 1960
Cleator Moor – Distington Junction	1st July 1963
Distington Junction – Harrington Junction	16th September 1963
Harrington Junction – Calva Junction	26th September 1965
Beckermet Mines Junction – Sellafield	18th January 1970
Lowca – Harrington Junction – Moss Bay	23rd May 1973
Parton – No. 4 Pit Siding, Lowca	ditto
Moor Row – Rowrah Hall Quarry	2nd February 1980
Corkickle No. 2 – Beckermet Mines	3rd October 1980
Loco Junction – Walney Ferry	1st July 1989

Siddick Junction – Broughton Moor	3rd June 1992
Vickers Gun Range siding to Eskmeals Gun Range	15th February 1995
Plumpton Junction – Glaxo	17th March 2000

On a positive note there was the Government Loan Guarantee Scheme, resulting from an Agreement with the Treasury dated 30th November 1935, which provided capital for railway improvement projects. A good example on the Furness Line was at Carnforth Station. An LMS Traffic Committee minute dated 28th April 1937 reads:

'The Chief Commercial and Chief Operating Managers reported that considerable delay and inconvenience is caused at Carnforth Station owing to there being only one platform for dealing with both Up and Down Furness trains. ... It is the view of the Chief Commercial Manager that with proper facilities at Carnforth, traffic could be developed to and from West Cumberland.'

A new Furness line platform, 890 feet long, with awning and waiting rooms, was agreed. The necessary signalling was to be provided, including the replacement of signalboxes Nos 1 & 2. The estimated cost was £53,000. This work resulted in the station of today. It is indeed fortunate that the work was completed before war traffic pressures brought major new projects to an end.

Under Traffic Committee minute of 27th April 1938 and the same financial arrangements, a new locomotive shed, with the latest mechanical coaling, was built to replace the old LNWR, MR and FR sheds at Carnforth. The cost, of what was later to become 'Steamtown', was £71,000.

Enemy action during the 1939-45 War largely destroyed the

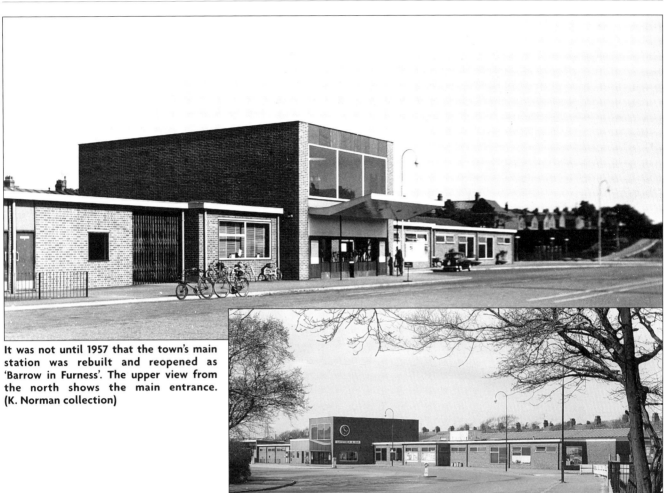

It was not until 1957 that the town's main station was rebuilt and reopened as 'Barrow in Furness'. The upper view from the north shows the main entrance. (K. Norman collection)

FR's principal passenger station, Barrow Central. Early in May 1941 German bombs wrecked the entrance hall and platform 1 of the station and inflicted damage on the venerable 'Coppernob' and destroyed her glass pavilion. The overall roof was removed and the station remained in a tattered state until a functional replacement was erected in the late 1950s.

The 1st January 1948 saw the birth of British Railways. On 25th September 1950 Furness Abbey station was closed. It had been used extensively during the 1939-45 war by Vickers' guests staying at the Company's Abbey House. There was very little other traffic. Lindal station, between Ulverston and Dalton, closed from 1st October 1951. In fact very few trains had called there since the working out of the Lindal mines and the village was well served by the Barrow – Ulverston joint Barrow Corporation and Ribble bus service. Eskmeals, a little used station just south of Ravenglass, closed from 3rd August 1959. The withdrawal of the passenger service between Grange and Kendal, on 4th May 1942, led to the closure of Sandside and Heversham stations. Sandside remained open for freight being served by a trip train from Carnforth, until this was withdrawn from 17th June 1968.

The two most significant (and most resisted) closures on the Furness Line were the Coniston and Lakeside branches into Lakeland. The rail journey to Coniston was admittedly a long way round but the scenic route remained popular with tourists until the use of the private car became widespread. The motor lorry more efficiently handled freight traffic. Passenger services were discontinued from 6th October 1958 and freight from 30th April 1962. The Lakeside passenger service was closed as a wartime economy measure. When the line reopened the trains were seasonal and did not call at Greenodd and Haverthwaite. This popular service was discontinued from 6th September 1965. However the Lakeside & Haverthwaite Railway, reopening in 1973, has splendidly restored that part of the line and steam trains now run in connection with the lake steamers.

The complex network of lines in the Barrow area, built to serve an extensive industry, and the FR steamers services to Belfast and Douglas, have been reduced to the siding between Salthouse Junction ground frame and the nuclear fuels sea terminal on Ramsden Dock.

The nuclear complex at Sellafield provides the Furness Line with its only remaining commercial freight movements, operated by Direct Rail Services (DRS) – the UK's only authorised carrier of irradiated material by rail. DRS have a major servicing depot at Sellafield from where regular services carry irradiated fuel between the Sellafield reprocessing plant and power stations across the UK as well as fuel from reactors on Royal Navy submarines and material imported through Barrow Docks from overseas customers. A siding, signalled from Sellafield box, has, in recent years, been installed north of Drigg Station to allow the direct transfer by rail of irradiated waste materials from the Sellafield site to the LLW repository on the land once occupied by the WW2 Drigg ROF on the seaward side of the Cumbrian Coast Line.

Freight traffic at Whitehaven has fallen away as the coal mines and their associated industries have run down and closed. In 1986 the Corkickle Brake – the last rope-worked incline on the UK rail system – ceased to carry traffic between the Corkickle sidings and the Albright & Wilson chemical plant on the high ground to the south of Whitehaven. Finally, on 15th

BRITISH RAILWAYS BOARD

PUBLIC NOTICE

TRANSPORT ACT - 1962

The London Midland Region of British Railways hereby give notice in accordance with Section 56 (7) of the Transport Act, 1962, that they propose to discontinue all railway passenger services between :—

Ulverston & Lake Side

AND TO CLOSE LAKE SIDE STATION

The railway passenger service concerned only operates during the currency of the British Railways Summer Timetable, June to September. The railway passenger service over this route during the Winter period was withdrawn in September, 1938.

It appears to the Board that following alternative services will be available:—

EXISTING SERVICES BY RAIL:—   NONE.

EXISTING SERVICES BY ROAD:—

     Ribble Motor Services Ltd.

     Services Nos. 514, 515, 517, 520 and 533 between Ulverston and Newby Bridge.

     Service No. 493 between Newby Bridge and Lakeside.

ADDITIONAL SERVICES PROPOSED BY ROAD:—

     Ribble Motor Services Ltd., have been given details of the passengers using the rail services proposed for withdrawal and they are satisfied that adequate arrangements can be made to cater for the displaced rail passengers, who consist predominately of holidaymakers using the Lake Windermere Steamer Services.

     Any users of the rail service which it is proposed to discontinue and anybody representing such users may lodge an objection within six weeks of 25th September, 1964, i.e. not later than 9th November, 1964, addressing the objection to:—

        The Secretary,
        Transport Users Consultative Committee for the North Western
        Area,
        Peter House,
        2, Oxford Street,
        MANCHESTER, 1.

     If any such objection is lodged, the service cannot be discontinued until the Transport Users Consultative Committee has considered the objection and reported to the Minister of Transport, and the Minister has given his consent to the closure under Section 56 (8) of the Transport Act, 1962.

     The Committee may hold a meeting to hear objections. Such a meeting will be held in public and any persons who have lodged an objection in writing may also make oral representation to the Committee.

     If no objections are lodged to the proposal, the service will not be re-introduced on 14th June, 1965.

September, 1964.   BR 35014.   HA 12.   Barrow Printing Company.

The public notice of the impending closure of the passenger service to Lakeside, September 1964. (Author: MAO0304)

Main Line from Yealand intermediate block signals to Gretna Junction and the Midland main line from Settle station to Carlisle. P. F. Winding, writing in *Modern Railways* for October and November 1965, gives the traffic and financial data of the Barrow Division. Winding revealed that the Barrow Division was to be abolished in a management review and its territory merged with Preston Division. Line Management was abolished on the LM Region after 1966. Station Masters were also withdrawn around this period and superseded by Station Managers, with larger areas. These in turn were replaced by Area Managers at Preston and Carlisle, with the boundary again at Yealand, on the West Coast Main Line, and Kent Viaduct, on the Furness Line.

The Transport Act 1968 created a number of functional divisions, for example shipping and workshops, to be managed separately. It also removed from the British Railways Board the responsibility for executive management of the railway. As a first step five executive directors were appointed, to build up a railway management team. It was not until 1974 that the structure of the new organisation was published in *Modern Railways*. There were to be eight territories replacing the five regions, and the managers were named. Barrow fell into the North West Territory based on Manchester with Manager R.B. Reid (the future Board Chairman). This reorganisation was based upon recommendations by the management consultants, McKinsey, who totally misjudged the scale of disruption and reaction this caused to staff. The 'Field Organisation' collapsed. By 1986 Preston Division had been abolished and the Area Managers reported to Regional HQ.

February 1997, Corkickle No. 1 and No. 2 boxes were closed and the extensive Corkickle sidings taken up, leaving only a single running line, between Bransty and St Bees worked by key token.

The FR Barrow General Offices at St George's Square continued into nationalisation. However, the 1950s saw the advent of 'Modernisation', which meant 'Reorganisation'. The London Midland Region proposed decentralisation, in which the huge Western, Midland and Central Divisions were broken down into smaller divisional units, reporting, from 1961, to Line Managers. Barrow Division was formed in 1958 and, in addition to the Furness & West Cumberland District, included the West Coast

A major reorganisation, implemented on 6th April 1992, saw the creation of separate vertically integrated businesses – Intercity, Network South-East, Regional Railway and Railfreight. The Furness Line became the responsibility of Regional Railways, managed from a District Office at Ladywell House, Preston. This was separate from the Intercity West Coast management at Preston station. The Area Manager, Trainload Freight, located at

Stanier 4-6-0 No. 44806 'Magpie' leaves Haverthwaite with a train for Lakeside under the auspices of the Lakeside & Haverthwaite Railway Co. formed in 1973. (K. Norman collection)

Railtrack. At the time of writing, the Furness Line is currently managed by General Manager, Lancs. and Cumbria, Network Rail, Preston, supported by Local Operations Managers, based at Carnforth, Barrow and Whitehaven.

The express passenger service between Barrow and Manchester Airport is operated by First TransPennine

Warrington, handled freight. These changes were in preparation for the privatisation of the railway in April 1996, with infrastructure being operated by Railtrack, and the passenger trains by Train Operating Companies.

Following a great deal of criticism regarding efficiency and safety, Network Rail, a non-profit making organisation, replaced

Express and the local services by Northern Rail. Nuclear flask traffic on the Furness Line is worked by Direct Rail Services (DRS), formerly a division of British Nuclear Fuels Ltd, and now a wholly owned subsidiary of the Nuclear Decommissioning Authority (NDA). The branch from Salthouse Junction ground frame to the trans-shipment berth at Ramsden Dock, Barrow is,

The last remnant of the FR rail network around the Barrow docks is the long siding from Salthouse Junction to the BNFL Marine Terminal at Ramsden Dock. Here, in the late 1980s, we see Class 31 diesel No. 31200 reversing a string of bogie wagons carrying nuclear flasks under the loading gantry. At this date the Sellafield freight services were still being provided by BR and the locomotive carries the decal of Railfreight's coal sector and the Cheshire Cat logo of Crewe Diesel Depot. (G. Holme collection)

Black 5 No. 45455 approaches the summit of Lindal Bank with a down express at Lindal Ore Sidings signalbox on 8th July 1967. This LMS box replaced the FR boxes at Lindal East and Lindal West in 1939. At this time the extensive up and down sidings remain in place but find use only for wagon and van storage. Close to here, in 1892, FR 0-6-0 No. 115 disappeared into an old mine working, where it remains to this day. (Author: MAA72)

as already noted, now the sole branch on the Furness Line. The cut-off loop between Park South and Dalton Junction (the 'Barrow Avoider') remains in use, carrying the regular service of DRS nuclear flask trains to and from several Magnox power stations as well as seasonal charter passenger trains, frequently employing steam haulage, between Carnforth and Ravenglass.

Reassuring, for the future of the line is the major repair work on the Leven Viaduct, completed in July 2006, and in 2011 on the Kent Viaduct, where, in each case, new decks have been installed on the refurbished piers during lengthy total line possessions. While services were suspended early in 2011 for the Kent viaduct repairs a substantial engineering project was undertaken on the

west portal of Lindal tunnel. The work entailed rock stabilisation, shortening the tunnel by approximately 20 metres to take the entrance back to a disused ventilation shaft and installing rock netting on the adjacent ground as a preventative measure against slippage. On the former W&FJR section, progressive heavy maintenance is proceeding on the various river crossings.

Track magnets and computer-controlled traffic management have been installed across the network but, on the Furness section, the signalling remains a mechanical operation from signalboxes, which, apart from Grange built to a BR design, were inherited from the Furness Railway, so while facing to the future, the line retains much of its old character.

CHAPTER 27 REFERENCES

1   Yeomans Godfrey A, 1995. *New Locomotives for the Furness Railway: 1890 to 1920* p.101.
2   PRO: Rail 418/7, Appendix to LMS Board Minutes.
3   *Whitehaven News*, 28th Mar. 1996, letter from J M Charters.

Barrow 2MT tank engine No. 41221 finds unusual employment on a down goods train at Furness Abbey. Between 1956 and 1959 a temporary signalbox was installed on the former down platform to control a section of gauntlet track through Furness Abbey tunnel to allow clearance for its relining. (Author: MAC1)

BIBLIOGRAPHY

PUBLICATIONS CONSULTED IN PREPARING THIS BOOK

Banks A.G.	*H.W. Schneider of Barrow and Bowness*	Kendal: 1984
Baughan Peter	*North of Leeds*	Harrow: 1966
Bradshaw's	*Railway Manual*	published annually
Bradshaw's	*General Railway Guide Timetables*	published monthly
Caine Caesar	*Cleator and Cleator Moor: Past & Present*	Whitehaven: 1916
Cavendish William	*7th Duke of Devonshire's Manuscript Diaries*	(at Chatsworth House)
CRA Journal	*Cumbrian Railways*	published quarterly
Davies Ken	*English Lakeland Steamers*	Chorley: 1984
Dickson R.W.	*General View of the Agriculture of Lancashire*	(at BL) 1815
Edgar S. & Sinton J.M.	*The Solway Junction Railway*	Headington: 1990
Fisher J.	*A Popular History of Barrow-in-Furness*	Barrow in Furness: 1891
Gale W.K.V.	*The British Iron & Steel Industry*	Newton Abbot: 1967
Gooderson P.J.	Article in *HSLC Transactions Vol. 122*	Chester: 1971
Gradon W McGowan	*Furness Railway: Its Rise and Development : 1846-1923*	Altrincham: 1946
Gradon W McGowan	*The Track of the Ironmasters*	Altrincham: 1952
Greville M.D.	Article in *HSLC Transactions*	Chester: 1953 (Later reprinted by R&CHS)
Hamilton J.A.B.	*British Railways in World War I*	London: 1967
Hamilton Ellis C.	*British Railway History 1877-1947*	London: 1959
Harris Alan	*Cumberland Iron*	Truro: 1970
Harris Nigel	*Portrait of a Shipbuilder: Barrow-Built Vessels from 1873*	St Michael's on Wyre: 1989
Hay Daniel	*Whitehaven: a Short History*	Whitehaven: 1966
Herapath's	*Railway Journal*	1839-1903
Hobbs J.L.	Article in *CWAAS Transactions NS Vol. LVI*	Kendal: 1956
Hopkins K.	*The Poetry of Railways*	London: 1966
Joy David	*A Regional History of the Railways of Great Britain, Vol. 14 The Lake Counties*	Newton Abbot: 1983
Kellett Jack	*James Ramsden: Barrow's Man of Vision*	Barrow: 1990
Kelly David	*The Red Hills*	Marton: 1994
Kendall W.B.	*Manuscript Papers*	(at BRO)
Lancaster J.Y. & Wattleworth D.R.	*The Iron & Steel Industry of West Cumberland*	Workington:1977
McNeill D.B.	*Coastal Steamers & Inland Navigation of the North of Ireland*	Belfast: 1960
Marshall John	*Biographical Dictionary of Railway Engineers*	Bewdley: 2003
Marshall J.D.	*Furness and the Industrial Revolution*	Barrow in Furness: 1958
Melville J. & Hobbs J.L.	*Early Railway History of Furness*	Kendal: 1951
Neele G. P.	*Railway Reminiscences*	London: 1904
Nock O.S.	*A History of the LMS: I. The First Years, 1923-30*	London: 1982
Parris Henry	*Government and the Railways in Nineteenth Century Britain*	London: 1965
Pearsall Alan W.H.	*North Irish Channel Services*	Belfast: 1962
Pettigrew W.F.	*History of the Furness Railway Locomotives.*	
	Article in Transactions of the Institution of Mechanical Engineers	London: 1901
Pollard S.	Article in *Economic History Review*	December 1955
Porter J.	*History of the Fylde of Lancashire*	Fleetwood: 1876
Pratt Edwin	*British Railways and the Great War*	London: 1921
RAIL Magazine		published fortnightly 1981 to present
Railway Magazine		published monthly 1897 to present
Reed Brian	*Crewe to Carlisle*	London: 1969
Richardson J.	*Furness Past and Present Vols 1 & 2*	Barrow in Furness: 1880
Rigg A. Neville	*John Barraclough Fell CE*	Penrith: 1996
Scott J.D.	*Vickers: a History*	London: 1962
Scott-Hindson Brian	Article in *CRA Journal Vol. 8*	Settle: 2004
Simmons Jack	*The Maryport & Carlisle Railway*	London: 1947
Stelfox James	*Manuscript Diaries*	(at Lancaster University Library)
Stileman F.C.	Article in *Proceedings of the Institution of Civil Engineers 1860*	
TTSJ	*Journal of the Transport Ticket Society*	
Taylor A.J.P.	*English History 1914-1945*	Oxford: 1965
Trescatheric Bryn	*Building Barrow*	Barrow in Furness: 1992

Tuck Henry	*The Railway Shareholders Manual 8th ed.*	London: 1848
VCH	*Victoria History of Cumberland Vols 1 & 2*	1901 & 1905
Williams F.S.	*The Midland Railway*	Nottingham: 1886
Yeomans G.A.	*New Locomotives for the Furness Railway: 1890 to 1920*	Derby: 1995

ADDITIONAL BIBLIOGRAPHY
OF PUBLICATIONS RELATING TO THE FURNESS RAILWAY

Bairstow Martin	*Railways in the Lake District*	Halifax: 1995
Barnes Fred	*Barrow & District: an Illustrated History*	Barrow in Furness: 1967
Battye Rock	*Dalton-in-Furness*	CRA: 2006
Bowtell Harold D.	*Over Shap to Carlisle*	Shepperton: 1983
Bowtell Harold D.	*Rails Through Lakeland*	St Michael's on Wyre: 1989
Broughton John R. & Harris Nigel	*British Railways Past & Present No. 1 Cumbria*	Carnforth: 1985
Broughton John R.	*The Furness Railway (in 'Past & Present' series)*	Wadenhoe: 1996
Butterworth D.	*The Coniston Branch of the Furness Railway*	1978
Davies W.J.K.	*The Ravenglass & Eskdale Railway*	Newton Abbot: 1968
Davey C.R.	*Reflections of the Furness Railway*	Barrow in Furness: 1984
Furness Railway Magazine: Volumes 1 to 3 (1921-1923) on a compact disc		CRA: 2010
Fryer C.E.J.	*British Baltic Tanks (Railway Monographs No 2)* Ch. 4 *Rutherford's Baltics for the Furness Line*	Sheffield: 1993
Gilpin Leslie R.	*A Cumbrian Railway Album – from the Cameras of Ian and Alan Pearsall*	CRA: 2011
Gilpin Leslie R.	*Grange over Sands*	CRA: 1997
Gilpin Leslie R.	*Ulverstone & Lancaster Railway*	CRA: 2008
Gradon W. McGowan	*Furness Railway: Its Rise & Development: 1846-1923*	Altrincham: 1946
Gradon W. McGowan	*Ratty – a History of the R & E R*	1947: 2nd edition 1997
Gradon W. McGowan	*A History of the Cockermouth Keswick & Penrith Railway*	Altrincham: 1948
Gradon W. McGowan	*The Track of the Ironmasters*	1952: reprint CRA: 2004
Joy David	*Railways of the Lake Counties*	Clapham: 1973
Joy David	*Cumbrian Coast Railways*	Clapham: 1968
Kelly David	*The Red Earth*	Barrow in Furness: 1998
Kirkman R. & van Zeller P.	*Rails round the Cumbrian Coast*	Clapham: 1988
Marsh J & Garbutt J.	*Cumbrian Railways*	Stroud: 1999
Marshall J.D.	*Old Lakeland*	Newton Abbot: 1971
Mellentin Julian	*Kendal and Windermere Railway*	Clapham: 1980
Norman Ken J.	*The Furness Railway ('Railway Heritage' series)*	Kettering: 2001
Owen Tim	*The Great Survivor*	CRA & FRT: 1999
Pearson Keith	*Fell Mountain Railways*	Brora: 2011
Pearson Michael	*The Cumbrian Coast ('Railway Rides' series)*	1992
Peascod Mike	*Cumbrian Engines in LMS Ownership* in LMS Journal No 14	Didcot: 2006
Pollard S	*North-West Coast Railway Politics*	CWAAS: 1953
Pollard S & Marshall J.D.	*The Furness Railway and the Growth of Barrow* in *Journal of Transport History Vol. 1 No. 2*	Leicester: 1953
Quayle Howard I.	*Furness Railway: a View from the Past*	Shepperton: 2000
Quayle Howard I.	*Whitehaven*	CRA: 2007
Quayle Howard I. & Jenkins S.C.	*Lakeside & Haverthwaite Railway*	Clapham: 1977
Robinson Peter W.	*Railways of Cumbria*	Clapham: 1980
Robinson Peter W.	*Cumbria's Lost Railways*	Catrine: 2002
Rush R.W.	*The Furness Railway 1843-1923*	Headington: 1973
Rush R.W.	*Furness Railway Locomotives & Rolling Stock*	Headington: 1973
Sankey R. & Norman Ken J.	*The Furness Railway: a Photographic Recollection*	Clapham: 1977
Smith Dick	*The Kendal & Windermere Railway*	CRA: 1998
Stileman Frank	*Barrow Docks and Approaches by Land and Sea.* Article in *Transactions of the Institution of Mechanical Engineers*	1901
Suggitt Gordon	*Lost Railways of Cumbria*	Newbury: 2008
van Zeller Peter	*Ravenglass*	CRA: 2001
Wade E.A.	*The Patent Narrow Gauge Railways of John Barraclough Fell*	NGRS: 1986
Western Robert	*The Cockermouth, Keswick & Penrith Railway*	Usk: 2001
Western Robert	*The Coniston Railway*	Usk: 2007
Western Robert	*The Ingleton Branch*	Headington: 1990

0-6-0 GOODS LOCOMOTIVE No 80, BUILT 1872, BY SHARP, STEWART & Co, MANCHESTER, FOR THE FURNESS RAILWAY
CLASS D1
THE BACKGROUND, THE NIGEL PIT, ROANHEAD

E.W. PAGET-TOMLINSON
OCTOBER 2002

Furness Railway No. 3 'Coppernob' at the National Railway Museum, York.

The Furness Railway War Memorial in the booking hall at Barrow Station.

The Furness Railway Trust's beautifully restored FR No. 20 seen here at 'Locomotion' – the National Railway Museum outstation at Shildon – on weekend shuttle service duty.

TransPennine Express Siemens 'Desiro' class 185 three-car unit departing Ulverston on 27th August 2010 with a Barrow in Furness to Manchester Airport service. The FR brackets that once supported the awning over platform 1 now serve as lighting pillars.

A Northern Rail class 144 unit takes the F&M line at Carnforth with a Leeds service on 15th August 2008. The abandoned Carnforth Station Jct signalbox on the right carries the Cavendish coat of arms on its gable.

The only regular freight traffic on the Furness section is provided now by services to and from the Sellafield nuclear complex. Here two DRS class 37 locomotives, in 'top-and-tail' mode, head east through Grange on 27th July 2011 with a single nuclear flask.

"COPPERNOB" FAREWELL

A peaceful scene at Barrow Central Station around 1910, taken from the Station Approach. On the right "Coppernob" can be glimpsed in her glass pavilion.
Photos: K. Norman collection

Peace was rudely shattered early in May 1941 when, during an air raid on Barrow, a German land mine demolished the Stationmaster's house, wrecked the station roof and buildings and brought down "Coppernob's" glass case about her boiler and chimney. Fortunately, the old engine was damaged only superficially.

The debris was quickly cleared from Platforms 1 and 2 and the station was able to continue to serve the town, albeit without its overall roof. The plinth on which locomotive No. 3 had rested since the early 1900s can be seen on the left, standing forlornly empty.
"Coppernob" was first taken to the safe haven of the Horwich workshops of the L&YR near Bolton. Still bearing her wartime scars, FR No. 3 is now the oldest inhabitant of the National Railway Museum in York.

FURNESS RAILWAY TICKETS

FIRST CLASS
Ticket numbers 37, 178, 856.
A selection of Furness Railway First class tickets in the design contemporary at the time of printing.

SECOND AND GOV CLASS TICKETS
Tickets 49 and 4934
49: Like most companies the Furness had second class accommodation in its early years abolishing it from 1st July 1898. Other companies retained it longer and a second class ticket was retained where any part of the journey was to be taken in a second class compartment. This example would be

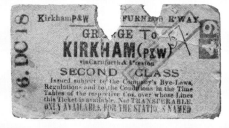 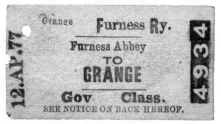

old stock when issued in 1896 as it has the fare written on by hand together with a stamp stating 'Fare'. 4934: Government or parliamentary tickets went out of use early on, this example being issued in 1877.

WALNEY FERRY
Ticket number 10028.
As well as the standard Edmondson card ticket the Furness issued tickets for its other activities. Illustrated is a thin paper ticket slightly larger than the standard Edmondson card tickets for use on the Walney Ferry. Tickets to be torn of rolls were in use at the Romney cottage and both roll and paper tickets were used at Barrow Central for platform tickets.

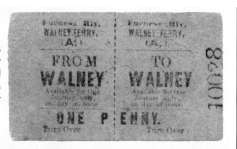

Tickets drawn from the Author's and other private collections. Text by Geoff Holme.

THIRD CLASS
Ticket numbers 7637, 9349, 8034, 2110, 1737, 2025, 384, 08, 9465.
The design of Furness tickets changed through the years and examples are shown here of several different designs. Initially no tickets carried audit numbers, but eventually in early 1906 in addition to the type of ticket and the destination station the audit number of the issuing station was included (1737, 8034). Before World War I inflation had been at a very low level but owing to wartime conditions it increased to levels rarely seen since and tickets were printed showing a revised and much higher fare (8034). As tickets issued at Newby Bridge halt showed 'Lake Side (N.B.62)' the only tickets seen to include Newby Bridge in either departure or destination were those between Lake Side and Newby Bridge. (1737) Return tickets were in two halves, the right hand outward half being surrendered at the destination station and the left hand half being retained for the return journey (9465). Single tickets to destination not on the Furness were usually green instead of the standard buff colour. They would always show which route had

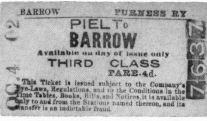 

to be followed which in the case of the Grimsby ticket was quite complex (08). These followed closely the style of the day for tickets issued for use within the Furness system.

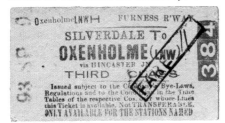 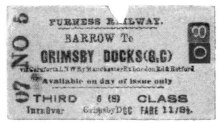 

EXCURSION TICKETS

Ticket numbers 129, 458, 16, 43, 38, 308.
A different design was used for the tickets for each of the circular tours. Illustrated are examples for tours 1 (129, 458), 2 (16), 5 (43) and 10 (38). Tours 1 and 2 could be taken from any station on the route in both an anti-clockwise (129) and clockwise (458) direction with separate tickets being provided for each direction. Like standard tickets each class also had its own colour distinction. Day excursion tickets at a discounted rate to normal full day return fare were also issued and the illustrated example was available from Seascale to Ambleside via rail and lake steamer – a grand day out (308). Where a private coach was used for part of the journey that part of the ticket would be retained by the coach operator who would forward it to Furness Railway Headquarters to claim his fare (38).

 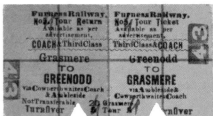

LAKE STEAMER TICKETS 99, 9995, 1051, 140.

Standard card tickets to the same designs as used on trains were issued for use on the Coniston and Windermere lake steamers (9995, 1051). For passengers wishing to upgrade their rail tickets to first class for the lake portion the illustrated excess ticket was available (99). A season ticket allowing unlimited travel on the steamers was produced, the large number showing quickly how many passengers this pass covered (140).

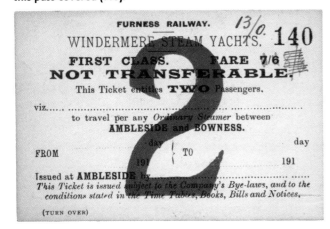

LONDON & NORTH WESTERN RAILWAY

Ticket number 11.
When a ticket was issued by a company that then required to use the Furness for part of its journey the ticket would be in the pattern of the company at the departure station. In this case the ticket was issued at Preston, the holder would then change to a Furness train at Carnforth as far as the end of the Furness line at Whitehaven to finish his journey by London and North Western train to Workington. This ticket sold in 1872 is unusual in that the old spelling of Ulverstone is used (11)

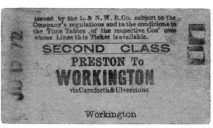

WORKMAN'S TICKETS

Ticket numbers 4534, 8649.

The company ran special trains for workmen, mainly to the shipyard at Barrow and special tickets were issued for these. The example shown is for the Millom to Barrow service and was valid on Thursday only (8649). Workmen could travel on ordinary services on payment of a supplement, for the illustrated example

from Foxfield to Barrow an extra 2d was charged. Following the Regulation of Railways Act all tickets had to show the fare and as this was increased it would be written by hand on existing stocks as in this example (4534).

ARTICLE TICKETS

Tickets number 24, 62, 26, 339.

Examples of tickets provided for the carriage of Dogs prams and bicycles. Many of these tickets saw little use at some stations and both examples from Roose were sold to the author when he went round the stations asking have you any old Furness Railway tickets as late as 20th October 1955 (24, 62), over 30 years after the Furness Railway ceased to exist as a separate identity.

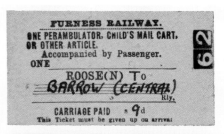

LNW & FURNESS JOINT LINES

Ticket numbers 4003, 8678.

For services on the ex Whitehaven, Cleator and Egremont Railway joint lines special tickets were produced with both companies names on. Tickets were based on both the Furness (8678) and the London and North Western (4003) styles.

CLEATOR & WORKINGTON JUNCTION RAILWAY Ticket numbers 079, 5013.

Like the other small companies in Cumbria that affect the story of the Furness Railway the Cleator and Workington Junction Railway issued its own tickets. A standard Parliamentary 3rd class example is shown (5013) together with a weekly workman's ticket to destinations on the line (079). Similar weekly tickets were also issued between Furness stations at reduced rates to normal fares.

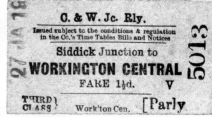

LONDON MIDLAND & SCOTTISH RAILWAY (FR) Ticket number 4982, 70, 02.

When the Furness Railway was amalgamated into the London Midland and Scottish Railway in 1923 many things only changed slowly and the style of tickets was one. Here we have examples from Silecroft where the destination had been added by hand presumably as the tickets to Millom had run out or insufficient were used to justify printed stock (70). Slightly changed tours using lines of previously rival companies required a new stock of tickets for those and this example was issued in Ambleside for a tour to Bowness by lake, by rail from Windermere to Lake Side by train via the former LNWR line Kendal and the FR branch line from Hincaster Junction to Arnside before travelling on back to Lake Side and the lake to the starting point at Ambleside. (02) The use of Lake Side(N.B.62) shows the ticket was issued at Newby Bridge Halt. (4982) During this interim period the old Furness Railway audit numbers were shown on all tickets.

FR TRACK DIAGRAMS

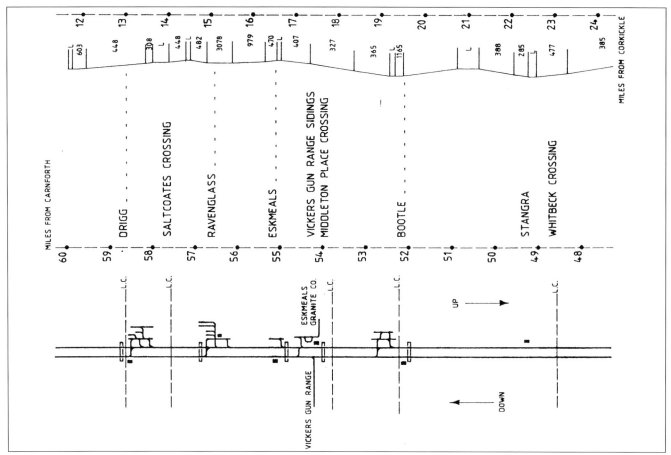

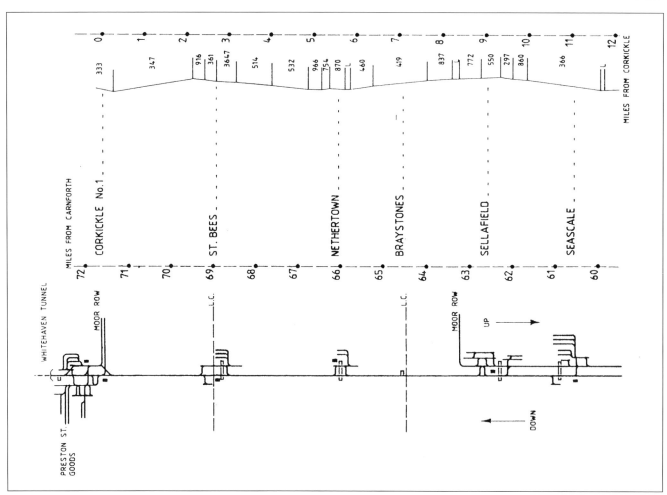

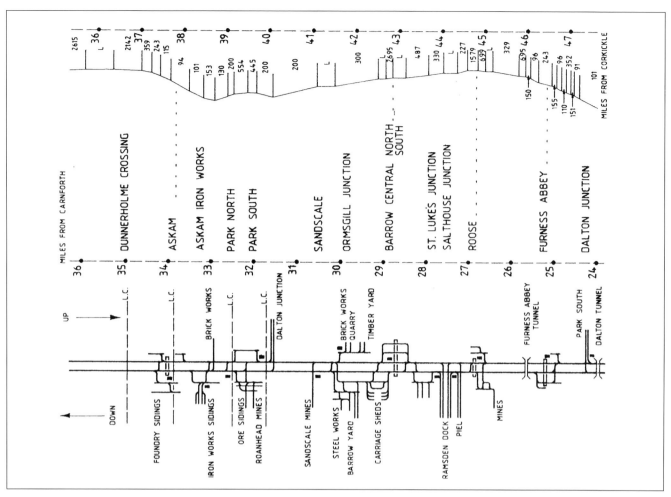

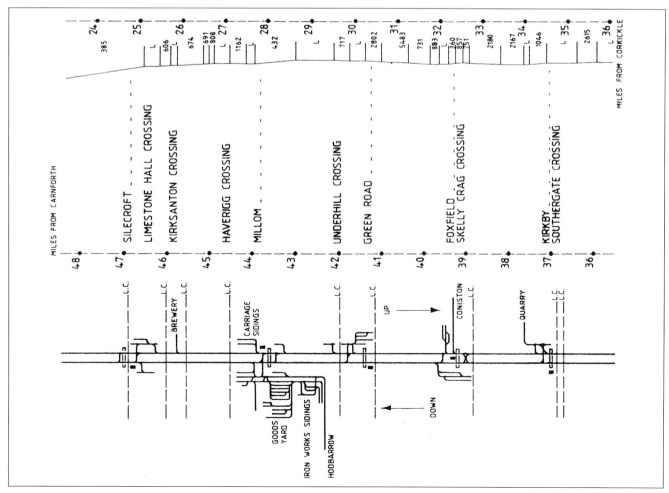

241

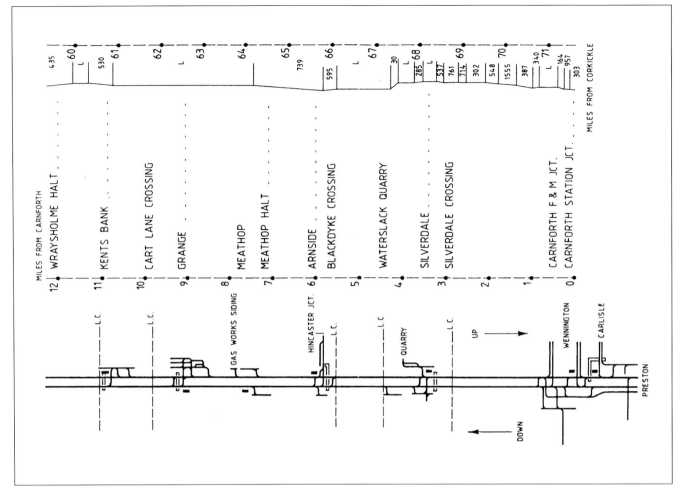

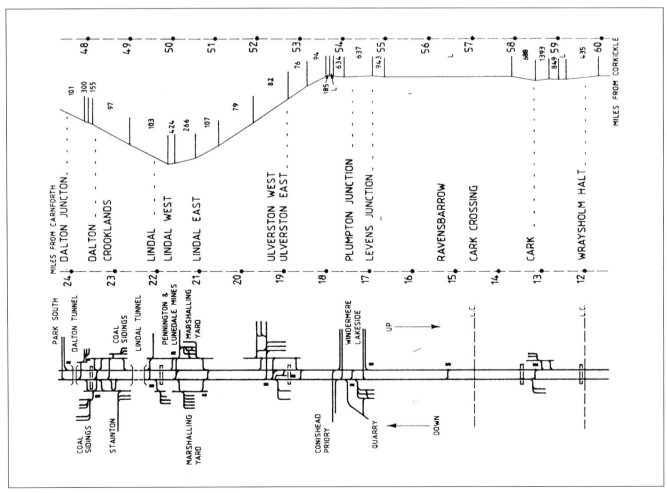

Furness Railway Standard Bearers

Cumbria Archive and Local Studies Centre 140 Duke Street, Barrow-in-Furness LA14 1XW Tel: 01229 407377 Fax: 01229 894364. This is the best source of research material on the Furness Railway and for access to local newspapers and family records for the Furness and South Cumberland area. The Centre staff are knowledgeable and helpful. Among its most interesting railway records is a collection of FR plans and other documents recovered by Michael Andrews when the former FR General Offices at St George's Square, Barrow were being vacated prior to demolition. Email: barrow.archives@cumbria.gov.uk

The **Furness Railway Trust** is a Registered Charity, based in North West England. It owns Furness Railway locomotive No. 20, built in 1863, which is currently the oldest operable main line locomotive in Britain, as well as a number of other locomotives, carriages and artefacts. The organisation has emerged as a leading hirer of locomotives and other rolling stock to heritage railways and museums, and is based at the Ribble Steam Railway at Preston, where new facilities to house and maintain its collection are being developed. www.furnessrailwaytrust.org.uk

In 2011 **FLAG** – the **Furness Line Action Group** – celebrated 25 years of promoting and protecting Cumbrian Coast rail services. Regular meetings with rail companies, MPs, local authorities and the Community Rail Partnership Steering Group ensure passengers' concerns and issues are represented effectively. A magazine is issued regularly to members with news of current developments. To help us fight for improvements, why not join FLAG now? Contact our Membership Secretary, Derek Walmsley, 116 Holker Street, Barrow-in-Furness LA14 5RU or E-mail: furnessline.actiongroup@btopenworld.com

CRUG – the **Copeland Rail Users Group** – was formed in 2003 as a result of anxieties over rail service levels on the former FR line within Copeland. The Group has worked ceaselessly with the various authorities to promote, protect and preserve the line between Whitehaven and Millom. The line now has a Community Rail Partnership which it is hoped will build on the improvements obtained by CRUG, such as the original 'Harrington Hump' and facilities for the disabled at Whitehaven. Membership Secretary: N Gilligan (01229 772726). www.crug.org.uk

The **Cumbrian Railways Association** is the county's railway history group founded in 1976. The Association publishes the quarterly magazine "Cumbrian Railways" and its other publications include several books relating to the Furness Railway. For further information visit the Association's website at www.cumbrianrailways.org.uk or send a stamped addressed envelope to the Membership Secretary at 95 Harrington Road, Workington CA14 2UE.

Since 1973 the **Lakeside & Haverthwaite Railway Company** has operated scheduled passenger services over part of the FR Lakeside branch, maintaining connections with steamer services on Windermere. Run by a dedicated team of paid and volunteer staff, the L&HR is based at Haverthwaite station which boasts a famous café, a well-stocked gift shop as well as all the necessary facilities for servicing and repairing their stud of locomotives and rolling stock. www.lakesiderailway.co.uk

From its earliest beginnings in 1875, the **Ravenglass & Eskdale Railway** has undergone many changes of fortune. For the past 50 years the 'Ratty' has returned from near extinction to become one of the Lake District's most popular tourist attractions. Its centre of operations at Ravenglass connects with trains on the FR line and through ticketing fares are available. Visitor attractions at Ravenglass include a museum, a gift shop and the new Turntable café. The Eskdale terminus at Dalegarth has its Fellbites Eatery and Scafell Gift Shop. www.ravenglass-railway.co.uk

The **FR's Gondola** continues to cruise Coniston Water during the tourist season under the auspices of the National Trust. www.nationaltrust.org.uk/gondola/. On Windermere, the successors of the FR's lake steamers continue to operate between Lakeside, Bowness and Ambleside with catering facilities at both Lakeside Pier and on board the steamers. www.windermere-lakecruises.co.uk

At Barrow Station the **Furness Railway War Memorial** from the 1914-18 conflict provides the focus for an annual ceremony of Remembrance each November conducted by the Railway Chaplain for the area.

Returning from Ravenglass, 'The Lakelander' steam-hauled special meets a Northern Rail class 156 unit as they cross the newly refurbished Kent Viaduct at Arnside in July 2011.

INDEX

INDEX OF PRINCIPAL PERSONAE

Items in **bold type** *indicate a photograph, map or plan*

INDEX OF SALIENT LOCATIONS

*Items in **bold type** indicate a photograph, map or plan*

AUTHOR'S ACKNOWLEDGEMENTS

Over a period of half a century, many people have helped in research for this book. Those such as John Campbell of the British Transport Historical Records, Porchester Road - a Maryport & Carlisle man and a helpful adviser of the author – are long gone. In more recent times Geoff Holme and Ken Norman have helped to complete the work. Both experienced Furness Railway researchers, their help has been invaluable. Various research facilities have provided information; these include the British Library, the Colindale Newspaper Library, the House of Lords Record Office, the Public Record Office (National Archives) and last but not least, the Barrow Record Office and Local History Library which has a great deal of Furness Railway material and a microfilm copy of the diary of William Cavendish, 7th Duke of Devonshire, who was chairman of the Furness Railway Company for forty years.

MJA

PUBLISHERS' APPRECIATION

It has been the aim of the present publishing team to use the final version of Michael's text together with the illustrative material and photographs, many from his own collection, that he had particularly selected. Being unaware of any arrangements already agreed by him with copyright holders, we have endeavoured to secure permission to use material that appeared to be in private ownership. We apologise for any shortcomings in these efforts.

Generous approval has been given by the Duke of Devonshire and the Chatsworth House Trust to publish the many illuminating extracts from the Diaries of the 7th Duke. Mr J.D. Sankey, custodian of the celebrated Sankey Collection of historical photographs, has kindly granted his permission to use copyright images from that archive. The Cumbrian Railways Association, through its Archivist, Peter Robinson, has been tireless in responding to requests for items from its notable photographic collections. The Archivist of the Institution of Civil Engineers granted permission to use their Lindal Tunnel illustration and Dr Paul Hindle allowed us to reprint the map of the Furness turnpike roads. David Cross kindly allowed us to include a photograph from the portfolio of his father, the late Derek Cross, whose work Michael had always admired. Mrs P L Paget-Tomlinson has given her consent for the use of her husband Edward's painting of FR No 80 on the cover of the book. Other sources of images and documents are indicated in the accompanying captions. Staff at the Barrow Archive & Local Studies Centre have dealt most patiently with many requests for help and advice. To all we express our thanks.

No matter how well-intention were our amateurish efforts, this book would not have seen the light of day without the talented and endlessly patient endeavours of Trevor Preece and Judith Kirkham, who have supervised the entire design and production phases. From their centre of operations overlooking the W&FJR section of the line at Seascale, they have guided the project to this conclusion, for which we record our gratitude.

The source references listed at each chapter end are almost wholly those recorded by Michael and we are relying on his legendary concern for accuracy that they and the extracts quoted are correct. The Bibliographies have, with the assistance of Howard Quayle, been extended to provide a reasonably comprehensive account of published material on and relating to the Furness Railway.

Our thanks go to the many friends of Michael and of the Furness Railway who have supported our efforts to give his *"The Furness Railway – A History"* this permanent form.

Geoff Holme, Ken Norman
Alan Johnstone, Alan Postlethwaite

Barrai Books · 17 Railway Terrace · Lindal in Furness · Ulverston · Cumbria LA12 0LQ

The Furness Railway lunchtime express for Euston, leaving Platform No. 2 at Barrow Central in around 1905, hauled by two FR 4-4-0 passenger locomotives. This drawing by David Fisher recreates one of the iconic images of the Furness line first captured in a classic Edward Sankey photograph.